Fodor's® FIRST New EDITION

Indonesia

The complete guide, thoroughly up-to-date

Packed with details that will make your trip

The must-see sights, off and on the beaten path

What to see, what to skip

Mix-and-match vacation itineraries

City strolls, countryside adventures

Smart lodging and dining options

Essential local do's and taboos

Transportation tips, distances and directions

Key contacts, savvy travel tips

When to go, what to pack

Clear, accurate, easy-to-use maps

Fodor's Travel Publications, Inc.
New York • Toronto • London • Sydney • Auckland
www.fodors.com/

Fodor's Indonesia

EDITOR: Laura M. Kidder

Editorial Contributors: David Brown, Mick Elmore, Helayne Schiff, M. T. Schwartzman, Holly S. Smith
Editorial Production: Melissa Klurman
Maps: David Lindroth, *cartographer*; Steven Amsterdam and Robert Blake, *map editors*
Design: Fabrizio La Rocca, *creative director*; Guido Caroti, *associate art director*; Jolie Novak, *photo editor*
Production/Manufacturing: Robert B. Shields
Cover Photograph: Blaine Harrington III
Database Production: Janet Foley

Copyright

First Edition

ISBN 0-679-00294-4

Special Sales

Fodor's Travel Publications are available at special discounts for bulk purchases for sales promotions or premiums. Special editions, including personalized covers, excerpts of existing guides, and corporate imprints, can be created in large quantities for special needs. For more information, contact your local bookseller or write to Special Markets, Fodor's Travel Publications, 201 East 50th Street, New York, NY 10022. Inquiries from Canada should be directed to your local Canadian bookseller or sent to Random House of Canada, Ltd., Marketing Department, 2775 Matheson Boulevard East, Mississauga, Ontario L4W 4P7. Inquiries from the United Kingdom should be sent to Fodor's Travel Publications, 20 Vauxhall Bridge Road, London SW1V 2SA, England.

PRINTED IN THE UNITED STATES OF AMERICA

10 9 8 7 6 5 4 3 2 1

CONTENTS

ON THE ROAD WITH FODOR'S

WHEN I PLAN A VACATION, the first thing I do is cast around among my friends and colleagues to find someone who's just been where I'm going. That's because there's no substitute for a recommendation from a good friend who knows your tastes, your budget, and your circumstances, someone who's just been there. Unfortunately, such friends are few and far between. So it's nice to know that there's *Fodor's Indonesia.*

In the first place, this book won't stay home when you hit the road. It will accompany you every step of the way, steering you away from wrong turns and wrong choices and never expecting a thing in return. Most important of all, it's written and assiduously updated by the kind of people you *would* hit up for travel tips if you knew them. They're as choosy as your pickiest friend, except they've probably seen a lot more of Indonesia. In these pages, they don't send you chasing down every town and sight on the islands but have instead selected the best ones, the ones that are worthy of your time and money. To make it easy for you to put it all together in the time you have, they've created short, medium, and long itineraries and, in cities, neighborhood walks that you can mix and match in a snap. Will this be the vacation of your dreams? We hope so.

About Our Writers

Our success in helping to make your trip the best of all possible vacations is a credit to the hard work of our extraordinary writers.

Mick Elmore drove a beat-up old Chrysler across seven Indonesian islands in 1991 and has returned many times since. His most recent visits include a trip to Central Java in 1996 to walk for a week with Tom Stone, who's on a seven-year stroll around the world; and trips to both Sumatra and Java in 1998 for Fodor's. Mick has been a journalist since 1984—first in Texas, then in Australia and Cambodia. He is now based in Bangkok, where he writes for wire services and magazines.

Indonesia (Bali, Nusa Tengarra, and Sulawesi) updater, **Holly S. Smith,** is a freelance writer whose articles on travel and Southeast Asian history and culture have appeared in various international magazines. She has also written several books including *Aceh: Art and Culture,* and *Java: Garden of the East.* Holly's current projects include a book on heroines in Aceh (a province in northern Sumatra) and a collection of short stories inspired by her backpacking adventures in Southeast Asia and South America.

We'd like to thank Amanresorts; Avis International; Holiday Inn hotels; Hotel Tugu; Hyatt hotels; Garuda Indonesia Airlines; Northwest Airlines; the Oberoi hotel; and Sheraton ITT.

Connections

We're pleased that the American Society of Travel Agents continues to endorse Fodor's as its guidebook of choice. ASTA is the world's largest and most influential travel trade association, operating in more than 170 countries, with 27,000 members pledged to adhere to a strict code of ethics reflecting the Society's motto, "Integrity in Travel." ASTA shares Fodor's devotion to providing smart, honest travel information and advice to travelers, and we've long recommended that our readers—even those who have guidebooks and traveling friends—consult ASTA member agents for the experience and professionalism they bring to your vacation planning.

On Fodor's Web site (www.fodors.com), check out the new Resource Center, an on-line companion to the Gold Guide section of this book, complete with useful hot links to related sites. In our forums, you can also get lively advice from other travelers and more great tips from Fodor's experts worldwide.

How to Use This Book

Organization

Up front is the **Gold Guide,** an easy-to-use section arranged alphabetically by topic. Under each listing you'll find tips and information that will help you accomplish what you need to in Indonesia. You'll also find addresses and telephone numbers of organizations and companies that offer destination-related services and detailed information and publications.

The first chapter in the guide, Destination: Indonesia, helps get you in the mood for your trip. What's Where gets you oriented, Pleasures and Pastimes describes the activities and sights that make Indonesia unique, New and Noteworthy cues you in on trends and happenings, Great Itineraries lays out a selection of complete trips, Fodor's Choice showcases our top picks, and Festivals and Seasonal Events alerts you to special events you'll want to seek out.

Each destination chapter in *Fodor's Indonesia* covers an island or group of islands. The first such chapter is Java, home of the nation's capital and major gateway city, Jakarta. From Java, the coverage moves eastward to Bali—perhaps the most popular destination—and then takes you off the beaten track to the islands of the Nusa Tengarra (Lombok, Sumbawa, Komodo, and Flores), which are still farther east. The last two chapters cover the islands suited to more intrepid travelers: Sulawesi, north of Nusa Tengarra, and Sumatra, west and north of Java. Each chapter is divided by geographical area; within each area, towns are covered in logical geographical order, and attractive stretches of road and minor points of interest between them are indicated by the designation *En Route*. And within town sections, all restaurants and lodgings are grouped.

To help you decide what to visit in the time you have, all chapters begin with our recommended itineraries. The A to Z section at the end of each region covers getting there and getting around. It also provides helpful contacts and resources.

Icons and Symbols

- ★ Our special recommendations
- ✕ Restaurant
- 🏨 Lodging establishment
- ✕🏨 Lodging establishment whose restaurant warrants a special trip
- 🦆 Good for kids (rubber duck)
- ☞ Sends you to another section of the guide for more information
- ✉ Address
- ☎ Telephone number
- ⏲ Opening and closing times
- 🎟 Admission (Owing to the instability of the rupiah, we do not list specific prices; the word "admission" appears when an entry fee is charged, the word "free" when one is not.)

Numbers in white and black circles (e.g., ③ or ❸) that appear on the maps, in the margins, and within the tours correspond to one another.

Dining and Lodging

The restaurants and lodgings we list are the cream of the crop in each price range. Price categories are cited below.

For restaurants:

CATEGORY	COST*
$$$$	over $30
$$$	$20–$30
$$	$10–$20
$	under $10

**per person for a three-course dinner, excluding tax, service, and drinks.*

For hotels:

CATEGORY	COST*
$$$$	over $150
$$$	$100–$150
$$	$75–$100
$	$40–$75

**for a standard double room in high season, excluding 10% service charge and 11% tax.*

Hotel Facilities

We always list the facilities that are available—but we don't specify whether you'll be charged extra to use them: When pricing accommodations, always ask what's included. In addition, assume that all rooms have private baths unless noted otherwise. In addition, when you book a room, be sure to mention if you have a disability or are traveling with children, if you prefer a private bath or a certain type of bed, or if you have specific dietary needs or other concerns.

Assume that hotels operate on the **European Plan** (EP, with no meals) unless we note that they use the **Continental Plan** (CP, with a Continental breakfast daily), **Breakfast Plan** (BP, with a full breakfast daily), **Modified American Plan** (MAP, with breakfast and dinner daily), or are **all-inclusive** (including all meals and most activities).

Restaurant Reservations and Dress Codes

Reservations are always a good idea; we mention them only when they're essential or are not accepted. Book as far ahead as you can, and reconfirm as soon as you arrive. Unless otherwise noted, the restaurants listed are open daily for lunch and dinner. We mention dress only when men are required to wear a jacket or a jacket and tie. Look for an overview of local dining-out habits in the Pleasures and Pastimes section that follows each chapter introduction.

Credit Cards

The following abbreviations are used: **AE**, American Express; **DC**, Diners Club; **MC**, MasterCard; and **V**, Visa.

Don't Forget to Write

You can use this book in the confidence that all prices and opening times are based on information supplied to us at press time; Fodor's cannot accept responsibility for any errors. Time inevitably brings changes, so always confirm information when it matters—especially if you're making a detour to visit a specific place.

Were the restaurants we recommended as described? Did our hotel picks exceed your expectations? Did you find a museum we recommended a waste of time? Keeping a travel guide fresh and up-to-date is a big job, and we welcome your feedback, positive *and* negative. If you have complaints, we'll look into them and revise our entries when the facts warrant it. If you've discovered a special place that we haven't included, we'll pass the information along to our correspondents and have them check it out. So send us your thoughts via e-mail at editors@fodors.com (specifying the name of the book on the subject line) or on paper in care of the Indonesia editor at Fodor's, 201 East 50th Street, New York, New York 10022. In the meantime, have a wonderful trip!

Karen Cure
Editorial Director

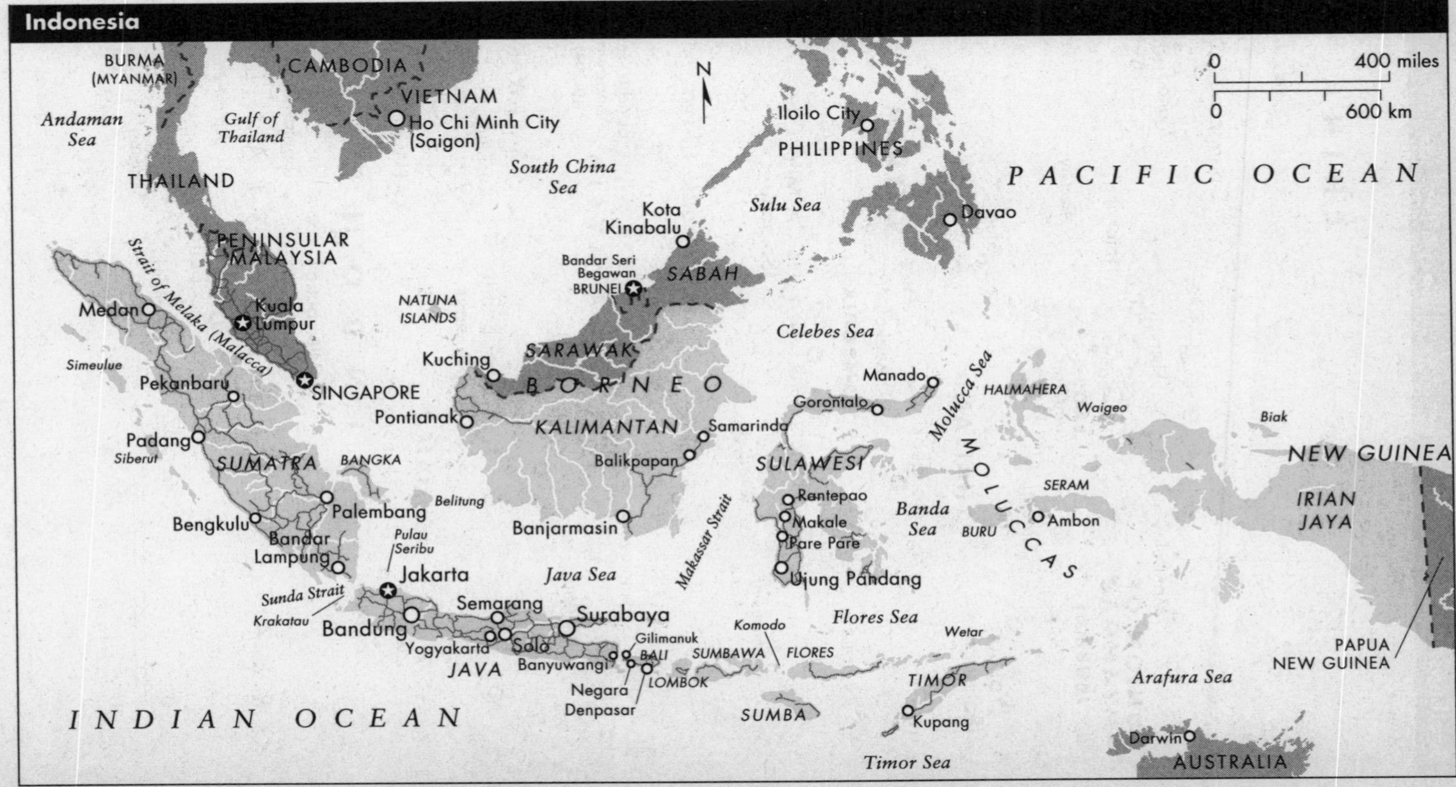
Indonesia
BURMA (MYANMAR)
CAMBODIA
VIETNAM
Ho Chi Minh City (Saigon)
Andaman Sea
Gulf of Thailand
THAILAND
South China Sea
PENINSULAR MALAYSIA
Kuala Lumpur
SINGAPORE
Strait of Melaka (Malacca)
Medan
Simeulue
Pekanbaru
Padang
Siberut
SUMATRA
BANGKA
Palembang
Bengkulu
Bandar Lampung
Belitung
Pulau Seribu
Jakarta
Sunda Strait
Krakatau
Bandung
Semarang
Yogyakarta
Solo
JAVA
Surabaya
Banyuwangi
Gilimanuk
BALI
Negara
Denpasar
LOMBOK
SUMBAWA
Komodo
FLORES
SUMBA
INDIAN OCEAN
NATUNA ISLANDS
Kuching
Pontianak
SARAWAK
BORNEO
KALIMANTAN
Kota Kinabalu
Bandar Seri Begawan
BRUNEI
SABAH
Samarinda
Balikpapan
Banjarmasin
Java Sea
Makassar Strait
N
Iloilo City
PHILIPPINES
Sulu Sea
Davao
Celebes Sea
Manado
Gorontalo
SULAWESI
Rantepao
Makale
Pare Pare
Ujung Pandang
Flores Sea
Molucca Sea
HALMAHERA
Waigeo
MOLUCCAS
SERAM
Ambon
BURU
Banda Sea
Wetar
TIMOR
Kupang
Timor Sea
Biak
NEW GUINEA
IRIAN JAYA
PAPUA NEW GUINEA
Arafura Sea
Darwin
AUSTRALIA
PACIFIC OCEAN
0 400 miles
0 600 km

Southeast Asia

CHINA
Guangzhou
Macao
HONG KONG
Hanoi
Haiphong
HAINAN
Mandalay
UNION OF MYANMAR (BURMA)
Luang Prabang
LAOS
Vientiane
Pegu
Chiang Mai
Yangon (Rangoon)
THAILAND
Hue
Danang
Bangkok
Angkor Wat
VIETNAM
CAMBODIA
Andaman Sea
Phnom Penh
Ho Chi Minh City (Saigon)
Isthmus of Kra
Gulf of Thailand
Songkhla
South China Sea
INDIAN OCEAN
Georgetown
PENINSULAR MALAYSIA
MALAYSIA
Bandar Seri Begawan
BRUNEI
SABA
Medan
Strait of Melaka (Malacca)
Kuala Lumpur
SARAWAK
Johor Bahru
SINGAPORE
Kuching
BORNEO
Karimata Strait
SUMATRA
KALIMANTAN
Jambi
KEPULAUAN
INDONESIA
Palembang
Banjarmasin
GREATER SUNDA ISLANDS
Jakarta
Java Sea
Bandung
Surabaya
Yogyakarta
JAVA
Malang
BALI
0
500 miles
0
750 km
N

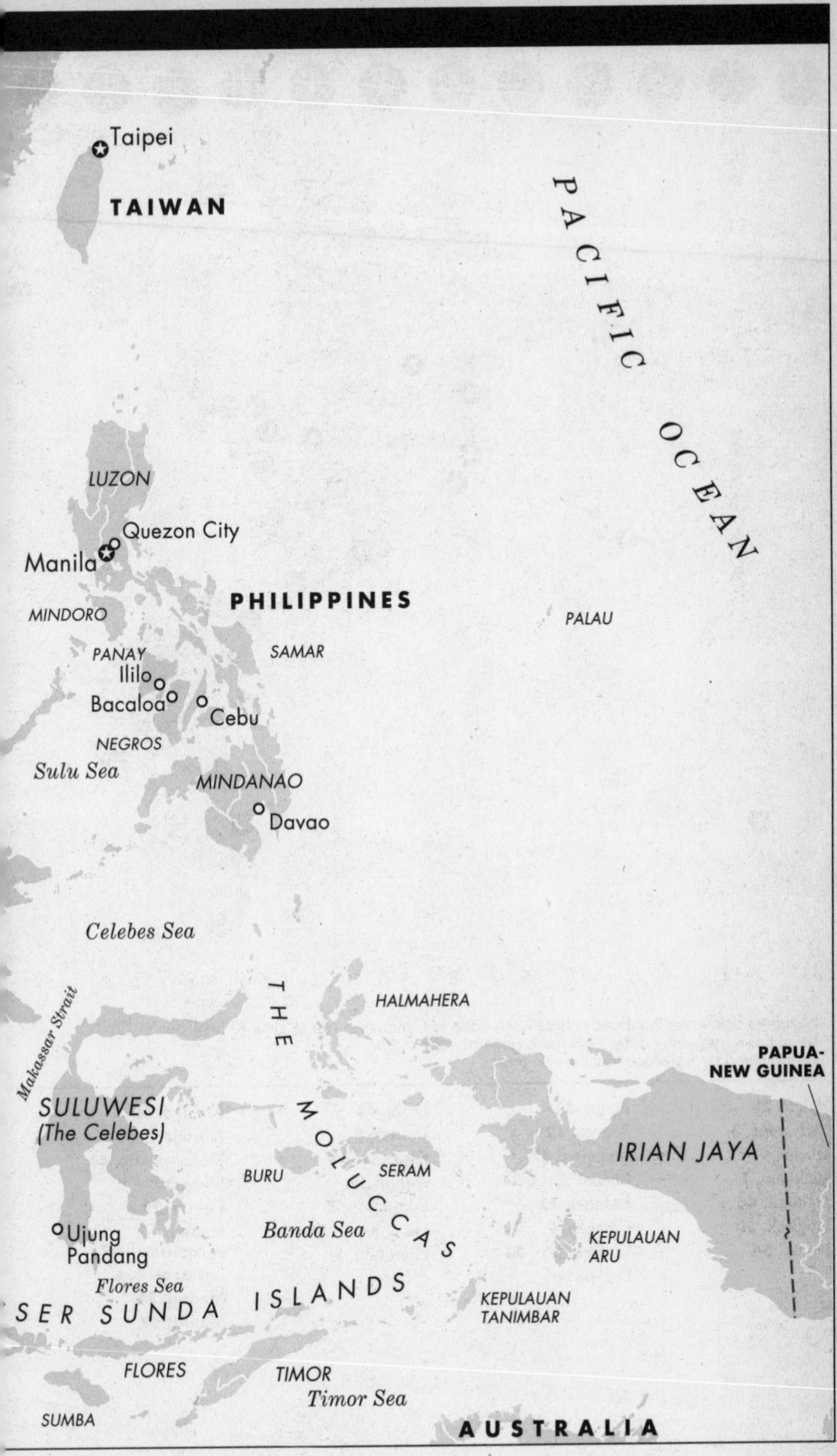

Taipei
TAIWAN
PACIFIC OCEAN
LUZON
Quezon City
Manila
PHILIPPINES
MINDORO
PALAU
PANAY
SAMAR
Ililo
Bacaloa
Cebu
NEGROS
Sulu Sea
MINDANAO
Davao
Celebes Sea
THE MOLUCCAS
HALMAHERA
Makassar Strait
PAPUA-
NEW GUINEA
SULUWESI
(The Celebes)
IRIAN JAYA
BURU
SERAM
Ujung
Pandang
Banda Sea
KEPULAUAN
ARU
Flores Sea
SER SUNDA ISLANDS
KEPULAUAN
TANIMBAR
FLORES
TIMOR
Timor Sea
SUMBA
AUSTRALIA

World Time Zones

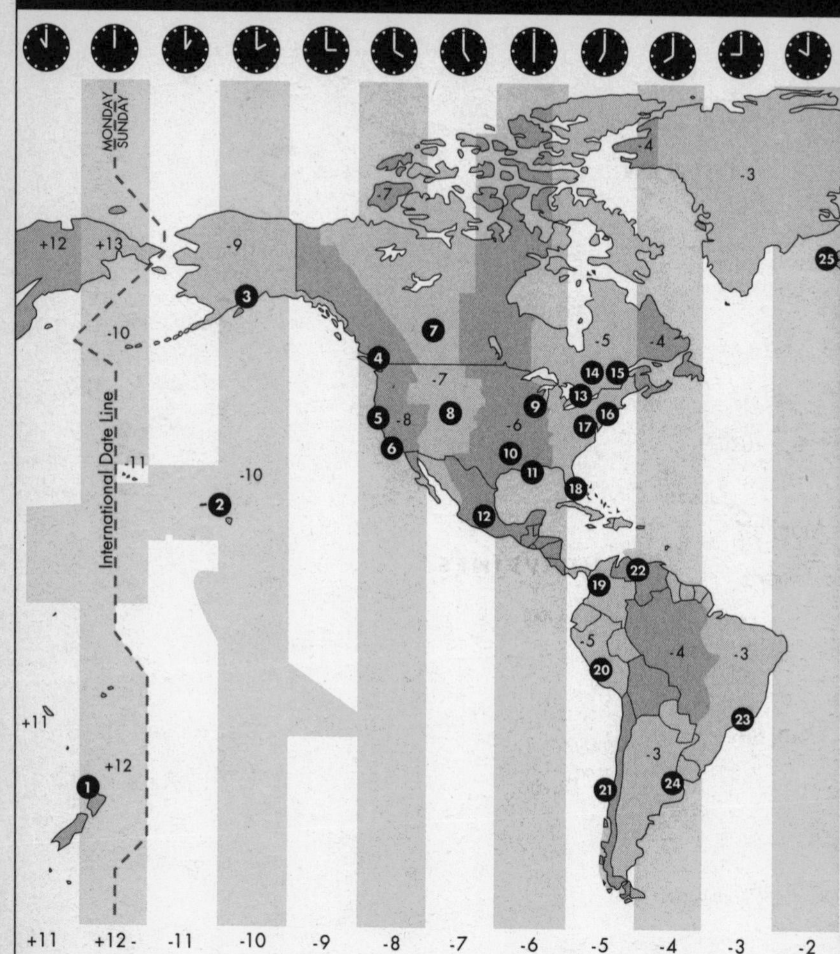

Numbers below vertical bands relate each zone to Greenwich Mean Time (0 hrs.).
Local times frequently differ from these general indications,
as indicated by light-face numbers on map.

Algiers, **29**
Anchorage, **3**
Athens, **41**
Auckland, **1**
Baghdad, **46**
Bangkok, **50**
Beijing, **54**
Berlin, **34**
Bogotá, **19**
Budapest, **37**
Buenos Aires, **24**
Caracas, **22**
Chicago, **9**
Copenhagen, **33**
Dallas, **10**
Delhi, **48**
Denver, **8**
Djakarta, **53**
Dublin, **26**
Edmonton, **7**
Hong Kong, **56**
Honolulu, **2**
Istanbul, **40**
Jerusalem, **42**
Johannesburg, **44**
Lima, **20**
Lisbon, **28**
London (Greenwich), **27**
Los Angeles, **6**
Madrid, **38**
Manila, **57**

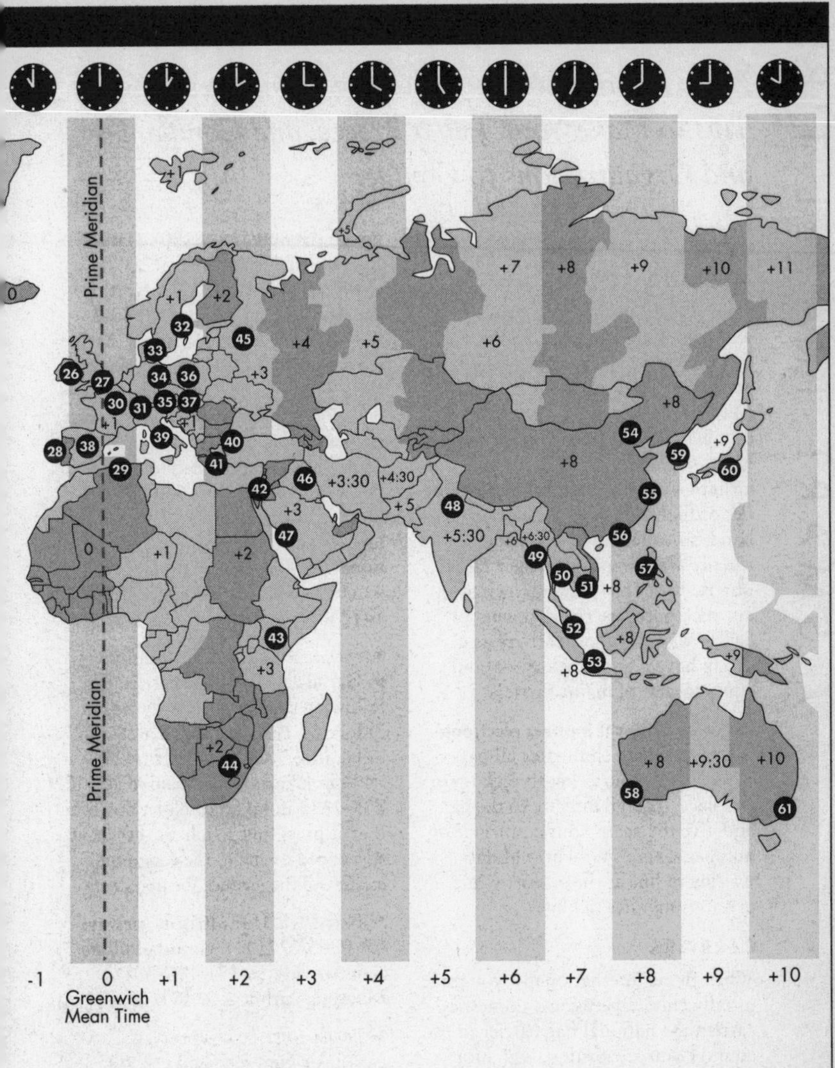

Mecca, **47**
Mexico City, **12**
Miami, **18**
Montréal, **15**
Moscow, **45**
Nairobi, **43**
New Orleans, **11**
New York City, **16**
Ottawa, **14**
Paris, **30**
Perth, **58**
Reykjavík, **25**
Rio de Janeiro, **23**
Rome, **39**
Saigon (Ho Chi Minh City), **51**
San Francisco, **5**
Santiago, **21**
Seoul, **59**
Shanghai, **55**
Singapore, **52**
Stockholm, **32**
Sydney, **61**
Tokyo, **60**
Toronto, **13**
Vancouver, **4**
Vienna, **35**
Warsaw, **36**
Washington, D.C., **17**
Yangon, **49**
Zürich, **31**

SMART TRAVEL TIPS A TO Z

Basic Information on Traveling in Indonesia, Savvy Tips to Make Your Trip a Breeze, and Companies and Organizations to Contact

AIR TRAVEL

BOOKING YOUR FLIGHT

Price is just one factor to consider when booking a flight: frequency of service and even a carrier's safety record are often just as important. Major airlines offer the greatest number of departures. Smaller airlines—including regional and no-frills airlines—usually have a limited number of flights daily. On the other hand, so-called low-cost airlines usually are cheaper, and their fares impose fewer restrictions, such as advance-purchase requirements. Safety-wise, low-cost carriers as a group have a good history—about equal to that of major carriers.

Ask your airline if it offers electronic ticketing, which eliminates all paperwork. There's no ticket to pick up or misplace. You go directly to the gate and give the agent your confirmation number. There's no worry about waiting in line at the airport while precious minutes tick by.

CARRIERS

When flying internationally, you must usually choose between a domestic carrier, the national flag carrier of the country you are visiting, and a foreign carrier from a third country. You may, for example, choose to fly Garuda Indonesian Airways to Indonesia. National flag carriers have the greatest number of nonstops. Domestic carriers may have better connections to your home town and serve a greater number of gateway cities. Third-party carriers may have a price advantage.

➤ MAJOR AIRLINES: **Air Canada** (☎ 800/776–3000 in the U.S., 514/393–3333 in Montreal, 416/925–2311 in Toronto). **Cathay Pacific** (☎ 800/233–2742 in the U.S. or 604/682–9747 in Vancouver). **China Airlines** (☎ 800/227–5118 in North America). **Continental** (☎ 800/525–0280). **Garuda Indonesian Airways** (☎ 212/370–0707 or 800/342–7832 in North America). **Japan Airlines** (☎ 800/525–3663 in North America). **Malaysia Airlines** (☎ 800/552–9264 in the U.S., 416/928–6670 in Toronto, 604/681–7741 in Vancouver). **Northwest Airlines** (☎ 800/225–2525 in North America). **Singapore Airlines** (☎ 800/742–3333 in the U.S., 604/682–9747 in Vancouver, 800/663–3046 toll-free in Canada). **Thai Airways International** (☎ 800/426–5204 in the U.S., 416/971–7907 in Toronto, 604/687–1412 in Vancouver).

➤ SMALLER AIRLINES: In addition to Garuda, the national carrier, the following smaller airlines fly within Indonesia: **Bouraq** (☎ 021/628–8827 in Jakarta), **Merpati** (☎ 021/424–7404 in Jakarta), and **Sempati** (☎ 021/835–1612 in Jakarta). Note, however, that at press time much air service was suspended owing to the economic crisis; call the airlines for updates.

➤ FROM THE U.K.: **British Airways** (☎ 0345/222111). **Garuda Indonesian Airways** ☎ 171/486–3011). **Malaysia Airlines** (☎ 181/740–2626).

➤ FROM AUSTRALIA AND NEW ZEALAND: **Air New Zealand** (☎ 9/357–3000 in Auckland). **Qantas** (☎ 13/1313).

CONSOLIDATORS

Consolidators buy tickets for scheduled international flights at reduced rates from the airlines, then sell them at prices that beat the best fare available directly from the airlines, usually without restrictions. Sometimes you can even get your money back if you need to return the ticket. Carefully read the fine print detailing penalties for changes and cancellations, and **confirm your consolidator reservation with the airline.**

➤ CONSOLIDATORS: **Cheap Tickets** (☎ 800/377–1000). **Up & Away Travel** (☎ 212/889–2345). **Discount Travel Network** (☎ 800/576–1600). **Unitravel** (☎ 800/325–2222). **World Travel Network** (☎ 800/409–6753).

CUTTING COSTS

The least-expensive airfares are priced for round-trip travel and usually must be purchased in advance. It's smart to **call a number of airlines, and when you are quoted a good price, book it on the spot**—the same fare may not be available the next day. Airlines generally allow you to change your return date for a fee. If you don't use your ticket, you can apply the cost toward the purchase of a new ticket, again for a small charge. However, most low-fare tickets are nonrefundable. To get the lowest airfare, **check different routings.** Compare prices of flights to and from different airports if your destination or home city has more than one gateway. Also price off-peak flights, which may be significantly less expensive.

Travel agents, especially those who specialize in finding the lowest fares (☞ Discounts & Deals, *below*), can be especially helpful when booking a plane ticket. When you're quoted a price, **ask your agent if the price is likely to get any lower.** Good agents know the seasonal fluctuations of airfares and can usually anticipate a sale or fare war. However, waiting can be risky: the fare could go *up* as seats become scarce, and you may wait so long that your preferred flight sells out. A wait-and-see strategy works best if your plans are flexible. If you must arrive and depart on certain dates, don't delay.

If you plan to visit other countries in Southeast Asia, **check into "Circle Pacific" fares or around-the-world "Globetrotter Fares."** These are flat-rate fares that are subject to advance-purchase restrictions, usually of 7–14 days, and other rules. "Circle Pacific" fares allow four stopovers, although travel may not be allowed to such countries as Vietnam, Burma, Laos, and Cambodia. Additional stopovers can be purchased for $50–$100. Around-the-world fares also have routing restrictions and require one transatlantic and one transpacific crossing. These tickets are based on either direction or mileage, and both have their advantages: direction-based fares can be less expensive, but mileage-based fares allow backtracking and multiple visits to a single city. If you only plan to travel to Indonesia, **consider buying Garuda Indonesia's "Visit Indonesia Pass"** (☞ Within Indonesia, *below*).

PICK YOUR ROUTE CAREFULLY

Nonstop flights from the United States to Indonesia are nonexistent. A direct flight, which requires at least one stop; or a connecting flight, which requires a change of airplanes, will often be your only choice. Some flights, especially nonstops, may be scheduled only on certain days of the week. Depending upon your destination, you may need to make more than one connection.

Flights to Indonesia may be transpacific or transatlantic. Westbound, the major gateway cities are Los Angeles, San Francisco, Seattle, Portland (Oregon), and Vancouver. Eastbound, the major gateways are New York, Detroit, Chicago, and Dallas. Stopover points may include Bangkok, Hong Kong, Kuala Lumpur, Seoul, Singapore, Taipei, or Tokyo. Your best bet is to **use Hong Kong, Singapore, or Tokyo for your stopover,** as many airlines fly nonstop to these cites from the west coast of the United States, and these cities have the greatest number of connecting flights. If you're leaving from the midwestern or eastern United States you can often **add a stopover in Europe or the Middle East to your transatlantic flight** for a small charge.

Many travelers take a major airline into an Asian capital, then transfer to one of the numerous smaller airlines that fly into Indonesia. Others take advantage of international routes that utilize less common entry points: Davao, the Philippines, to Manado, Sulawesi; Darwin, Australia, to Kupang, Timor; Kuching, Malaysia, to Pontianak, Kalimantan (on Borneo); and Port Moresby, New Guinea, to Jayapura, Irian Jaya—although the latter requires a special visa.

CHECK IN & BOARDING

Airlines routinely overbook planes, assuming that not everyone with a ticket will show up, but sometimes everyone does. When that happens, airlines ask for volunteers to give up their seats. In return these volunteers usually get a certificate for a free flight and are rebooked on the next flight out. If there are not enough volunteers, the airline must choose who will be denied boarding. The first to get bumped are passengers who checked in late and those flying on discounted tickets, so **get to the gate and check in as early as possible,** especially during peak periods.

Although the trend on international flights is to drop reconfirmation requirements, many airlines still ask you to reconfirm each leg of your international itinerary. Failure to do so may result in your reservation being canceled.

Always **bring a government-issued photo ID to the airport.** You may be asked to show it before you are allowed to check in.

ENJOY THE FLIGHT

For more legroom, **request an emergency-aisle seat**; don't however, sit in the row in front of the emergency aisle or in front of a bulkhead, where seats may not recline. If you don't like airline food, **ask for special meals when booking.** These can be vegetarian, low-cholesterol, or kosher, for example.

Those traveling with children are usually offered the bulkhead seat when available. **Note that although bulkhead seats offer more legroom, carry-on baggage must be stored overhead,** which can be inconvenient for those with toddlers who frequently need diapers, food, toys, and other items. **If you're flying with an infant, ask the agent for a bassinet,** which hooks up to the bulkhead wall or hangs from the ceiling. Flight attendants will usually heat up or refrigerate bottles and provide other services for young ones if the request is made ahead of time.

Some carriers have prohibited smoking throughout their systems; others allow smoking only on certain routes or even certain departures from that route. For flights within Asia, many airlines still have smoking sections, so **contact your carrier regarding its smoking policy.**

FLYING TIMES

Transpacific flying times to Bali are approximately 19 hours from Los Angeles, 23 hours from Chicago, 25 hours from New York, and 22 hours from Vancouver. Flying the eastbound route, the flight time from New York is 23 hours to Jakarta and 25 hours to Bali. Allowing for stops, it's 26 hours from Toronto and Montréal to Jakarta and 28 to Bali. From London it's 16 and 18 hours to Jakarta and Bali, respectively. From Sydney and Melbourne, it's 7 and 4 hours to Bali and 9 and 6 hours to Jakarta. From Auckland, it takes 9 hours to reach Bali and 11 hours to Jakarta.

HOW TO COMPLAIN

If your baggage goes astray or your flight goes awry, complain right away. Most carriers require that you **file a claim immediately.**

➤ AIRLINE COMPLAINTS: U.S. Department of Transportation **Aviation Consumer Protection Division** (✉ C-75, Room 4107, Washington, DC 20590, ☎ 202/366–2220). **Federal Aviation Administration Consumer Hotline** (☎ 800/322–7873).

WITHIN INDONESIA

If you're island hopping, or even just seeing the highlights one one of the larger islands, much of your travel is likely to be by air. Unless you are a very savvy traveler or have the time to examine your options after you arrive, it's best to **buy all your air tickets for travel within Indonesia before you leave home.** First, **compare the cost of buying one ticket that includes all of your stopovers with the cost of buying individual tickets for each leg of your trip.** Garuda Indonesia offers a "Visit Indonesia Pass" for $300, good for three flights within Indonesia, and additional flight coupons for $100 each. It's best to buy the pass before your arrival (allow at least a week for processing), but if you don't have time to purchase one before your trip, you can buy one in Indonesia if you show a local airline office a copy of your international tickets. One hitch to the deal, though, is that you must fly in and out of the country on Garuda Indonesia; otherwise, a surcharge of $60 is added.

Flying within Indonesia requires patience and flexibility, as schedules run on the infamous *jam karet,* or "rubber time," and long hauls may incorporate unscheduled stops. From Jakarta it's 40 minutes to Bandung, 1¼ hours to Yogyakarta, and 1½ hours to Surabaya on Java; 1½ hours to Denpasar on Bali; 2 hours to Ujung Pandang on Sulawesi; 2¼ hours to Medan on Sumatra; and 2¼ hours to Mataram on Lombok. From Denpasar, it's 40 minutes to Mataram and almost 1½ hours to Ujung Pandang.

AIRPORTS & TRANSFERS

AIRPORTS

International flights to Jakarta's Soekarno Hatta Airport land at Terminal One, with the exception of Garuda Indonesia Airways flights, which are processed through Terminal Two. Bali's Ngurah Rai International Airport and Medan's Polonia Airport are also major international gateways. There's an airport tax of Rp 25,000 for international departures and one of Rp 5,500 to 11,000, depending on the airport, for domestic departures.

➤ AIRPORT INFORMATION: **Ngurah Rai International Airport** (☎ 0361/751026). **Polonia Airport** (☎ 061/538444). **Soekarno Hatta Airport** (☎ 021/550–5307).

TRANSFERS

The only way into Medan from the airport is by taxi. A fixed rate of Rp 4,800 applies. Most hotels can arrange for a car or minivan to meet you at Ngurah Rai International Airport. Otherwise, order a taxi at the counter outside customs; the fixed fare varies anywhere from around Rp 5,000 to Kuta to Rp 40,000 to Ubud depending on the location of your hotel; count on about Rp 2,000 per mile. You can also catch a bemo outside the airport, but make sure that you're going in the right direction and that if you enter an empty van you're not hiring it for yourself—unless that's your intention.

Soekarno Hatta Airport is 35 km (20 mi) northwest of Jakarta. To be safe, allow a good hour for the trip on weekdays. Taxis *from* the airport add a surcharge of Rp 2,300 and the road toll (Rp 4,000) to the metered fare. The surcharge doesn't apply going *to* the airport. The average fare to a downtown hotel is Rp 20,000. However, if it's raining and there are likely to be traffic jams, you'll need to negotiate a fare—Rp 40,000 should do it.

BAJAJ

Although scooting through traffic in these three-wheel orange contraptions can be faster, more exciting, and less expensive than taxis, keep in mind that they are also hot (no air-conditioning) and loud (no glass in the windows). A few blocks will cost Rp 500–Rp 1,000; a half-mile will run Rp 2,000–Rp 5,000, depending on your negotiating skills. Drivers are notorious for overcharging, so bargain hard—and finalize the price *before* you get in.

BECAKS

These three-wheeled pedicabs are useful for short distances. In Jakarta they're permitted only in the outlying neighborhoods, but elsewhere in Indonesia they're plentiful. A few blocks will cost Rp 200–Rp 500; a half-mile can run Rp 1,000–Rp 3,000. Becak drivers are tough bargainers, but if one doesn't meet your price, another may. Just be sure to sort out the fare with the driver beforehand.

BEMOS

A bemo is a converted pickup truck or minivan—a standard form of transport for short trips. Most bemos follow regular routes and will stop anywhere along the way to pick up or discharge passengers. You pay when you get out. Try to learn the fare (they vary according to distance) from another passenger; otherwise you'll be overcharged. An empty bemo will often try to pick up Western travelers, but beware: unless you clarify that it's on its regular route, you will be chartering it as a taxi.

BOAT TRAVEL

High-speed ferries depart Monday–Saturday from Penang, Malaysia, and arrive in Belawan (the port of Medan), Sumatra, five hours later. Return trips depart around noon from Belawan every day except Monday. Contact Express Bahagia or Perdana Express in Medan, or Kuala Perlis-Langkawi Ferry Service in Penang. Another popular ferry route is that from Singapore to the Riau Archipelago's Batam—there are departures every hour from Singapore's World Trade Center docks to Sekupang, Batam during the day—where you can pick up a domestic flight to other points in Indonesia. Another ferry route from Singapore is to Tanjung Pinang, in the Riau Archipelago and just a 90-minute ferry ride, and from there you can take a Merpati flight to another Indonesian destination. The state-owned Pelni company has many passenger boat routes throughout the country. For more details on boat travel between Indonesia's islands, *see* the Essentials section *in* the individual chapters.

➤ BOAT COMPANIES: **Express Bahagia** (Jln. Sisingamangaraja 92A, Medan, ☏ 061/720954; PPC Building, Jln. Pasara King Edward, Penang, ☏ 04/263–1943). **Kuala Perlis-Langkawi Ferry Service** (PPC Building, Jln. Pasara King Edward, Penang, ☏ 04/262–5630). **Pelni** (Jln. Angkasa 18, Jakarta, ☏ 021/421–1921; Jln. Martadinata 38, Ujung Pandang, ☏ 0411/331393). **Perdana Express** (Jln. Katamso 35C, Medan, ☏ 061/545803).

BUS TRAVEL

As many Indonesians don't own cars, bus travel is comprehensive throughout much of the country. It's also inexpensive: the 14-hour trip between Jakarta and Yogyakarta, for instance, costs Rp 17,500. Comfort levels vary, however. Buses for long-distance trips often have extra-wide, reclining seats; air-conditioning; videos; box or buffet meals; and rest rooms. Local buses are usually crowded and lack any amenities, including air-conditioning. The main stumbling block for local bus travel is language. Even if you know your route, city buses can still be confusing, so get written instructions/directions from a hotel staff member to show a bus driver—just in case.

Tickets and schedules are available from terminals, travel desks, or travel agencies. Tourist offices also provide schedules. The only international land crossing from Indonesia is between Kuching, Malaysia and Pontianak, Kalimantan.

➤ BUS COMPANIES: For Java and Sumatra, contact **Antar Lintas Sumatra** (Jln. Jati Baru 87A, Jakarta, ☏ 021/320970) or **Bintang Kejora** (Jln. K. H. Mas Mansyur 59, Jakarta, ☏ 021/336677). For Java, Bali, and Sumatra, try **PT. ANS** (Jln. Senen Raya 50, Jakarta, ☏ 021/340494), **Java Indah Express** (Jln. Diponegoro 14, Denpasar, ☏ 361/227329), or **Lorena** (Jln. Hasannudin 3, Denpasar, ☏ 361/234941). To book a seat on one of the smaller vehicles that run east through Nusa Tenggara, try the numerous Denpasar transport agencies on Jalan Diponegoro and Jalan Hasannudin; otherwise, you can ask the drivers at any ferry terminal if seats are available. **Liman Express** (Jln. Timor, Ujung Pandang, ☏ 0411/315851) makes daily runs to Tanatoraja on Sulawesi.

BUSINESS HOURS

Banks are open from around 9 AM to 3 PM or 4 PM, but they may close during the lunch hour. Bank branches in hotels may stay open later. **Government offices** are open Monday–Thursday from approximately 8–3 and Friday 8–11:30 AM. Some are also open on Saturday 8–2. **Offices** have varied hours, usually around 9–5 weekdays and a half day on Saturday. Most **museums** are open Tuesday–Thursday and weekends 9–2 (although some larger museums stay open until 4 or 5), Friday 9–noon. **Shops** are generally open Monday–Saturday 9–5. Offices and stores in Muslim areas are only open until 11 AM on Friday.

CAMERAS & COMPUTERS

EQUIPMENT PRECAUTIONS

Always **keep your film, tape, or computer disks out of the sun.** Carry an extra supply of batteries, and **be**

prepared to turn on your camera, camcorder, or laptop to prove to security personnel that the device is real. Always **ask for hand inspection of film,** which becomes clouded after successive exposure to airport X-ray machines, and **keep videotapes and computer disks away from metal detectors.**

TRAVEL PHOTOGRAPHY

➤ PHOTO HELP: Kodak Information Center (☎ 800/242–2424). ***Kodak Guide to Shooting Great Travel Pictures,*** available in bookstores or from Fodor's Travel Publications (☎ 800/533–6478; $16.50 plus $4 shipping).

CAR RENTAL

Given the traffic situations within the city limits of major Indonesian destinations, it's probably best to **leave the driving to the cabbies and chauffeurs** who rule the roads here. Self-drive cars are available through large rental agencies, hotels, or travel agencies in major cities and tourist hubs, including Jakarta, Yogyakarta, and Bali. **If you must rent a car, use common sense about when to do so.** On Bali, renting cars is common practice and relatively safe, but in other locales traffic conditions and poor roads can make driving hazardous. Although hiring a car and driver (through your hotel or a travel agent) generally costs 25%–50% percent more than simply renting a car (rates start at about $45 a day), it's still relatively inexpensive.

Gas prices are higher than in the States, the equivalent of around $1.65 for a U.S. gallon. Stations are few and far between, so **don't set out with less than a quarter tank,** and **check your fuel gauge frequently to make sure that it works.** Pertamina is a major gas station chain, though there are numerous small vendors as well; however, **be sure you know how to ask for the right type of fuel.**

➤ MAJOR AGENCIES: Avis (☎ 800/331–1084, 800/879–2847 in Canada, 008/225533 in Australia). Hertz (☎ 800/654–3001, 800/263–0600 in Canada, 0345/555888 in the U.K., 03/9222–2523 in Australia, 03/358–6777 in New Zealand). National InterRent (☎ 800/227–3876; 0345/222525 in the U.K., where it is known as Europcar InterRent).

➤ SMALL AGENCIES: For smaller agencies *see* the Essentials sections for specific regions *in* individual chapters.

CUTTING COSTS

To get the best deal, **book through a travel agent who is willing to shop around.**

Also **ask your travel agent about a company's customer-service record.** How has the company responded to late plane arrivals and vehicle mishaps? Are there often lines at the rental counter? If you're traveling during a holiday period, does a confirmed reservation guarantee you a car?

INSURANCE

When driving a rented car you are generally responsible for any damage to or loss of the vehicle. You also are liable for any property damage or personal injury that you may cause while driving. Before you rent, **see what coverage you already have** under the terms of your personal auto-insurance policy and credit cards.

REQUIREMENTS

Most Indonesian car rental companies require (or would like you to have) your license from home *and* an International Driver's License. You can get one through the American or Canadian automobile associations, or, in the United Kingdom, through the Automobile Association or Royal Automobile Club. Most Western companies also have age requirements. For example, Avis requires that you be at least 25 years old, Hertz 21 years old, and National 18 years old.

Always discuss your itinerary with the agent before signing the contract. Some rental contracts may limit the areas to which you can drive. For example, you need a special permit—really just a letter from the rental agency—to cross from Bali to Lombok.

SURCHARGES

Before you pick up a car in one city and leave it in another, **ask about drop-off charges or one-way service fees,** which can be substantial. Note, too, that some rental agencies charge extra if you return the car before the time specified in your contract. To avoid a hefty refueling fee, **fill the tank just before you turn in the car,** but be aware that gas stations near the rental outlet may overcharge.

CHILDREN & TRAVEL

CHILDREN IN INDONESIA

Youngsters are not only welcomed in Indonesia—they're embraced with delight in most areas. Only the strictest business establishments and stiffest upscale hotels and restaurants (ask before you book) frown upon children; otherwise, they're seen as a natural complement to life. You will be amazed at how many people will want to hold and play with your kids, and at how their presence will actually open conversations and cut through cultural boundaries. Because they'll be the center of attention, if your youngsters are very young or particularly shy, plan outings for off-peak hours. Many large hotels have playgrounds and special menus and activities for children; smaller places often have more personalized services. **Check to see what types of kid-friendly amenities a hotel offers.**

Be sure to plan ahead and **involve your youngsters** as you outline your trip. When packing, include things to keep them busy en route. On sightseeing days try to schedule activities of special interest to your children. If you are renting a car don't forget to **arrange for a car seat** when you reserve. Most hotels in Indonesia allow children under a certain age to stay in their parents' room at no extra charge, but others charge them as extra adults; be sure to **ask about the cutoff age for children's discounts.**

➤ BABY-SITTING: There are few formal sitting agencies in Indonesia. Large hotels and resorts have their own activity programs and baby-sitting services; smaller establishments will usually recruit a trusted family member or neighbor to provide any assistance you need. Some families hire a nanny from an au pair service before they depart.

FLYING

If your children are two or older, **ask about children's airfares.** As a general rule, infants under two not occupying a seat fly at greatly reduced fares or even for free.

In general the adult baggage allowance applies to children paying half or more of the adult fare. When booking, **ask about carry-on allowances for those traveling with infants.** In general, for babies charged 10% of the adult fare you are allowed one carry-on bag and a collapsible stroller, which may have to be checked; you may be limited to less if the flight is full.

Experts agree that it's a good idea to use safety seats aloft for children weighing less than 40 pounds. Airlines, however, can set their own policies: U.S. carriers allow FAA-approved models but usually require that you buy a ticket, even if your child would otherwise ride free, since the seats must be strapped into regular seats. Airline rules vary, so it's important to **check your airline's policy about using safety seats during takeoff and landing.** Safety seats cannot obstruct the movement of other passengers in the row, so get an appropriate seat assignment as early as possible.

When making your reservation, **request children's meals or a free-standing bassinet** if you need them; the latter are available only to those seated at the bulkhead, where there's enough legroom. Remember, however, that bulkhead seats may not have their own overhead bins, and there's no storage space in front of you—a major inconvenience.

GROUP TRAVEL

If you're planning to take your kids on a tour, look for companies that specialize in family travel.

➤ FAMILY-FRIENDLY TOUR OPERATORS: **Rascals in Paradise** (✉ 650 5th St., Suite 505, San Francisco, CA 94107, ☎ 415/978–9800 or 800/872–7225, FAX 415/442–0289).

CONSUMER PROTECTION

Whenever possible, **pay with a major credit card** so you can cancel payment or get reimbursed if there's a problem, provided that you can provide documentation. This is the best way to pay, whether you're buying travel arrangements before your trip or shopping at your destination.

If you're doing business with a particular company for the first time, **contact your local Better Business Bureau and the attorney general's offices** in your state and the company's home state, as well. Have any complaints been filed?

Finally, if you're buying a package or tour, always **consider travel insurance** that includes default coverage (☞ Insurance, *below*).

➤ LOCAL BBBS: **Council of Better Business Bureaus** (✉ 4200 Wilson Blvd., Suite 800, Arlington, VA 22203, ☎ 703/276–0100, FAX 703/525–8277).

CRUISING

If you're interested in visiting a variety of Southeast Asian cities, **consider a cruise to the region.** Southeast Asia is one of the hottest destinations in cruising, and you can sail in many different styles. Choices range from a traditional ocean liner to a clipper-type tall ship to a luxury yacht. To get the best deal, **book with a cruise-only travel agency.**

➤ CRUISE LINES: **Crystal Cruises** (✉ 2121 Ave. of the Stars, Los Angeles, CA 90067, ☎ 800/446–6620). **Cunard Line Limited** (✉ 555 5th Ave., New York, NY 10017, ☎ 800/528–6273). **Orient Lines** (✉ 1510 S.E. 17th St., Suite 400, Fort Lauderdale, FL 33316, ☎ 305/527–6660 or 800/333–7300). **Princess Cruises** (✉ 10100 Santa Monica Blvd., Los Angeles, CA 90067, ☎ 310/553–1770). **Radisson Seven Seas Cruises** (✉ 600 Corporate Dr., Suite 410, Fort Lauderdale, FL 33334, ☎ 800/333–3333). **Renaissance Cruises** (✉ 1800 Eller Dr., Suite 300, Box 350307, Fort Lauderdale, FL 33335-0307, ☎ 800/525–2450). **Royal Caribbean Cruise Line** (✉ 1050 Caribbean Way, Miami, FL 33132, ☎ 305/539–6000). **Seabourn Cruise Line** (✉ 55 Francisco St., San Francisco, CA 94133, ☎ 415/391–7444 or 800/929–9595). **Silversea Cruises** (✉ 110 E. Broward Blvd., Fort Lauderdale, FL 33301, ☎ 305/522–4477 or 800/722–9955). **Star Clippers** (✉ 4101 Salzedo Ave., Coral Gables, FL 33146, ☎ 800/442–0551).

CUSTOMS & DUTIES

When shopping, **keep receipts** for all of your purchases. Upon reentering the country, **be ready to show customs officials what you've bought.** If you feel a duty is incorrect, appeal the assessment. If you object to the way your clearance was handled, get the inspector's badge number. In either case, first ask to see a supervisor, then write to the appropriate authorities, beginning with the port director at your point of entry.

ON ARRIVAL

Two liters of liquor and 200 cigarettes may be brought into Indonesia duty-free. Restrictions apply on the import of radios and television sets. Of course, no drugs, weapons, or pornography are allowed; neither are cassette players or printed matter in Indonesian or Chinese. Note: carry all prescription medicines in their original containers and keep a copy of the doctor's slip with you.

ON DEPARTURE

You may not export more than 50,000 rupiah per person. Other forbidden exports include antiques (generally more than 100 years old and worth more than $100; check with Customs for current specifications), artifacts, cultural treasures, and products made from endangered plants and animals, such as furs, feathers, and the tortoiseshell items sold in Bali.

IN AUSTRALIA

Australia residents who are 18 or older may bring back $A400 worth of souvenirs and gifts (including jewelry), 250 cigarettes or 250 grams of tobacco, and 1,125 ml of alcohol (including wine, beer, and spirits). Residents under 18 may bring back $A200 worth of goods.

➤ INFORMATION: **Australian Customs Service** (Regional Director, ✉ Box 8, Sydney, NSW 2001, ☎ 02/9213–2000, FAX 02/9213–4000).

IN CANADA

Canadian residents who have been out of Canada for at least 7 days may bring in C$500 worth of goods duty-free. If you've been away less than 7 days but more than 48 hours, the duty-free allowance drops to C$200; if your trip lasts 24–48 hours, the allowance is C$50. You may not pool allowances with family members. Goods claimed under the C$500 exemption may follow you by mail; those claimed under the lesser exemptions must accompany you. Alcohol and tobacco products may be included in the 7-day and 48-hour exemptions but not in the 24-hour exemption. If you meet the age requirements of the province or territory through which you reenter Canada, you may bring in, duty-free, 1.14 liters (40 imperial ounces) of wine or liquor *or* 24 12-ounce cans or bottles of beer or ale. If you are 16 or older you may bring in, duty-free, 200 cigarettes and 50 cigars.

You may send an unlimited number of gifts worth up to C$60 each duty-free to Canada. Label the package UNSOLICITED GIFT—VALUE UNDER $60. Alcohol and tobacco are excluded.

➤ INFORMATION: **Revenue Canada** (✉ 2265 St. Laurent Blvd. S, Ottawa, Ontario K1G 4K3, ☎ 613/993–0534, 800/461–9999 in Canada).

IN NEW ZEALAND

Although greeted with a *Haere Mai* ("Welcome to New Zealand"), homeward-bound residents with goods to declare must present themselves for inspection. If you're 17 or older, you may bring back $700 worth of souvenirs and gifts. Your duty-free allowance also includes 4.5 liters of wine or beer; one 1,125-milliliter bottle of spirits; and either 200 cigarettes, 250 grams of tobacco, 50 cigars, or a combo of all three up to 250 grams.

➤ INFORMATION: **New Zealand Customs** (✉ Custom House, 50 Anzac Ave., Box 29, Auckland, New Zealand, ☎ 09/359–6655, ☎ 09/309–2978).

IN THE U.K.

From countries outside the EU, including Indonesia, you may import, duty-free, 200 cigarettes or 50 cigars; 1 liter of spirits or 2 liters of fortified or sparkling wine or liqueurs; 2 liters of still table wine; 60 milliliters of perfume; 250 milliliters of toilet water; plus £136 worth of other goods, including gifts and souvenirs.

➤ INFORMATION: **HM Customs and Excise** (✉ Dorset House, Stamford St., London SE1 9NG, ☎ 0171/202–4227).

IN THE U.S.

U.S. residents may bring home $400 worth of foreign goods duty-free if they've been out of the country for at least 48 hours (and if they haven't used the $400 allowance or any part of it in the past 30 days).

U.S. residents 21 and older may bring back 1 liter of alcohol duty-free. In addition, regardless of your age, you are allowed 200 cigarettes and 100 non-Cuban cigars. Antiques, which the U.S. Customs Service defines as objects more than 100 years old, enter duty-free, as do original works of art done entirely by hand, including paintings, drawings, and sculptures.

You may also send packages home duty-free: up to $200 worth of goods for personal use, with a limit of one parcel per addressee per day (and no alcohol or tobacco products or perfume worth more than $5); label the package PERSONAL USE, and attach a list of its contents and their retail value. Do not label the package UNSOLICITED GIFT, or your duty-free exemption will drop to $100. Mailed items do not affect your duty-free allowance on your return.

➤ INFORMATION: **U.S. Customs Service** (Inquiries, ✉ Box 7407, Washington, DC 20044, ☎ 202/927–6724; complaints, Office of Regulations and Rulings, ✉ 1301 Constitution Ave. NW, Washington, DC 20229; registration of equipment, Resource Management, ✉ 1301 Constitution Ave. NW, Washington DC 20229, ☎ 202/927–0540).

DISABILITIES & ACCESSIBILITY

ACCESS IN INDONESIA

Those with disabilities who are planning a trip to Indonesia will find facilities woefully inadequate or nonexistent. However, the situation is quickly changing at many hotels and sights as the need for access is universally recognized. On Bali, for example, the Four Seasons Jimbaran, the Grand Hyatt Bali, and the Amandari resorts all offer wheelchair access and other amenities. International airlines can generally accommodate people with disabilities, though smaller regional airlines may not offer the same standards of access or comfort; check before you book.

MAKING RESERVATIONS

When discussing accessibility with an operator or reservations agent, **ask hard questions.** Are there any stairs, inside *or* out? Are there grab bars next to the toilet *and* in the shower/tub? How wide is the doorway to the room? To the bathroom? For the most extensive facilities meeting the latest legal specifications, **opt for newer accommodations,** which are more likely to have been designed with access in mind. Older buildings or ships may have more limited facilities. Be sure to **discuss your needs before booking.**

TRANSPORTATION

➤ COMPLAINTS: **Disability Rights Section** (✉ U.S. Department of Justice, Civil Rights Division, Box 66738, Washington, DC 20035–6738, ☎ 202/514–0301 or 800/514–0301, TTY 202/514–0383 or 800/514–0383, FAX 202/307–1198) for general complaints. **Aviation Consumer Protection Division** (☞ Air Travel, *above*) for airline-related problems. **Civil Rights Office** (✉ U.S. Department of Transportation, Departmental Office of Civil Rights, S-30, 400 7th St. SW, Room 10215, Washington, DC, 20590, ☎ 202/366–4648, FAX 202/366–9371) for problems with surface transportation.

TRAVEL AGENCIES & TOUR OPERATORS

As a whole, the travel industry has become more aware of the needs of travelers with disabilities. In the U.S., the Americans with Disabilities Act requires that travel firms serve the needs of all travelers. Note, though, that some agencies and operators specialize in making travel arrangements for individuals and groups with disabilities.

➤ TRAVELERS WITH MOBILITY PROBLEMS: **Access Adventures** (✉ 206 Chestnut Ridge Rd., Rochester, NY 14624, ☎ 716/889–9096), run by a former physical-rehabilitation counselor, offers tours throughout Asia, including Indonesia. **Flying Wheels Travel** (✉ 143 W. Bridge St., Box 382, Owatonna, MN 55060, ☎ 507/451–5005 or 800/535–6790, FAX 507/451–1685), an agency for wheelchair-bound travelers, coordinates trips to a number of countries in Asia.

➤ TRAVELERS WITH DEVELOPMENTAL DISABILITIES: **New Directions** (✉ 5276 Hollister Ave., Suite 207, Santa Barbara, CA 93111, ☎ 805/967–2841, FAX 805/964–7344) offers packages throughout Asia.

DISCOUNTS & DEALS

Be a smart shopper and **compare all your options** before making any choice. A plane ticket bought with a promotional coupon may not be cheaper than the least expensive fare from a discount ticket agency. For high-price travel purchases, such as packages or tours, keep in mind that what you get is just as important as what you save. Just because something is cheap doesn't mean it's a bargain.

CLUBS & COUPONS

Many companies sell discounts in the form of travel clubs and coupon books, but these cost money. You must use participating advertisers to get a deal, and only after you recoup the initial membership cost or book price do you begin to save. If you plan to use the club or coupons frequently, you may save considerably. Before signing up, find out what discounts you get for free.

➤ DISCOUNT CLUBS: **Entertainment Travel Editions** (✉ 2125 Butterfield Rd., Troy, MI 48084, ☎ 800/445–4137; $20–$51, depending on destination). **Great American Traveler** (✉ Box 27965, Salt Lake City, UT 84127, ☎ 801/974–3033 or 800/548–2812; $49.95 per year). **Moment's Notice Discount Travel Club** (✉ 7301 New Utrecht Ave., Brooklyn, NY 11204, ☎ 718/234–6295; $25 per year, single or family). **Privilege Card International** (✉ 237 E. Front St., Youngstown, OH 44503, ☎ 330/746–5211 or 800/236–9732; $74.95 per year). **Sears's Mature Outlook** (✉ Box 9390, Des Moines, IA 50306, ☎ 800/336–6330; $19.95 per year). **Travelers Advantage** (✉ CUC Travel Service, 3033 S. Parker Rd., Suite 1000, Aurora, CO 80014, ☎ 800/548–1116 or 800/648–4037; $59.95 per year, single or family). **Worldwide Discount Travel Club** (✉ 1674 Meridian Ave., Miami Beach, FL 33139, ☎ 305/534–2082; $50 per year family, $40 single).

CREDIT-CARD BENEFITS

When you use your credit card to make travel purchases you may get free travel-accident insurance, collision-damage insurance, and medical or legal assistance, depending on the card and the bank that issued it. American Express, MasterCard, and Visa provide one or more of these services, so **get a copy of your credit card's travel-benefits policy.** If you are a member of an auto club, always **ask hotel and car-rental reservations agents about auto-club discounts.** Some clubs offer additional discounts on tours, cruises, and admission to attractions.

DISCOUNT RESERVATIONS

To save money, **look into discount-reservations services** with toll-free numbers, which use their buying power to get a better price on hotels, airline tickets, even car rentals. When booking a room, always **call the hotel's local toll-free number** (if one is available) rather than the central reservations number—you'll often get a better price. Always ask about special packages or corporate rates.

When shopping for the best deal on hotels and car rentals, **look for guaranteed exchange rates,** which protect you against a falling dollar. With your rate locked in, you won't pay more, even if the price goes up in the local currency.

➤ AIRLINE TICKETS: ☎ 800/FLY–4–LESS.

➤ HOTEL ROOMS: **Steigenberger Reservation Service** (☎ 800/223–5652).**Travel Interlink** (☎ 800/888–5898). **VacationLand** (☎ 800/245–0050).

PACKAGE DEALS

Packages and guided tours can save you money, but don't confuse the two. When you buy a package, your travel remains independent, just as though you had planned and booked the trip yourself. Fly/drive packages, which combine airfare and car rental, are often a good deal.

ELECTRICITY

The electrical current in Indonesia is 220 volts, 50 cycles alternating. **If you're coming from North America bring an adapter and a converter.** Electricity may flicker out at any time, even in Jakarta and Bali. Carry a small flashlight with extra batteries and keep computers charged at all times just in case.

If your appliances are dual-voltage, you'll need only an adapter. Don't use 110-volt outlets, marked FOR SHAVERS ONLY, for high-wattage appliances such as blow-dryers. Most laptops operate equally well on 110 and 220 volts and so require only an adapter.

EMBASSIES & CONSULATES

➤ AUSTRALIAN: **Denpasar Consulate** (Jln. Prof. Mochtar Yamin Kav 51, Renon,, ☎ 0361/235092), and **Jakarta Embassy:** (Jln. H. R. Rasuna Said Kav. C15–16, ☎ 021/522–7111).

➤ CANADIAN: **Jakarta Embassy** (Jln. Jendral Sudirman Kav. 29, 5th floor, Wisma Metropolitan 1, ☎ 021/510709).

➤ NEW ZEALAND: **Jakarta Embassy** (Jln. Diponegoro 41, ☎ 021/330680).

➤ UNITED KINGDOM: **Jakarta Embassy** (Jln. M. H. Thamrin 75, ☎ 021/330904); **Medan Consulate** (Jln. Ahmad Yani 2, ☎ 061/518699).

➤ UNITED STATES: **Denpasar Consulate** (Jln. Hayam Wuruk 188,

☎ 0361/233605), **Jakarta Embassy** (Jln. Medan Merdeka Selatan 5, ☎ 021/3442211), **Medan Consulate** (Jl. Imam Bonjol 13, ☎ 061/322200), **Sanur Consulate** (Jln. Segara Ayu 5, ☎ 0361/288478), and **Surabaya Consulate** (Jln. Raya Dr. Sutomo 33, ☎ 031/568–2287).

FURTHER READING

Anthology of Modern Indonesian Poetry, edited by B. Raffle, provides insight into Indonesian society. Christopher Koch's *The Year of Living Dangerously* is a historical novel of the chaotic state of Indonesia in 1965. *The Religion of Java,* by Clifford Geertz, is a modern classic that describes the religious and social life of the Javanese.

Underwater Indonesia, by Kal Muller, is the best guide to diving in the archipelago—a must-read for anyone planning to scuba dive or snorkel here. Anne Richter's *The Arts & Crafts of Indonesia* is a beautifully photographed guide to handicrafts, costumes, and arts throughout the islands. *Adventuring in Indonesia,* by Holly S. Smith, is a guide to the nature and culture of the islands, including many national parks. Eliot Elosofan's *Java Diary,* Frances Yeager's *Jungle Woman,* and John MacKinnon's *In Search of the Red Ape* are classic accounts of explorers discovering wildlife and culture on Java, Sumatra, and Borneo, respectively.

GAY & LESBIAN TRAVEL

Gay and lesbian travelers should practice discretion, even on relatively carefree Bali. Homosexuality is not readily accepted in this overwhelmingly Muslim country

➤ LOCAL CONTACT: For advice and information on gay and lesbian activities, contact the organization **Gaya Nusantara** (Jln. Mulyosari Timur 46, Surabaya, ☎ 031/593–4924).

➤ TOUR OPERATORS: **Hanns Ebensten Travel** (✉ 513 Fleming St., Key West, FL 33040, ☎ 305/294–8174), one of the oldest operators in the gay market, offers packages such as "The Islands of Indonesia," which covers Java, Bali, and Kalimantan. **Toto Tours** (✉ 1326 W. Albion Ave., Suite 3W, Chicago, IL 60626, ☎ 773/274–8686 or 800/565–1241, FAX 773/274–8695) is currently coordinating trips to the region that may include a cruise around Bali.

➤ GAY- AND LESBIAN-FRIENDLY TRAVEL AGENCIES: **Advance Damron** (✉ 1 Greenway Plaza, Suite 800, Houston, TX 77046, ☎ 713/850–1140 or 800/695–0880, FAX 713/888–1010). **Club Travel** (✉ 8739 Santa Monica Blvd., West Hollywood, CA 90069, ☎ 310/358–2200 or 800/429–8747, FAX 310/358–2222). **Islanders/Kennedy Travel** (✉ 183 W. 10th St., New York, NY 10014, ☎ 212/242–3222 or 800/988–1181, FAX 212/929–8530). **Now Voyager** (✉ 4406 18th St., San Francisco, CA 94114, ☎ 415/626–1169 or 800/255–6951, FAX 415/626–8626). **Yellowbrick Road** (✉ 1500 W. Balmoral Ave., Chicago, IL 60640, ☎ 773/561–1800 or 800/642–2488, FAX 773/561–4497). **Skylink Women's Travel** (✉ 3577 Moorland Ave., Santa Rosa, CA 95407, ☎ 707/585–8355 or 800/225–5759, FAX 707/584–5637), serving lesbian travelers.

HEALTH

STAYING WELL

Although the islands of Indonesia do not require or suggest vaccinations before traveling, the United States Centers for Disease Control offer the following recommendations:

Tetanus-diphtheria and polio vaccinations should be up-to-date—if you haven't been immunized since childhood, **consider bolstering your tetanus vaccination.** You should also be immunized against (or immune to) measles, mumps, and rubella. If you plan to visit rural areas, where there's questionable sanitation, you'll need to **get an immune-serum globulin vaccination as protection against hepatitis A.** If you are staying for longer than three weeks and traveling into rural areas, antimalarial pills and a typhoid vaccination are recommended. If staying for a month or more, you should be vaccinated against rabies and Japanese encephalitis; for six months or more, against hepatitis B as well. For news on current outbreaks of infectious diseases, ask your physician and check with your state or local department of health.

In Indonesia the major health risk is traveler's diarrhea, caused by eating contaminated fruit or vegetables or drinking contaminated water. So **watch what you eat.** Stay away from ice, uncooked food, and unpasteurized milk and milk products, and **drink only bottled water** or water that has been boiled for at least 20 minutes. Mild cases may respond to Imodium (known generically as loperamide) or Pepto-Bismol (not as strong), both of which can be purchased over the counter. Drink plenty of purified water or tea—chamomile is a good folk remedy. In severe cases, rehydrate yourself with a salt-sugar solution (½ teaspoon salt and 4 tablespoons sugar per quart of water).

According to the National Centers for Disease Control (CDC) there is a limited risk of malaria and dengue in certain areas of Indonesia, including Lombok, northern Sumatra, Kalimantan, and Irian Jaya. In most urban or easily accessible areas you need not worry. However, if you plan to visit remote regions or stay for more than six weeks, **check with the CDC's International Travelers Hotline.** In areas where malaria and dengue, both of which are carried by mosquitoes, are prevalent, use mosquito nets, wear clothing that covers the body, apply repellent containing DEET, and use spray for flying insects in living and sleeping areas. Also **consider taking antimalarial pills.** There is no vaccine that combats dengue.

➤ HEALTH WARNINGS: **National Centers for Disease Control** (✉ CDC, National Center for Infectious Diseases, Division of Quarantine, Traveler's Health Section, 1600 Clifton Rd., M/S E-03, Atlanta, GA 30333, ☎ 404/332–4559, FAX 404/332–4565).

MEDICAL PLANS

No one plans to get sick while traveling, but it happens, so **consider signing up with a medical-assistance company.** Members get doctor referrals, emergency evacuation or repatriation, 24-hour telephone hot lines for medical consultation, cash for emergencies, and other personal and legal assistance. Coverage varies by plan, so **review the benefits of each carefully.**

➤ MEDICAL-ASSISTANCE COMPANIES: **International SOS Assistance** (✉ 8 Neshaminy Interplex, Suite 207, Trevose, PA 19053, ☎ 215/245–4707 or 800/523–6586, FAX 215/244–9617; ✉ 12 Chemin Riantbosson, 1217 Meyrin 1, Geneva, Switzerland, ☎ 4122/785–6464, FAX 4122/785–6424; ✉ 10 Anson Rd., 14-07/08 International Plaza, Singapore, 079903, ☎ 65/226–3936, FAX 65/226–3937).

DIVERS' ALERT

Do not fly within 24 hours of scuba diving.

➤ SCUBA-DIVING INFORMATION: For scuba-diving information, contact the Indonesian diving organization, **Possi** (Jln. Prapatan 38, Jakarta, ☎ 021/348685).

HOLIDAYS

Start of Ramadan, the Islamic month of fasting (Dec. 9, 1999; Nov. 27, 2000); New Year's Day; Idul Fitri, the end of Ramadan (Jan. 19, 1999; Jan. 8, 2000); Isra Miraj Nabi Mohammed, Mohammed's Ascension (Feb./Mar.); Good Friday (Apr. 2, 1999; Apr. 21, 2000); Ascension Day (May 13, 1999; June 1, 2000); Waicak, Birth of Buddha, (May/June); Haji, commemorating Mecca pilgrimages (July); Independence Day (Aug. 17); Birth of Mohammed (Oct.); Christmas Day.

HORSE CARTS

Horse-drawn carts are disappearing fast, but they remain a popular way to get around on Lombok, Sumbawa, and other tourist areas. The typical fare for distances up to a kilometer is Rp 200–Rp 500.

INSURANCE

Travel insurance is the best way to **protect yourself against financial loss.** The most useful plan is a comprehensive policy that includes coverage for trip cancellation and interruption, default, trip delay, and medical expenses (with a waiver for preexisting conditions).

Without insurance, you will lose all or most of your money if you cancel your trip, regardless of the reason. Default insurance covers you if your tour operator, airline, or cruise line goes out of business. Trip-delay covers unforeseen expenses that you may incur due to bad weather or mechanical delays. It's important to compare the fine print regarding trip-delay coverage when comparing policies.

For overseas travel, one of the most important components of travel insurance is its medical coverage. Supplemental health insurance will pick up the cost of your medical bills should you get sick or injured while traveling. U.S. residents should note that Medicare generally does not cover health-care costs outside the United States, nor do many privately issued policies. Residents of the United Kingdom can buy an annual travel-insurance policy valid for most vacations taken during the year in which the coverage is purchased. If you are pregnant or have a pre-existing condition, make sure you're covered. British citizens should buy extra medical coverage when traveling overseas, according to the Association of British Insurers. Australian travelers should buy travel insurance, including extra medical coverage, whenever they go abroad, according to the Insurance Council of Australia.

Always **buy travel insurance directly from the insurance company**; if you buy it from a cruise line, airline, or tour operator that goes out of business you probably will not be covered for the agency or operator's default, a major risk. Before you make any purchase, **review your existing health and home-owner's policies** to find out whether they cover expenses incurred while traveling.

➤ TRAVEL INSURERS: In the U.S., **Access America** (✉ 6600 W. Broad St., Richmond, VA 23230, ☎ 804/285–3300 or 800/284–8300). **Travel Guard International** (✉ 1145 Clark St., Stevens Point, WI 54481, ☎ 715/345–0505 or 800/826–1300). In Canada, **Mutual of Omaha** (✉ Travel Division, 500 University Ave., Toronto, Ontario M5G 1V8, ☎ 416/598–4083, 800/268–8825 in Canada).

➤ INSURANCE INFORMATION: In the U.K., **Association of British Insurers** (✉ 51 Gresham St., London EC2V 7HQ, ☎ 0171/600–3333). In Australia, the **Insurance Council of Australia** (☎ 613/9614–1077, FAX 613/9614–7924).

LANGUAGE, CULTURE, & ETIQUETTE

Although some 300 languages are spoken in Indonesia, Bahasa Indonesia has been the national language since independence. English is widely spoken in tourist areas.

Indonesians are extremely polite. Begin encounters with locals by saying "*Selamat pagi*" ("Good morning"), "*Selamat siang*" ("Good day"), "*Selamat sore*" ("Good afternoon"), or "*Selamat malam*" ("Good evening"), depending on the time of day. Two phrases you'll use often are "*Terima kasih*" ("Thank you") and "*Ma'af*" ("Excuse me" or "I'm sorry"). Shaking hands has become a common practice, and Indonesians are very tactile, so expect to be touched often in conversation. Smiling is the national pastime, so do it frequently and you'll have a much easier time transcending language barriers. Some etiquette no-nos are pointing with your index finger (gesture with your whole hand instead), crossing your arms, and placing your hands on your hips (signs of anger). Most important, avoid touching food or people with your left hand, which is considered unclean.

The more formal or sacred an occasion, the more formally dressed you should be. When visiting mosques, women should wear something on the head and shouldn't enter during menstruation. Men should wear long trousers and have at least their upper arms covered. Don't walk in front of those who are praying. At Balinese temples, you must wear a sash to enter; these are usually rented on-site for a few rupiah. Shorts (and other above-the-knee clothing) are considered improper temple attire, so avoid them or borrow a sarong when visiting any holy place.

LODGING

Accommodations in Indonesia range from shoebox-size rooms with shared or "squat" toilets, to five-star luxury. Every major city and important resort has at least one international-style hotel (many are part of such chains as Sheraton, Regent, Hyatt, Hilton, Holiday Inn, and Inter-Continental) that is famous for its service and amenities. If you can afford to splurge, this is the place to do it. The prices of even the very top hotels are still far lower than comparable digs in Europe—particularly with the recent drop in exchange rates and airfares to the region.

A good rule for medium and large hotels in popular areas is to **reserve your rooms at least two months prior to arrival.** This is especially true in December and January, during Chinese New Year, at the end of Ramadan, and during the Western summer holidays and local school breaks. The international chains have U.S. reservations offices. If you do arrive in an Asian capital without a hotel reservation, you will generally find a reservations desk at the airport that may be able to provide an immediate booking. This service is usually efficient and free, and often special discounts are available.

Most bottom-end accommodations are clustered in particular areas of cities or tourist hubs—and they're usually a little off the beaten path. Always **ask to see the room before committing to a stay in a budget hotel.** and **comparison-shop for the best deal.** In Jakarta, Jalan Jaksa is the budget hub, as are the *gangs* (alleys) around the train station in Yogyakarta, the backstreets of Kuta beach on Bali, and the outskirts of Rantepao in the Toraja area of south-central Sulawesi.

Small hotels aren't the only type of budget accommodation in Indonesia; you'll also find the *wisma* (a comfortable hotel/homestay type of establishment), the *losmen* (a budget hotel with simple rooms and shared baths and living areas), and the *penginapan* (a bare-bones losmen, the simplest type of accommodation available). No reservations are necessary for these establishments; just show up and ask for a room, and move on to the next if the first one is full. Be sure to arrive early around holidays, however, because rooms can fill up quickly.

APARTMENT & VILLA RENTALS

If you want a home base that's roomy enough for a family and comes with cooking facilities, **consider a furnished rental.** These can save you money, especially if you're traveling with a large group of people. Home-exchange directories list rentals (often second homes owned by prospective house swappers), and some services search for a house or apartment for you (even a castle if that's your fancy) and handle the paperwork. Some send an illustrated catalog; others send photographs only of specific properties, sometimes at a charge. Up-front registration fees may apply. Travel agencies, property management companies, and private business owners are the best sources for information about home rentals in Asia. Many international companies also rent homes for their expatriate employees, so they may also be able to provide leads.

➤ RENTAL AGENTS: **InTouch** (✉ Jln. Raya Seminyak 22, Seminyak 80361, ☎ 0361/731047, FAX 0361/731683) in Bali and **Private Villas International** (✉ HK Diamond Exchange Building, 8–10 Duddell St., Central, Hong Kong, ☎ 0852/525–1336, FAX 0852/537–7181) have listings in Indonesia. **Hideaways International** (✉ 767 Islington St., Portsmouth, NH 03801, ☎ 603/430–4433 or 800/843–4433, FAX 603/430–4444) is a travel club whose members arrange rentals among themselves; yearly membership is $99.

HOSTELS

No matter what your age, you can **save on lodging costs by staying at hostels.** In some 5,000 locations in more than 70 countries around the world, Hostelling International (HI), the umbrella group for a number of national youth hostel associations, offers single-sex, dorm-style beds and, at many hostels, "couples" rooms and family accommodations. Membership in any HI national hostel association, open to travelers of all ages, allows you to stay in HI-affiliated hostels at member rates (one-year membership is about $25 for adults; hostels run about $10–$25 per night). Members also have priority if the hostel is full; they're eligible for discounts around the world, even on rail and bus travel in some countries.

➤ Hostel Organizations: **Hostelling International—American Youth Hostels** (✉ 733 15th St. NW, Suite 840, Washington, DC 20005, ☎ 202/783–6161, FAX 202/783–6171). **Hostelling International—Canada** (✉ 400-205 Catherine St., Ottawa, Ontario K2P 1C3, ☎ 613/237–7884, FAX 613/237–7868). **Youth Hostel Association of England and Wales** (✉ Trevelyan House, 8 St. Stephen's Hill, St. Albans, Hertfordshire AL1 2DY, ☎ 01727/855215 or 01727/845047, FAX 01727/844126); membership in the U.S. $25, in Canada C$26.75, in the U.K. £9.30).

MAIL

POSTAL RATES

Two kinds of airmail are available: *pos udara* (regular) and *kilat* (express). Kilat rates to the United States or the United Kingdom are Rp 1,200 and Rp 1,300 respectively for postcards and Rp 1,600 and Rp 1,700 for 1 gram (.035 oz.) letters. Postcards are Rp 600 to all foreign countries. Pos udara letters less than 21 grams are Rp 1,600 to North America and Europe and Rp 1,200 to Australia and New Zealand.

RECEIVING MAIL

For letters or packages to reach you in any major town in the islands, have them sent to the main post office—usually open Monday through Thursday 8–4, Friday 8 AM–11 AM, and Saturday 8 AM–12:30 PM. You can have mail sent to you "poste restante" care of local post offices. Just be sure that letters addressed to you have your surname (underlined and in capital letters), followed by your name, to avoid filing confusion. A small fee may be charged to pick up a letter. Most hotels will also accept mail and hold it. Do not have anyone send cash.

WRITING TO INDONESIA

Indonesian addresses are straightforward. All you need is for a proper address are the name, street address (Jln. stands for "Jalan," or road), number (though many addresses in small towns won't have this), town, island, and postal code. Finally, be sure to follow all this information with "Republik Indonesia."

MONEY

COSTS

Prices in Indonesia depend on what you're buying. The basic cost of living is low and domestic labor is cheap, but you'll pay a premium for anything imported. Thus, camera film is expensive, food is not. Regionally, costs rise in direct relation to tourism and business development. Prices in Bali and Jakarta are relatively high, particularly at deluxe hotels and restaurants. Sumatra and Sulawesi, by contrast, are bargains.

Major cities have shopping complexes and department stores where prices are fixed, but at small shops and street stalls bargaining is not only expected but part of the whole shopping experience. Bargaining is, in fact, having a dialogue with the vendor, and a certain respect is established between you and the seller. It's also an art, so try to develop your own technique. Start by offering half the asking price, even a third in the tourist areas. You'll finish somewhere in between. Shops with higher-quality merchandise are likely to take credit cards, but payment in cash puts you in a better bargaining position. The keys to good negotiation in Asia are a positive attitude and flexibility.

➤ Sample Prices: Cup of coffee: 25¢–$2; small bottle of beer, $1–$4; small bottled water, 25¢–$2; can of soda: 50¢–$3; bottle of house wine: $7–$15; sandwich: $2–$7; 1-mi (½-km) taxi ride, 75¢–$3 (depending on traffic); city bus ride: 10¢–$2; museum: 25¢–$3.

SERVICE CHARGES, TAXES, AND TIPPING

High-end hotels charge 21% tax, of which only 10% is the regular government tax also seen on the bill at moderate hotels; the rest comprises various service charges. Departing passengers on international flights pay an airport departure tax of around Rp 25,000. Domestic airport taxes are from Rp 6,500–Rp 11,000, depending on the point of departure.

The more expensive tourist restaurants include a service charge; if not, tip 10%. Above the hotel service charge, plan to tip bellboys Rp 10,800 per bag; you may also want to tip room-service personnel if you request a special service. Porters at the airport should receive about Rp 5,400 per bag. Taxi drivers aren't tipped except in Jakarta and Surabaya, where Rp 500, or the small change, is the minimum. For a driver of a hired car, Rp 21,600 for half a day would be the minimum tip. Private guides expect a gratuity, perhaps Rp 32,400–Rp 54,000 per day.

CREDIT & DEBIT CARDS

Should you use a credit card or a debit card when traveling? Both have benefits. A credit card allows you to delay payment and gives you certain rights as a consumer (☞ Consumer Protection, *above*). A debit card, also known as a check card, deducts funds directly from your checking account and helps you stay within your budget. When you want to rent a car, though, you may still need an old-fashioned credit card. Although you can always *pay* for your car with a debit card, some agencies will not allow you to *reserve* a car with a debit card.

Otherwise, the two types of plastic are virtually the same. Both will get you cash advances at ATMs worldwide if your card is properly programmed with your personal identification number (PIN). Both offer excellent, wholesale exchange rates. And both protect you against unauthorized use if the card is lost or stolen. Your liability is limited to $50, as long as you report the card missing.

➤ ATM LOCATIONS: **Cirrus** (☎ 800/424–7787). **Plus** (☎ 800/843–7587) for locations, or visit your local bank.

➤ REPORTING LOST CARDS: To report lost or stolen credit cards, call the following toll-free numbers: **American Express** (☎ 800/327–2177); **Diners Club** (☎ 800/234–6377); **Master Card** (☎ 800/307–7309); and **Visa** (☎ 800/847–2911).

CURRENCY

Indonesia's unit of currency is the rupiah. Bills come in denominations of 100, 500, 1,000, 5,000, 10,000, 20,000, 50,000, and 100,000 Rp, coins in 25, 50, 100, 500, and 1,000 Rp. The exchange rate at press time was Rp 10,800 to the U.S. dollar, Rp 6,940 to the Canadian dollar, Rp 18,000 to the U.K. sterling, Rp 6,300 to the Australian dollar, and Rp 5,300 to the New Zealand dollar.

EXCHANGING MONEY

For the most favorable rates, **change money through banks.** Although fees charged for ATM transactions may be higher abroad than at home, Cirrus and Plus exchange rates are excellent, because they are based on wholesale rates offered only by major banks. You won't do as well at exchange booths in airports or rail and bus stations, in hotels, in restaurants, or in stores, although you may find their hours more convenient. To avoid lines at airport exchange booths, **get a bit of local currency before you leave home.**

➤ EXCHANGE SERVICES: **Chase *Currency To Go*** (☎ 800/935–9935). **International Currency Express** (☎ 888/842–0880 on the East Coast, 888/278–6628 on the West Coast). **Thomas Cook Currency Services** (☎ 800/287–7362 for telephone orders and retail locations).

TRAVELER'S CHECKS

Do you need traveler's checks? It depends on where you're headed. If you're going to rural areas and small towns, go with cash; traveler's checks are best used in cities. Lost or stolen checks can usually be replaced within 24 hours. To ensure a speedy refund, buy your own traveler's checks—don't let someone else pay for them: irregularities like this can cause delays. The person who bought the checks should make the call to request a refund.

PACKING

LUGGAGE

How many carry-on bags you can bring with you is up to the airline. Most allow two, but the limit is often reduced to one on certain flights. Gate agents will take excess baggage—including bags they deem oversize—from you as you board and add it to checked luggage. To avoid this situation, make sure that everything you carry aboard will fit under your seat. Also, get to the gate early, and request a seat at the back of the plane; you'll probably board first, while the overhead bins are still empty. Since big, bulky baggage attracts the attention of gate agents and flight attendants on a busy flight, make sure your carry-on is really a carry-on. Finally, a carry-on that's long and narrow is more likely to remain unnoticed than one that's wide and squarish.

If you are flying internationally, note that baggage allowances may be determined not by piece but by weight—generally 88 pounds (40 kilograms) in first class, 66 pounds (30 kilograms) in business class, and 44 pounds (20 kilograms) in economy.

Airline liability for baggage is limited to $1,250 per person on flights within the United States. On international flights it amounts to $9.07 per pound or $20 per kilogram for checked baggage (roughly $640 per 70-pound bag) and $400 per passenger for unchecked baggage. You can buy additional coverage at check-in for about $10 per $1,000 of coverage, but it excludes a rather extensive list of items, shown on your airline ticket.

Before departure, **itemize your bags' contents** and their worth, and label the bags with your name, address, and phone number. (If you use your home address, cover it so that potential thieves can't see it readily.) Inside each bag, **pack a copy of your itinerary.** At check-in, **make sure that each bag is correctly tagged** with the destination airport's three-letter code. If your bags arrive damaged or fail to arrive at all, file a written report with the airline before leaving the airport.

PACKING LIST

Pack light, because porters can be hard to find and baggage restrictions are tight on international flights—be sure to check on your airline's policies before you pack. And either leave room in your suitcase or bring expandable totes for all your bargain purchases.

If you'll be traveling through several different types of climate, your wardrobe will have to reflect this. Light cotton or other natural-fiber clothing is appropriate for any Indonesian destination; drip-dry is an especially good idea, because the tropical sun and high humidity encourage frequent changes of clothing. Avoid exotic fabrics, because you may have difficulty getting them laundered.

Indonesia is generally informal: a sweater, shawl, or lightweight linen jacket will be sufficient for dining and evening wear, except for top international restaurants, where men will still be most comfortable in (and may in fact be required to wear) a jacket and tie. A sweater is also a good idea for cool evenings or overly air-conditioned restaurants. An umbrella can be helpful for shielding against both rain and sun.

The paths leading to temples can be rough; in any case, a pair of sturdy and comfortable walking shoes is always appropriate when traveling. Slip-ons are preferable to lace-ups, as shoes must be removed before you enter most shrines and temples. Women will also need shawls to enter. Pack a flashlight and extra batteries for trips to caves—and for when the occasional power outage turns your hotel room into a cave.

It's wise to **bring your favorite toilet articles** (in plastic containers, to avoid breakage and reduce the weight of luggage). Allow for the tropical sun by bringing along a hat and sunscreen. Mosquito repellent is a good idea, and toilet paper is not always supplied in public places, so small tissue packets are handy. Moist towelettes are great for cleaning off tropical grime and sweat while traveling, as well as for quick wash-ups before meals in more remote establishments where soap and water aren't always available.

In your carry-on luggage **bring an extra pair of eyeglasses or contact lenses** and **enough of any medication you take** to last the entire trip. You may also want your doctor to write a spare prescription using the drug's generic name, since brand names may vary from country to country. **Never put prescription drugs or valuables in luggage to be checked.** To avoid customs delays, carry medications in their original packaging. And don't forget to copy down and carry addresses of offices that handle refunds of lost traveler's checks.

PASSPORTS & VISAS

Once your travel plans are confirmed, **check the expiration date of your passport.** It's also a good idea to **make photocopies of the data page**; leave one copy with someone at home and keep another with you, separated from your passport. If you lose your passport, promptly call the nearest embassy or consulate and the local police; having a copy of the data page can speed replacement.

The Indonesian government stipulates that passports must be valid for at least six months from arrival date, and all travelers must have proof of onward or return passage. For stays up to 60 days, visas are not required for citizens of Australia, Canada, New Zealand, the United Kingdom, and the United States as long as you enter the country through one of the major gateways. These include the airports at Ambon, Bali, Balikpapan, Bandung, Batam, Biak, Jakarta, Kupang, Manado, Mataram, Medan, Padang, Pekanbaru, Pontianak, and Surabaya, as well as sea ports of Ambon, Balikpapan, Batam, Belawan, Benoa, Jakarta, Kupang, Manado, Padangbai (Bali), Pontianak, Semarang, Surabaya, and Tanjung Pinang. The only international land crossing allowed is between Kuching, Malaysia, and Pontianak, Kalimantan. Other ports of entry may require a visa.

PASSPORT OFFICES

The best time to apply for a passport or to renew is during the fall and winter. Before any trip, be sure to check your passport's expiration date and, if necessary, renew it as soon as possible. (Some countries won't allow you to enter on a passport that's due to expire in six months or less.)

➤ AUSTRALIAN CITIZENS: **Australian Passport Office** (☎ 13/1232).

➤ CANADIAN CITIZENS: **Passport Office** (☎ 819/994–3500 or 800/567–6868).

➤ NEW ZEALAND CITIZENS: **New Zealand Passport Office** (☎ 04/494–0700 for information on how to apply, 0800/727776 for information on applications already submitted).

➤ U.K. CITIZENS: **London Passport Office** (☎ 0990/21010), for fees and documentation requirements and to request an emergency passport.

➤ U.S. CITIZENS: **National Passport Information Center** (☎ 900/225–5674; calls are charged at 35¢ per minute for automated service, $1.05 per minute for operator service).

SAFETY

If you're a hiker or diver, be aware that these islands are home to a number of dangerous and poisonous creatures—know what to watch out for before you head into the wild.

Owing to the downward spiral of the Indonesian economy and general political dissatisfaction, large public demonstrations have occurred in major cities throughout the islands, including riots in Jakarta and Bandung. Tourists should be safe in any case, but be wary of the social climate before you travel, pay attention to travelers' advisories, and steer clear of areas embroiled in political upheaval, especially during elections.

Crime against travelers mainly occurs in large cities and tourist areas, where small-time thieves prey on unseasoned visitors, so a little caution in how you act can go a long way. Dress modestly and don't flash your money around. Carry travelers checks and keep large amounts of cash in a hidden money pouch or locked in hotel safes. Pickpockets haunt crowded transport hubs, and scam artists love to draw in naive travelers. Check out what you buy before you lay down the money—fake jewels, fake name-brand items (handbags, shoes, perfume), bait-and-switch gifts "pre-wrapped" for customs, and bogus shipping promises are the typical tricks of this region.

SENIOR-CITIZEN TRAVEL

There's no reason that active, well-traveled senior citizens shouldn't visit Indonesia, whether on an independent (but prebooked) vacation, an escorted tour, or an adventure vacation. Before you leave home, however, determine what medical services your health insurance provider will cover outside the United States; note that Medicare does not provide for payment of hospital and medical services outside the United States. If you need additional travel insurance, buy it (☞ Insurance, *above*).

To qualify for age-related discounts, **mention your senior-citizen status up front** when booking hotel reservations (not when checking out) and before you're seated in restaurants (not when paying the bill). Note that discounts may be limited to certain menus, days, or hours. When renting a car, **ask about promotional car-rental discounts,** which can be cheaper than senior-citizen rates.

➤ ADVENTURE TRAVEL: **Overseas Adventure Travel** (✉ Grand Circle Corporation, 625 Mt. Auburn St., Cambridge, MA 02138, ☎ 617/876–0533 or 800/221–0814, FAX 617/876–0455) offers tours to Java, Bali, Sumatra, Sulawesi, Nusa Tenggara, and Komodo Island in Indonesia, as well as to Malaysia, Singapore, Thailand, and Vietnam.

➤ EDUCATIONAL TRAVEL PROGRAMS: **Elderhostel** (✉ 75 Federal St., 3rd floor, Boston, MA 02110, ☎ 617/426–8056) coordinates trips to Indonesia, Malaysia, the Philippines, Thailand, and Vietnam.

STUDENTS

To save money, **look into deals available through student-oriented travel agencies.** To qualify you'll need a bona fide student ID card. Members of international student groups are also eligible.

➤ STUDENT I.D.S & SERVICES: **Council on International Educational Exchange** (✉ CIEE, 205 E. 42nd St., 14th floor, New York, NY 10017, ☎ 212/822–2600 or 888/268–6245, FAX 212/822–2699), for mail orders only, in the United States. **Travel Cuts** (✉ 187 College St., Toronto, Ontario M5T 1P7, ☎ 416/979–2406 or 800/667–2887) in Canada.

➤ STUDENT TOURS: **Contiki Holidays** (✉ 300 Plaza Alicante, Suite 900, Garden Grove, CA 92840, ☎ 714/740–0808 or 800/266–8454, FAX 714/740–2034). **AESU Travel** (✉ 2 Hamill Rd., Suite 248, Baltimore, MD 21210-1807, ☎ 410/323–4416 or 800/638–7640, FAX 410/323–4498).

TAXIS

Registered taxis and hired cars may be hailed on city streets—look for the yellow number plates. Except in Jakarta, Surabaya, parts of Bali, and at most airports, you negotiate the fare with the driver before setting out. Most hotels have taxi stands.

TELEPHONES

CALLING INDONESIA

To call Indonesia from overseas, dial the country code, 62, and then the area code, omitting the first 0.

LOCAL CALLS

Although Jakarta's telephone system has been improved in recent years, the same cannot be said for service in the rest of the country. In most cases you're better off using hotel phones despite the small surcharges; that way you don't need to amass quantities of coins, and an operator can help with translation and information. Your best chance of finding a phone is in hotel lobbies and Telekom offices. Some travel agencies have phones you can use for local calls, and the staff will let you send and receive faxes for a small fee.

For local calls, 3 minutes costs Rp 100. Older public phones take Rp 100 coins, but the newer ones accept only phone cards—a recent introduction restricted to the larger cities and tourist areas. For long distance, dial the area code before the number. For operator and directory assistance, dial

108 for local calls, 106 for the provinces.

LONG-DISTANCE AND INTERNATIONAL CALLS

Major Indonesian cities are now hooked into the International Direct Dialing (IDD) system via satellite. Dial 001 plus the respective country code. For towns without the IDD hookup, go through the operator (in tourist destinations many speak English). If you want to avoid using hotel phones, the most economical way to place an IDD call is from the nearest Kantor Telephone & Telegraph office. For international directory assistance, dial 102.

You can make collect calls to Australia, Europe, and North America; for other countries, you need a telephone credit card. Reduced rates on international phone calls are in effect 9 PM–6 AM daily. For most Western countries, Indonesia also has special "home country" phones in its Telekom offices and many hotels. With these you can contact an operator in your home country just by pushing a button. Like a collect call, the bill is charged to whomever you're calling, or you can use one of the calling cards that are sold everywhere.

AT&T, MCI, and Sprint international access codes make calling the United States relatively convenient, but you may find the local access number blocked in many hotel rooms. First ask the hotel operator to connect you. If the hotel operator balks, ask for an international operator, or dial the international operator yourself. One way to improve your odds of getting connected to your long-distance carrier is to travel with more than one company's calling card (a hotel may block Sprint, for example, but not MCI). If all else fails, call from a pay phone in the hotel lobby.

➤ ACCESS CODES: AT&T (☎ 001–801–10). MCI (☎ 001–801–11). Sprint (☎ 001–801–15).

TOUR OPERATORS

Buying a prepackaged tour or independent vacation can make your trip to Indonesia less expensive and more hassle-free. Because everything is prearranged, you'll spend less time planning.

Operators that handle several hundred thousand travelers per year can use their purchasing power to give you a good price. Their high volume may also indicate financial stability. But some small companies provide more personalized service; because they tend to specialize, they may also be more knowledgeable about a given area.

BOOKING WITH AN AGENT

Travel agents are excellent resources. In fact, large operators accept bookings made only through travel agents. But it's a good idea to **collect brochures from several agencies,** because some agents' suggestions may be influenced by relationships with tour and package firms that reward them for volume sales. If you have a special interest, **find an agent with expertise in that area**; ASTA (☞ Travel Agencies, *below*) has a database of specialists worldwide.

Make sure your travel agent knows the accommodations and other services. Ask about the hotel's location, room size, beds, and whether it has a pool, room service, or programs for children, if you care about these. Has your agent been there in person or sent others you can contact?

Do some homework on your own, too: Local tourism boards can provide information about lesser-known and small-niche operators, some of which may sell only direct.

BUYER BEWARE

Each year consumers are stranded or lose their money when tour operators—even very large ones with excellent reputations—go out of business. So **check out the operator.** Find out how long the company has been in business, and ask several travel agents about its reputation. If the package or tour you are considering is priced lower than in your wildest dreams, **be skeptical.** Try to **book with a company that has a consumer-protection program.** If the operator has such a program, you'll find information about it in the company's brochure. If the operator you are considering does not offer some kind of consumer protection, then ask for references from satisfied customers.

In the U.S., members of the National Tour Association and United States Tour Operators Association are required to set aside funds to cover your payments and travel arrangements in case the company defaults. It's also a good idea to choose a company that participates in the American Society of Travel Agent's Tour Operator Program (TOP). This gives you a forum if there are any disputes between you and your tour operator; ASTA will act as mediator.

➤ TOUR-OPERATOR RECOMMENDATIONS: **American Society of Travel Agents** (☞ Travel Agencies, *below*). **National Tour Association** (✉ NTA, 546 E. Main St., Lexington, KY 40508, ☎ 606/226–4444 or 800/755–8687). **United States Tour Operators Association** (✉ USTOA, 342 Madison Ave., Suite 1522, New York, NY 10173, ☎ 212/599–6599 or 800/468–7862, FAX 212/599–6744).

COSTS

The more your package or tour includes, the better you can predict the ultimate cost of your vacation. Make sure you know exactly what is covered, and **beware of hidden costs.** Are taxes, tips, and service charges included? Transfers and baggage handling? Entertainment and excursions? These can add up.

Prices for packages and tours are usually quoted per person, based on two sharing a room. If traveling solo, you may be required to pay the full double-occupancy rate. Some operators eliminate this surcharge if you agree to be matched with a roommate of the same sex, even if one is not found by departure time.

GROUP TOURS

Among companies that sell tours to Indonesia, the following are nationally known, have a proven reputation, and offer plenty of options. The classifications used below represent different price categories, and you'll probably encounter these terms when talking to a travel agent or tour operator. The key difference is usually in accommodations, which run from budget to better, and better-yet to best.

➤ SUPER-DELUXE: **Abercrombie & Kent** (✉ 1520 Kensington Rd., Oak Brook, IL 60521-2141, ☎ 630/954–2944 or 800/323–7308, FAX 630/954–3324). **Absolute Asia** (✉ 180 Varick St., New York, NY 10014, ☎ 212/627–1950 or 800/736–8187).

➤ DELUXE: **Globus** (✉ 5301 S. Federal Circle, Littleton, CO 80123-2980, ☎ 303/797–2800 or 800/221–0090, FAX 303/347–2080). **Maupintour** (✉ 1515 St. Andrews Dr., Lawrence, KS 66047, ☎ 785/843–1211 or 800/255–4266, FAX 785/843–8351). **Tauck Tours** (✉ Box 5027, 276 Post Rd. W, Westport, CT 06881-5027, ☎ 203/226–6911 or 800/468–2825, FAX 203/221–6866).

➤ FIRST-CLASS: **Brendan Tours** (✉ 15137 Califa St., Van Nuys, CA 91411, ☎ 818/785–9696 or 800/421–8446, FAX 818/902–9876). **General Tours** (✉ 53 Summer St., Keene, NH 03431, ☎ 603/357–5033 or 800/221–2216, FAX 603/357–4548). **Orient Flexi-Pax Tours** (✉ 630 Third Ave., New York, NY 10017, ☎ 212/692–9550 or 800/545–5540, FAX 212/661–1618). **Pacific Bestour** (✉ 228 Rivervale Rd., River Vale, NJ 07675, ☎ 201/664–8778 or 800/688–3288, FAX 201/722–0829). **Pacific Delight Tours** (✉ 132 Madison Ave., New York, NY 10016, ☎ 212/684–7707 or 800/221–7179, FAX 212/532–3406).

➤ BUDGET: **Cosmos** (☞ Globus, *above*).

PACKAGES

Like group tours, independent vacation packages are available from major tour operators and airlines. The companies listed below offer vacation packages in a broad price range.

➤ AIR/HOTEL: **Absolute Asia** (☞ Groups, *above*). **Orient Flexi-Pax Tours** (☞ Groups, *above*). **Pacific Bestour** (☞ Groups, *above*). **Pacific Delight Tours** (☞ Groups, *above*).

➤ IN THE U.K.: **Bales Tours** (Bales House, Junction Rd., Dorking, Surrey RH4 3HB, ☎ 01306/876881 or 01306/885991). **British Airways**

Holidays (✉ Astral Towers, Betts Way, London Rd., Crawley, West Sussex RH10 2XA, ☎ 01293/723171). **Hayes and Jarvis** (Hayes House, 152 King St., London W6 0QU, ☎ 0181/748–5050). **Kuoni Travel** (✉ Kuoni House, Dorking, Surrey RH5 4AZ, ☎ 01306/740500).

THEME TRIPS

➤ CUSTOMIZED PACKAGES: **Pacific Experience** (✉ 63 Mill St., Newport, RI 02840, ☎ 401/849–6258 or 800/279–3639, FAX 401/849–6158).

➤ ADVENTURE: **Asia Pacific Adventures** (826 S. Sierra Bonita Ave., Los Angeles, CA 90036, ☎ 323/935–3156 or 800/825–1680). **Geographical Expeditions** (2627 Lombard St., San Francisco, CA 94123, 415/922–0448 or 800/777–8183). **Himalayan Travel** (✉ 110 Prospect St., Stamford, CT 06901, ☎ 203/359–3711 or 800/225–2380, FAX 203/359–3669). **Mountain Travel-Sobek** (✉ 6420 Fairmount Ave., El Cerrito, CA 94530, ☎ 510/527–8100 or 800/227–2384, FAX 510/525–7710). **Naturequest** (✉ 934 Acapulco St., Laguna Beach, CA 92651, ☎ 714/499–9561 or 800/369–3033, FAX 714/499–0812).

➤ ARCHAEOLOGY: **Archeological Tours** (✉ 271 Madison Ave., New York, NY 10016, ☎ 212/986–3054, FAX 212/370–1561).

➤ BICYCLING: **Backroads** (✉ 801 Cedar St., Berkeley, CA 94710-1800, ☎ 510/527–1555 or 800/462–2848, FAX 510-527–1444).

➤ CULINARY: **Geographical Expeditions** (☞ Adventure, *above*).

➤ LEARNING: **Earthwatch** (✉ Box 9104, 680 Mount Auburn St., Watertown, MA 02272, ☎ 617/926–8200 or 800/776–0188, FAX 617/926–8532) organizes research expeditions.

➤ SCUBA DIVING: **Rothschild Dive Safaris** (900 West End Ave., #1B, New York, NY 10025-3525, ☎ 800/359–0747, FAX 212/749–6172). **Tropical Adventures** (111 2nd Ave. N, Seattle, WA 98109, ☎ 206/441–3483 or 800/247–3483, FAX 206/441–5431).

➤ WALKING/HIKING: **Backroads** (☞ Bicycling, *above*).

➤ YACHT CHARTERS: **Ocean Voyages** (✉ 1709 Bridgeway, Sausalito, CA 94965, ☎ 415/332–4681 or 800/299–4444, FAX 415/332–7460).

TRAIN TRAVEL

Java is the only island with reliable train service. The line runs from Jakarta through Yogyakarta to Surabaya and Banyuwangi, and it's a worthwhile mode of transport if you have time. Executive and business classes include air-conditioning, comfortable swivel seats, TV, and meals. Economy offers fan-cooled cars and open windows that let you view the lush countryside as it slides by. Early morning departures are best for avoiding the midday heat. Night trains are also a viable alternative, though sleeper cars are rarely offered. Schedules and tickets are available through hotel travel desks, travel agencies, or at the train stations; be sure to get tickets well in advance. Between Jakarta and Yogyakarta, it's around Rp 55,000 in executive class, Rp 23,000 in business, and Rp 14,000 in economy; to Surabaya, it's around Rp 57,000 in executive, Rp 38,000 in business, and Rp 10,000 in economy.

➤ INFORMATION: **Regional Operational Office** (KADAOPS; Jln. Taman Stasiun 1, Jakarta Kota, Jakarta, ☎ 021/692–9083).

TRAVEL AGENCIES

A good travel agent puts your needs first. Look for an agency that has been in business at least five years, emphasizes customer service, and has someone on staff who specializes in your destination. In addition, **make sure the agency belongs to the American Society of Travel Agents** (ASTA). If your travel agency is also acting as your tour operator, *see* Buyer Beware in Tour Operators, *above*.

➤ LOCAL AGENT REFERRALS: **American Society of Travel Agents** (ASTA, ☎ 800/965–2782 24-hr hot line, FAX 703/684–8319). **Alliance of Canadian Travel Associations** (✉ Suite 201, 1729 Bank St., Ottawa, Ontario K1V 7Z5, ☎ 613/521–0474, FAX 613/

521–0805). **Association of British Travel Agents** (✉ 55–57 Newman St., London W1P 4AH, ☎ 0171/637–2444, FAX 0171/637–0713).

TRAVEL GEAR

Travel catalogs specialize in useful items, such as compact alarm clocks and travel irons, that can **save space when packing.** They also offer dual-voltage appliances, currency converters, and foreign-language phrase books.

➤ MAIL-ORDER CATALOGS: **Magellan's** (☎ 800/962–4943, FAX 805/568–5406). **Orvis Travel** (☎ 800/541–3541, FAX 540/343–7053). **TravelSmith** (☎ 800/950–1600, FAX 800/950–1656).

U.S. GOVERNMENT

The U.S. government can be an excellent source of inexpensive travel information. When planning your trip, **find out what government materials are available.**

➤ ADVISORIES: **U.S. Department of State** (✉ Overseas Citizens Services Office, Room 4811 NS, Washington, DC 20520); enclose a self-addresses, stamped envelope. **Interactive hot line** (☎ 202/647–5225, FAX 202/647–3000). **Computer bulletin board** (☎ 301/946–4400).

➤ PAMPHLETS: **Consumer Information Center** (✉ Consumer Information Catalogue, Pueblo, CO 81009, ☎ 719/948–3334) for a free catalog that includes travel titles.

VISITOR INFORMATION

➤ OUTSIDE INDONESIA: **Indonesian Embassy in Australia** (8 Darwin Ave., Yarralumla ACT 2600, ☎ 06/273–3222) and an **Indonesian Tourist Office in Australia**(Level 10, S. Elizabeth St., Sydney NSA 2000, ☎ 02/9233–3630). **Indonesian Embassy in Canada** (287 MacLaren St., Ottawa, Ontario, Canada K2P 0L9, ☎ 613/236–7403). **Indonesian Embassy in New Zealand** (70 Glen Rd., Kelburn, Wellington, ☎ 04/475–8697).. **Indonesian Tourist Office in the United Kingdom** (3 Hanover St., London W1R 9HH, ☎ 0171/493–0030). **Indonesia Tourist Board in the United States** (3457 Wilshire Blvd., Los Angeles, CA 90010, ☎ 213/387–2078).

➤ WITHIN INDONESIA: **Directorate General of Tourism in Indonesia** (Jln. Merdeka Barat 16–19, Jakarta 10110, ☎ 021/386–7588). For regional tourist offices, *see* the Essentials section *in* individual chapters.

WHEN TO GO

CLIMATE

Indonesia's low-lying regions are uniformly hot and humid year-round. Temperatures can reach 90°F (32°C) soon after midday, and they drop no lower than 70°F (21°C) at night. The weather at higher altitudes is up to 20°F (11°C) cooler.

The best months to visit Indonesia are April–May and September–October, when crowds are lighter and you're not so likely to get drenched: the west monsoon, from November through March, brings heavy rains. It can drizzle for several days in a row or pour half the day, with only occasional dry spells. Since most of Indonesia's attractions are under the open sky—temples and other architecture, beaches, and outdoor festivals—the monsoon can very literally dampen your enjoyment. Like many locals, you may want to keep an umbrella on hand at all times for protection from both rain and sun.

In the peak tourist months, June and July, popular areas (especially Tanatoraja) are crammed with visitors. Bali hotels also tend to be fully booked around Christmas and New Year's; transport and accommodations in the rest of the country are full around Muslim holidays. Unless you plan to stay only on Bali, consider carefully before visiting during Ramadan, the Islamic month of fasting, when many restaurants, offices, and tourist attractions are closed until sundown.

CLIMATE

The following are average temperatures in Jakarta:

Jan.	84F	29C	May	88F	31C	Sept.	88F	31C
	74	23		74	23		74	23
Feb.	84F	29C	June	88F	31C	Oct.	88F	31C
	74	23		74	23		74	23
Mar.	85F	30C	July	88F	31C	Nov.	85F	30C
	74	23		74	23		74	23
Apr.	86F	30C	Aug.	88F	31C	Dec.	85F	30C
	74	23		74	23		74	23

➤ FORECASTS: **Weather Channel Connection** (☎ 900/932–8437), 95¢ per minute from a Touch-Tone phone.

1 Destination: Indonesia

A NATION OF ISLANDS

THE SHEER SIZE OF INDONESIA is mind-boggling. This world's fourth most populous country covers more than 17,000 islands (over one-third of them uninhabited) that stretch for more than 5,161 km (3,200 mi) from the Pacific to the Indian Ocean. From north to south, the islands form a 1,774-km-long (1,100-mi-long) bridge—the largest archipelago in the world—between Asia and Australia. If the country were created only of land, it would span the distance from New York to Los Angeles and have the depth of a line from Seattle to San Francisco, with a land mass nearly equal to that of Australia. However, nearly three-quarters of its area is water, including the Indian Ocean, the South China Sea, and the Pacific. On the nation's bicolored flag: the stripe of red on top symbolizes land and the white base represents water in a clever play on its nickname "Tanah (land) Air (water)."

From Jakarta's tall steel-and-glass office buildings to Irian Jaya's thatched huts, Indonesia embraces an astonishing array of cultures. Today, Indonesia's 210 million people—Asmat, Balinese, Batak, Dayak, and on down through the alphabet—speak more than 300 languages. The national language, Bahasa Indonesia, is officially recognized as a means of binding the population together under a fitting national motto: "*Bhinneka Tunggal Ika,*" or "Unity in Diversity."

It's this size and diversity that make Indonesia so fascinating. You can relax in one of Bali's luxury resorts or take a river trip through the jungles of Borneo. If you do venture off the beaten path—really the way to fall in love with the country's charms—remember that patience is a key to enjoying your trip. Since tourism is a new priority for Indonesia, the infrastructure is often rudimentary. Only in areas slated for tourist development can you expect to find services approaching international standards. Elsewhere, expect only modest accommodations and casually scheduled transport.

The Land and Its Flora and Fauna

Centered atop the famous "Ring of Fire," Indonesia is a geological enigma where change has been continuous throughout the centuries. More than 400 volcanoes rise to form the archipelago's backbone; close to 100 of these are active today. Donau Toba (Lake Toba) in northern Sumatra, the largest and deepest lake in Southeast Asia, is the remnant of the most devastating explosion in history and now shelters 630-sq-km (391-sq-mi) Samosir, the world's largest lake island. Other mountains whose eruptions have echoed worldwide are Sumbawa's Gunung Tambora (in 1815), Java's Krakatau volcano (in 1883), and Bali's Gunung Agung (in 1963).

Indonesia's islands are unique for their rich natural resources. The archipelago's 144 million hectares of rain forest are second in size only to those of Brazil and comprise 10% of the world's remaining rain forest areas. More than 40,000 plants, 4,000 varieties of trees, and 1,500 types of flowers are found here, and the country harvests more than 300 rare and pharmaceutical species each year. Many are beauties, such as the 170 types of orchids that grow in Kalimantan (on Borneo) alone; others are beastly, such as the giant orange Raffelesia, the world's largest flower, which is as memorable for its stench as it is for its 6-foot width. Beneath the earth is a literal treasure chest of gold, silver, and diamonds found in the hills of Sumatra, Kalimantan, and Sulawesi. Oil is a prime source of income throughout the islands.

Even more striking than the country's flora, though, is its fauna. Indonesia protects more than 600 endemic mammals, reptiles, and birds—creatures found nowhere else in the world. Many reside in just one region or on just one island, such as the Sumatran and Javan rhinos; the Sumatran elephant; the Bali starling; the Sumatran and Borneo orangutans; the Sulawesi anoa, babirusa, and macaque; the Komodo dragon; and the birds of paradise from Irian Jaya. A majority of these animals are also endangered. In fact, Indonesia is the guardian for more than 60 creatures on the international lists for protection, giving the islands more rare species than any other country in the world.

The Land and Its People

The earliest evidence of inhabitants have been found on Java, where the remains of a Homo habilis child are believed to be the oldest in Southeast Asia (they date from around 1.9 million years). Relics dated 2,000 BC–500 BC show seafaring cultures, which has been confirmed by records kept by Chinese and Indian traders who began sailing through the area between 400 AD and 600 AD.

The nation has seen a succession of conquerors and revolutions, even receiving its name from one of its earliest colonizers: "Indonesia" comes from two Greek words—"indos," meaning Indian, and "nesos," meaning islands—a testament to the Indian traders who roamed the islands in the 1st century AD. The great Buddhist monument of Borobudur and the Hindu Prambanan temples were constructed around 200 years later as hallmarks of east Java's Saliendra dynasty, one of the most powerful kingdoms in Southeast Asian history. From the 9th to 12th centuries, Saliendra and northern Sumatra's Srivijaya kingdom were the ruling trade centers, until the Majapahit kingdom ushered in a "Golden Age" of cultural revolution on Java. However, at the same time, Sumatra was welcoming Arabic traders to the northern province of Aceh, where the religion of Islam took hold and would soon sweep through the region to bind the islands in faith.

Contact with the west came in 1509, when Portuguese traders arrived. A century later they were displaced by the Dutch, and by the 18th century, Dutch rule encompassed most of Indonesia, known to the West as the Dutch East Indies. Except for a brief interlude of British rule during the Napoleonic Wars of 1811–16, the Dutch remained in power until the outbreak of World War II. After the surrender of the occupying Japanese in 1945, a bloody fight for Indonesian independence ensued. In 1949 Indonesia won its sovereignty, and the name Dutch East Indies became one more piece of colonial history.

The Land and Its Politics

The man behind the independence movement was Sukarno (many Indonesians have only one formal name), who became president of the new republic and implemented a leftist nationalist policy. He forcibly prevented ethnic groups from forming their own republics and extended Indonesia's borders by annexing part of New Guinea, now the province of Irian Jaya. Despite imprisoning his opposition, he lost control of the movement, the economy suffered under an annual inflation rate of 650%, and Indonesia dissolved into chaos.

On the night of September 30, 1965, Communists (or so it was said) abducted and murdered six top generals and their aides and, it is alleged, were about to seize power. Major-General Suharto intervened, and blood flowed by the gallon. Anyone accused of being a Communist was slaughtered. Rampaging mobs massacred thousands—some estimates place the number of dead at 500,000.

Suharto became president in 1967 and ruled for seven consecutive terms until the growing economic and social turmoil that began with the 1997 Asian financial crisis—and the consequent devaluation of the rupiah by more than 75%—had the country riding waves of anxiety and expectation. Repressive policies toward the independence-minded people of Timor, the one island that remained more Portuguese than Dutch, didn't help either, particularly since Timor freedom fighters Bishop Carlos Ximenes Belo and José Ramos-Horta attracted the international spotlight when they shared the 1996 Nobel Peace Prize.

In May 1998, after weeks of student demonstrations against Suharto's government, (these culminated in riots that ricocheted throughout the islands), Suharto allowed Vice President B. J. Habibie to assume interim rule of the country. However, for the students and general public, Habibie—a known Suharto supporter—is only an interim solution at best, and at press time, the country was drawing up new electoral parties and candidates. As for Indonesia's political and economic future, everything will depend on how Habibie handles his power and how strongly his opponents are supported by the masses. At worst, the country could fall into a far more fragmented archipelago of isolated, individualist islands; at best, it could pull together as a stronger, more experienced, and more enthusiastic nation of islands—united in their diversity.

WHAT'S WHERE

Java

Java is the archipelago's economic and political core, and it's also the most crowded island; 14 million people live in the capital area of Jakarta alone. Yet this is still a land of great natural power, with more than two dozen active volcanoes—including the infamous Krakatau—and 15 peaks that rise above 1,860 ft. The Great Britain–size isle is also a natural haven, with nearly two dozen national parks and reserves. Between these are found clusters of five main cultural groups: the Islamic Sundanese and the reclusive Badui of West Java, the traditional Javanese of the central areas, the Tenggerese of the east, and the Madurese of Madura Island.

Bali

Bali is the country's most popular getaway, just a pint-size nub of land 140 km by 80 km (87 mi by 50 mi) in size. Its distinction is that it is the only Hindu island in an overwhelmingly Islamic country, yet the religions peacefully coexist. The dominant natural force in Bali is Gunung Agung, the "mother mountain," which the Balinese worship as the abode of the gods. Temples are built facing the volcano, and rituals are regularly performed in its honor.

Nusa Tenggarra

Of the more than 500 islands trickling eastward from Bali in the Nusa Tenggara archipelago, the main stepping stones are Lombok, Sumbawa, Komodo, and Flores. Lombok, the lush, mountainous home of the majestic Gunung Rinjani volcano, has in fact been deemed "little Bali"; in essence, the Island of the Gods plus Muslim Sasak cultures and minus the tourists. Sumbawa could well be called "little Java" for its scenic coastlines, open forests, and small Islamic towns. Komodo, of course, is the infamous center for dragon-spotting, and Flores is quickly gathering fame for its fabulous dive sites.

Sulawesi

Sulawesi is one of the world's most uniquely shaped islands; its four arms are bits of Australia, Antarctica, Borneo, and New Guinea that smashed together over the eons. As these islands slowly came together, they created a haven for some of the world's most unusual species, such as the anoa "dwarf buffalo," the babirusa "pig deer," and the black Celebes macaque. The island is also a shelter for unusual cultures, from the Bajau and Bugis sea gypsies in the south to the Christian Minihasans in the north. Perhaps the best-known and most intriguing culture here, though, is that of the Tanatoraja, where highland villages in the southwest peninsula are still the site of elaborate funeral celebrations, cliffside graves, and life-size effigies of the dead.

Sumatra

Sumatra, the world's sixth-largest island, has more than 100 volcanoes that stretch 2,000 km (1,240 mi) north to south. Over 15 are currently active, including Gunung Leuser near Medan and Gunung Marapi near Jambi. This island also has some very large tracts of pristine rain forest, and much of its southern swamps have yet to be explored. The westernmost point in the archipelago is here, at Pulau Weh at the tip of the northern province of Aceh, where Arabic traders originally landed in the 13th century. Sumatra also encompasses Nias Island and the Mentawais in the Indian Ocean, where primitive cultures still exist, and the Riau Archipelago in the Melaka Strait, home to seafaring peoples. Near Medan is 1,797-square-km (1,114-square-mi) Lake Toba, the largest lake in Southeast Asia, where the Christian Batak culture thrives. The Bukittinggi area just to the west is the home of the matriarchal Minangkabau tribe.

PLEASURES AND PASTIMES

Dance

Dance is everywhere on the islands: at celebrations, purification ceremonies, temple rituals, weddings, birthdays, processions to the sea. On Java, court dances are still performed at the sultan's palace in Yogyakarta and, in the summer, dance troupes of several hundred performers act out the Hindu legend of the Ramayana by full-moon light at the Prambanan Temple. For the Javanese, the slow, smooth movements are almost like a ballet in which each subtle turn of the head or lift of the finger has meaning. Sumatra's dance traits have the added elements of liveliness and simultaneous movements that include claps, snaps, kneeling dances, and chanting as music is played in the background for performances like the *saudati.* Other dances symbolize offerings of peace, such as northern Sumatra's *meusekat*; or, like the *tob daboh,* they can mimic battlelike action using dancers who are armed with real daggers.

On Bali, perhaps the island best known for its colorful and elegant performing arts, dancers move low to the ground, with bent knees, arched backs, and controlled steps, arms at right angles with elbows pointing up and fingers spread wide. The female dancers flutter their long-nailed fingers. They move slowly across the stage, then turn quickly but precisely with a staccato movement. Head movements are staccato, too, without facial expression except for their darting and flashing eyes. They wear petaled or gold headdresses. The men have to do battle and get killed, and their movements are more varied.

Most dances are accompanied by the traditional gamelan orchestra of gongs, drums (mostly hand-beaten), a type of xylophone with bronze bars, violin-like instruments, and a flute. Balinese dancing is far more exuberant than Javanese, and the Balinese gamelan is sharper and louder, with more crescendo. Behind every dance is a legend with a moral theme.

BARONG➢ The Barong is a dance of Good versus Evil. The Good is Barong, a dragon with a huge, bushy, lionlike head and a long flower-bedecked beard. Bells ring as he snaps his head. The two dancers inside the costume use complicated motions to make Barong humorous and good natured, but ferocious when he meets Evil, in the form of the witch Rangda. Rangda's horrifying mask is white, with bulging eyes and tusks extending from her mouth. Her long braided hair sweeps down to the floor amid menacing, red, mirrored streamers. She rushes threateningly back and forth across the stage. There are also beautiful female dancers with petaled headdresses, tasseled girdles, and gold-and-green sarongs, and male warriors whose prince is crowned with gold and flowers. Rangda forces the warriors to turn their kris (dagger) blades on themselves, but Barong's powers keep the blades from harming them. A bird dancer enters and is killed—the required sacrifice to the gods—and Rangda is banished.

LEGONG➢ The Legong is a glittering classical dance. The story involves a young princess kidnapped by an enemy of her father. Three young girls in tight gold brocade and frangipani headdresses perform several roles. Their movements are rapid and pulsating; they punctuate the music with quick, precise movements and flashing eyes. It's an exacting dance—girls start training for the roles at five and retire before they're 15.

KECAK➢ The dramatic Kecak, the Monkey Dance, depicts the monkey armies of Hanuman, who rescued Rama and his love, Sita, from the forests of Ceylon in the *Ramayana,* the great Hindu epic. No gamelan is used; all sound comes from the chorus, who, in unison, simulate both the gamelan and the chattering, moaning, bellowing, and shrieking of monkeys. This dance is often performed at night under torchlight. The dark figures, again in unison, make wild arm gestures and shake their fingers. (The Kecak isn't a classical dance but a product of this century.)

Dining

The choice of foods in Indonesia is wide ranging: Indonesian, Chinese, and Western cooking are available in every major town and resort. To meet the needs of an increasing number of Japanese tourists, you'll also find Japanese restaurants in Jakarta and on Bali.

Warungs are Indonesian street-food stalls, sometimes with benches and tables in the open, under canvas, or sheltered by a sheet of galvanized tin. The food here varies from drab to tasty, but it's always cheap: you can eat well for Rp 1,000. Warungs are often clustered together at a *pasar malam,* or night bazaar.

Rumah makan are just like warungs, only with fixed walls and roofs. Another step up is the *restoran,* a very broad category of small dining establishments. Most are Chinese-owned and serve both Indonesian and Chinese cuisine. Hotel dining rooms generally offer Chinese, Indonesian, and Western fare; the native specialties are usually toned down. If you enjoy spicy food, you'll be happier at more authentic eateries.

Nasi (rice) is the staple of the Indonesian diet. It's eaten with breakfast, lunch, and dinner, and as a snack, but it mainly serves as a backdrop to an exciting range of flavors. Indonesian food can be very hot, particularly in Sumatra. Your first sample might be *sambal,* a spicy relish made with chilies that's placed on every restaurant table. Indonesians cook with garlic, shallots, turmeric, cumin, ginger, fermented shrimp paste, soy sauce, lime or lemon juice, lemongrass, coconut, other nuts, and hot peppers. Peanut sauce is common; two dishes frequently encountered are *gado gado,* a cold vegetable salad dressed with spiced peanut sauce, and *saté* (or *satay*), slices of skewered meat charcoal-broiled and dipped in a flavored peanut sauce. *Mie* (noodles) are also used in a variety of popular fare, such as *mie goreng,* an entrée of stir-fried noodles with meat and vegetables.

You'll find dishes with such meats as *ayam* (chicken), *babi* (pork), *daging* (beef), and *kambing* (lamb), though, naturally, fresh fish and shellfish abound. *Ikan* (fish) is often baked in a banana leaf with spices, grilled with a spicy topping, or baked with coconut. *Udang* (shrimp) come cooked in coconut sauce, grilled with hot chilies, made into prawn-and-bean-sprout fritters, or, in Sulawesi, with butter or Chinese sweet-and-sour sauce. *Cumi-cumi* (squid) and *kepiting* (crab) are also featured.

For dessert, Indonesians eat fresh fruit: papaya, pineapple, rambutan, salak, and mangosteen. Because this is a mostly Muslim country, wine and alcohol—when available—are expensive additions to a meal; beer is your best bet. Hard liquor is generally only available in popular bars and Western restaurants in the major cities, although local whiskey brews, called *arak,* are found throughout the islands.

Most food comes cut into small pieces, and finger bowls are provided. Even in Jakarta, you'll see well-dressed Indonesians eating with their fingers. Visitors normally receive forks, although the combination of a spoon (held in the right hand to eat with) and a fork (held in the left hand to help push food into the spoon) is commonly used as well. In more remote areas, the right hand is the main eating implement. (The left hand, traditionally used in Asian lavatory hygiene, is considered unclean and is never used for dining, touching, or pointing.) Note that water in Indonesia is not potable, so stick with the bottled variety. Ice used in restaurants and hotels is supposed to be the kind made under government supervision with the claim that it's safe; as you have no way to check whether or not the proper ice is used, you may want to forego it.

Here are a few more food terms that appear frequently on Indonesian menus:

bakmi goreng—fried noodles with bits of beef, pork, or shrimp; tomatoes; carrots; bean sprouts; cabbage; soy sauce; and spices
dendeng ragi (or rendang)—thin squares of beef cooked with grated coconut and spices
gudeg—chicken with jackfruit
kelian ayam—Sumatran chicken curry
nasi campur—steamed rice with bits of chicken, shrimp, or vegetables with sambal; often topped with a fried egg and accompanied by *krupok,* delicious puffy prawn crisps
nasi goreng—fried rice with shallots, chilies, soy sauce, and ketchup; it may include pork (in Bali), shrimp, onions, cabbage, mushrooms, or carrots; it's often studded with tiny fiery green peppers in Sumatra
nasi rames—a miniature rijsttafel
rijsttafel—literally, "rice table"; steamed rice with side dishes such as sayur lodeh, gudeg, or kelian ayam
sayur lodeh—a spicy vegetable stew
soto ayam—chicken soup, varying from region to region but usually including shrimp, bean sprouts, spices, chilies, and fried onions or potatoes; mie soto ayam is chicken noodle soup.

Lodging

You'll find superb resorts—such as the Four Seasons on Bali and the Mandarin Oriental in Jakarta—that cost half what you might pay in the Caribbean. All such establishments generally include room service and air-conditioning as part of their long lists of amenities. New hotels open all the time in Bali's popular areas; Ubud doesn't yet have any mammoth hotels, which has helped it maintain a small-town feel, but the number of small hotels (20–50 rooms) multiplies every year.

The government classifies hotels with star ratings, five stars being the most luxurious. Its criteria are somewhat random, however. (No hotel without a garage gets four stars, for example, despite the fact that many visitors don't need a garage.) Besides hotels, most Indonesian towns offer three types of rooming houses: *penginapan, losmen,* and *wisma.* Theoretically, the penginapan is cheapest, with thin partitions between rooms, and the wisma most expensive, with thicker walls. The term "losmen" is often used generically to mean any small rooming house. Facilities vary widely throughout the islands: some Bali losmen are comfortable and social, with shared living areas and rest rooms; others are quieter and more private, with separate sitting areas and individual baths. At the bottom range in the less touristed areas you'll usually get a clean room with a shower and an Asian toilet—either an in-ground porcelain "squatter" or a seatless Western "throne"—for less than $5 a night. Losmen on Bali often include a light breakfast, and free tea, coffee, and snacks are part of the hospitality in many areas. Note that although there a few luxury exceptions, as a rule the standards in accommodations on Lombok and islands farther east as well as in some parts of Sumatra and Sulawesi often fall below those in, say, Jakarta or Bali—be prepared to rough it.

Scuba Diving and Snorkeling

Scuba diving is becoming popular, and licensed diving clubs have sprung up around the major resort areas. Bali (off Sanur and the north coast), Lombok's Gili Islands, Flores, and North Sulawesi have some of the world's best diving. The best times for diving in Indonesia are March–June and October–November.

Shopping

Arts and crafts in Indonesia are bargains by U.S. standards. If you have the time, custom-made items can be commissioned. Consider bringing pictures or samples of items that you'd like built or reproduced—anything from clothing and jewelry to furniture and board games.

From Java the best buys are batik cloth and garments, traditional jewelry, musical instruments, leather *wayang* puppets, and leather accessories. In Bali, look for batiks, stone and wood carvings, bamboo furniture, ceramics, silver work, traditional masks, and wayang puppets. Sumatra is best for thick, handwoven, cotton cloth; carved-wood panels and statues, often in primitive, traditional designs; and silver and gold jewelry. Sulawesi is known for its silver-filigree jewelry, handwoven silks and cottons, hand-carved wood panels, and bamboo goods. Be aware that machine-produced goods are sometimes sold to visitors as handcrafted.

NEW AND NOTEWORTHY

In 1998, Indonesia's failing economy and its citizens' cries for reforms led to student demonstrations. These, in turn, escalated into mass protests and then riots in Jakarta, Medan, and Solo that left more than 1,000 dead. On May 22, in response to the unrest, President Suharto resigned, ending a 32-year-long rule. His replacement was then–Vice President B. J. Habibe, who appointed a new cabinet and promised change. However, many feel that Habibe, a long-time Suharto protégé, is not the right man to lead the nation through its difficulties. Although at press time it did not look as if Habibe would resign, he did call for elections in May 1999.

Unlike many countries that are rife with unrest, the violence in Indonesia is not directed at foreign visitors. Further, there are places—Yogyakarta on Java and the islands of Bali, Nusa Tengarra, and Sulawesi—that have remained peaceful. If you're planning a trip to Indonesia, scan the newspapers for updates, contact the Indonesian tourism board for assessments of the current situation, and check with the state department about any warnings. Realize, also, that the money generated by tourism may well help Indonesia overcome some its economic woes; that while taking advantage of low (sometimes criminally low) prices, you may be helping a troubled nation. Let your conscience be your guide.

There are many **new hotels and resorts** throughout the country, including Jakarta's Regent and Shangri-La hotels and Borobudur's Amanjiwo resort on Java; the Oberoi resort on Lombok; Jimbaran Bay's Ritz-Carlton, Bukit Peninsula's Bali Cliff, and Ubud's Four Seasons on Bali; and Ujung Padang's Radisson on Sulawesi.

Many tour and adventure companies now offer **trips farther afield,** including those to central Sulawesi, the secluded homeland of the Toraja culture; northern Sumatra, where rain forests and volcanoes provide a stunning backdrop to serene Lake Toba and Gunung Leuser National Park; and eastern Kalimantan with its Dayak river cultures. Although luxury amenities are out of the question in these far reaches, simple yet comfortable accommodations are being built. Indonesia is the keeper of the world's third-largest rain forest area—filled with unique and rare species. The country's numerous **national parks** are receiving more attention than ever before, and much is being done to provide educational and ecosensitive facilities.

Booklovers take note: Indonesia recently exempted all books from a 10% sales tax. The exemption, which once only applied to religious and educational titles, is an attempt to make more books accessible to more people.

GREAT ITINERARIES

It could easily take an active traveler years to explore all of Indonesia, and even to see the limited number of destinations covered in this book would still require a whirlwind month or two. This guide discusses only those areas that have a range of amenities for all travelers and have sights or attractions that are of particular interest.

If you haven't been to Bali, then that island should be on your itinerary. It would be very easy to spend an entire vacation at one of Bali's resorts—Kuta, Nusa Dua, and Sanur are the best known—but assuming that you have the itch to see more, then Java's Yogyakarta and the famed temple of Borobudur should be your second destinations. Or consider visiting Lombok and the western islands of Nusa Tenggara as an extension of a holiday in Bali. North Sumatra, including the peaceful Lake Toba area and the rain forest of Gunung Leuser National Park, and south-central Sulawesi, including the beaches and waterfalls around Ujung Pandang and the mountainous Toraja highlands, are also recommended options. Jakarta, while enmeshed in the typical trappings of big-city traffic and smog, is actually worth a look for its cultural and historical sites, including a variety of museums, a cobblestone neighborhood known as Old Batavia, and a waterfront that has for centuries been a crux of Southeast Asian trade.

If You Have 7 Days

Fly into Bali and spend the first two days exploring the temples and villages, using **Ubud** as your base; be sure to see at least one dance performance. Then take an hour's flight to **Yogyakarta** and spend two nights there, making sure to visit **Borobudur, Prambanan,** and the sultans' palaces in Yogyakarta and **Solo.** Return to Bali for a couple of days at a beach resort before flying out.

If You Have 10 Days

Enter Indonesia by way of **Medan,** taking three days to visit **Brastagi** and **Lake Toba.** Depart from Sumatra and spend one night in **Jakarta.** On the fifth day take the early morning flight into **Yogyakarta** and visit **Prambanan** in the afternoon. The next morning drive out to **Borobudur** and then take the late afternoon flight to Bali. Split your final days between the beach and sightseeing around the island. Be sure to visit Ubud and other craft and cultural villages clustered southeast of the island's center.

If You Have 14 Days

With two weeks in Indonesia, you could follow the 10-day itinerary and add a side trip from Bali to Sulawesi. Fly into **Ujung Pandang** for a night, taking the afternoon to explore the natural beauty of Bantimurung park, then proceed to **Rantepao** for a three-day exploration of Toraja. If time permits, head north and take a two-day dive trip on the coral reefs of Bunaken Marine Park near Manado before heading home.

If You Have 15–21 Days

TEMPLES AND ANCIENT CULTURES➢ Fly into Jakarta and spend the night; hire a car and driver the next morning, and take in the Botanic Gardens and Presidential

Palace in Bogor. From the capital, fly to Yogyakarta that evening and spend two full days visiting the Sultan's Palace, the ruins of Taman Sari, and the Prambanan and Borobudur temples. From Yogyakarta, fly to Bali for two days and hire a car to visit Besakih, Tanah Lot, Ulu Watu, and some of the island's smaller temples. Next, fly to Ujung Pandang, where you can spend the afternoon at the massive Ft. Rotterdam before flying up to Tanatoraja the next morning. After two days in Toraja, head back to Ujung Pandang and catch a connecting flight to Balikpapan, where you can spend three days learning about the Dayak river cultures and seeing the longhouses. From Balikpapan, head back to your international gateway.

NATIONAL PARKS AND WILDLIFE OVERVIEW➢ Fly into Medan, hire a car, and head south for Gunung Leuser National Park, where you can spend three days viewing orangutans and rain-forest life. Next, fly to Jakarta and spend the night; the next morning catch a boat to Ujung Kulon National Park, for three days of snorkeling, hiking, and spotting wildlife on Pulau Peucang and the mainland. Using Jakarta as your base, fly to Labuanbajo, Flores, and catch a boat for a three-day Komodo adventure. Back in Jakarta, fly to Ujung Pandang and then Poso, where you can spend three days exploring Lore Lindu National Park; then head north to Manado, for three days of diving or snorkeling around the beautiful reefs or Pulau Bunaken Marine Park before flying home.

THE GRAND DIVE TOUR➢ Fly into Jakarta and head down to Ujung Kulon National Park by boat, where you can spend three days diving the many reefs around Pulau Peucang. Head back to Jakarta and fly or travel overnight by road to Bali, where you can take four days to explore the numerous reefs and wrecks along the eastern coast. Cross over to Lombok by ferry and spend three days diving the reefs around northwest Senggigi and the Gili islands. Cross back to Denpasar and then fly to Manado for five days of diving the excellent reefs of Bunaken Manado Tua National Marine Reserve. Finally, fly to Ambon, hire a boat, and spend three days diving the Maluku reefs before flying back to Jakarta. (Caution: If you follow this itinerary be sure to rest or just snorkel rather than dive within 24 hours of flying.)

FODOR'S CHOICE

Beaches

★ **Balina, Bali.** This serene, curving stretch of sand has the feel of an upscale resort area.

★ **Carita, Java.** This quiet resort area is a great place to gets some sun and spend a night before a visit to the Krakatau volcano.

★ **Jimbaran Bay, Bali.** Here you'll find white sand, sapphire waves, and startling sunsets.

★ **Lombok Island.** Magnificent waves roll in on the deserted south-coast beaches.

★ **Lovina, Bali.** Gentle waves lap the black-sand shores at Lovina.

★ **Pangandaran, Java.** Although the surf from the Indian Ocean here can be dangerous, the black sands of the beach are almost irresistible.

Dining

★ **Xin Hwa, Jakarta, Java.** Here spicy Szechuan dishes are served in refined surroundings. *$$$$*

★ **Telaga Naga, Sanur, Bali.** This is *the* place on Bali for Szechuan and Cantonese fare. *$$$*

★ **Sari Kuring, Jakarta, Java.** Very good Indonesian seafood is typified by the grilled prawns, which practically melt in your mouth. *$$*

★ **Ny Suharti, Yogyakarta, Java.** Forget charm and atmosphere and all the other items on the menu: you're here for the best fried chicken on the island, perhaps in all of Indonesia. *$*

★ **Pondok Torsina, Tanatoraja, Sulawesi.** Here you can feast on Indonesian fare on a veranda overlooking rice paddies in the "Land of the Kings." *$*

Lodging

★ **Amandari, near Ubud, Bali.** The peaceful gardens and luxurious cottages here are in a private village setting overlooking the lush Ayung River valley. *$$$$*

★ **Amanjiwo, Borobudur, Java.** The 35 suites all have views of Borobudur temple from their private patios, 14 of which have swimming pools. *$$$$*

★ **Four Seasons, Sayan, Bali.** Given the captivating view of the Ayung River, you may never want to leave your private villa and pool to explore the rest of the island. $$$$

★ **Hotel Tugu, near Denpasar, Bali.** Art and artifacts abound here—in the public areas, the guest quarters, and the on-site museum. You can contemplate these works in your private cottage surrounded by quiet gardens. $$$$

★ **Mandarin Oriental, Jakarta, Java.** Expect refined, personal service in an atmosphere of understated elegance. $$$$

★ **The Oberoi, Medan Beach, Lombok.** The ultimate secluded retreat has private thatched cottages at the shores of Medana Beach and within sight of Gili Air. $$$$

★ **Kusuma Sahid Prince Hotel, Solo, Java.** A former prince's residence becomes your home away from home. $$$

★ **Majapahit Hotel, Surabaya, Java.** The large grounds and personal service here make you feel as if you're in a bygone era. $$$

★ **Puri Komodo Resort, Labuanbajo, Flores.** From your beach bungalow at this back-to-nature hideaway you can contemplate a day trip to Komodo Island. $

Museums

★ **Puppet Museum, Jakarta, Java.** Watch a shadow-puppet play or view an extensive collection of traditional Indonesian puppets, as well as examples from Thailand, China, Malaysia, India, Cambodia, and elsewhere.

★ **Puri Lukisan Museum, Ubud, Bali.** Bali's "palace of paintings" incorporates an overview of the island's famed artisan immigrants and native talents in a setting of tropical gardens and Balinese folklore.

The Natural World

★ **Bunaken Manado Tua National Marine Reserve, Sulawesi.** Just off the shore from Manado the marine life is vibrant and colorful, the diving memorable.

★ **Danau Toba, Sumatra.** The largest lake in Southeast Asia and one of the highest in the world, Lake Toba sits nearly 3,000 ft above sea level, surrounded by green mountains that plunge into its 1,500-ft deep waters.

★ **Gunung Bromo, Java.** You can stand on the rim of this active volcano just before dawn and watch it spew steam from a bubbling cauldron of water, ash, and sulphur.

★ **Keli Mutu, Flores.** Inside an extinct volcano cone, a triad of lakes mysteriously change colors.

Palaces and Unique Structures

★ **The Kraton Sultans' Palace of Yogyakarta, Java.** The original palace of Javanese sultans, built in 1757, is an extensive open complex of gardens and pavilions where there are performances of traditional Javanese dance and gamelan music daily.

★ **Traditional Clan Houses of the Toraja, Sulawesi.** The carved and painted *tongkonans* are built on piles and topped by massive roofs shaped like a ship or buffalo horns.

Sacred Places

★ **Borobudur Temple, Central Java.** It took perhaps 10,000 men 100 years to build this giant stupa, which illustrates the earthly and spiritual life of the Buddha with thousands of relief carvings and statues.

★ **Prambanan Temple Complex, Central Java.** These remarkable 9th-century temples celebrate the Hindu pantheon.

Shopping

★ **Antique wayang kulit on Bali or in Yogyakarta on Java.** These puppets conjure up the shadows of Hindu epics.

★ **Batiks and leather in Yogyakarta, Java.** Fabulous designs on batik and crafted bags in leather are real temptations.

★ **Silver filigree on Bali and in Yogyakarta on Java.** Delicate spiderwebs of creations in dainty, intricate shapes.

★ **Stone and wood carving on Bali.** Guardians sculpted in stone and masks in wood are essential to keep evil spirits at bay.

FESTIVALS AND SEASONAL EVENTS

Festival dates depend on the type of calendar prevalent in the region where they take place. Most of Indonesia uses the Islamic calendar; the Balinese use a lunar calendar. The **Indonesia Calendar of Events,** with listings for the entire archipelago, is available at Garuda airline offices, or contact tourist information offices.

WINTER

DEC.–JAN.➢ **Idul Fitri,** two days marking the end of Ramadan (a month of fasting during daylight), is the most important Muslim holiday. Festivals take place in all the villages and towns of Muslim Indonesia.

Kesodo ceremonies are held by the Hindu Tenggerese at the crater of Mt. Bromo on Java.

MAR.➢ **Nyepi,** the Balinese New Year, falls on the vernal equinox, usually around March 21. New Year's Eve is spent exorcising evil spirits, which are first attracted with offerings of chicken blood, flowers, and aromatic leaves, then driven away with noise as masked youths bang gongs and tin pans. The island falls silent: no fires or lamps may be lit, and traffic is prohibited.

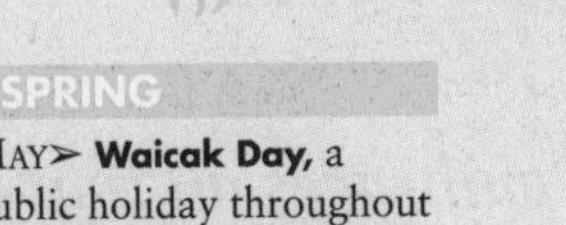

SPRING

MAY➢ **Waicak Day,** a public holiday throughout Indonesia, celebrates the Buddha's birth, death, and enlightenment. The **Ramayana Ballet Festival** is held at the Prambanan temple near Yogyakarta during the full-moon week each month, beginning in May and continuing through October. A cast of 500 performs a four-episode dance-drama of the *Ramayana* epic.

SUMMER

JULY➢ **Galungan,** Bali's most important festival, celebrates the creation of the world, marks a visit by ancestral spirits, and honors the victory of good over evil. Celebrants make offerings in family shrines and decorate their villages. On the 10th and last day they bid farewell to the visiting spirits with gifts of *kuningan,* a saffron-yellow rice.

AUG.➢ **Independence Day** is celebrated on the 17th throughout Indonesia with flag-raising ceremonies, sports events, and cultural performances.

AUTUMN

OCT.➢ The town of Pamekasan on Java holds **bull-racing finals** in mid–October. A jockey stands on skids slung between two yoked bulls. The animals are decorated, and there's mass dancing before they run. The winner is the bull whose feet cross the finish line first. **Sekaten** commemorates the birth of Mohammed. In Yogyakarta the sultan's antique gamelan—a unique Indonesian musical instrument—is played only on this day. The concert is performed in the gamelan pavilion of the kraton, the sultan's palace complex. Then the celebrants form a parade, carrying enormous amounts of food from the kraton to the mosque, where they distribute it to the people.

2 Java

Java embraces all that is beloved about Indonesia. There are exciting Asian cityscapes; lavender slopes of silent, smoking volcanoes that unfold into verdant rice terraces; ancient temples and palaces; and a people whose beliefs are threaded with Islam, Buddhism, Hinduism, and mysticism passed down through the centuries by ruling kingdoms.

JAVA COULD BE A BIG COUNTRY all by itself. It's the heart, soul, and financial center of Indonesia. And with more than 100 million people squeezed into an area about the size of Louisiana, it's the world's most populous island. Strangely enough, however, you can still find places of great solitude. This thin isle—about 1,100 km (684 mi) from east to west and between 100 km (62 mi) and 200 km (124 mi) wide—is full of volcanoes (many of them active), pounded by big surf from the Indian Ocean, and buffeted by the much calmer Java Sea. Divided into three provinces—West, Central, and East Java—and two special territories—Jakarta the capital and Yogyajakarta the cultural center—it's easy to see in bite-size sections. The road and rail systems are extensive (although in places they're pushed to their limits), the people are friendly, and English isn't as foreign a tongue as you might expect.

It seems that every bit of land—from the fertile valleys to the steep mountain slopes—is cultivated, taking advantage of the rich volcanic soil. But such landscaping is one of the few constants here. Java's long and varied history is evident in Borobudur, the world's largest Buddhist monument; Cirebon, a city on the north coast that dates back more than 500 years; ancient Hindu sites; and remnants of old Javanese empires. Islam, which arrived in the 13th century and remains the most prominent religion, has its share of monuments, too. The Dutch made Java one of their colonies in the early 1800s, and their influence is still reflected in such cities as Bandung and Bogor in West Java. The capital, Jakarta—with its tall modern buildings casting shadows on shacks and shanties—seems a tribute to a contemporary age in which the collision of old ideas and new ones has caused confusion and upheaval.

Indonesia, with Java leading the way, is entering an exciting yet worrying time. Exciting because of the promise of new freedoms and opportunities and worrying because of the uncertainty of economic crisis. As you travel, you'll notice a huge gulf between rich and poor—particularly in Jakarta—and it may take some getting used to. Further, the floating rupiah and inflation are playing havoc with prices. With this come great bargains, but also considerable commercial instability. Companies—including travel agencies, airlines, and other tourism-related businesses—open and close seemingly overnight. Some tolerance will be needed. Your patience and compassion, however, will be amply rewarded by the rich sights and experiences that Java, and the rest of Indonesia, offer.

Pleasures and Pastimes

Architecture

Java is the home of several world-renowned temples and palaces, each of which offers an architectural sample from a different era and religious background. Many are near Yogyakarta, including Borobudur, the world's largest Buddhist temple, the Hindu temples of Prambanan, and the sultans' palaces of Yogyakarta and Solo.

Dining

As the site of the archipelago's capital and the business and transport crossroads of the islands, Java offers an endless selection of Western and Asian fare—including just about every Indonesian dish ever invented. Celebrated chefs often make guest appearances to prepare meals at larger hotels in Jakarta, Yogyakarta, and Surabaya. To find a true taste of Java, though, follow the Javanese (or at least ask for their recommendations).

Javanese fare leans toward the spicy. Chili peppers, shallots, garlic, and ginger are frequently used, and the fiery *sambal* sauces accompany every meal as does *nasi putih* (steamed rice)—the perfect complement to the island's famed thick stews and rich curries. For appetizers try *gado gado* (a medley of steamed vegetables topped by spicy peanut sauce); *soto ayam* (chicken soup); or *satay* (also spelled "sate"), small skewers of grilled meat dipped in peanut sauce and accompanied by spicy peppers, onions, and soy sauce. Main courses include *goreng* (fried) or *bakar* (grilled) dishes as well as such succulent fare as *rendang daging* (beef simmered in coconut milk and spices), *sayur lodeh* (spicy vegetable stew), and *opor ayam* (chicken simmered in coconut milk and spices, a specialty of Yogyakarta). To sample several dishes in one meal, try *nasi campur* or *nasi rames,* both of which feature several small meat and vegetable portions served around sa scoop of steamed rice. Or, go for the all-out rijsttafel (literally, "rice table") buffet—a full spread of Indonesian rice and noodle dishes that was popularized by the Dutch and is still found at many restaurants. (Note: You won't find pork here, since this is an Islamic island, and outside of the large cities you won't find much alcohol, either.)

Lodging

Accommodations on this heavily touristed island run the gamut from all-out luxury resorts to simple (sometimes sparse) *losmen* with shared facilities. You'll find all the major international chain hotels in Jakarta, with branches of most in Surabaya and Yogyakarta; most towns have at least one top-class or business hotel. Something new to the island is the "boutique hotel," a type of small luxury establishment with such personal touches as museum-quality selection of island artwork and antiques throughout. Whichever type of accommodation you choose, be aware of national and religious holidays before arriving and book well ahead if you will be traveling during these times.

Nightlife

You'll find something going on at all hours—particularly on *malam Minggu* (Saturday night)—in Jakarta, Bandung, Yogyakarta, and Surabaya. All three towns have flashy dance clubs and bars. In smaller towns, night markets offer after-dark tastes of local atmosphere.

Scuba Diving and Snorkeling

Divers with limited schedules often head for the islands of Pulau Seribu, where countless coral reefs and abundant undersea life are accessible on short notice. Pulau Peucang, off the shore of Ujung Kulon National Park, offers several reefs and a classic tropical setting.

Trekking

With landscapes that range from stark volcanic slopes to rain-forest jungle, mangrove swamps, and tropical beaches, Java is one of the archipelago's best islands to explore by foot. Every national park has a network of trails to follow, a system of open shelters for camping, and guides available either from the park office or the nearby villages. Ujung Kulon and Gunung Gede–Pangrango each have basic visitor facilities and accommodate hundreds of guests every year. Java is also one of the few places on earth where you can safely (at press time, anyway) climb a number of active volcanoes, including Krakatau on the west coast and the summits of Bromo, Tengger, and Semeru in the east.

Exploring Java

The myriad opportunities for exploring history, nature, and culture on this versatile island attract tourists, short-term business travelers, and long-term backpackers alike. Its limitless activities and limited boundaries allow for many different experiences within each small area, or a more broad view of a single pursuit across the whole of the island.

Great Itineraries

IF YOU HAVE 3-4 DAYS

Fly into **Jakarta** ①–⑬ and take a day tour of the major historical sites, including Sunda Kelapa, Old Batavia, and a museum or a selection of monuments. The next morning, drive to **Bogor** ⑰ and view the Botanic Gardens and the Presidential Palace, then head through the Puncak Pass to **Bandung** ⑱ and catch a late afternoon flight to **Yogyakarta** ㉑–㉕. Take a night tour around the city by horse-drawn cart or bicycle pedicab, including the open markets and restaurants of Jalan Malioboro and the palace area, where you might be able to view a wayang kulit puppet show or a performance of the gamelan orchestra. The next day, take a morning tour of the Kraton and Taman Sari, then make a quick visit to **Prambanan** ㉗ and finish at **Borobudur Temple** ㉖ for the sunset. Have dinner along Jalan Malioboro and take in a local dance performance—or, if you're traveling between May and October, catch a performance of the Ramayana ballet at the Prambanan temple by moonlight—before returning to Jakarta the next morning.

IF YOU HAVE 7 DAYS

Fly into **Jakarta** ①–⑬ and take a day tour of city sights, spend the night, then head south for **Carita Beach** for two nights, where you can spend your time trekking, exploring the **Pulau Krakatau** ⑮ volcano offshore, or just relaxing with a massage on the beach. Next, head northeast for **Bogor** ⑰ and spend the night, taking time to tour the Botanic Gardens and/or the Presidential Palace. The next morning, head through the Puncak Pass for **Bandung** ⑱ then catch an afternoon flight to **Yogyakarta** ㉑–㉕, where you can spend two days exploring the town and surrounding temples before heading back to the capital.

IF YOU HAVE 10 DAYS

Starting with a day tour and a night in **Jakarta** ①–⑬ proceed to **Carita Beach, Bogor** ⑰, and **Bandung** ⑱ as described in the seven-day tour above. Then head southeast for **Pangandaran** ⑲ spending town nights to enjoy the beaches and thriving fishing village setting. Continue northeast to **Yogyakarta** ㉑–㉕ for three nights as above before returning to Jakarta. Or, skip Pangandaran and fly from Bandung to Yogyakarta, spend three nights, then fly east to Malang and spend two days exploring **Mt. Bromo** ㉜ before heading back to the capital.

IF YOU HAVE 14 DAYS

After two nights and a full day tour of **Jakarta** ①–⑬ sights, head for **Carita Beach** for two days, then continue on to **Bogor** ⑰, **Bandung** ⑱, and **Pangandaran** ⑲ as described in the seven- and ten-day tours above. Take an additional day to explore **Yogyakarta** ㉑–㉕, then fly to Malang and spend two nights and a full day trekking the **Mt. Bromo** ㉜ area. Finally, head northeast to **Surabaya** ㉛ and take an afternoon to tour the city before flying back to Jakarta the next morning.

JAKARTA

Indonesia's capital is a place of extremes. Modern multistory buildings look down on shacks with corrugated-iron roofs. Wide boulevards intersect with unpaved streets. Elegant hotels and high-tech business centers stand just a few blocks from overcrowded kampongs. BMWs accelerate down the avenues while pedicabs (which are officially banned from the city) plod along backstreets.

Although the government has tried to prepare for the 21st century, Jakarta has had trouble accommodating the thousands who have flocked to it each year from the countryside. Because of the number of migrant workers who arrive each day, it's difficult to accurately estimate the city's population. The census reports 8.5 million, but the true number is closer to 14 million. The crowds push the city's infrastructure to the limit. Traffic often grinds to a standstill, and a system of canals, built by the Dutch to prevent flooding in below-sea-level Jakarta, can't accommodate the heavy monsoon rains, so the city is sometimes under water for days. The heat and humidity take getting used to, though air-conditioning in the major hotels, restaurants, and shopping centers provides an escape. Early morning and late afternoon are the best times for sightseeing.

Exploring Jakarta

At Jakarta's center is the vast, parklike Merdeka Square, where Sukarno's 433-ft National Monument is topped with a gold-plated flame symbolizing national independence. Wide boulevards border the square, and the Presidential Palace (the president doesn't live here), the army headquarters, City Hall, Gambir Railway Station, the National Museum, and other government buildings are here.

Immediately south of the square along Jalan M. H. Thamrin (*jalan* means "street") is the Menteng district with many international hotels and embassies. Farther south (after Jalan Thamrin changes its name to Jalan Jentral Sudirman) is the downtown of New Jakarta, home to most banks, large corporations, and more international hotels. This area is also known as the Golden Triangle.

North and west of Merdeka Square, around the port of Sunda Kelapa at the mouth of the Ciliwung River, is the Kota area, known as Old Batavia. This is where the Portuguese first arrived in 1522. A century later, in 1619, the Dutch secured the city, renamed it Batavia, and established an administrative center for their expanding Indonesian empire.

Dutch rule came to an abrupt end when, in World War II, the Japanese occupied Batavia and changed its name back to Jayakarta. The Dutch returned after Japan's surrender, but by 1949 Indonesia had won independence and, abbreviating the city's old name, established Jakarta as the nation's capital.

Old Batavia

Old Batavia, or Kota, is down by the port, where the Dutch administration was centered. As Jakarta expanded after World War II, Old Batavia was neglected. Its stately colonial buildings fell into decay, its streets and sidewalks caved in, and its shophouses became warehouses and repair shops. Prior to the economic crisis, an appreciation for Jakarta's heritage was awakened, and a revitalization of Old Batavia began. Many of the old buildings were restored and the area experienced an economic rejuvenation and beautification. (Note that despite gentrification, it's best to visit Old Batavia by day; some of the streets are scary to walk along at night.)

A GOOD TOUR

To cover a lot of ground before the midday heat, a combination of walking and taking cabs is prudent for this tour. Start by taking a taxi to the **fish market** ①, which is best seen early in the day. If you walk through the back of the market, you can save on the entrance fee to **Sunda Kelapa Harbor,** where vessels dock with goods from Indonesia's outer islands. Head south and stop at the **Maritime Museum** ②, then veer left, over to Jalan Tongkol, which becomes Jalan Cengkeh. Turn right onto

Jalan Kunir, and follow it a short distance to Jalan Pintu Besar Utara. Turn left and head down to the heart of Old Batavia, **Fatahillah Square** ③. On the west side of the square, which was the city's central plaza in the days of the Dutch, is the **Puppet Museum** ④ (often called the Wayang Museum); on the east side is the **Jakarta Fine Art Gallery** ⑤, in the former Palace of Justice. The old Town Hall, on the square's south side, is now the **Museum of Old Batavia** ⑥. Behind the Town Hall, on Jalan Pangeran Jayakarta and opposite the Kota Railway Station, is the **Portuguese Church** ⑦, the oldest in Jakarta. From the square head south to explore **Glodok,** Old Batavia's Chinatown; wander around and marvel at all the activity in its narrow streets.

TIMING

To experience the frenetic activity of the fish market, start your tour early, at around 7 AM. If you're visiting on a Sunday, there's an abbreviated wayang *kulit,* or shadow-puppet play, performed at 10 AM at the Puppet Museum. Since the heat builds as the day progresses, try to finish your walk soon after midday.

SIGHTS TO SEE

❸ **Fatahillah Square.** At the heart of the old city is Fatahillah Square, cobbled with ballast stones from old Dutch trading ships. In its center is a fountain, a reproduction of one originally built here in 1728. Near the fountain, criminals were beheaded while their judges watched from the balconies of Town Hall (☞ Museum of Old Batavia, *below*). Just to the north is an old Portuguese cannon whose muzzle tapers into a clenched fist, a Javanese fertility symbol; dless women have been known to straddle the cannon for help in conceiving.

❶ **Fish Market.** The Pasar Ikan is as remarkable an introduction to the denizens of Indonesia's seas as a visit to an aquarium—and more chaotic and exciting. It's colorful, noisy, smelly, and slimy, and there are great photo opportunities. Be sure to come early, when it's in full swing. ✉ *Sunda Kelapa Harbor.*

Glodok. Much of Chinatown has been demolished, but there are still sights and smells that evoke the days when Chinese were brought in as laborers and worked like slaves to become merchants. Many now run successful businesses, and this has caused resentment in other ethnic groups. During the riots that rocked the capital in May 1998, ethnic Chinese were targeted by furious mobs who felt that the Chinese received unfair government protection. Though businesses were looted and burned throughout the city, Glodok was, obviously, hit hard. More than 1,000 people died in the rioting (mostly looters who were trapped in torched shopping malls), and many Chinese fled to neighboring countries. Some came back, but many of those who lost homes and/or loved ones vowed never to return. Today, there's little evidence of the riots, but for locals, they're a powerful part of the area's history. Wander around Glodok Plaza (a landmark shopping center and office building), and you can still find small streets crowded with Chinese restaurants and shops that sell herbal medicines. Glodok is also an entertainment district at night, but unless you know your way around, it's better left to the locals.

❺ **Jakarta Fine Art Gallery.** The Belai Seni Rupa Jakarta is in the former Palace of Justice, built between 1866 and 1870, on the east side of Fatahillah Square. The gallery's permanent collection includes paintings by Indonesia's greatest artists; contemporary works, such as wood sculptures; and the Chinese ceramic collection of Adam Malik, a former Indonesian vice-president. A museum in the southeast of the Menteng district, the **Adam Malik Museum** (✉ Jl. Diponegoro 29, ☎ 021/

Emmanuel Church, **11**
Fatahillah Square, **3**
Fish Market, **1**
Istiqlal Mosque, **10**
Jakarta Cultural Center (TIM), **12**
Jakarta Fine Art Gallery, **5**
Maritime Museum, **2**
Museum of Old Batavia, **6**
National Monument (MONAS), **8**
National Museum, **9**
Portuguese Church, **7**
Puppet Museum, **4**
Textile Museum, **13**

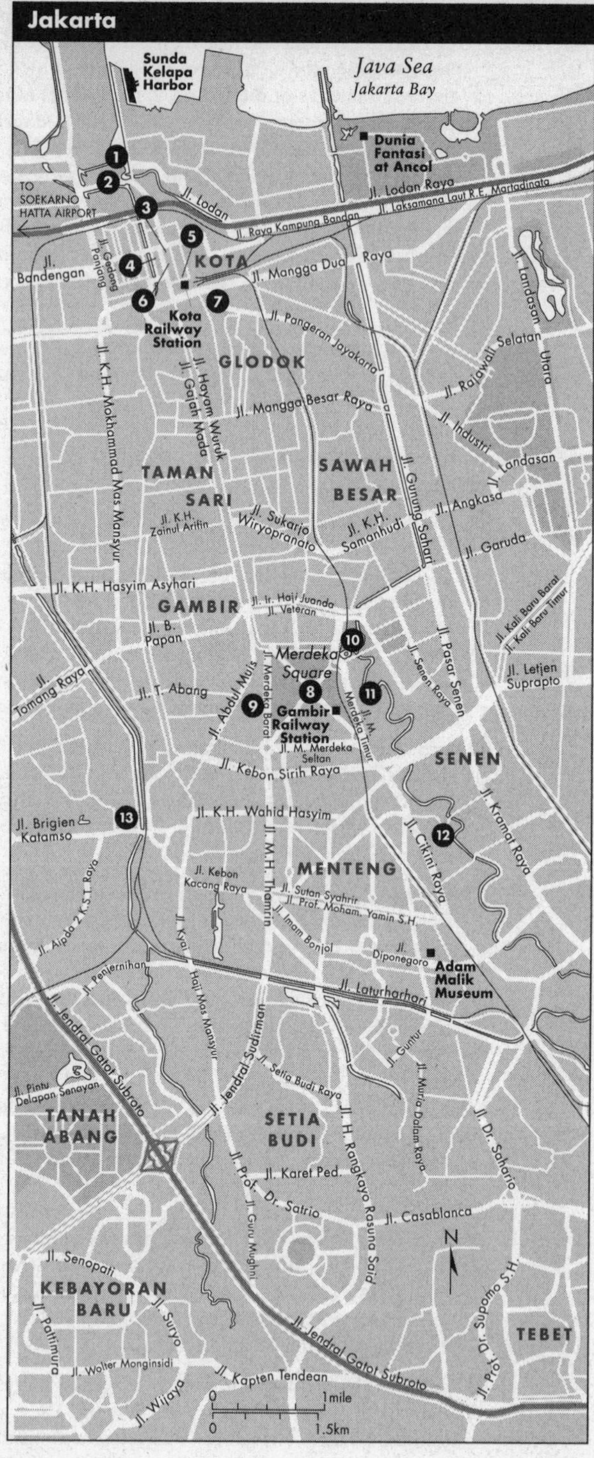

337400 or 021/337388), displays even more of his works. ✉ *Jl. Taman Fatahillah 2,* ☎ *021/676090.* 💳 *Admission.* ⏲ *Tues.–Sun. 9–2.*

NEED A BREAK?

Café Batavia (✉ Jl. Taman Fatahillah 2, ☎ 021/691-5531), on the north side of Fatahillah Square, is a friendly place in which to enjoy Indonesian hors d'oeuvres, an Indonesian or European entrée, or a bit of ice cream. Its collection of nostalgic bric-a-brac, including a sketch of Winston Churchill, makes it quite cheerful. Choose a table by the window and watch the goings-on in the square below.

❷ **Maritime Museum.** Two former Dutch East Indies warehouses have been restored to house the Museum Bahari. One warehouse is devoted to models of Indonesian sailing vessels; the other contains ancient maps and documents that tell the history of the spice trade. Neither exhibit is very thorough. ✉ *Jl. Pasar Ikan 1,* ☎ *021/669-0518.* 💳 *Admission.* ⏲ *Tues.–Sun. 9–2.*

❻ **Museum of Old Batavia.** On the south side of Fatahillah Square is the old Town Hall, built by the Dutch in 1707. Preserved as an historic building, it now houses the Museum Sejarah Jakart, commonly known as the Jakarta Museum. The history of Batavia is chronicled with antique maps, portraits, models of ancient inscribed Hindu stones, antique Dutch furniture, weapons, and coins. Unfortunately, the exhibits have few explanations in English, and the museum is rather gloomy. Beneath the halls are the dungeons where criminals once awaited trial. Prince Diponegoro, the Indonesian patriot who nearly evicted the Dutch from Java in 1830, was imprisoned here on his way to exile in Manado. All you see of the dungeons are the double-barred basement windows along Jalan Pintu Besar. ✉ *Jl. Taman Fatahillah 1,* ☎ *021/679101.* 💳 *Admission.* ⏲ *Tues.–Thurs. 9–2:30, Fri. 9–noon, Sat. 9–1, Sun. 9–3.*

❼ **Portuguese Church.** Opposite the Kota Railway Station, behind the Museum of Old Batavia, is the oldest church in Jakarta. It was built by the Portuguese—among the first Europeans to arrive in Indonesia—in the 17th century. Its exterior is plain, but inside you'll see carved pillars, copper chandeliers, solid ebony pews, and plaques commemorating prominent Dutch administrators. ✉ *Jl. Pangeran Jayakarta.*

★ 👶 ❹ **Puppet Museum.** On the west side of Fatahillah Square, in a former Protestant church, is the Museum Wayang. Here you'll find an extensive collection of traditional Indonesian wayang kulit figures, the intricately cut leather shadow puppets used to perform stories from the Hindu epics the *Ramayana* and the *Mahabarata.* The museum also has wayang *golek* figures (wooden puppets used in performing Arabic folk tales or stories of Prince Panji, a legendary Javanese prince associated with the conversion of Java to Islam), as well as puppets from Thailand, China, Malaysia, India, Cambodia, and elsewhere. An abbreviated wayang kulit is performed on Sunday morning at 10. Also on display are puppets that are employed in social education projects, including those used by the Yogyakarta family-planning program. ✉ *Jl. Pintu Besar Utara 27,* ☎ *021/679560.* 💳 *Admission.* ⏲ *Tues.–Thurs. and weekends 9–2, Fri. 9–1.*

Sunda Kelapa Harbor. At the back of the fish market is the wharf, where Makassar and Bugis *prahus* (sailing ships) are docked at oblique angles to the piers. They look like beached whales, but they still sail the Indonesian waters as they have for centuries, trading between the islands. You can negotiate a small punt (about Rp 2,500–3,000) to take you on a 30-minute tour of the harbor. Government plans to develop a tourist marina here are on hold owing to Indonesia's fiscal crisis, so the evocative setting is safe for a while yet. *Admission.* *Daily 8–6.*

New Jakarta

In many developing countries, the capital becomes a symbol of national pride in shaking off the yoke of economic, and often colonial, servitude. In pre–economic crisis Jakarta, this attitude led to the construction of wide avenues, tall skyscrapers (many of which are bank offices), palatial government buildings, and extravagant monuments. Modern Jakarta has little aesthetic appeal, but it's an interesting example of how an evolving nation attempts to thrust itself into the modern age.

A GOOD TOUR

New Jakarta is almost impossible to cover on foot. The distances between sights are long, the streets aren't pedestrian-friendly, and the equatorial heat will melt you. Taxis are very cheap. Use them to get from one sight to another.

Start your tour in vast Merdeka Square, at the towering **National Monument** ⑧, taking its interior elevator up to the top for a bird's-eye view of the city. Then head for the monument's basement to visit the Museum of National History. Next head west to the **National Museum** ⑨ and its outstanding collection of Indonesian antiquities and ethnic artwork. From the museum, you may want to ride around the square in a taxi. On the northwest corner is the Presidential Palace; on the northeast corner is the **Istiqlal Mosque** ⑩, Indonesia's largest (guided tours are available); and a bit farther down the east side is **Emmanuel Church** ⑪. Keep the taxi and continue south down Jalan Cikini Raya to the **Jakarta Cultural Center** ⑫, known by the acronym TIM, where you're bound to find a cultural performance of some kind in progress. (If you walk, it's about 15 minutes from the south side of the square.) Directly west from TIM and about 10 minutes by taxi is the **Textile Museum** ⑬, with a collection of more than 300 kinds of Indonesian textiles and a small workshop where batik making is demonstrated.

TIMING

It shouldn't take much more than a half a day to cover these sights. Do plan to spend at least a couple of hours in the National Museum. If possible, time your visit to coincide with one of the free tours given in English—Tuesday, Wednesday, and Thursday at 9:30 AM—and you'll appreciate the museum a thousand times more; on Sunday morning there's Javanese or Sundanese gamelan music from 9:30 to 10:30.

SIGHTS TO SEE

11 **Emmanuel Church.** This classical Dutch Protestant church, off Merdeka square in the shadow of the ☞ **National Monument,** was built in 1835. Today its modest simplicity seems wonderfully incongruous in contrast to the grandeur of the surrounding monuments. ✉ *Jl. Merdeka Timur 10.*

10 **Istiqlal Mosque.** On the northwest corner of Merdeka Square is Indonesia's largest mosque. If you haven't come to pray, you probably won't be encouraged to enter on your own. To appreciate the mosque's size and open layout, however, you can arrange to join a guided tour through your hotel or a travel agent. ✉ *Jl. Veteren.*

12 **Jakarta Cultural Center.** There's something happening at the Taman Ismail Marzuki (TIM) from morning to midnight. Most evenings, either the open-air theater or the enclosed auditorium stages some kind of performance, from Balinese dance to imported jazz, from gamelan concerts to poetry readings. Your hotel will have a copy of the monthly program. Two art galleries display paintings, sculpture, and ceramics.

Also within the complex are an art school, an art workshop, a cinema, a planetarium, and outdoor cafés. ⊠ *Jl. Cikini Raya 73,* ☎ *021/ 342605.* 🎟 *Admission.* ⊙ *Daily 8–8. Planetarium shows: Tues.–Sun. at 7:30; Sun. at 10, 11, and 1.*

8 **National Monument.** Merdeka Square is dominated by the towering Monument Nasional (MONAS). Local wags have taken to calling the Russian-built tower commemorating Indonesia's independence "Sukarno's last erection." Some of this bitterness may stem from the fact that the World Bank supplied funds for 77 pounds of pure gold to coat the "flame of freedom" atop the column while many Indonesians starved. Regardless of how you feel about it, the monument serves as a useful landmark. Take its interior elevator up to just below the flame for a panoramic view of the city.

In the basement is the **Museum of National History,** with a gallery of 48 dioramas that illustrate Indonesia's history and struggle for independence. The Hall of Independence contains four national treasures: the flag raised during the independence ceremony in 1945; the original text of the declaration of independence; a gilded map of the Indonesian Republic; and the Indonesian coat of arms, which symbolizes the five principles of the Indonesian Republic (belief in one supreme god; a just and civilized humanity; unity of Indonesia; consensus arising from discussion and self-help; and social justice). ⊠ *Jl. Silang Monas, Merdeka Square,* ☎ *021/681512 museum.* 🎟 *Admission (one price for both monument and museum).* ⊙ *Monument: Sat.–Thurs. 9–4, Fri. 9–11. Museum: Tues.–Thurs. and Sat. 9–2:30, Fri. 9–11:30* AM.

★ 9 **National Museum.** On the west side of Merdeka Square stands the Museum Nasional, recognizable by the bronze elephant in front—a gift from the King of Siam (Thailand) in 1871. The museum has the most complete collection of Indonesian antiquities and ethnic artwork in the country. There are five sections: Hindu and Buddhist stone carvings from the 7th to 15th centuries; an exhibit of prehistoric skulls, weapons, and cooking utensils dating back 4,000 years; Indonesian ethnic crafts; a treasure room with gold trinkets, jeweled weapons, and Buddhist statues; and one of the largest collections of Chinese ceramics outside China. Free tours are given in English on Tuesday, Wednesday, and Thursday at 9:30 AM, and on Sunday morning you can hear gamelan music from 9:30 to 10:30. To the right, as you face the museum, is the **museum shop,** which sells such items as shadow puppets and books on Indonesia. ⊠ *Jl. Merdeka Barat 12,* ☎ *021/381–2346.* 🎟 *Admission.* ⊙ *Tues.–Thurs. and weekends 8:30–1, Fri. 8:30–11.*

13 **Textile Museum.** With its rich collection of Indonesian fabrics and small workshop where batik-making is demonstrated, the Museum Tekstil will give you an idea of what to expect by way of design and quality in the textiles you'll come across as you travel about the country. ⊠ *Jl. K. Sasuit Tubun 4,* ☎ *021/365367.* 🎟 *Admission.* ⊙ *Tues.–Thurs. and Sun. 9–2, Fri. 9–11, Sat. 9–1.*

Jakarta's Green Spaces

Jakarta has made an attempt to attract visitors and to give local residents recreational opportunities. At the same time, the government has wanted to make Jakarta an example of the diversity that is Indonesia. Thus, many of the city's parks are celebrations of the nation's different ethnic and cultural groups.

A GOOD ROUTE

You may not want to visit both of these recreational attractions—choose the one that best satisfies your interests. North of Kota and stretching east along the bay is **Dunia Fantasi at Ancol**; billed as Southeast Asia's largest recreation area, it provides entertainment around the clock. About 12 km (7 mi) southeast of Merdeka Square and 30 minutes by taxi is the **Beautiful Indonesia in Miniature Park.** Its 250 acres hold 27 full-size traditional houses, as well as various museums.

TIMING

You may want to spend the afternoon at Dunia Fantasi at Ancol after touring Old Batavia, since it's north of Kota. However, avoid it on the weekends, when it's thronged with Jakarta families. You'll want to allow a good half a day at Beautiful Indonesia in Miniature Park, perhaps arriving in time for lunch.

SIGHTS TO SEE

Beautiful Indonesia in Miniature Park. The Batak house of North Sumatra, the Redong longhouse of the Kalimantan Dayaks, the cone-shape hut of Irian Jaya, and the Toraja house of South Sulawesi are just a few of the 27 full-size traditional houses—one from each Indonesian province—on display at the Taman Mini Indonesia Indah. There are even miniature Borobudur and Prambanan temples. Other attractions at the 250-acre park include a 30-minute movie, *Beautiful Indonesia,* shown daily from 11 to 5; the Museum Indonesia, with traditional costumes and handicrafts; a stamp museum; the Soldier's Museum, honoring the Indonesian struggle for independence; the Transportation Museum; and Museum Asmat, highlighting the art of the master carvers of the Asmat people of Irian Jaya. The park also has an orchid garden, an aviary, a touring train, cable cars, horse-drawn carts, paddleboats, and places for refreshment. English-speaking guides are available, if you call in advance. The park is about 12 km (7 mi) southeast of Merdeka Square and 30 minutes by taxi. ✉ *12 km (7 mi) south of central Jakarta, off Jagorawi Toll Rd.,* ☎ *021/849525.* *Admission.* ⏲ *Museums, daily 9–3; outdoor attractions, daily 9–4.*

Dunia Fantasi at Ancol. A village unto itself, this 24-hour park has hotels, nightclubs, shops, and amusement centers, including an oceanarium with dolphin and sea lion shows, a golf course, a race-car track, a four-pool complex with a wave pool, and water slides. Africa is represented by a comedy of mechanized monkeys, America by a Wild West town, Europe by a mock Tudor house, and Asia by buildings from Thailand, Japan, India, and Korea. Rides, shooting galleries, and food stalls surround these attractions, all set on 1,360 acres of land reclaimed from the bay in 1962. ✉ *Taman Impian Jaya Ancol,* ☎ *021/681512.* *Admission.* ⏲ *Daily.*

Dining

All the major hotels have Western and Indonesian restaurants, and many of the latter also offer Chinese food. Outside the hotels, dining options range from restaurants with a formal atmosphere and fine cuisine to Western fast-food outlets, including the more upscale ones such as TGI Friday's and Planet Hollywood, to inexpensive street stalls.

Chinese

$$$$ ★ ✕ **Xin Hwa.** The Malay chef at this elegant 100-seat restaurant in the Mandarin Oriental hotel (☞ Lodging, *below*) prepares spicy Szechuan specialties, including sliced, braised chicken with hot-pepper oil and abalone soup with fermented black beans. Try the excellent bird's nest soup and the stir-fried lobster in a hot black-bean sauce. Dinner reservations are highly recommended. ✉ *Jl. M. H. Thamrin,* ☎ *021/391-6438. AE, DC, MC, V. No lunch weekends.*

Dining ●
Asiatique, **21**
Brasserie, **29**
Le Bistro, **9**
Gandy, **15**
Green Pub, **8,23**
Handayani, **6**
Manari, **24**
Mira Sari, **27**
Nadaman, **19**
Natrabu, **7**
Oasis, **10**
Omar Khayam, **3**
Paregu, **25**
Pondok Laguna, **2**
Sari Kuring/Sari Nusantara, **5**
Tamnak Thai, **14**
Xin Hwa, **17**

Lodging ○
Grand Hyatt, **12**
Hotel Borobudur InterContinental, **4**
Hotel Wisata International, **16**
Interhouse, **26**
Jayakarta Tower, **1**
Kebayoran Inn, **28**
Mandarin Oriental, **18**
Marcopolo, **13**
President Hotel, **11**
Regent, **22**
Shangri-La, **20**

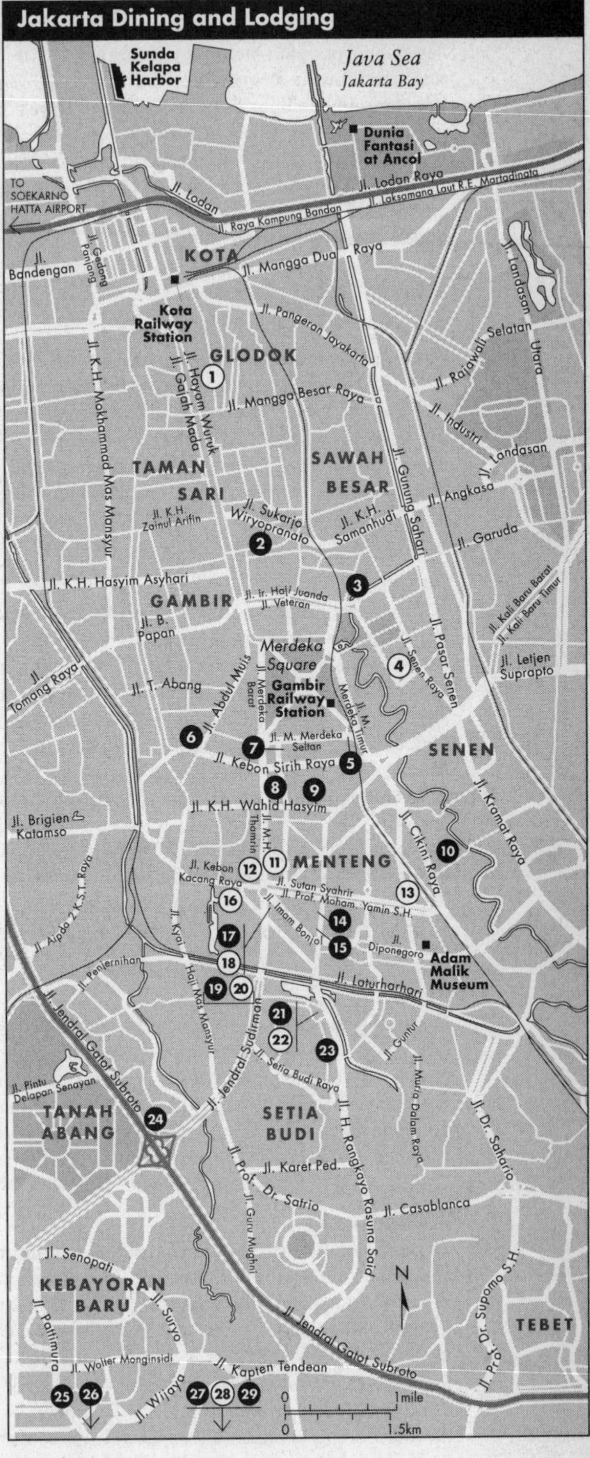

Contemporary

$$$ ✕ **Asiatique.** The concept of marrying Asian spices with Western culinary concepts isn't new in California, but it is in Jakarta. At this restaurant in the Regent hotel (☞ Lodging, *below*), chefs Kenji Salz (formerly of the Four Seasons Bali) and Derek Watanabe (a graduate of New York's Culinary Institute of America) are the innovators. They blend elements from different Asian cuisines to produce tempting combinations. You can order most dishes as an appetizer or a main course; a broad selection of appetizers is a good way to satisfy your curiosity. Especially tasty are the lemongrass-spiked tandoori salmon and the fried chili and lobster with peppers and lotus root. ✉ *Jl. H. R. Rasuna Said,* ☎ *021/252–3456. AE, DC, MC, V. No lunch.*

Eclectic

$$$ ✕ **Oasis.** Fine international cuisine, as well as a traditional rijsttafel, ensure that, even after decades, the Oasis remains popular with Western visitors. A specialty is medallions of veal Oscar—served in a cream sauce with mushrooms, crabmeat, and asparagus. The atmosphere lives up to the cuisine in this lovely old house decorated with tribal art and textiles. A combo alternates with Batak singers to provide music nightly. ✉ *Jl. Raden Saleh 47,* ☎ *021/326397. Reservations essential. AE, DC, V. Closed Sun.*

French

$$$ ✕ **Brasserie.** French-born Gil D'Harcour opened this cozy restaurant in 1997 in Kemang, a trendy neighborhood in the south of the city where many expats live. The atmosphere in the dining room and on the patio is casual, and the food—traditional French dishes made with fresh, local ingredients—is good. The wine list has an extensive selection of French varieties. ✉ *Plaza Bisnis, Jl. Kemang Raya 2,* ☎ *021/718–3422. AE, MC, V.*

$$$ ✕ **Le Bistro.** Candlelit and intimate, with checked tablecloths and copper pots, the ambience here puts you in the mood for the classic Provençal menu—simple food, prepared with herbs, from the south of France. Try the roast chicken with rosemary and thyme. The circular piano bar at the back of the dining room is the perfect spot for an after-dinner liqueur. ✉ *Jl. K. H. Wahid Hasyim 75,* ☎ *021/364272. AE, DC, V.*

Indian

$ ✕ **Omar Khayyam.** In addition to an Indian buffet lunch, this restaurant offers such specialties as curries and tandoori dishes. The decor pays homage to the eponymous Persian poet: some of his poetry is inscribed on the walls. Try the chicken *tikka makhanwalla*—boneless tandoori chicken with tomato, butter, and cream sauce—or the marinated fish that's wrapped in a banana leaf and deep-fried. ✉ *Jl. Antara 5–7,* ☎ *021/356719. Reservations not accepted. No credit cards.*

Indonesian

$$ ✕ **Handayani.** This true neighborhood restaurant has friendly service and some English-speaking staffers. Decor isn't its strong point—lines of tables and chairs fill a bare room—but Handayani draws locals for its food rather than its sparse interior. You may have to be a bit bold to sample some of the dishes, such as chicken bowels steamed in banana leaves, beef intestine satay, and goldfish fried or grilled. If you're timid try the lobster-size king prawns cooked in a mild chili sauce or the nasi goreng Handayani, a special version of the Indonesian staple. ✉ *Jl. Abdul Muis 35E,* ☎ *021/373614. DC, V.*

$$ ✕ **Manari.** Locals often bring their foreign guests here. The menu is primarily Indonesian, though there are dishes from China (Canton) and Thailand, too. The food is really secondary, however, to the varied dinnertime cultural performances—dances and songs that demonstrate Indonesia's multiethnic heritage. ✉ *Jl. Jendral Gatot Subroto 14,* ☎ *021/516102. Reservations essential. AE, MC, V.*

$$ ✕ **Mira Sari.** Comfortable rattan chairs with soft pillows, fresh flowers, and friendly service make this a congenial spot. Regional Indonesian specialties are served in the air-conditioned dining room, in the garden, or on the terrace. The menu includes a very good version of Indonesian chicken soup; excellent spiced, grilled fish; prawns grilled with spices and chilies; and roast or fried spiced chicken. ✉ *Jl. Kemang Utara 1, 33 Patiunus 15,* ☎ *021/799–7997. Reservations essential. No credit cards.*

$$ ✕ **Natrabu.** Decor at this popular Padang (the spicy cuisine of the Minangkabau people in the Padang area of West Sumatra) restaurant is minimal: bare tabletops and side booths, red Sumatran banners hanging from the ceiling, and a model of a Minangkabau house set in a corner. Padang waiters wearing head scarves from the region deliver bowls of food from the moment you sit down. You can order, or you can select from the dishes they bring—you pay for the ones you try. ✉ *Jl. H. A. Salim (often called Jl. Sabang) 29A,* ☎ *021/335668. Reservations not accepted. MC, V.*

$$ ★ ✕ **Pondok Laguna.** Here, the large dining room, divided by water pools and falls, is always crowded with families and young couples. The noise level is fairly high and the service casual. Some of the staff speaks English; all are anxious to help foreign guests. Fish is the specialty—either fried or grilled and accompanied by different sauces ranging from hot to mild. Whatever you choose, expect it to be fresh and cooked to perfection. ✉ *Jl. Batu Tulis Raya 45,* ☎ *021/359994. Reservations not accepted. AE, DC, MC, V.*

$$ ★ ✕ **Sari Kuring.** This restaurant near Merdeka Square serves very good Indonesian seafood, especially the grilled prawns and the Thai fish à la Sari Kuring, marinated in spices then quickly fried. The restaurant is large, but connected on many levels by stone steps, so there's some feeling of intimacy. If you can't get a table here, try next door at Sari **Nusantara,** where the fare is similar except for a slight Chinese influence in the cooking and fewer spices in the sauces. ✉ *Jl. Silang Monas Timur 88,* ☎ *021/352972. AE, V.*

Japanese

$$$ ✕ **Nadaman.** This restaurant in the Shangri-La hotel (☞ Lodging, *below*) offers a varied selection of traditional and newer Japanese dishes. The 56-seat main dining room is decorated with rice-paper lanterns and black lacquer tables; there are also private rooms, some with tatami mats and one with tables and a sushi bar. ✉ *Jl. Jendral Sudirman Kav 1,* ☎ *021/570–7440. AE, DC, MC, V.*

Mexican

$$ ✕ **Green Pub.** The two branches of the Green Pub are recommended not only for their Mexican food but for their live country-and-western music (6:30–9) and jazz (9:30–1). The decor is somewhere between a Western saloon and a Mexican ranch, with tapestries adorning the walls. The burritos and enchiladas are quite authentic, and the menu also includes such Tex-Mex dishes as barbecued spareribs. ✉ *Jakarta Theater Building, Jl. M. H. Thamrin 9,* ☎ *021/359332. Reservations not accepted. AE, V.* ✉ *Jl. H. R. Rasuna Said, Setia Budi Building 1,* ☎ *021/517983. Reservations not accepted. AE, V.*

Steak House

$$ ✕ **Gandy.** There are several Gandys in Jakarta, but this one is the most interesting. Stepping into this popular place is like stepping back into the 1960s: the staff wears uniforms that seem outdated by about 30

years but fit in well with the wooden decor and steak-house setting. Some of the beef and imported lamb dishes—the specialities here—arrive on a hot plate and keep cooking at your table. Things become lively after 7 PM or 8 PM, when a jazz band with a singer starts to perform. ✉ *Jl. Hos. Cokroaminoto 90,* ☎ *021/629–0539. AE, DC, MC, V.*

Thai

$$ ✕ **Tamnak Thai.** The friendly staff here serves good, standard Thai food in the comfortable, 30-odd-table dining room or the separate VIP room. The menu includes pictures—for the uninitiated—and the chef will prepare dishes for you as if you were in Thailand or tone down the spices if you like. Seafood dishes are standouts. ✉ *Jl. Hos. Cokroaminoto 78,* ☎ *021/315–0833. MC, V.*

Vietnamese

$$ ✕ **Paregu.** This place serves the best Vietnamese food in town. The decor is simple, with Asian embellishments, and the service is top-notch. Try the Vietnamese version of spring rolls; the fried rice with scrambled eggs, chicken, shrimp, and a blend of herbs and spices; or the herbed seafood. ✉ *Jl. Sudan Cholagogue 64,* ☎ *021/774892. No credit cards.*

Lodging

Jakarta has many world-class hotels with all the modern amenities and countless budget establishments with few frills. Most accommodations are just south of Merdeka Square.

$$$$ **Grand Hyatt.** Glitter and shining-marble modernity characterize this 1992 hotel. You enter the four-story atrium lobby and climb a palatial staircase (or take the escalator) to the reception area. One more short flight up brings you to the expansive Fountain Lounge, where you can watch the stalled traffic on Jalan M. H. Thamrin. On the fifth floor is the pool garden, an extensive area of greenery with a seafood terrace restaurant. Rooms are spacious, and each has two bay windows; bathrooms have separate shower stalls and toilets. Furnishings are in the ubiquitous pastels, but pleasant nonetheless. Beneath the Hyatt is the Plaza Indonesia (☞ Shopping, *below*), with restaurants, nightclubs, and more than 250 shops. In a city that sprawls, this proximity to a "social center" is an advantage. ✉ *Jl. M. H. Thamrin (Box 4546), 10045,* ☎ *021/390–1234; 800/233–1234 in the U.S.;* FAX *021/310–7300. 413 rooms, 47 suites. 6 restaurants, bar, pool, massage, 6 tennis courts, health club, jogging, squash, business services. AE, DC, MC, V.*

$$$$ **Hotel Borobudur Inter-Continental.** Billed as "your country club in Jakarta," this large, modern complex sits on 23 acres of landscaped gardens and has excellent facilities. Floor-to-ceiling windows at the back of the Pendopo Lounge look out onto the greenery, making it a delightful place for afternoon tea, cocktails, or snacks. Most of the compact guest rooms have a modern Javanese design; the Garden Wing has suites with kitchens. Request a room that overlooks the gardens and the pool or risk staying in one that faces the parking lot. ✉ *Jl. Lapangan Banteng Selatan (Box 329), 10710,* ☎ *021/380–5555; 800/327–0200 in the U.S.;* FAX *021/380–9595. 712 rooms, 140 suites. 5 restaurants, 2 bars, room service, pool, miniature golf, 8 tennis courts, badminton, health club, jogging, racquetball, squash, dance club, playground, business services, meeting rooms. AE, DC, MC, V.*

$$$$ ★ **Mandarin Oriental.** Jakarta's most sophisticated hotel was completely renovated in mid-1997. The elegant circular lobby has three tall, beautifully carved Batak roofs, each housing a Sumatran statue. An open mezzanine above the lobby provides comfortable seating for tea or cocktails and some fine shops, including a gallery for Ida Bagus Tilem, Bali's

master wood-carver. Guest rooms are spacious and have top-quality furnishings: thick russet carpeting, floral bedspreads, off-white draperies on picture windows, and dark wood furniture. Complimentary afternoon tea and hors d'oeuvres are delivered to your room. Most rooms are "executive," with butler service; for a nominal extra fee you can have complimentary breakfast and cocktails as well as use of the executive lounge and concierge services. The hotel's location is central, and with the Plaza Indonesia shopping complex (☞ Shopping, *below*) and the Grand Hyatt (☞ *above*) across the square, there are shops, restaurants, and bars within a two-minute walk. On-site restaurants include the Xin Hwa (☞ Dining, *above*). ✉ *Jl. M. H. Thamrin (Box 3392), 10310,* ☎ *021/314–1307; 800/526–6566 in the U.S.;* FAX *021/314–8679. 438 rooms. 4 restaurants, bar, pool, sauna, health club, business services, meeting rooms. AE, DC, MC, V.*

$$$$ ★ **Regent.** The architects made the most of space and natural light at this property, which sits on 6 acres in the Golden Triangle, the city's booming business district. In the lobby, 10 shades of granite and marble are set off by honey-color teak paneling and Indonesian art. Guest rooms are large—a minimum of 500 square ft—and double layers of masonry between them keep things soundproof. Double-glazed, sliding glass doors lead out onto small balconies; framed Indonesian tapestries adorn the walls; and marble baths have deep tubs and separate shower stalls. Phones have two lines, modems, and voice mail. The Regent Club, on the 17th floor, has a commodious lounge where complimentary breakfast and evening cocktails are served amid a backdrop of great city views. Service throughout the hotel is friendly and enthusiastic. ✉ *Jl. H. R. Rasuna Said, 12920,* ☎ *021/252–3456; 800/545–4000 in the U.S.;* FAX *021/252–4480. 378 rooms. 3 restaurants, bar, pool, sauna, 2 tennis courts, health club, business services, meeting rooms. AE, DC, MC, V.*

$$$$ **Shangri-La.** At this opulent hotel, chandeliers adorn the huge lobby, where a string quartet plays classical music during much of the day. Rooms are spacious and comfortable; baths have tubs as well as separate shower stalls. A stay here includes free use of the well-equipped Horizon Health Club, which is like a resort in and of itself and has one of the city's best pools. The hotel's location in the Golden Triangle area makes it a convenient place for business travelers. ✉ *Jl. Jendral Sudirman Kav 1, 10220,* ☎ *021/570–7440; 800/942–5050 in the U.S.;* FAX *021/570–3530. 628 rooms, 40 suites. 6 restaurants, 2 bars, pool, massage, putting green, 3 tennis courts, health club, jogging, business services, meeting rooms. AE, DC, MC, V.*

$$$ **Hotel Wisata International.** Ranked as a three-star hotel by the government, the ungainly Wisata is off Jakarta's main thoroughfare. Corridors are long and narrow, guest rooms compact but clean. Each has a king-size bed; a TV and a safe take up most of the remaining space. Rooms on the executive floor are only marginally larger. Still, the price, the convenient coffee shop off the lobby, and the central location make the Wisata a reasonable choice. ✉ *Jl. M. H. Thamrin, 10230,* ☎ *021/230–0406,* FAX *021/324597. 165 rooms. Bar, coffee shop, meeting rooms. AE, DC, MC, V.*

$$$ **President Hotel.** Like many hotels in the Japanese Nikko Hotel group, the President has a spare, utilitarian atmosphere but is equipped with all the modern amenities. Guest rooms are simple, with blue-and-navy striped fabrics, plain wood furniture, and small bathrooms. The on-site Ginza Benkay restaurant serves Japanese food, the Kahyangan serves Japanese and Indonesian, and the Golden Pavilion serves Chinese. ✉ *Jl. M. H. Thamrin 59, Jakarta 10350,* ☎ *021/230–1122,* FAX *021/314–3631. 354 rooms. 3 restaurants, bar, coffee shop, meeting rooms. AE, DC, MC, V.*

$$ ★ **Jayakarta Tower.** This moderately priced hotel is within walking distance of Old Batavia. The marble lobby is accented with hand-blown-glass chandeliers and carved-wood panels. Each spacious room has a double or two twin beds, with Javanese-pattern spreads, plus a table and two chairs and a vanity/desk. Executive rooms have minibars. For on-site meals your choices are the Dragon (a Chinese restaurant), as well as a coffee shop that serves Western and Indonesian specialties; ask to see the Thai menu at both. The hotel is affiliated with KLM's Golden Tulip properties, so you can make reservations through the airline. ✉ *Jl. Hayam Wuruk 126 (Box 803), 11001,* ☎ *021/629–4408,* FAX *021/626–5000. 435 rooms. 2 restaurants, coffee shop, room service, pool, health club, meeting rooms. AE, DC, MC, V.*

$ **Interhouse.** This hotel is in the Kebayoran expatriate neighborhood and shopping district. Rooms are comfortable, though not large, and have air-conditioning; pleasant, homey furnishings; and pastel color schemes. ✉ *Jl. Melawai Raya 18–20 (Box 128/KBYB), 10305,* ☎ *021/270–0408,* FAX *021/720–6988. 130 rooms. Restaurant. AE, V.*

$ **Kebayoran Inn.** Just south of the center of Jakarta is this quiet, residential-type lodging. The clean, air-conditioned rooms are simply decorated, with an Indonesian batik or ikat here and there. ✉ *Jl. Senayan 87, Jakarta 12180,* ☎ *021/716208,* FAX *021/560–3672. 61 rooms. Restaurant. AE, V.*

$ ★ **Marcopolo.** The staff at this basic, economical hotel is helpful, and although the carpeted rooms are plain, they're clean, adequate, and air-conditioned. The restaurant serves good Chinese and European food. ✉ *Jl. T. Cik Ditiro 19, 10350,* ☎ *021/325409,* FAX *021/310–7138. 181 rooms. Restaurant, pool, nightclub. AE, DC, MC, V.*

Nightlife and the Arts

Nightlife

Owing to the economic crisis, Jakarta's night scene is surely in for some volatile times; nightspots will, no doubt, quickly come and go. When you arrive, you'll have to check out what's happening. Hotel staffers are terrific resources, and concierges can make reservations for you if necessary. Another good resource is *Jakarta Week,* which lists upcoming events and is found at most hotels. The places detailed below seemed, at press time, the ones most likely to survive the test of both time and economics.

Green Pub. After dinner at this pub-restaurant consider hanging out with the expats and listening to music performed by local bands. ✉ *Jakarta Theater Building, Jl. M. H. Thamrin 9,* ☎ *021/359332.*

Hard Rock Cafe. You'll find the same American fare and rock-and-roll paraphernalia here as at its brethren in cities around the world. The live music starts at about 9 PM. The stage has a huge, stained-glass-window backdrop that depicts Elvis Presley. ✉ *Sarinah Building, 2nd floor, Jl. M. H. Thamrin 11,* ☎ *021/390–3565.* ⏲ *Daily 11 AM–1 AM.*

Harry's Captain's Bar. This comfortable spot in the Mandarin Oriental hotel (☞ Lodging, *above*) is good for a relaxed evening of music by a small international or local group. ✉ *Jl. M. H. Thamrin,* ☎ *021/321307.* ⏲ *Nightly 8 PM–1 AM.*

Jaya Pub. This long-established piano bar is across from the Sarinah department store. It's popular with older expats and Indonesians alike, in part because the owners are two former Indonesian movie stars, Rimi Melati and Frans Tumbuan. ✉ *Jl. M. H. Thamrin 12,* ☎ *021/327508.* ⏲ *Daily noon–2 AM.*

O'Reiley's Pub and Bar. Built to resemble an Irish pub, this spot in the Grand Hyatt hotel (☞ Lodging, *above*) offers beer on tap. Stop by for a few drinks and some conversation early in the evening or a few pints and some live music later at night. ✉ *Jl. M. H. Thamrin,* ☎ *021/390-1234.* ⏲ *Daily 11 AM–1 AM.*

Planet Hollywood. You can't, it seems, have the Fashion and Hard Rock cafes without also having a Planet Hollywood. You can dine amid the movie memorabilia or just sip drinks and chat about your favorite films. There's live entertainment on Thursday, Friday, and Saturday after 10 PM. As it's in the east section of sprawling Jakarta, it's best to take a taxi. ✉ *Jl. Gatot Subroto Kav 16,* ☎ *021/526-6727.*

Tanamur. Here's a place that just about every hotel staff member will suggest when asked for tips on nightspots. (Many staffers smile about Tanamur, and some say they don't go because their boyfriend or girlfriend would frown on it—though most have been at least once.) This Jakarta institution has good jazz and soft rock and is usually the most crowded disco in town. What goes on as couples huddle against the dimly lit walls is better left unsaid; a bevy of hostesses is ready to dance and drink with guests who don't have a date. ✉ *Jl. Tanah Abang Timur 14,* ☎ *021/353947.* ⏲ *Nightly 9 PM–2 AM.*

The Arts

For information on Jakarta's art events, check the daily *Indonesian Observer* newspaper or the monthly *What's On* magazine (available in many hotels) or contact the City Visitor Information Center (☞ Visitor Information *in* Jakarta Essentials, *below*).

DANCE AND THEATER

Beautiful Indonesia in Miniature Park. This park offers various regional dances on Sunday and holidays from 10 to 2 (☞ Jakarta's Green Spaces *in* Exploring Jakarta, *above*). ✉ *Off Jagorawi Toll Rd.,* ☎ *021/849525.*

Bharata Theater. Every night but Monday and Thursday, from 8:15 to midnight, this theater stages performances of traditional wayang *orang* (dance-dramas), depicting stories from the *Ramayana* or the *Mahabharata.* Sometimes the folk play *Ketoprak,* based on Javanese history, is also performed. ✉ *Jl. Kalilio, no phone.*

Jakarta Hilton Cultural Program. Each week, the Hilton offers regional dance programs. Every afternoon from 4 to 6, the famous and very old Cakra Dalem Raya gamelan orchestral set is played. ✉ *Indonesia Bazaar, Jakarta Hilton, Jl. Jendral Sudirman and Jl. Jendral Gatot Subroto,* ☎ *021/583051.*

Taman Ismail Marzuki. This arts center hosts plays, music and dance performances, art shows, and films. Monthly schedules of events are distributed to hotels. ✉ *Jl. Cikini Raya 73,* ☎ *021/342605.*

PUPPET SHOWS

National Museum. Here there are biweekly performances using leather shadow puppets to depict stories from the *Ramayana* or the *Mahabharata,* or wood puppets to depict Islamic legends. ✉ *Jl. Merdeka Barat 12,* ☎ *021/360976.*

Puppet Museum. This museum frequently offers performances; check with the staff for dates and times. ✉ *Jl. Pintu Besar Utara 27,* ☎ *021/679560.*

Outdoor Activities and Sports

Diving

Dive Indonesia (✉ Hotel Borobudur Inter-Continental, Jl. Lapangan Banteng Selatan, ☎ 021/370108) specializes in underwater photography and arranges trips to Flores and Sulawesi. **Jakarta Dive School and Pro Shop** (✉ Indonesia Bazaar, Shop 32, Jakarta Hilton, Jl. Jendral Sudiman and Jl. Jendral Gatot Subroto, ☎ 021/583051 ext. 9008) offers open-water lessons and equipment rental.

Golf

At last count greater Jakarta had 20 golf courses. The Indonesia Golf Course Association, together with the Indonesia Tourism Promotion Board, publishes *The Official Golf Map of Indonesia,* available free at travel agencies and tourist offices. There are two well-maintained, 18-hole courses open to the public, though both are extremely crowded on weekends. Greens fees are generally Rp 150,000 on weekdays and Rp 250,000 on weekends; caddy fees run Rp 25,000 (tips are appreciated). The **Ancol Golf Course** (✉ Dunia Fantasi at Ancol, Taman Impian Jaya Ancol, ☎ 021/681511) has pleasant sea views. **Kebayoran Golf Club** (✉ Jl. Asia-Afrika, Pintu 9, ☎ 021/654–1156) is popular with expats.

Health and Fitness Centers

The **Clark Hatch Physical Fitness Center** has two facilities (✉ Hotel Borobudur Inter-Continental, Jl. Lapangan Banteng Selatan, ☎ 021/370108; ✉ Jakarta Hilton, Jl. Jendral Sudirman and Jl. Jendral Gatot Subroto, ☎ 021/583051) with up-to-date equipment, as well as massage, heat treatments, a sauna, and a whirlpool.

Other gyms are: **Club Olympus Fitness Center** (✉ Fifth floor, Grand Hyatt, Jl. M. H. Thamrin, ☎ 021/390–1234), **Executive Fitness Center** (✉ Ground floor, South Tower, Kuningan Plaza, Jl. H. R. Rasuna Said, ☎ 021/578–1706), **Medical Scheme** (✉ Setia Budi Bldg. L, Jl. H. R. Rasuna Said, Kuningan, ☎ 021/515367), and **Pondok Indah Health and Fitness Center** (✉ Jl. Metro Pondok Indah, ☎ 021/764906).

Running

The **Hash House Harriers/Harriettes,** a world-wide club known for mixing outrageous antics into its runs, has a chapter in Jakarta (✉ HHH Box 46/KBY, Jakarta, ☎ 021/799–4758). Men run Monday at 5 PM, women Wednesday at 5 PM, and there's socializing in between. Write or call for meeting places and routes.

Tennis and Squash

Many of Jakarta's hotels have tennis and/or squash courts where nonguests can play. Call first to reserve a court. The **Grand Hyatt** (✉ Jl. M. H. Thamrin, ☎ 021/390–1234), the **Hotel Borobudur Inter-Continental** (✉ Jl. Lapangan Banteng Selatan, ☎ 021/370108), and the **Jakarta Hilton** (✉ Jl. Jendral Sudirman and Jl. Jendral Gatot Subroto, ☎ 021/583051) have both tennis and squash facilities.

Shopping

Indonesia became a shoppers' paradise when the rupiah's value went from about 2,500 to the U.S. dollar in mid-1997 to 17,000 in the first half of 1998. (At press time, it was hard to tell where the rupiah's value would go and what inflation would do to prices.) All this has been bad news for Indonesians; indeed, when import prices increased, it put a lot of items out of reach for many citizens. But for visitors with dollars, such locally produced items as batik fabric, wood carvings, and clothing were, at press time, nearly criminally cheap.

Department Stores

Pasaraya (✉ Jl. Iskandarsyah 1½, in Blok M, ☎ 021/739–0170). Jakarta's largest department store tempts you to visit its multistory complex to see Indonesia's latest in women's fashions and handicrafts by paying your taxi fare if you're staying at a five-star hotel. Check with your hotel's concierge for a coupon.

Plaza Indonesia (✉ Jl. M. H. Thamrin, ☎ 021/310–7272). Under the Grand Hyatt and across the square from the Mandarin Oriental, this is a central and convenient shopping center. Among its 250 stores are upscale boutiques, art and antiques galleries, bookshops, travel agents, Sogo's food store, and restaurants.

Plaza Senayan (✉ Jl. Asia-Africa 8, ☎ 021/572–5555). One of the city's newest shopping complexes has upscale boutiques with designer-label fashions.

Sarinah Mataram (✉ Jl. M. H. Thamrin 11, Menteng, ☎ 021/327425). This four-story department store not only sells a variety of goods from its convenient location, but is also connected to the Hard Rock Cafe—a great place to rest your feet after all that shopping.

Markets

Jalan Surabaya Antiques Stalls (✉ Pasar Barang Antik Jalan Surabaya, in Menteng residential area). The city's daily (9–6) "flea market," sells mundane goods at either end, but in the middle you might find delftware, Chinese porcelain, old coins, old and not-so-old bronzes, and more. You *must* bargain.

Pasar Melawai (✉ Jl. Melawai, in Blok M). This series of buildings and stalls offers everything from clothing to toys, cosmetics, and fresh foods. English is spoken; hours are daily 9–6.

Specialty Stores

ANTIQUES

For serious antiques shopping, try the stores along Jalan Paletehan I (Kebayoran Baru); Jalan Maja Pahit and Jalan Gajah Mada (Gambir/Kota); Jalan Kebon Sirih Timur and Jalan H. A. Salim (Mentang); and Jalan Ciputat Raya (Old Bogor Road).

Cony Art Antiques (✉ Jl. Malawai Raya 180E, ☎ 021/716554). This shop in the Kebayoran district is worth a visit for antique Chinese porcelain.

Madjapahit Art and Curio (✉ Jl. Melawai III/4, ☎ 021/715878). This reputable store is behind the Sarinah Jaya, near Blok M.

Nasrun (✉ Jl. Kebon Sirih Rimur Dalam) has a large collection of Chinese porcelain, antique batik, and Javanese and Sumatran wood carvings.

NV Garuda Arts, Antiques (✉ Jl. Maja Pahit 12, Kota, ☎ 021/342712). NV Garuda is another reliable shop.

HANDICRAFTS

Sarinah Mataram (✉ Jl. M. H. Thamrin 11, Menteng, ☎ 021/327425). The third floor of this department store is devoted entirely to handicrafts, which you can also find in abundance at its larger sister store, Pasaraya (☞ *above*).

TEXTILES

Batik Berdikari (✉ Jl. Masjid in Palmerah, southwest of Merdeka Sq., ☎ 021/548–2814). This shop (and factory) sells various types of Indonesian batik and has demonstrations of the ways in which batik is made (either hand-drawn or printed).

Batik Danar Hadi (✉ Jl. Raden Saleh 1A, ☎ 021/342748). The batik selection here is quite large.

Batik Mira (✉ Jl. Mar. Raya 22, ☎ 021/761138). This is the place for expensive but excellent-quality batik. Its tailors will do custom work, and you can also ask to see the factory at the rear of the store.

Batik Semar (✉ Jl. Tornang Raya 54, ☎ 021/567–3514). Here you'll find top-quality batik with many unusual designs.

Bin House (✉ Jl. Panarukan 33, ☎ 021/335941). This shop carries Indonesian handwoven silks and cottons, including ikat, as well as antique textiles and objects d'art.

Plaza Indonesia (✉ Jl. M. H. Thamrin, ☎ 021/310–7272). This is a good place for chic, fashionable batiks, especially on the first floor.

PT Ramacraft (✉ Jl. Panarukan 25, ☎ 021/333122). PT Rarnacraft is the name of both the label and company run by Iwan Tirta, a famous designer of batik fabrics and clothing for men and women.

Jakarta Essentials

Arriving and Departing

BY AIRPLANE

Jakarta's airport, **Soekarno Hatta** (☎ 021/550–5307), is a modern showpiece, with glass-walled walkways and landscaped gardens. Although most of it isn't air-conditioned, it's breezy and clean. There's a small duty-free shopping area. Terminal One handles international flights, and Terminal Two serves all Garuda Indonesia Airways flights (both international and domestic) and all other domestic airlines. (For information on carriers and flights, ☞ Air Travel *in* Gold Guide.) Between the two terminals, a **Visitor Information Center** (☎ 021/550–7088) is usually open Monday through Saturday 8 AM–10 PM, though sometimes it's closed seemingly because the staff feels like it. In both terminals there are **Indotel desks** (☎ 021/550–7179) where you can make hotel reservations, often at discounted rates.

From the Airport to Downtown: The airport is 35 km (20 mi) northwest of Jakarta. A toll expressway takes you three-quarters of the way to the city quickly, but the rest is slow going. To be safe, allow a good hour for the trip on weekdays.

Taxis *from* the airport add a surcharge of Rp 2,300 and the road toll (Rp 4,000) to the fare on the meter. The surcharge doesn't apply going *to* the airport. Blue Bird Taxi (☞ By Taxi under Getting Around, *below*) offers a 25% discount on the toll charge either way. The average fare to a downtown hotel is Rp 20,000. However, if it's raining and there are likely to be traffic jams, you'll need to negotiate a fare—Rp 40,000 should do it. On request, some hotels, such as the Mandarin Oriental, will arrange to have a chauffeur-driven car waiting for you. The cost is Rp 55,000.

Air-conditioned buses, with DAMRI in big letters on the side, operate every 20 minutes between the airport and six points in the city, including the Gambir Railway Station, Rawamangun Bus Terminal, Blok M, and Pasar Minggu Bus Terminal. The cost is Rp 3,000.

BY BUS

Bus terminals are off Merdeka Square and Blok M; buy tickets at the terminals or at travel agencies. **Pulo Gadang** (✉ Jl. Perintis Kemerdekaan, ☎ 021/489–3742) serves Semarang, Yogyakarta, Solo, Surabaya, Malang, and Denpensar. Use **Cililitan** (✉ Jl. Raya Bogor, ☎ 021/809–3554) for Bogor, Sukabumi, Bandung, and Banjar. **Kalideres** (✉ Jl. Daan Mogot) is the depot for Merak, Labuhan, and major cities in Sumatra (which include a ferry ride as part of a bus journey).

BY TRAIN

Use the **Tanah Abang Railway Station** (✉ Jl. KH Wahid Hasyim, southwest of Merdeka Sq., ☎ 021/340048) for trains to Sumatra. (You get off the train for the ferry across the Sunda Straight to Sumatra, and then catch another train in Bandarlampang.) Trains for destinations other than Sumatra—to Bogor and Bandung or to the east Java cities of Semarang, Yogyakarta, Solo, Surabaya, Madiun, and Malang—start from one of two other stations: the **Kota Railway Station** (✉ Jl. Stasiun Kota, south of Fatahillah Sq., ☎ 021/678515 or 021/679194) or the **Gambir Railway Station** (✉ Jl. Merdeka Timur, east side of Merdeka Sq., ☎ 021/342777 or 021/348612). You can buy tickets from travel agencies (☞ Contacts and Resources, *below*) or at the station at least an hour before departure.

Getting Around

BY BUS

Non-air-conditioned public buses charge a flat Rp 350; the (green) air-conditioned buses charge Rp 600. All are packed during rush hours, and pickpockets abound. The routes can be labyrinthine, but you can always give one a try and get off when the bus veers from your desired direction. For information, contact these companies: **Hiba Utama** (☎ 021/413626 or 021/410381), **P. P. D.** (☎ 021/881131 or 021/411357), or **Mayasari Bhakti** (☎ 021/809–0378 or 021/489–2785).

BY CAR

Though rental cars are available, they're not advised. Traffic is horrendous, and parking is very difficult. If you do decide to rent a car, be aware that traffic police supplement their income by stopping you, even for infractions that you never knew you made. The police will suggest Rp 70,000 to forget the matter; you're expected to negotiate, and Rp 30,000 should make you both happy.

You can rent cars from: **Avis** (✉ Jl. Doponegoro 25, ☎ 021/331974), **Hertz** (✉ Jl. Tenku, C. K. Ditoro 11E, ☎ 021/332610), or **National** (✉ Hotel Kartika Plaza, Jl. M. H. Thamrin 10, ☎ 021/333423).

You can hire air-conditioned, chauffeur-driven cars for a minimum of two hours, at hourly rates of Rp 11,375 for a small Corona or Rp 21,000 for a Mercedes. Daily charters cost Rp 105,000 and Rp 210,000, respectively. Try Blue Bird Taxi (☞ *below*) or Hertz (☞ *above*).

BY MOTOR BECAK

These dirty, little, orange put-puts are, believe it or not, very good for short, one-way trips. Flag them down on the street. Most rides are Rp 2,000 to 5,000. You sit in the back, though it's a bit of a squeeze for anyone bigger than average.

BY TAXI

A cheap and efficient way of getting around, Jakarta's metered taxis charge Rp 900 for the first kilometer (½ mi) and Rp 450 for each subsequent 100 meters. You can flag taxis on the streets, and most hotels have cab stands. Be sure that the meter is down when you set off, and avoid taxis with broken meters or none at all, or you will be seriously overcharged. For a radio-dispatched taxi, call **Blue Bird Taxi** (☎ 021/798–9000 or 021/798–9111).

Contacts and Resources

EMERGENCIES

Ambulance: ☎ 118. **City Health Service:** ☎ 119.

Doctors and Dentists. A group-practice clinic, Bina Medica (✉ Jl. Maluku 8–10, ☎ 021/344893) provides 24-hour service and English-speaking doctors. Doctors-on-Call (☎ 021/683444, 021/681405, or 021/514444) has English-speaking doctors who make house calls. Payment in cash is required. Dental services are provided at the Metropolitan Medical Center (✉ Wisata Office Tower, 1st floor, Jl. M. H. Thamrin, ☎ 021/320408). English-speaking staff (including dentists) are available at the 24-hour clinic and pharmacy SOS Medika Vayasan (✉ Jl. Prapanca Raya 32–34, Kebayoran Baru, ☎ 021/771575 or 021/733094).

Pharmacies. Melawai Apotheek (✉ Jl. Melawai Raya 191, ☎ 021/716109) has a well-stocked supply of American medicines. SOS Medika

Vayasan (☞ *above*) also has a pharmacy. **Police:** ☎ 110. **Traffic accidents:** ☎ 118.

ENGLISH-LANGUAGE BOOKSTORES

Major hotel shops carry magazines, newspapers, paperbacks, and travel guides in English. For a wide book selection, try **PT Indira** (✉ Jl. Melawi V/16, Blok M, ☎ 021/770584). The **Family Book Shop** (✉ Kemang Club Villas, Jl. Kelurahan Bangka, ☎ 021/799–5525) has quite a few titles. The largest selection is at the **Times Bookshop** (✉ Jl. M. H. Thamrin 28–30, ☎ 021/570–6581), on the lower floor of Plaza Indonesia.

TOUR OPERATORS AND TRAVEL AGENTS

Hotel tour desks will book the following tours or customize outings with a chauffeured car: "City Tour" (6 hrs) covers the National Monument, Pancasila Monument, Beautiful Indonesia in Miniature Park, and Museum Indonesia; "Indocultural Tour" (5 hrs) visits the Central Museum, Old Batavia, the Jakarta Museum, and a batik factory; "Beautiful Indonesia Tour" (3–4 hrs) takes you by air-conditioned bus through the Beautiful Indonesia in Miniature Park; and "Jakarta by Night" (5 hrs) includes dinner, a dance performance, and a visit to a nightclub. Tours beyond Jakarta include the following: a nine-hour trip to Pelabuhanratu, a former fishing village that's now a resort; an eight-hour tour to the safari park at Bogor and the Botanical Gardens, 48 km (30 mi) south of Jakarta at a cool 600 ft above sea level, and to the Puncak Mountain Resort; and a two-day tour into the highlands to visit Bandung and its volcano, with stops at Bogor and Puncak.

Gray Line (✉ Jl. Hayam Wunuk 3–P, ☎ 021/639–0008) covers most of Jakarta and its surrounding attractions. If you show up at **Jakarta City Tourist Center** (✉ Lapangan Binteng, Bantung Square, no phone), which opens at 8 AM, you can join any of the tours operating that day, usually at a discounted rate.

Travel agencies arrange transportation, conduct guided tours, and can often secure hotel reservations more cheaply than you could yourself. **Natourin** (✉ 18 Buncit Raya, Jakarta 12790, ☎ 021/799–7886) has extensive facilities and contacts throughout Indonesia. Although the following agents specialize in train travel, they can also help you with other travel needs: **Carnation** (✉ Jl. Menteng Raya 24, ☎ 021/384–4027 or 021/386–5728), **P. T. Bhayangkara** (✉ Jl. Kebon Sirih 23, ☎ 021/327387), and **Iwata Nusantara** (✉ Jl. Riau 19, ☎ 021/314–8957).

Large government-owned travel agencies with branch offices at most Indonesian tourist destinations include the following: **Nitour** (✉ Duta Merlin, Jl. Gajah Mada 3–5, ☎ 021/346346); **Satriavi** (✉ Jl. Prapatan 32, ☎ 021/380–3944); and **Pacto Ltd. Tours and Travel** (✉ Jl. Surabaya 8, ☎ 021/332634), the Indonesian representative of American Express.

VISITOR INFORMATION

The comprehensive *Falk City Map of Jakarta* is available at bookstores for Rp 9,200. The *Jakarta Program,* available at most hotel newsstands for Rp 4,000, is a monthly magazine listing attractions and events.

The **City Visitor Information Center** (✉ Jakarta Theatre Building, Jl. M. H. Thamrin 9, ☎ 021/354094) has brochures, maps, and information on bus and train schedules to other Java destinations. The center is open Monday–Thursday 8–3, Friday 8–11:30 AM, and Saturday 8–2.

The **Indonesian tourist office** (✉ Jl. K. H. Abdurrohim 1, at Dimas Pariwisata, Kuningan Barat, ☎ 021/525–1316) is charged with dispensing information on destinations across the archipelago, but it's difficult to find and the assistance given is minimal.

WEST JAVA

Java's western province has coastline, mountains, and fertile valleys that are intensively farmed. The province also has the impressive Ujung Kulon National Park, which is set on a peninsula in the island's southwestern corner. Just north of the park is Pulau Krakatau, an active island volcano. There are wild areas in the southeast corner, too, around the resort town of Pangandaran. Cosmopolitan Bandung, Indonesia's third-largest city, has a few reminders of the days when the Dutch flocked here to escape Jakarta's sweltering heat.

Most of the people in West Java are Sundanese and have their own language and cuisine (for a long time, the region was known as Sunda). The people are friendly and inquisitive; all also speak Bahasa Indonesia, Indonesia's national language, and many speak some English.

The Thousand Islands

14 *16 km–32 km (10 mi–20 mi) northwest of Jakarta; an hour or two by boat.*

In the Java Sea, northwest of Jakarta, are the little Thousand Islands—really a misnomer, because there are only 113 of them. Their white-sand beaches, lined with coconut palms, offer a retreat from the heat and bustle of the capital. If the concrete and noise of Jakarta are getting to you, consider a day trip to **Pulau Seribu** (*pulau* means island) to walk on the sands in a sea breeze. You can hire a motorboat from the **Marina Jaya Ancol** (✉ Jakarta, ☎ 021/681512), or take a **hovercraft** (✉ the port is at Jl. Donggala 26A, Tanjun Priok, Jakarta, ☎ 021/325608).

Lodging

Several islands have rustic getaways; accommodations are available on **Pulau Putri** (☎ 021/828–1093), **Pulau Matahari** (☎ 021/380–0521), **Pulau Bidadari** (☎ 021/680048), and **Pulau Laki** (☎ 021/314–4885). Contact each island's Jakarta office (listed above) to make reservations and to arrange transport to the island. Room rates are usually quoted as all-inclusive packages that include food and transport.

$$$ **Kotok Island Resort.** Set on 42 unspoiled acres of coconut groves and tropical foliage, this resort owns all but the island's very eastern tip, which belongs to a private Japanese club. In this back-to-nature environment, the accommodations are rustic, the plumbing primitive. The 22 bungalows have bamboo walls, basic bamboo furniture, and tiled baths with showers. Eight units are air-conditioned, but thanks to the sea breezes, the rest are comfortable with just overhead fans. The dining room—an open-air pavilion over the water—serves well-prepared Indonesian specialties. Licensed instructors give scuba-diving courses, and there's good snorkeling. The resort provides a launch service from Jakarta; the run takes 90 minutes. ✉ *Reservation office: Duta Merlin Shopping Arcade, 3rd floor, Jl. Gajah Mada 3–5, Jakarta,* ☎ *021/634–2948,* FAX *021/633–6120. 22 rooms. Restaurant, bar, beach, dive shop, snorkeling. No credit cards.*

Pulau Krakatau

15 *2 to 4 hours by boat from Carita Beach, which is 150 km (95 mi) southwest of Jakarta.*

You'll need to make an overnight trip to see the famous Krakatau (Krakatoa) Island, in the Sunda Strait between Sumatra and Java. The active volcano, Anak Krakatau, is actually the child of Krakatau, a volcano

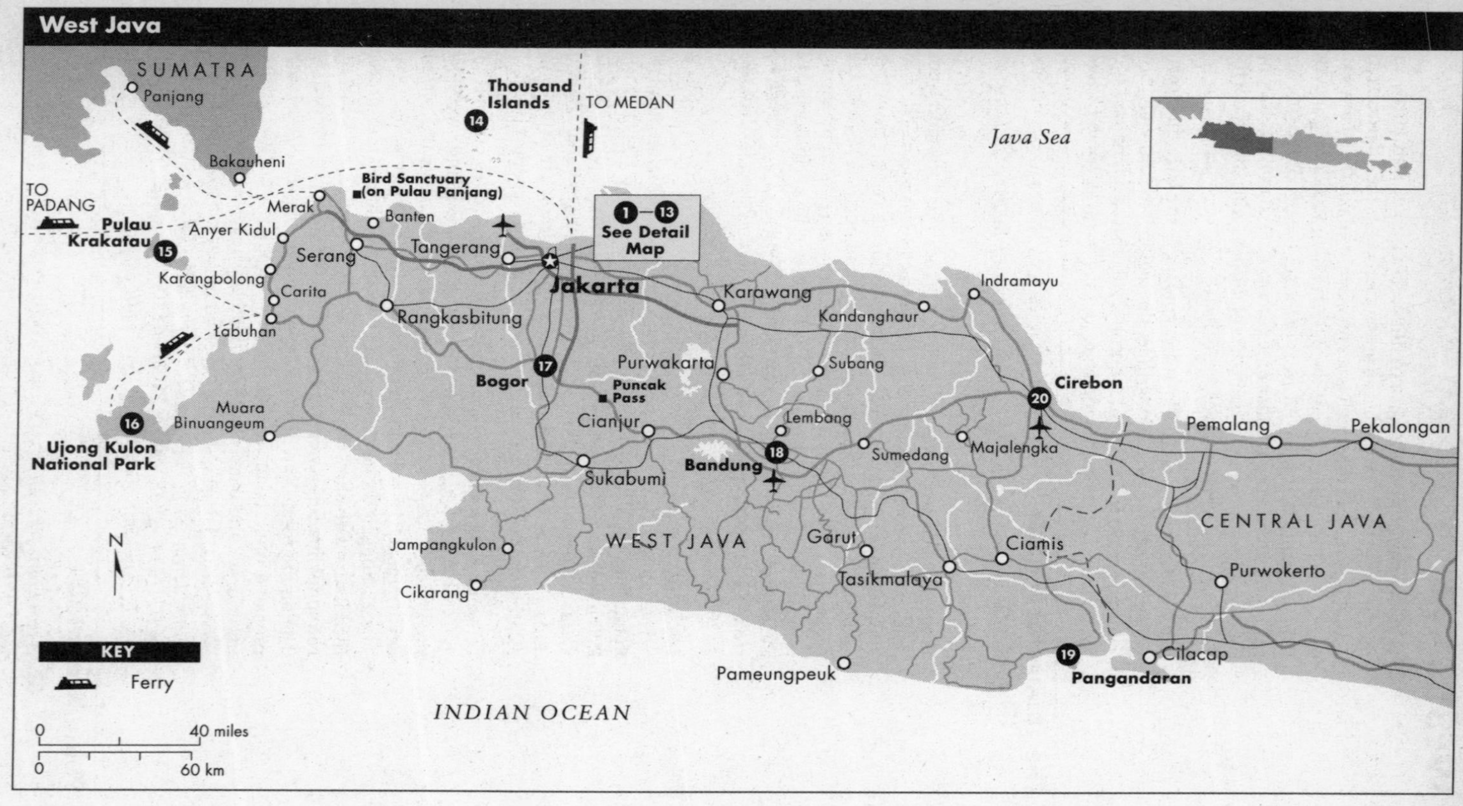

West Java
SUMATRA
Panjang
Bakauheni
TO PADANG
Pulau Krakatau
15
Thousand Islands
14
TO MEDAN
Java Sea
Bird Sanctuary (on Pulau Panjang)
Merak
Anyer Kidul
Banten
Serang
Tangerang
Karangbolong
Carita
Labuhan
Jakarta
1—13 See Detail Map
Rangkasbitung
Karawang
Indramayu
Kandanghaur
Purwakarta
Subang
Bogor
17
Puncak Pass
Cirebon
20
Muara Binuangeum
16
Ujong Kulon National Park
Cianjur
Lembang
Pemalang
Pekalongan
18
Sumedang
Majalengka
Sukabumi
Bandung
CENTRAL JAVA
N
WEST JAVA
Garut
Ciamis
Jampangkulon
Purwokerto
Tasikmalaya
Cikarang
KEY
19
Cilacap
Ferry
Pameungpeuk
Pangandaran
INDIAN OCEAN
0
40 miles
0
60 km

that erupted in 1883, killing 36,000 people and creating marvelous sunsets around the world for the next two years. Anak Krakatau emerged from the sea between three other islands by early 1928—45 years after its predecessor's eruption. (Note: Access by boat is an on-again, off-again venture as the volcano has been erupting intermittently since 1993. If you do go, take care; people have been injured by flying rocks and debris.) The popular place to overnight is **Carita Beach,** a quiet resort that's pleasant in its own right.

Lodging

$$ **Carita Krakatau Beach Hotel.** There are two advantages to this hotel: air-conditioned buses leave daily from its reservation office in Jakarta, and the hotel arranges trips (including the two-hour sea crossing) to the volcano. The rooms are modest, but most of the time you're out on the beach or taking refreshment at the terrace restaurant. The historic Krakatau photos and news clippings in the lobby breezeway, as well as the seaside vistas of the volcano, make a visit here worthwhile even if you don't plan to spend the night. ✉ *Carita Beach; reservations office at Hotel Wisata International, Jl. M. H. Thamrin, ground-floor arcade, Jakarta,* ☎ *0254/21043; 021/314–0252 in Jakarta. 45 rooms. Restaurant, beach, waterskiing. MC, V.*

Ujung Kulon National Park

★ 16 *200 km (124 mi) southwest of Jakarta.*

Forty or so endangered Javan rhinos still hide in the jungles of Ujung Kulon National Park, a World Heritage Site with nearly 800 square km (340 square mi) of peninsular and island wilderness that few people venture to see. It's a great place to trek (the snorkeling is good, too), but getting here is tough; the easiest way is by boat. If you're adventurous and have the time (at least two or three days, though four days or more is best) and the gear, you can arrange a tour with guide in Jakarta or Carita or go on your own. Note that you'll need to buy supplies before setting out; there are no facilities in the park, although there are basic guest bungalows, a few small stores, and a new World Wildlife Fund visitors center at the main entrance in Taman Jaya. Hotels in Jakarta can recommend tour operators (☞ Tour Operators *in* West Java Essentials, *below*); a four-day, three-night trek usually costs between $200–$300 per person. You can also hire a guide at the park office in Taman Jaya.

Bogor

17 *60 km (36 mi) south of Jakarta.*

The sprawling, smoky city of Bogor hides several attractions. Drop in at Jalan Pancasan 17 to see a **gong foundry,** one of the few remaining on Java, where instruments of the gamelan orchestra are still made using traditional methods.

The white-porticoed **Presidential Palace**—first built in 1745 by Dutch Governor General Gustav Willen Baron Van Imhoft and then rebuilt in 1856 after being destroyed by an earthquake—has a fine collection of paintings and sculptures. The palace is on the west side of Bogor's main attraction, the **Kebun Raya Bogor** (Botanical Gardens) founded in 1817 by the first English governor-general of Indonesia, maintained by the Dutch, and adopted by Sukarno. The 275-acre garden has 15,000 species of plants, hundreds of trees, an herbarium, cactus gardens, and ponds with enormous water lilies. The monument in the park is of Olivia Raffles, first wife of Sir Stanford Raffles, who died here at the Bogor Palace. Guides are available at Rp 6,000 an hour. *Admission.* ⏲ *Daily 9–5.*

Lodging

$$$ **Novotel Bogor.** Bogor's best hotel looks like an alpine resort, albeit one that's surrounded by banana trees. The grounds are so lush that you can't help but think that the city's beautiful botanical garden provided inspiration. Rooms are spacious, and you can lounge by the pool or play golf or tennis. The hotel's only drawback is its location 4 km (3 mi) from town. ✉ *Golf Estat Gogor Raya, 16710,* ☎ *251/271555; 800/221–4542 in the U.S.;* FAX *251/271333. 180 rooms. Restaurant, pool, 18-hole golf course, 2 tennis courts, health club, jogging, business services. AE, DC, MC, V.*

En Route The road from Bogor to Bandung winds through tea plantations and rain forests, past waterfalls and lakes. This is the Puncak region, where on clear days you'll get views of the Gede, Pangrango, and Salak mountains. Just over the summit of Puncak Pass is the **Puncak Pass Hotel,** a famous stop for travelers that serves excellent afternoon teas and vistas.

Bandung

18 *187 km (120 mi) southeast of Jakarta, 127 km (84 mi) southeast of Bogor.*

Situated on a plateau at 2,500 ft and shadowed by majestic volcanoes, Bandung was transformed into a Dutch oasis at the turn of the last century. European architects put up Art Deco buildings, café society copied fashions from Paris and Amsterdam, and Bandung became Indonesia's cultural and intellectual heart. There was even speculation that the capital might be transferred from steamy Jakarta to this mountain-fresh hill town.

The city's status waned after World War II. With independence, the political focus shifted to the tightly centralized government in Jakarta, and the Sundanese reasserted their own complex language and customs. Today, Bandung is an appealing mix of European and Asian cultures. With overcrowding burdening Jakarta's infrastructure, Bandung has, in recent years, attracted high-tech businesses with its intellectual environment and its 13 universities, including the prestigious Institute Teknologi Bandung. Although brochures exaggerate the city's attractions, it does have a pleasant climate—warm days and cold nights—and it's small and pedestrian-friendly enough to cover on foot.

In the days when Bandung called itself the "Parijs van Java," **Jalan Braga** was the "Rue St. Honoré." In the last few years the city made a successful attempt to rejuvenate the area, and it's once again a nice place to walk. There aren't many remnants of Bandung's glory days, but the classic, Art Deco **Savoy Homann** hotel (☞ Lodging, *below*) has been restored at great pains by its current owners. Near the Savoy hotel on Jalan Asia-Africa is the **Freedom Building** (Gedung Merdeka), where in 1955 Chou En-lai, Ho Chi Minh, Nehru, Nasser, and U Nu attended the famous Asia-Africa Conference of nonaligned nations.

Walking north back past the Savoy Homann, you'll reach the ***alun-alun*** (town square), the heart of Bandung. Just off the square is **Market Street,** which is worth a stroll at night, when book and magazine sellers take over one side and food stalls popular with locals take over the other. If you continue north along Jalan Braga you'll pass several cafés that offer great cakes and coffee for a break. If you're looking for evening entertainment, karaoke bars have taken over some of the side streets in this area.

At the **Geological Museum** (✉ Jl. Diponegoro), which is open daily 9–5 and is free, you'll find replicas of the fossils of Java Man (*Homo erectus*; a predecessor of Homo sapiens). North of the Geological Museum is the **Institut Teknologi Bandung,** designed by Maclaine Pont, a proponent of the Indo-European integrated style, exemplified here by the upturned, Minangkabau-style roofs; beyond the institute are the Dago Tea House and a waterfall with a splendid panorama of the city.

The hills surrounding Bandung are known as Parahyangan (Abode of the Gods) and are sacred to the Sundanese. The first stop on a tour of this area is usually the pleasant hill town of Lembang, just less than 10 km (6 mi) north of Bandung. The **Tangkuban Perahu Nature Reserve,** 10 km (6 mi) north of Lembang, contains Indonesia's only active volcano whose rim is accessible by car. From the preserve's entrance, the narrow road winds 4 km (2½ mi) to the crater's edge. The souvenir stands and hawkers are a nuisance, but the crater, boiling and seething with sulfurous steam, is dramatic. Several kilometers southeast of the crater are the **Crater Hot Springs,** with public baths where you can soothe your soul.

Dining and Lodging

$$$ ✕ **Braga Permai.** You can sit at tables on a streetside patio and order from the large selection of Indonesian and Western dishes that make this restaurant popular with both locals and tourists. It's a good place for lunch, dinner, or a break from a walk along Jalan Braga (the cakes are great). At night a piano player adds to the ambiance. ✉ *Jl. Braga 58,* ☎ *022/420–1831. AE, DC, MC, V.*

$$ ✕ **Sari Sunda.** This Sundanese restaurant first opened in the early 1990s and proved so successful with locals that now there are three branches. This branch is in a wooden building with bamboo furniture and lots of plants—very relaxing. The Sundanese dishes are spicy but not spicy enough to stun your taste buds. You can't go wrong with the fried fish covered in sweet-spicy topping or the chicken steamed in bamboo. The fruit drinks are also highly recommended. ✉ *Jl. Lengkong Sesar 77,* ☎ *022/438125. AE, DC, MC, V.*

$ ✕ **Naripan Steak.** A 10-minute walk off Jalan Braga will bring you to this open-to-the-street, meat-lovers grill. The dining room, with its basic tables and hard-back chairs, is sparse, but the food is tops. The satay beef and chicken are real treats. ✉ *Jl. Naripan 30,* ☎ *022/426–4453. No credit cards.*

$$ ★ **Savoy Homann.** It's neither the priciest nor the most up-to-date hotel in town, but the Savoy Homann is loaded with character. Built in the 1880s, it acquired its Art Deco details in 1930. In the evening, guests gather at the bar in the central courtyard to listen to a band. Superior rooms are the size of small suites; most have sitting areas and look onto either the street (windows are double-glazed) or the courtyard. The English-speaking staff is very friendly. ✉ *Jl. Asia-Afrika 112, 40261,* ☎ *022/250–0303,* FAX *022/250–0301. 153 rooms. Restaurant, bar, coffee shop. AE, DC, MC, V.*

$$ **Sheraton Inn.** Though this hotel is in a residential neighborhood 15 minutes by taxi from downtown, many travelers are drawn by its modern facilities, its well-trained staff, and its tranquility. The best rooms overlook the circular courtyard and its pool. Dining is a relaxed affair, either on the terrace by the pool or inside with air-conditioning. The Sheraton-style architecture and ambience are more American than Indonesian. ✉ *Jl. Ir. H. Juanda 390 (Box 6530), 40065,* ☎ *022/210303; 800/325–3535 in the U.S.;* FAX *022/210301. 111 rooms. Restaurant, pool, 2 tennis courts, business services. AE, DC, MC, V.*

$ **Lembang Grand Hotel.** Built in 1926 and used by the Dutch as a hill resort, the Grand still stands and offers simple accommodation just north of Bandung. ✉ *Jl. Raya Lembang 228, Lembang,* ☎ *022/82393. 26 rooms. Pool, 2 tennis courts. MC, V.*

Outdoor Activities and Sports

In many villages near Bandung, Sunday morning is the time for the weekly *adu domba* (ram fights). Facing off two at a time, prize rams bang, crash, and lock horns until one contestant decides that enough is enough and scampers off. It's as much a social event as a serious sport (though the wagerers take it seriously); don't miss it if you're around on a weekend.

Pangandaran

★ 19 *210 km (130 mi) southeast of Bandung, 370 km (230 mi) southeast of Jakarta.*

Pangandaran, a beach resort on a peninsula about halfway between Bandung and Yogyakarta, is popular with Bandung residents on weekends. If possible, visit during the week when you share it only with the local fisherfolk. The surf from the Indian Ocean pounds the black sandy beaches and can be dangerous. Still, there are sections protected by the bulb at the end of the peninsula—great places to splash about in calmer waters.

Though the peninsula is small enough to see on foot, there are plenty of becaks if you get tired. You might take one to the entrance of the small national park, passing rows of booths that sell mostly clothing along the way. The staff at your hotel can recommend a guide who's familiar with the park's jungled terrain; they can also arrange longer trips to Green Canyon, a larger and more spectacular wilderness area a couple hours away (☞ Tour Operators *in* West Java Essentials, *below*).

Dining and Lodging

$$ ✕ **Bunga Laut Restaurant.** Though this small restaurant in a bungalow doesn't look like much, it has great Sundanese food—a bit spicy but yummy. ✉ *Jl. Bulak Laut 2, no phone. No credit cards.*

$ ★ ✕ **Fish Market.** If you hanker for seafood, check out the collection of open-air restaurants here. Good choices include **Ditha,** in a bamboo building next to the road, and **Risma,** a concrete structure (its walls stop at waist level) next to the gravel parking area. At both you get to choose your fish and then have it cooked however you want. ✉ *Jl. Pantai Timur, about halfway up the peninsula, no phone. No credit cards.*

$$$ **Pantai Indah Timur.** This resort and its sister property, **Pantai Indah Barat** (on the peninsula's west side), are the most upscale in the region. The grounds at both are very well kept, with lots of trees and brick footpaths. The wooden one- and two-story buildings fit in well with the environment. Rooms are spacious and comfortable though not luxurious. ✉ *Jl. Kidang Pananjung 139,* ☎ *265/379004,* FAX *265/379327. 21 rooms, 2 suites, 7 bungalows. 2 restaurants, pool, 2 tennis courts. AE, DC, MC, V.*

$$ **Adam's Home Stay.** The air-conditioned bungalows here are grouped near the pool and just a two-minute walk from the beach. There are also fan-cooled rooms in the old Dutch-era main house, which faces the ocean. The view and sound of the ocean from these rooms can't be beat, and the library-bookshop—which has English-language titles—is just down the stairs next to the restaurant. You can have a cappuccino and stock up on reading material. ✉ *Jl. Pamugaran Bulak Laut,*

46396, ☎ 265/639164, FAX 265/639164. 9 rooms, 3 bungalows. Restaurant, bar, pool, bicycles, library. MC (sometimes).

Cirebon

20 *130 km (81 mi) northeast of Bandung, 250 km (155 mi) southeast of Jakarta.*

Cirebon is situated on a mangrove coast where, unfortunately, there are no beaches and few remaining mangroves. Over the centuries this port town has been influenced by many cultures; today it's something of a commercial crossroads and, as such, is a little wealthier than most Indonesian cities. The people here are friendly, and the distances between sights are manageable on foot. There are also plenty of fancy, painted becaks; you can catch a ride to almost anywhere in town for less than a dollar. City Hall, near the train station, is an Art Deco building right out of old Los Angeles or Miami. Cirebon also has a couple of cinemas that show slightly dated Hollywood movies, so, if you missed something in the past year or two, this could be your chance to catch up.

Start your tour in the south of the city at the **Kraton Kesepuhan,** a walled palace built in 1529 and set on 30 acres of peaceful grounds. The 13th generation of sultans still lives in a section that's closed to the public. You can still get a look inside by visiting the museum. The ornate carriage (circa 1549) on display is alone worth the visit. Just north of here is **Mesjid Agung,** one of Java's oldest and most interesting mosques—note its tiered roof. From the mosque, it's a few minutes' walk north along Jalan Lemah Wungkuk to the **Kraton Kanoman,** a palace with tranquil grounds and a huge banyan tree in its courtyard. A few minutes up the road from here is the **Vihara Dewi Welasasih,** a colorful temple that's a testament to the Chinese influence in the city. On the coast near the temple there's an odd little **amusement park** with a few rides and a rickety old boardwalk out over the water.

Dining and Lodging

$$ ✕ **Helena.** Seafood tops the menu at this big, air-conditioned, dining hall; if you want it spicy the chef will cook it Thai style. You'll also find a wide selection of Indonesian rice and chicken dishes. ✉ *Jl. Ade Irma Suryani Nasution, ☎ 231/201882. No credit cards.*

$$ ✕ **Jumbo Restaurant and Sea Food.** This restaurant in the heart of Cirebon has an extensive seafood menu as well as other chicken and meat dishes. The dark-wood dining room is quite comfortable. ✉ *Jl. Siliwangi 191, ☎ 231/203606. MC, V.*

$$$ 🏨 **Bentani.** Here you'll find all the amenities of a world-class hotel, but with more homegrown, personal service. Guest rooms are comfortable and spacious, and there are several on-site nightlife options, including karaoke. ✉ *Jl. Siliwangi 69, 45121, ☎ 231/207526, FAX 231/207527. 64 rooms, 20 suites. 2 restaurants, 2 bars, pool, sauna, health club, dance club. AE, MC, V.*

$$–$$$ 🏨 **Hotel Prima.** This hotel opened in 1991 across from the city hall. The rooms are comfortable, and the staff is friendly. ✉ *Jl. Siliwangi 107, 45124, ☎ 231/205411, FAX 231/205407. 88 rooms, 8 suites. Restaurant, bar, pool, 2 tennis courts. AE, MC, V.*

$$ 🏨 **Hotel Sidodadi.** Air-conditioning, clean rooms, and complimentary breakfast are all part of the package at this moderately priced establishment in in Cirebon's hotel row. ✉ *Jl. Siliwangi 72, ☎ 231/202305, FAX 231/204821. 50 rooms. Restaurant. MC, V.*

West Java Essentials

Arriving and Departing

BY AIRPLANE

Jakarta is the hub for flights to points in West Java (☞ Arriving and Departing By Airplane *in* Jakarta Essentials, *above*). There has been talk of making Bandung more of a gateway, but with the economic turmoil of the late 1990s, it may be a while till anything gets off the ground (so to speak).

BY BOAT

Boat travel between Jakarta and Sumatra is an option, albeit a slow one. The KM *Lawit,* and KM *Kerinci* make a 40-hour trip between Jakarta and Padang about every two weeks. There are also ferries every hour between Merak (110 km/68 mi west of Jakarta) to Bakauheni on the southern tip of Sumatra.

BY TRAIN

The trip to Bandung from Yogyakarta is eight hours, and there are three or more trains a day. The night train has *ekeskutif* (first-class) compartments with reclining seats, air-conditioning, and blankets. The day train lacks these amenities but offers *biznis* (business) class, with padded seats and windows that you can open.

Getting Around

BY AIRPLANE

There are flights to Bandung's Husein Sastranegara airport from Jakarta with **Merpati** and **Garuda** (✉ Jl. Asia Afrika 73, ☎ 022/441226), which share an office across from the Savoy Homann in Bandung.

BY BOAT

Each of the Thousands Islands resorts has its own boat transport; contact them directly to make arrangements. Boats for Pulau Krakatau leave Carita Beach at around 8 AM; the trip takes 2½ hours by speedboat (Rp 100,000), 4 hours on a slower boat (about Rp 40,000). It's best to visit with a reputable tour operator, and you can make arrangements for this in Jakarta or Carita. Don't venture out if the waters are rough, even though there are plenty of boatmen in Carita who will offer to take you despite high seas (these are the people to avoid). Note also that sometimes you won't be able to visit Pulau Krakatau owing to volcanic activity.

Boats to Ujung Kulon National Park leave from Labuan, just south of Carita. You can take the *Wanawisata,* which costs about Rp 324,000 one way and takes about six hours. (You'll have to ask about its schedule, which is ever-changing). Alternatively, you can charter a boat (about Rp 400,000) that can carry as many as 20 people. Another option, and probably the best one, is to organize a three- or four-day tour with a travel agent in Carita (ask your hotel staff for recommendations).

BY BUS

The road from Jakarta to Bandung offers spectacular views, and many minibuses make the trip each day—though fretful passengers may spend more time watching the next curve than the scenery. The larger air-conditioned buses are a better bet. You can travel from Jakarta to Carita Beach by public bus in about three hours, but the minivans of **P. J. Krakatau** (✉ Ujung Kulon Tours, Hotel Wisata International, Jakarta, ☎ 021/314–0252) are a lot more comfortable.

BY CAR

You can rent a car and drive yourself, but unless you know the language and the country it's not recommended. Its best to hire a car with a driver to take you from major hubs to surrounding sights. Such arrangements don't cost very much, and they leave you free to watch the scenery.

BY TRAIN

There are numerous trains between Jakarta's Gambir Station and Bogor each day (it's almost like a commuter service as many people live along the hour-long route). Four express trains make the four- to six-hour trip from Gambir to Cirebon daily. Trains between Surabaya and Jakarta also pass through Cirebon. The trip from Jakarta to Bandung—approximately three hours from Gambir Station, with nine departures daily—is quite scenic: the train travels through flat rice lands before climbing mountains along a curving track and over trestle bridges built by the Dutch. Rates are Rp 20,000 for executive class with air-conditioning and reclining seats, RP 7,000 for business class with open windows and padded seats, and *really* cheap for third class, in which case you get what you pay for.

Contacts and Resources

EMERGENCIES

Hospital: Adventist Hospital (✉ Jl. Cihampelas 161, Bandung, ☎ 022/234-386).

ENGLISH-LANGUAGE BOOKSTORES

In central Bandung there are several book shops along Jalan Braga.

TOUR OPERATORS

The **Bandung City Tour** (☎ 022/520–4650) is a half-day bus trip to Bandung's major sites. Contact the **Indonesian Guide Association** (✉ Jl. Kidang Pananjung 21, Pangandaran, ☎ 265/639296) to arrange for treks to wilderness areas around Pangandaran. Sudrajad Pujo Adi at **Kirana Wisata** (✉ Wisata International Hotel, Jl. M. H. Thamrin 48, ☎ 021/390–8008) has been taking visitors to Ujung Kulon National Park since 1990.

VISITOR INFORMATION

Bandung Tourist Information Office (✉ Alun-alun, Jl. Asia Afrika, no phone). **Bogor Tourist Information Office** (✉ Jl. Merak 1, ☎ 251/325701)). **West Java Provincial Tourist Office** (✉ Jl. Soekarno-Hatta, Km 11, Bandung, ☎ 022/780–5739).

CENTRAL AND EAST JAVA

Central Java—and the special province of Yogyajakarta within its borders—is the cultural heart of Indonesia. The region nurtured some of the country's great Indian kingdoms in the 8th and 9th centuries, including the Buddhist Sailendras, who built the Borobudur temple, and the Hindu Sanjayans, who made Prambanan their religious center. Today visitors generally use Yogyakarta as a base for seeing these temples. However, if you prefer less commercialism and tourist hustling, the ancient city of Solo, 64 km (40 mi) to the east, is a good bet. From this quiet city you can easily drive out to Sukuh Temple and to Sangiran, the site where Java Man was discovered.

Five hours northeast of Yogyakarta is Surabaya, a good base from which to explore East Java, a free-spirited province ideally suited to adventurous, unorthodox travelers. It has three regions; the north coast, including Madura Island; the Brantas River basin; and the volcanoes that dominate the south. Mt. Bromo, an active volcano from whose rim you can peer down into nature's cauldron, is a provincial highlight.

Central and East Java

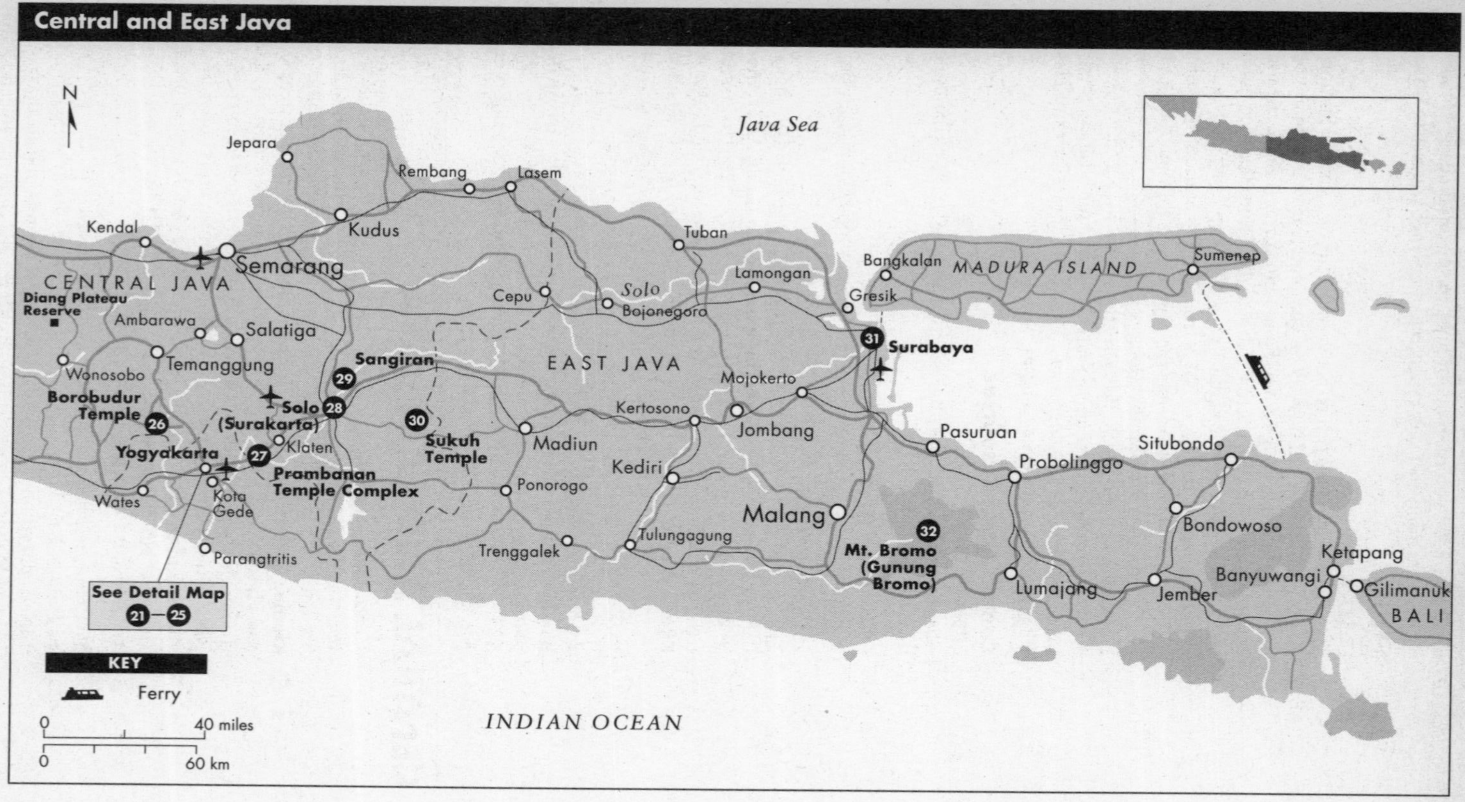

Yogyakarta

21–25 *618 km (371 mi) southeast of Jakarta, 431 km (251 mi) southeast of Bandung.*

Every Indonesian has a soft spot for Yogyakarta, or Yogya (pronounced *joeg-jakarta* or *joeg-ja*), a city of some 300,000 on a fertile plain in the shadow of three volcanoes. Students from Yogya's Gajah Mada University account for some 20% of the city's population, and dance and choreography schools, wayang troupes, and poetry workshops make it an artist's mecca. Every evening, classical drama and dance performances are staged somewhere in the city. Leading Indonesian painters and sculptors display their work in numerous galleries, and crafts shopping is a major activity. The batik here and in Solo (☞ *below*) is said to be superior even to that found on Bali.

Exploring Yogyakarta

Yogya sprawls. Unless you stay at the Garuda (☞ Lodging, *below*) or one of the less expensive city hotels, chances are you'll be a few miles from Jalan Malioboro, the main thoroughfare.

SIGHTS TO SEE

25 **Affandi Museum.** Out toward the airport, about 8 km (5 mi) southeast of Yogya, is the home and studio of Indonesia's best-known painter, Affandi (1907–90). A permanent collection of his works, along with paintings by young artists, is exhibited in an oval, domed extension to the traditional paddy-field house. ✉ *Jl. Laksda, Adisucipto 67, no phone.* 🎫 *Free.* ⏲ *Daily 9–3.*

24 **Diponegoro Monument.** This is the reconstructed residence of Prince Diponegoro, who rebelled against the Dutch and led a bloody guerrilla battle in the Java War (1825–30). The house is now a museum, displaying the prince's krises, lances, and other revered possessions. ✉ *Tegalrejo (4 km/2½ mi west of Yogyakarta),* ☎ *0274/563068.* 🎫 *Donation appreciated.* ⏲ *Open by appointment only.*

Jalan Malioboro. This is where the action is, day and night. It's the main shopping street, not only for established stores but also for sidewalk vendors. They set up cardboard stands that sell handicrafts until about 9 PM, then convert to food stalls serving Yogya's specialties: *nasi gudeg* (rice with jackfruit in coconut milk) and *ayam goreng* (marinated fried chicken). Malioboro is a fascinating street; arrive by 8 PM, and you can catch both the shops and the food. Haggle for prices over items on the street or look for good deals at the indoor market, **Pasar Beringharjo,** at the top of the street; it's worth visiting just to see the stacked merchandise—everything from jeans to poultry.

★ 21 **Kraton.** At the southern end of Malioboro stands the Kraton, or Sultan's Palace. The large, grassy square in front of it—a walled city within the city—is the **alun-alun,** where the townspeople formerly gathered to trade, gossip, and hear the latest palace news. The Yogya Kraton has special significance to Indonesians as the bastion against Dutch colonialism. During the War of Independence (1945–49), Yogya's Sultan Hamengku Buwono allowed the Indonesian freedom fighters—including guerrilla commander Suharto—to use the Kraton as a base. Built in 1756, it's a vast complex of pavilions and buildings, part of which—strictly off-limits to the public—is home to the present sultan. The complex is protected by 400 guards (in blue shirts) and maintained by 1,000 servants (in red shirts).

At the center of the white, green-trimmed palace is the **Bengsal Kengono** (Golden Pavilion), an open hall with carved teak columns and a black-and-gold interior, where weddings, cremations, and coronations

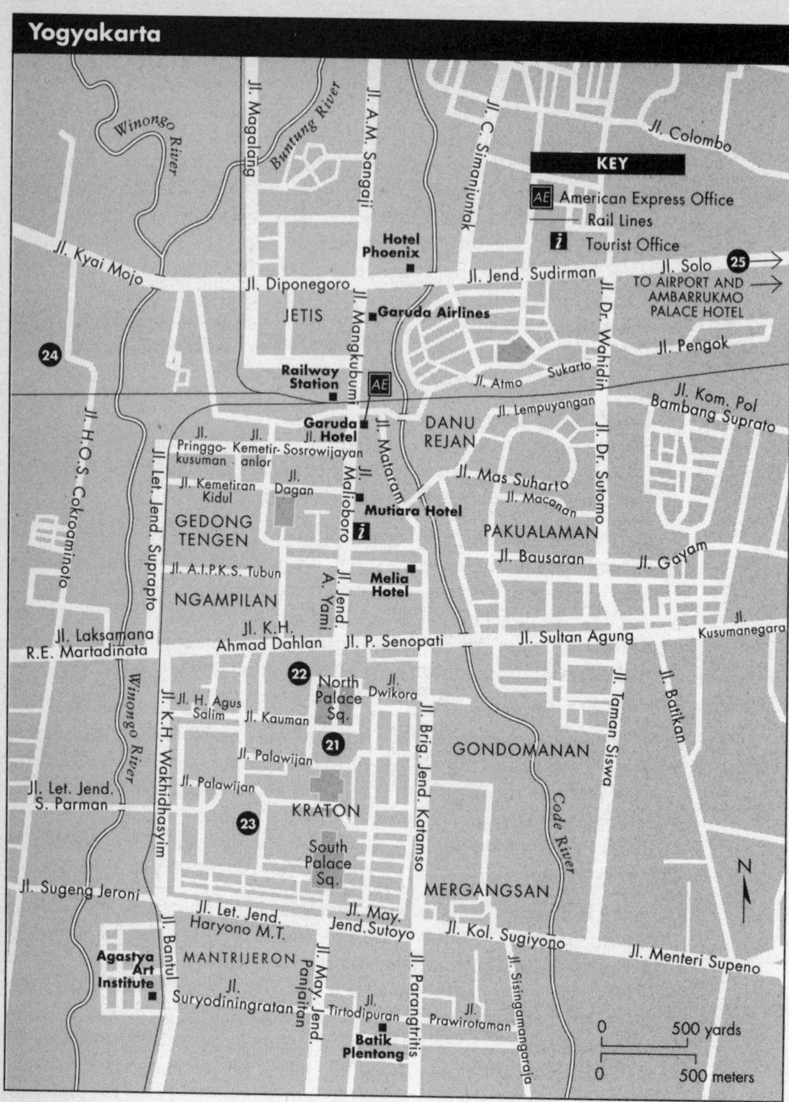

Affandi Museum **25**
Diponegoro Monument, **24**
Kraton, **21**
Sono Budoyo Museum, **22**
Taman Sari, **23**

are held. The complex includes a gallery that displays a collection of gamelan instruments. Try to time your visit to catch the Sunday classical dance rehearsal (10:30 and noon, except during Ramadan). In another pavilion is a collection of sedan chairs. The last one was used in 1877; now a Rolls-Royce transports the sultan on ceremonial occasions. *No phone.* 🎫 *Admission.* ⏲ *Sun.–Thurs. 8:30 AM–1 PM, Fri.–Sat. 8:30 –11:30 AM.*

22 **Sono Budoyo Museum.** Of Yogya's several museums, the most interesting and well-maintained is the Sono Budoyo Museum, on the square in front of the Kraton. Inside this traditional Javanese-style building is a collection of crafts and batiks from Java and Bali. Its archaeological treasures include a small gold Buddha, and the display of wayang golek, the wood puppets used in Muslim theater, is charming. ☎ *0274/562775.* 🎫 *Admission.* ⏲ *Tues.–Thurs. 8 AM–1 PM, Fri. and Sun. 8–11 AM, Sat. 8–noon.*

23 **Taman Sari.** Behind the Kraton is the recreational Water Palace constructed by the same sultan who built the main palace. A large artificial lake, sunken bathing pools, underground passageways, and towers where gamelan orchestras serenaded the royal party were all part of this noble retreat. It was abandoned in the 18th century and fell into ruin; the restored sections give a sense of what the privileged enjoyed. Visit the ornate bathing pools used by the princesses, the underground mosque, and the tower from which the sultan watched his concubines lounge by the water. *No phone.* 🎫 *Admission.* ⏲ *Sun.–Thurs. 8 AM–1 PM, Fri. 8–11 AM.*

Dining

For Western food, you can dine at the major hotels. Many also offer a performance of segments from the *Ramayana,* charging an extra fee to see the show. The Indonesian fare at local restaurants is inexpensive and good.

$$ ★ ✕ **Pesta Perak.** This smartly decorated restaurant has wrought-iron furniture and a sultan-costumed maître d', as well as excellent Javanese cuisine. Its rijsttafel includes satays, gudeg, and fish wrapped in banana leaves. An à la carte menu is also offered, but customers rarely choose this. A gamelan trio plays traditional music. Use a becak to get there, and have it wait for you; the fare from Jalan Malioboro, including waiting time, is less than Rp 4,000. ✉ *Jl. Tentura Rakyat Mataran 8,* ☎ *0274/586255. MC, V.*

$$ ✕ **Pringsewu Garden Restaurant.** For relaxed alfresco dining at tables tucked between shrubs and trees, this restaurant is a delight. It offers some of the best fare in the region, served by a friendly staff attired in colorful batiks. The cooking is from West Sumatra. Try the ayam goreng *mantega* (with a butter sauce) or the ikan *mas baket* (grilled and served in ginger sauce). ✉ *Jl. Magelang, Km 6,* ☎ *0274/564993. AE, DC, MC, V.*

$$ ✕ **Sintawang.** Though the tables are Formica, the restaurant is clean and offers a wide range of outstanding seafood, either cooked Javanese-style or grilled for Western palates. Try the udang *bakar* (marinated and grilled), udang *pais* (spiced and grilled in a banana leaf), or ikan *asam manis* (in a sweet-and-sour sauce). ✉ *Jl. Magelang 9,* ☎ *0274/512901. Reservations not accepted. AE, DC.*

$ ✕ **Legian Garden Restaurant.** Choose a table next to the open windows at the edge of its terrace and watch fellow tourists *jalan jalan* (amble around) on the street below. Since the food is pretty average (primarily Western, with a few Indonesian alternatives), you may just want to stop by for a beer. ✉ *Jl. Perwakilan 9 (off Jl. Malioboro), 1st floor,* ☎ *0274/564644. Reservations not accepted. No credit cards.*

$ ★ ✕ **Ny Suharti.** It's worth the Rp 3,500 cab ride here from Malioboro for the best fried chicken in Java. Forget charm and atmosphere and the other items on the menu: you're here for a bird—boiled, marinated in spices, then cooked up crisp. Order one for two people, with rice on the side, and enjoy it out on the veranda. If you pay by credit card, a 3% surcharge will be added to your bill. ✉ *Jl. Laksda Adisucipto, Km 7,* ☎ *0274/515522. Reservations not accepted. MC, V.*

$ ★ ✕ **Via Via.** This little restaurant sets the standard for backpacker fare of cheap, simple cuisine. The small Indonesian and Western menu is very good, as are the fruit shakes. This is also a good place to pick up travel information. ✉ *Jl. Prawirotaman 24, no phone. No credit cards.*

Lodging

In the 1990s, the number of hotels in Yogyakarta grew in leaps and bounds, and the quality of existing establishments improved greatly. Now there are accommodations to meet every pocketbook. The world-class Amanjiwo, which opened in 1997 near the Borobudur Temple, is one of the best hotels in Southeast Asia (with prices to match its reputation). In Yogya itself there are countless new medium-range hotels as well as 2 blocks of guest houses in the southern part of town. Just off Jalan Malioboro (across from the Garuda and 2 blocks from the railway station), there's a good selection of small, budget hotels. With so many lodging options, prices are competitive. There are discounts of as much as 50% on offer—just be sure to ask about them.

$$$$ ★ 🏨 **Amanjiwo.** Superlatives don't do this hotel justice. Designed by American Ed Tuttle, who also created Bali's Amankila and the Amanpuri in Phuket, Thailand, it has 35 suites, each in its own building; 14 of them have private pools of a reasonable size, though there's also a 40-meter communal pool. Rooms are spacious and airy with king-size beds; big, sliding-glass doors; outdoor sunken tubs; indoor showers; and two dressing areas with closets. The grounds are at the base of steep mountains, and there are views of Borobudur Temple from each suite. You can continue to pay homage to the temple while swimming laps in the pool, dining in the open-air restaurant, or relaxing in the bar. To top it off, the hotel offers a sunrise tour of Borobudur (reservations are recommended). ✉ *About 6 km (4 mi) south of Borobudur Temple and up a slight incline (Box 333, Magelang 56553),* ☎ *0293/88333,* FAX *0293/88355. 35 suites. Restaurant, bar, café, pool, massage, bicycles, travel services. AE, DC, MC, V.*

$$$$ 🏨 **Ambarrukmo Palace.** Yogyakarta's premier in-town hotel is built on the grounds of a former royal country retreat. Guest rooms are large, decorated with light Indonesian-pattern fabrics and mahogany furniture, and full of amenities. The best rooms have balconies that overlook the gardens. This hotel is very popular with American tour groups, and some rooms are little worn; if yours isn't up to standard, don't be shy about asking for another. Every evening sees some type of entertainment, usually dances from the *Ramayana.* ✉ *Jl. Laksda Adisucipto, 55281,* ☎ *0274/566488,* FAX *0274/563283. 266 rooms. 2 restaurants, bar, minibars, pool, travel services. AE, DC, MC, V.*

$$$–$$$$ 🏨 **Melia.** Part of the Spanish-owned Sol Melia chain, this hotel is conveniently close to Jalan Malioboro. Some of its spacious, comfortable rooms have doors that connect them with other rooms—perfect options for families or other groups. The hotel is built around a big pool and garden area, where you can get a foot massage and take it really easy. ✉ *Jl. Suryotomo 31, 55122,* ☎ *0274/589521,* FAX *0274/588070. 295 rooms. Restaurant, coffee shop, pool, massage, health club, meeting rooms, shops, travel services. AE, DC, MC, V.*

$$–$$$ **Garuda.** The draws at this imposing old hotel are its central location and its moderate prices. Standard guest rooms are plainly furnished but do have all the latest conveniences, including a TV with a VCR and a minibar. Ask for one of the newer rooms as the older ones have a faint musty odor; note, however, that all rooms have suffered from the steady stream of tour groups (there are black scrape marks on walls and stains on carpets). The restaurants offer Indonesian and Western food. ✉ *Jl. Malioboro 60, 55271,* ☎ *0274/566353,* FAX *0274/563074. 235 rooms. 2 restaurants, coffee shop, minibars, pool, tennis court, exercise room, business services, travel services. AE, DC, MC, V.*

$$ **Radisson Yogya Plaza.** New in 1996, there is a pleasing freshness to this hotel, which calls itself a resort within a city. Guest rooms, most with king-size beds, are modern and functional; the best for light and peace are those overlooking the courtyard, where you'll find the pool and a café and terrace off to the side. In the evenings, a local band plays—sometimes a string quartet, sometimes a gamelan orchestra—and later a performance of the *Ramayana* is given. Off the large atrium lobby, which contains a comfortable sitting area, the dining room serves Western and Indonesian fare and excellent buffet breakfasts. The downside to this property is that it's more than a 30-minute walk to downtown Yogyakarta; a shuttle bus does run back and forth, but distance precludes a spontaneous walk. ✉ *Jl. Gejayan, Complex Columbo, 55821,* ☎ *0274/584222,* FAX *0274/584200. 120 rooms. 2 restaurants, bar, pool, massage, 2 tennis courts, health club, business services, meeting rooms. AE, DC, MC, V.*

$ **Batik Palace Hotel.** For modest accommodations in the center of Yogya, this hotel offers worn but clean rooms, each with twin beds, table, and chair. The lobby, decorated with batiks and crafts, is a comfortable place to relax. ✉ *Jl. Mangkubumi 46 (Box 115), 55153,* ☎ *0274/562229,* FAX *0274/562149. 38 rooms. Restaurant, pool. V.*

$ **Data Guest House.** Along Jalan Prawirotaman to the south of the Kraton are a score of inexpensive guest houses. Data is one of the best, with clean rooms and reasonable prices, and its position down a narrow street makes it one of the quietest. The very basic double rooms (around $15) have two narrow beds, cold-water showers, and fans—there are, however, no windows. Twice as much will get you a "garden view" (the guest house's fancy term for the courtyard), air-conditioning, and a hot-water shower. Since there are only eight of these deluxe rooms, reserve ahead. The owners speak excellent English and are only too happy to assist in travel planning. Prices include a modest American buffet breakfast. (Be sure you find Data Guest House—many other hotels in the neighborhood have "Data" in their names.) ✉ *Jl. Prawirotaman 26/1, 55153,* ☎ *0274/372064. 32 rooms. Breakfast room. AE, DC, MC, V.*

$ **Mutiara.** Two buildings on Jalan Malioboro make up this hotel. The newer south wing has fresher rooms that, despite their pale-green-and-orange-flecked decor, are worth the extra $5. Cracked plaster and stained carpets notwithstanding, all the rooms are swept clean, fresh towels are supplied though the day, and the cheerful staff is always ready to give advice. The restaurant serves meals all day long, but stick to the breakfast. A small combo plays every evening on the ground floor. ✉ *Jl. Malioboro 18, 55153,* ☎ *0274/563814,* FAX *0274/561201. 109 rooms. Restaurant, coffee shop, pool. AE, DC, MC, V.*

$ **Rose Guest House.** The rooms here are very modest, but they do have private baths and either air-conditioning or overhead fans. The rates include breakfast and airport transfers, so this hotel is an extremely good value. ✉ *Jl. Prawirotaman 22, 55153,* ☎ *0274/727991. 29 rooms. Restaurant, pool. No credit cards.*

Nightlife and the Arts

If you hanker for a beer and maybe some local music, try the restaurants along Jalan Prawirotaman or Jalan Malioboro. Indeed, after dark Jalan Malioboro is transformed from a crowded market street into one long, open restaurant—the hub of social life in the city. Magicians perform tricks and singers wander between tables strumming guitars, and conversations and coffee continue long after the last dish has been cleared from the table.

Most often there will be a gamelan orchestra playing in your hotel, but a performance in the sultan's palace is not to be missed. Portions of the *Ramayana* are performed at different venues throughout the city, but the most dramatic setting is at the Prambanan Temple Complex (☞ *below*). Wayang kulit shows, usually based on stories from the *Ramayana,* are also given.

DANCE, MUSIC, AND THEATER

The **Kraton,** the sultan's palace, hosts traditional gamelan music on Monday and Wednesday from 10:30 to noon. In addition, every Sunday from 10:30 AM to 12:30 PM, the **Kraton Classic Dance School** rehearses here. Actors perform stories from the *Ramayana* nightly at 7 in **Taman Hiburan Rakyat** (People's Park; ⊠ Jl. Brig. Jen. Katamso). Shows last about two hours.

PUPPET SHOWS

Wayang kulit shows take place Sunday through Friday from 3 to 5 PM at the **Agastya Art Institute** (⊠ Jl. Gedongkiwo MDIII/237, no phone).

Eight-hour wayang kulit performances of the full *Ramayana* or *Mahabharata* are usually held every second Saturday of the month at **Sasono Hinggil,** a theater just south of Yogya's Kraton, on the opposite side of the alun-alun. These plays begin at 9 PM and last until dawn. Shorter versions lasting two to three hours are given at other times. Your hotel should have the schedule, or check at the information booth outside the theater.

At the **Ambar Budaya** (Yogyakarta Crafts Center; ⊠ Jl. Laksda Adisucipto, opposite the Ambarrukmo Palace Hotel), hour-long wayang kulit performances take place every Monday, Wednesday, and Saturday at 9:30 PM.

Shopping

Shopping for batiks is a delight, and you should make the time to watch batik being made at one of the many small factories. Yogyakarta is also a center for painters, and their works are displayed in scores of galleries. Leather goods here are usually well made and inexpensive. Yogyakarta may be a shopper's dream, but be selective—there's a lot of tacky merchandise alongside the treasures—and bargain gracefully. After you've offered your next-to-last price, walk away; you'll probably be called back. There are any number of scams to lure you into shops—for instance, the claim that a student art exposition is being held and the works are being sold without commercial profit. Don't believe it!

Jalan Malioboro is lined with shops; the handicraft stalls turn into food stalls around 9 PM. Most of the merchandise is junk, but it's worth picking through. This is a convenient area to buy T-shirts or shorts, but prices are on the high side.

You'll find good prices—prices that locals may pay—at the modern indoor market, **Pasar Beringharjo,** at the top end of Jalan Malioboro, across from the Kraton. This fascinating market offers countless spices and foodstuffs, as well as pots and pans, clothes, and electronics.

HANDICRAFTS

In addition to batik, Yogya handicrafts include small hand-tooled leather goods, pottery (items decorated with brightly colored elephants, roosters, and animals from mythology are made in Kasongan, just south of Yogya), and wayang kulit and wayang golek. All the shops and stalls on Jalan Malioboro and around the Kraton sell puppets and other handicrafts. The **Yogyakarta Handicrafts Center** (✉ Jl. Adisucipto, no phone), not far from the Ambarrukmo Palace hotel (☞ Lodging, *above*), sells handicrafts by artisans with disabilities.

The patterned Indonesian textiles called batik—made by drawing on fabric with wax, then dyeing the unwaxed areas—can be found in all the stalls in Yogyakarta. Many prints with batik design are machine-made, however, so beware. Before you buy, try to visit a batik factory where you can watch the process and browse the showrooms.

One place to see batik being created is **Batik Plentong** (✉ Jl. Tirtodipurun 28, ☎ 0274/562777), which has everything from yard goods to pot holders and batik clothing—all hand-stamped and hand-drawn. Visit **Iman Batik Workshop** (✉ Jl. Dagen 76B, just off Jl. Malioboro, no phone), where Iman Nuryanto, the owner, holds changing exhibitions of local artisans. Don't pay more than 50% of the asking price. The **Koperasi (Cooperative) Fine Arts School** (✉ Jl. Kemetiran Kidul, no phone), south of the railway station, has batik designed by talented artisans—just be sure to bargain.

You'll find high-quality leather goods **Kusuma** (✉ Jl. Kauman 50, parallel to Malioboro, ☎ 0274/565453). There's room for modest bargaining, but no credit cards are accepted.

If you're interested in ceramics and pottery, head for **Kansongan,** 8 km (5 mi) southwest of Yogya. There are more than 30 pottery workshops in the little town, which is slowly being engulfed by Yogya but still far enough away to keep its identity. Pottery isn't the easiest merchandise to transport, but there are many pots and sculptures that are truly worth buying. Taxis all know where Kansongan is, or you can take a bus heading toward Bantul, get out at the town entrance, and walk the last kilometer.

Many silversmiths have workshops and salesrooms in **Kota Gede,** 6 km (3½ mi) southeast of Yogya. The largest in Kota Gede, **Tom's Silver** (✉ Jl. Ngaksi Gondo, Kota Gede 3-1 A, ☎ 0274/525416) also offers the best workmanship. Also try **MD Silver** (✉ Jl. Keboan, Kota Gede, ☎ 0274/375063).

Borobudur Temple

★ ㉖ *42 km (26 mi) northwest of Yogyakarta.*

That the temple of Borobudur took perhaps 10,000 men 100 years to build becomes credible the moment you set eyes on its cosmic structure, in the shadow of the powerful volcanoes that the Javanese believe are the abode of God. Try to go early in the morning—plan to end your two- to three-hour visit before noon, while the temperature is still relatively cool. Guided coach tours run from Yogya hotels, or you can hire a minibus and guide (usually more informed) through a Yogya travel agency. If you'd like to visit on your own, take the public bus that heads toward Samarung, then change at Muntilan for the Ramayana bus to Borobudur.

Borobudur was abandoned (the reasons are still debated) soon after completion in AD 850, and the forest moved in. The man who founded modern Singapore, Thomas Stamford Raffles (then the English lieutenant-governor of Java), and his military engineer, H. C. C. Cornelius, rediscovered the temple in 1814. A thousand years of neglect had left much of it in ruins, and the temple has undergone two mammoth restorations, first from 1907 to 1911, and then again from the 1960s to the 1980s with the help of UNESCO and $25 million.

The temple is a giant stupa (dome-shape structure): five lower levels contain 1,500 relief carvings depicting the earthly life of Siddhartha in his passage to enlightenment. Start at the eastern staircase on the first level and walk clockwise around each gallery to follow the sequence of Lord Buddha's life.

Above the reliefs are 432 stone Buddhas. Even higher, above the square galleries, are three circular terraces with 72 latticed stupas that hide statues depicting the Buddha's departure from the material world and existence on a higher plane. The top stupa symbolizes the highest level of enlightenment. Looking out at the surrounding mountains from the upper level of Borobudur, you feel some of the inspiration that created this grand monument. If you go around each of the nine galleries, you will have walked roughly 5 km (3 mi) closer to heaven. On weekends the complex is fairly crowded—another reason to come early. There is a museum on the grounds, charging an additional admission that its contents do not justify. *No phone.* 🎫 *Admission.* ⏲ *Daily 6:15–5.*

OFF THE BEATEN PATH

CANDI PAWON AND MENDUT – About 1.5 km (1 mi) east of Borobudur, on the way back to the main road, is a small temple, **Candi Pawon,** built around the same time as Borobudur. It's thought that worshipers purified themselves here on their way to Borobudur. Another kilometer or so farther east is the small temple **Mendut,** also from the 9th century. The exterior of this friendly temple is superbly carved with some 30 large relief panels depicting scenes from the Buddha's previous incarnations. Inside stands a magnificent 10-ft statue of Buddha, flanked by the bodhisattvas Avalokitesvara and Vajrapani.

Prambanan Temple Complex

★ 27 *16 km (10 mi) northeast of Yogyakarta, a 30-min drive via the Solo road.*

When the Sanjayan kingdom evicted the Buddhist Sailendras, the Sanjayans wanted to memorialize the return of a Hindu dynasty and, supposedly, undermine Borobudur. To this end they built Prambanan. When the 9th-century complex was rediscovered in 1880, it was in ruins from centuries of neglect and enveloping vegetation. In 1937 reconstruction began, and the work continues to this day.

The temple was built with an outer stage for commoners, a middle stage for high-ranking nobility, and a main temple area for royalty. Of the original 244 temples, eight major and eight minor temples are still standing, in the highest central courtyard of the Prambanan plain.

The center temple, dedicated to Shiva the Destroyer, is the highest (155 ft) and the best-restored; Vishnu's is to the north; and Brahma's to the south. Originally the temples were painted—Shiva's red, Brahma's white, Vishnu's a dark gray—but only traces of the paint remain. To the east of these temples are three smaller ones, which contained the "vehicles" of each god: Shiva's bull, Vishnu's elephant, and Brahma's goose. Only the bull survives.

In part because the complex was dedicated to Shiva, and in part because Shiva's temple is the best restored, this is where you'll want to spend most of your time. Over the entrance is the head of Kali, a protection against evil from land. On the balustrade, the *naga* (serpent) guards against evil from the sea. The base has medallions with lions (an imported figure) as well as half-bird, half-human figures flanked by trees of good hope. Above these, on the outer balustrade, are carvings of classical Indian dancers and celestial beings.

The inner wall of the balustrade is carved with lively, sometimes frivolous, reliefs that tell the story of the *Ramayana*. From the east gate, walk around the temple clockwise to follow the story in sequence. The reliefs show free-flowing movement, much humor, and a love of nature. In contrast to Borobudur's reliefs, these carvings combine a celebration of the pleasures and pains of earthly life with scenes from Hindu mythology. They're more fun to look at (monkeys stealing fruit and bird-women floating in air), but the drama they portray—the establishment of order in the cosmos—is just as serious.

In the main chamber, at the top of the east stairway, a four-armed statue of Shiva the creator and destroyer stands on a lotus base. In the south chamber, Shiva appears as divine teacher, with a big beard and big stomach. The statue in the western chamber is Ganesha, Shiva's elephant-headed son. And in the northern chamber, Shiva's consort, Durga, kills the demon buffalo. An **archaeological museum** was opened in 1990, but its exhibits won't add much to your appreciation of the imposing architecture of the temples. However, you may want to stop at the information desk at the entrance to clarify any questions you have about the complex. Note that if you book through a tour operator, you can combine Prambanan with a visit to Borobudur or to Solo, 46 km (29 mi) northeast of Yogya. Minibuses go out to Prambanan from the Jalan Solo terminus in Yogya. If you hire a taxi, the round-trip will cost Rp 35,000. *No phone.* 🎫 *Admission.* ⏲ *Daily 6–5.*

OFF THE BEATEN PATH

CANDI SAMBISARI – The numerous other Buddhist and Hindu temples between Yogyakarta and Prambanan are in various states of ruin but merit at least a day of exploring. A great way to see them is to rent a bike and pack a lunch. Signs on the Yogya–Solo road point the way to the temples. Most are off the road, down small paths, and charge a small admission. Candi Sambisari, a small temple off the highway and 3 km (2 mi) back toward Yogya, is set in a sunken garden and is usually deserted—ideal for a quiet rest.

The Arts

Within walking distance of the temple is the **Prambanan theater complex,** where performances of the *Ramayana* are given in the evening, either at the Ramayana Theatre (open-air) or the Trimurti Theatre (indoor). The Ramayana ballet—an elaborate presentation with scores of dancers, a full-blown orchestra, and armies of people in monkey costumes strutting around the stage—is performed at various times throughout the year. From January through March, shows are usually once a week on Thursday. April through June and October through December, there are at least three performances (Tuesday, Wednesday, and Thursday). July through September features up to five performances a week—always on Tuesday, Wednesday, and Thursday, and usually on Saturday and Sunday. Hotel tour desks can arrange tickets and transportation, or you can share a taxi from the Tourist Information Center in Yogyakarta (☞ Visitor Information *in* Central and East Java Essentials, *below*) at 6:30. Public buses pass the theater's entrance, but they can be unreliable, and the drivers tend to gouge foreigners. ✉ *Jl. Raya Yogya-Solo, Km 16,* ☎ *0274/63918.* 🎫 *Admission.*

Solo

28 *60 km (38 mi) northeast of Yogyakarta, 40 km (25 mi) northeast of Prambanan.*

Solo (also known as Surakarta or Sala) is less Westernized than Yogya, with fewer tourists and much less hustling. The city has its own traditional batik designs and its own style of dance. And although its people are devoutly Muslim, their daily life is less religious. During the unrest that led to Suharto's resignation, Solo was the scene of widespread looting, and many banks and businesses were torched. As was the case in Jakarta, the ethnic Chinese were singled out, partly because of an economic imbalance and partly because of cultural tensions that go way back. Conflict with the Chinese-Indonesians started in Solo in the 18th century when Chinese merchants supported a rebellion against Keraton Kartosuro. Then, in 1965, the "year of living dangerously," there were conflicts between political factions dominated by the Chinese and other groups. A riot on November 19, 1983, again targeted Chinese, and much of their property was damaged or destroyed.

On the west side of town is the **Kraton Mangkunegaran,** a palace complex of carved, gilded, teak pavilions. The outer center pavilion, or *pendopo,* serves as the audience hall and is typical of a Javanese royal building. The Italian marble floor laid in 1925, the guardian lions from Berlin, and the 50-ft roof supported by teak pillars make the pendopo very grand. Its ceiling is painted with a flame motif bordered by symbols from the Javanese zodiac, designed with the eight mystical colors (yellow to ward off sleep, green to subdue desire, purple to keep away bad thoughts, etc.). The effect is gaudy but dramatic.

The museum, in the ceremonial pavilion just behind the main pendopo, displays dance ornaments, masks, jewelry, chastity belts for men and women, and wayang kulit and wayang golek. At center stage is the enclosed bridal bed (originally a room reserved for offerings to the rice goddess). To the left of the museum are the official reception rooms: a formal dining room, with a Javanese-style stained-glass window (made in Holland) and an ivory tusk with carvings that depict the wedding of Arjuna, one of the heroes of the *Mahabharata*; a mirrored parlor area; and a "bathing" room for royal brides. ✉ *Jl. Sugiyopranoto, no phone.* 🎫 *Admission.* ⏲ *Mon.–Thurs. and Sat. 9–noon, Fri. 9–11 AM.*

Solo's second palace, **Kraton Kasuhunan** (sometimes called Kraton Solo), is being rebuilt because it suffered terrible damage (its elaborate ceremonial pavilion was gutted) during a fire in 1985. Luckily, the museum—one of Central Java's best—was unharmed by the blaze. It contains a priceless collection of silver and bronze Hindu figures and Chinese porcelain, but the real treat is three royal carriages given to the sultanate by the Dutch in the 18th century. The English-speaking guide will help you appreciate the collection. ✉ *Jl. Coyudan,* ☎ *0271/44046.* 🎫 *Admission.* ⏲ *Sat.–Thurs. 9–noon.*

Dining and Lodging

$$ ✕ **Kusuma Sari.** This spotless restaurant is excellent for Indonesian fare, be it ayam goreng or a snack such as *resoles ragout* (chicken wrapped in a soft pancake)—and you can dine until 11 PM nightly. The tile floors, glass-topped wood tables, and plate-glass windows don't offer a lot of atmosphere, but choose a table by the window and watch the flow of pedestrians and becaks on the town's main street. ✉ *Jl. Slamet Riyadi 111,* ☎ *0271/37603. Reservations not accepted. No credit cards.*

$ ✕ **Ramayana.** For good, inexpensive local cuisine try this plain dining room a two-minute walk from the Kusuma Sahid Prince Hotel (☞

below). Dishes include such Indonesian staples as nasi goreng and satays. ✉ *Jl. Imam Bonjol 49,* ☎ *0271/46643. No credit cards.*

$$$ ★ ✕ 🏨 **Kusuma Sahid Prince Hotel.** Here three two-story buildings and outlying bungalows are set back from the street on 5 acres of landscaped gardens. The lobby veranda—the original *pendopo agung* (prince's courtyard)—is a wonderful place for tea or a cool drink. The quiet guest rooms are well maintained, and all the accoutrements—from the linens to the orchids—are quite fresh. Some rooms have a view of the enormous pool; those in the newer wing have up-to-date furnishings and always-welcome climate control. The formal Kasuma Sahid restaurant is light and airy, with white linen and polished silver. The menu includes such Indonesian specialities as chicken with jackfruit and fish wrapped in banana leaves—with the restaurant's own special blend of spices. Western dishes with nouvelle French influences and Indonesian accents are featured as well. ✉ *Jl. Sugiyopranoto 22,* ☎ *0271/46356,* FAX *0271/44788. 103 rooms. Restaurant, bar, pool, shops, meeting rooms, travel services. AE, DC, MC, V.*

$ 🏨 **Wisata Indah.** Though the plastered walls have hand smudges and the bathrooms are *mandi* style (a tub of water with a small bucket used to throw water over yourself; it doesn't sound like much, but it works quite well), the hot water is hot, the sheets are freshly laundered, and the staff is friendly and helpful. Outside each room are tables and chairs for breakfast (included in the price) and other meals that you can order from the bellboys. Negotiate the room rate before you sign in. ✉ *Jl. Slamet Riyadi 173,* ☎ *0271/46770. 27 rooms. MC, V.*

The Arts

At Solo's **Mangkunegaran Palace,** a gamelan orchestra performs each Saturday from 9 to 10:30 AM. Dance rehearsals are held on Wednesday from 10 to noon and on Monday and Friday afternoons.

Shopping

Solo's main shopping street is **Jalan Secoyudan.** In addition to a score of goldsmiths, you'll find antiques stores selling curios from the Dutch colonial days, as well as krises and other Javanese artifacts. Between Jalan Slamet Riyadi—which has many antiques shops—and Mangkunegaraan Palace, and just off Diponegoro is **Pasar Triwindu,** Solo's daily flea market, where hundreds of stalls sell everything from junk to old coins to batik. Bargain like crazy.

Solo has its own batik style, often using indigo, brown, and cream, as opposed to the brighter colors of Yogya's batiks. Prices are better in Solo, and you have some 300 batik factories to choose from. Aside from the shops along Jalan Secoyudan, visit **Pasar Klewer,** a huge batik market just outside the Kraton Solo with a fine selection of goods on the second floor. An established shop that sells batik and has batik-making demonstrations is **Dinar Hadi Batik Shop** on Jalan Dr. Rajiman (there's no phone).

Sangiran

29 *15 km (9 mi) north of Solo.*

In the late 19th century, Sangiran was the center for excavations in search of evidence to support Charles Darwin's theory of evolution. In 1891 Dutch physician Eugene Dubois discovered what he called "Java Man" (*Homo erectus*) in East Java not far from Sangiran, and the paper he published on his find rocked the scientific community. Afterward, older and more important Java Man finds were made, mostly around Sangiran. (Note that Sangiran is not to be confused with Sanggarahan, a village just outside Yogya known for its pleasure houses.) The museum here contains good exhibits about these discoveries, including a replica of a Java Man cranium (the originals are in musuems around the world); models of these ancestors of the Homo sapiens who lived some 250,000 years ago; and fossils of other forms of life, such as now-extinct elephants. To get here you can take a bus to Kaliso, then walk 30 minutes to the site; or take a taxi (Rp 15,000 round-trip from Solo). *No phone. 🎫 Admission. ⌚ Mon.–Sat. 9–4.*

Sukuh Temple

30 *35 km (21 mi) east of Solo.*

Sukuh Temple stands mysteriously and exotically alone and contains elements of Hinduism, Buddhism, and animism. Looking like an abbreviated pyramid, the delightful temple is full of cult symbols and objects with erotic suggestions. The structure dates from the 15th century, but no one knows who built it or what traditions were practiced in it. The place has a mystical atmosphere, enhanced by the lush surrounding rice terraces. A hired car (Rp 20,000) is the most convenient way to get here; the journey takes a good hour along winding, hilly roads. You can also come by bus, but it requires three changes: at Tertomoyo catch the bus to Tawangmangu, then get off at Karangpandan for a minibus to Sukuh. *🎫 Admission. ⌚ Daily 9–4.*

Surabaya

31 *260 km (150 mi) northeast of Solo, 320 km (198 mi) northeast of Yogyakarta.*

Surabaya isn't on the traditional tourist route, but with a rapidly expanding business and industrial base—it's Indonesia's second-largest city and for centuries its most important eastern seaport—it's looking for visitors. Hope springs eternal in the human breast.

The city's rich history includes its capture by Kublai Khan in the 13th century and by the Japanese during World War II. On November 10, 1945, the Dutch and their allies virtually flattened the community while trying to reclaim it after the Japanese surrender. The Surabayans resisted and raised the red-and-white Indonesian flag above the Hotel Majapahit (☞ Dining and Lodging, *below*). (November 10 is now celebrated throughout Indonesia as Revolutionary Heroes' Day, symbolizing the country's determination to throw off the colonial yoke.) Despite all the history here, the Hotel Majapahit and a 1950s Soviet submarine on display by the river are the only real sights.

Surabaya is the maritime jumping-off point for the little-visited island of Madura (famous for its bullfights) and for Sulawesi (☞ *below*); a transfer point for flights to Singapore, Hong Kong, and cities in Japan; and a good base from which to visit Mt. Bromo.

Dining and Lodging

$$$ ✕ **Indigo Restaurant and Bar.** Connected to the Hotel Majapahit (☞ *below*) and done in the same art-deco style, this 130-seat restaurant—with its long, dark-wood bar and its booths—feels like a posh café. The good "Euro-Asian" food includes such dishes as pizza cooked in a wood-burning oven. The baked goods are delicious, and the coffee is strong. *✉ Jl. Tunjungan 65, ☎ 031/545–4333. AE, DC, MC, V*

$$$ ✕ **Kuningan.** Fish is the specialty here, particularly shellfish. The traditional Chinese-style dining room is a comfortable place to peruse the extensive menu. *✉ Jl. Kalimantan, ☎ 031/534–5103. MC, V.*

$$–$$$ ✕ **Cafe Venezia.** Set in a charming old villa that has a garden, this eatery is a great place to take a break from the hectic streets. The intriguing mix of tasty food includes steaks and hamburgers as well as Japanese and Korean cuisine. ✉ *Jl. Ambengan 16,* ☎ *031/534–3335. MC, V.*

$$$ ★ **Hotel Majapahit.** Built in the center of town in 1910 by the Sarkies brothers (of Singapore's Raffles fame), this is one of Indonesia's few heritage hotels. Its expansive courts and green lawns became derelict after World War II, but in 1994 the Mandarin Oriental Hotel Group took over; a $27 million restoration was completed in 1996. Although modern luxuries were added, many of the original details were retained, including stained-glass windows, terrazzo floors, and colonial-style balconies and verandas. Rooms on the ground floor are large, but those upstairs are slightly quieter. The Presidential Suite, the largest of its kind in Indonesia, is more than 8,600 square ft. Furnishings are Javanese, and some are antiques. Batiks from Yogyakarta add splashes of color. There's a pool bar as well as three restaurants: Sarkies for Oriental seafood, Indigo for Eurasian, and Shima for Japanese. ✉ *Jl. Tunjungan 65, 60011,* ☎ *031/545–4333,* FAX *031/545–4111. 135 rooms, 15 suites. 3 restaurants, bar, pool, tennis court, health club, business services, meeting rooms. AE, DC, MC, V.*

$$$ **Hyatt Regency Surabaya.** This large, modern hotel has an 11-story wing and the 27-story Regency Tower with Regency Club rooms, meeting rooms, two business centers, and offices. An added convenience is an airline ticketing office. Rooms are typical Hyatt—comfortable; beige; fairly large; and furnished with wooden cabinets, king-size beds, and ferns in huge clay pots. The main lobby is popular with locals who come to drink and listen to a trio that plays sentimental favorites. Expats gather in the Tavern for drinks and light meals. ✉ *Jl. Jendral Basuki Rakhmat 106-128, 60275,* ☎ *031/531–1234; 800/233–1234 in the U.S.;* FAX *031/532–1508. 500 rooms. 2 restaurants, lobby lounge, coffee shop, pool, exercise room, shops, business services, meeting rooms, travel services. AE, DC, MC, V.*

Mt. Bromo

★ 32 *Tosari, a village on the mountain, is 90 km (55 mi) southeast of Surabaya.*

It's truly a thrill to approach the circular crater of this active volcano, one of a triad of precipitous peaks, and then look down into what seems like the depths of hell—a bubbling cauldron of water, ash, and sulphur that spews clouds of hot steam. The elemental eeriness of this sight is compounded by having to get up very early in the morning, hike to the top through the chilly air, and worship the sun as it comes up.

Part of the pleasure of visiting Mt. Bromo (Gunung Bromo) is that you're allowed much closer to the rim than at other volcanoes (those in Hawaii, for example), but be surefooted: in 1994 one American peering down the 350 ft to the crater's bottom fell in and never came out. Additionally, before you make any Bromo-related travel plans, verify that the mountain is open: sometimes the volcano is so active that the government prohibits people from visiting. However, the Tengger and Semaru peaks, which also surround the dusty valley here, are popular alternatives for trekking.

One way to visit Mt. Bromo is on an organized tour (☞ Guided Tours *in* Central and Eastern Java Essentials, *below*) that gets you to the rim of the caldera just before dawn. You can either leave Surabaya in the afternoon and stay overnight in a small bungalow hotel, or leave in the wee hours of the morning and return by lunchtime. Either way, the predawn walk will be chilly, so bring a sweater.

Central and Eastern Java Essentials

Arriving and Departing

BY AIRPLANE

Adisucipto Airport (☏ 274/566666) is 10 km (6 mi) east of Yogyakarta. From Jakarta's Soekarno-Hatta Airport, **Garuda** (☏ 0274/563706 in Yogyakarta; 031/545–7747 in Surabaya; 021/334425 in Jakarta) offers several daily flights; flying time is about 45 minutes. Seats fill up quickly, so reservations are essential. There are also flights into Yogya from Denpasar (Bali) and Surabaya on **Merpati** (☏ 0274/514272 in Yogyakarta; 031/568–8111 in Surabaya; 021/424-3608 in Jakarta). There are flights to Surabaya's **Juanda Airport,** about 20 km (12 mi) from downtown, on Garuda and Merpati from most Javanese cities, as well as from Bali and Lombok.

Between the Airport and Yogyakarta. A minibus runs until 6 PM from airport to the terminal on Jalan Senopati for Rp 250; from here you can catch a three-wheel becak to your hotel. Taxis to or from downtown charge Rp 5,500. The major hotels send their own minibuses to the airport.

Between the Airport and Surabaya. A taxi to town is your best bet. Cabs cost about Rp 15,000 and work on a coupon system so you need not bargain with the driver.

BY BUS

Night buses from Jakarta to Yogyakarta take about 14 hours and cost about Rp 12,250. Buses also run from Denpasar on Bali (12 hours), Bandung (7 hours), and Surabaya (8 hours). For information in Jakarta, contact: **Antar Lintas Sumatra** (✉ Jl. Jati Baru 87A, ☏ 021/320970) or **PT. ANS** (✉ Jl. Senen Raya 50, ☏ 021/340494).

BY CAR

Although the scenery may be beautiful, the long drive from Jakarta is slow going, and service areas are few and far between. It is advisable to hire a driver when traveling through Indonesia.

BY TRAIN

Trains from the Gambir Railway Station in Jakarta leave several times daily for Yogya's **Tugu Railway Station** (✉ Jl. Pasar Kembang, ☏ 274/514270 or 274/513785). The trip takes 7–12 hours and costs Rp 6,700–Rp 21,500, depending on whether the train is an express or a local and on the class of the ticket. The most comfortable trip is via the *Senja Utama Express,* which has sleeping cars and leaves Gambir at 7:20 PM and arrives in Yogya at 4:50 AM. The fares are Rp 18,000 for B class, Rp 21,000 for A class, and Rp 44,000 for executive class. There are also day and night trains from Bandung (an eight-hour trip) and from Surabaya (seven hours) as well as service to Surabaya from Jakarta, Yogyakarta, and Solo. (Note: Trains to and from Jakarta and points east and west use Surabaya's Pasar Turi terminal on Jalan Gresik in the north of the city; the Gubeng Train Station, on Jalan Gubeng Sumatra in the central part of Surabaya is used by trains going to and from Solo, Yogya, and Bandung.)

Another line links Surabaya (from the Pasar Turi terminal) to Banyuwangi, on the eastern tip of Java; from here ferries depart every 30 minutes for the 20-minute crossing to Bali. This is a slow train, though, and most non–air travelers to Bali prefer the night express buses. The train between Jakarta and Surabaya takes 14 hours overnight but, oddly, sleepers aren't available. The executive class (Rp 21,000), however—with air-conditioning, reclining seats, and dinner service—is quite comfortable. Business and Economy cost less, but you'll feel worse for wear after an overnight trip. Another option is to break the trip in Cirebon, a charming coastal town four hours east of Jakarta on the fast train, and about 10 hours west of Surabaya.

Getting Around

BY BECAK

Becaks (three-wheel pedicabs) are the main form of public transportation in most Javanese towns and cities (except Surabaya and Jakarta, where they're banned). Yogya alone has about 25,000 of them, most with paintings of mountains on their fenders. Solo has quite a few, as well. In nice weather, they're a relaxing way to travel. The proper fare is about Rp 1000 per km (½ mi); be sure to negotiate with your driver before starting out.

BY BICYCLE

In Yogya, you can rent bicycles for Rp 4,000 a day from the **Hotel Indonesia** (✉ Sosromenduran IV, ☎ 0274/587659). The **Restaurant Malioboro** (✉ Jl. Malioboro 67, no phone) also has bikes for rent.

BY BUS

As a rule, you can simply go to the bus station in any Javanese city and catch a bus for most anywhere on the island. The shorter bus trips are tolerable; for longer hauls it's best to stick with trains. For day trips between cities minibuses are a favored way to go. They leave for Solo throughout the day (7–5) from Yogyakarta's **Terminal Terban** (✉ Jl. Diponegoro near Jl. P.Mangkubumi) or from Jalan Sudirman or Jalan Solo. From Solo's **Gilligan minibus station,** which is next to the main Tirtonadi Bus Terminal on Jalan Dr. Setiabudi in the northwest of town, take a *bemo,* or minivan (Rp 300), or a becak (Rp 750) the 3 km (1.8 mi) into town. To reach Mt. Bromo, you can take a bus from Surabaya's **Bungurasih Bus Station** to Probolinggo and change for a bemo up to Pasuruan; from there take a minibus up to Tosari. To get from Tosari to the crater's rim, another 7½ km (4½ mi), you can rent a four-wheel-drive vehicle or, if you're fit, make the two-hour uphill trudge.

BY TAXI

In Yogya you can catch taxis in front of the larger hotels; in general, they don't cruise the streets. Taxis are metered; the flag-fall charge is Rp 800 and covers the first kilometer. A shared taxi from Yogya to Solo costs Rp 2,500 per person.

BY TRAIN

The train from Yogya to Solo takes about one hour; from Solo to Surabaya takes about four. The train is a great way to watch Java pass by. Executive class is air-conditioned and has comfortable reclining seats, business has padded seats but no air-conditioning, and third class can be like chaos on the rails.

Contacts and Resources

EMERGENCIES

Ambulance: ☎ 118. **Hospitals:** Bethesda Hospital (✉ Yogyakarta, ☎ 0274/588876), Dr. Sardjito Hospital (✉ Yogyakarta, ☎ 0274/587333), RS Budi Mulia (✉ Surabaya, ☎ 031/534–1821), RS Darmo (✉ Surabaya, ☎ 031/561–8824), and RSUD Dr. Soetomo (✉ Surabaya, ☎ 031/550–1111). **Fire:** ☎ 113. **Police:** ☎ 110.

ENGLISH-LANGUAGE BOOKSTORES

There are several stores with used books along Jalan Prawirotaman in the south of Yogyakarta. In Surabaya the best bookshops are in the three main malls:

Surabaya Mall (✉ Jl. Kusuma Bangsa 116, ☎ 031/534-3002), **Surabaya Plaza** (✉ Jl. Pemuda 31-37, ☎ 031/531–5088), and **Tunjungan Plaza** (✉ Jl. Basuki Rachmat 8-12, ☎ 031/531–1507).

GUIDED TOURS

Hotels and travel agencies in Yogya can arrange the following tours, either in a private chauffeured car or as a group tour by bus:

Art and Handicrafts. A five-hour tour of the local craft centers for leather puppets, wood carving, silver work, batik, and pottery.
Borobudur. An eight-hour tour of Yogyakarta; the countryside; and the Borobudur, Mendut, and Pawon temples.
Prambanan. A three-hour tour of the temple complex.
Yogya City. A three-hour tour including the sultan's palace, Sono Budoyo Museum, Kota Gede silver works, and batik and wayang workshops.
Yogya Dieng Plateau. A 10-hour tour of the Dieng Plateau, with its spectacular scenery, sulfur springs, and geysers, plus a visit to Borobudur.

In Surabaya, the largest tour agency is **Orient Express** (✉ Jl. Jendral Basuki Rakhamat 78, ☎ 031/515253), which will meet you at the airport or anywhere else in Surabaya. Day tours (Rp 436,000 per person) depart Surabaya at 1 AM. Overnight tours (Rp 927,000 per person) depart at 3 PM for the Bromo Cottages in Tosari, where the accommodation is simple, modern, and clean. You rise at 3:30 AM and travel by Jeep up Mt. Penanjakan (9,088 ft) for spectacular sunrise views. Afterward the Jeep takes you to the sea of sand—an area of fine volcanic ash bleached by the sun—and then to the stairway to the rim of the Bromo crater; finally it's back to the cottages for breakfast before returning to Surabaya.

You can also rent a chauffeured car and do the trip independently for about Rp 100,000, plus the fee for a Jeep on the last leg of the journey. Try **P. T. Zebra Nusantart** (✉ Jl. Tegalsari 107, Surabaya, ☎ 031/511777); the firm also has a representative at the Surabaya Hyatt.

TRAVEL AGENCIES

Yogya's main companies include **Nitour** (✉ Jl. K. H. A. Dahlan 71, ☎ 0274/375165) and **Satriavi** (✉ Hotel Ambarrukmo Palace, ☎ 0274/566488 ext. 7135). American Express cardholders can contact **Pacto Ltd. Tours and Travel** (✉ Garuda Hotel, Jl. Malioboro 60, ☎ 0274/565345). The locally operated **Intan Pelangi** (✉ Mutiara Hotel, Jl. Malioboro 18, ☎ 0274/562895) is also helpful.

In Surabaya: American Express cardholders can contact **Pacto Ltd. Tours and Travel** (✉ Jl. Jendral Basuki Rachmad 106, ☎ 031/532–6385) and **Nitour Incorporation** (✉ Jl. Urip Sumoharjo 63, ☎ 031/534–1247).

VISITOR INFORMATION

Yogyakarta's **Tourist Information Office** (✉ Jl. Malioboro 16, ☎ 0274/562811) has maps, schedules of events, bus and train information, and a helpful staff. It's open Monday through Saturday from 8 to 8. There's also a tourist booth at the railway station. The **Solo Tourist Information Office** (✉ Jl. Slamet Riyadi 275, ☎ 0271/46501) is open Monday–Saturday 8–5.

In Surabaya you can try the **Surabaya Tourist Office** (✉ Jl. Darmakali 35, ☎ 031/575448) or the **East Java Tourist Office** (✉ Jl. Pemuda 118, ☎ 031/532–4499). Both are open weekdays 8:30 to 5.

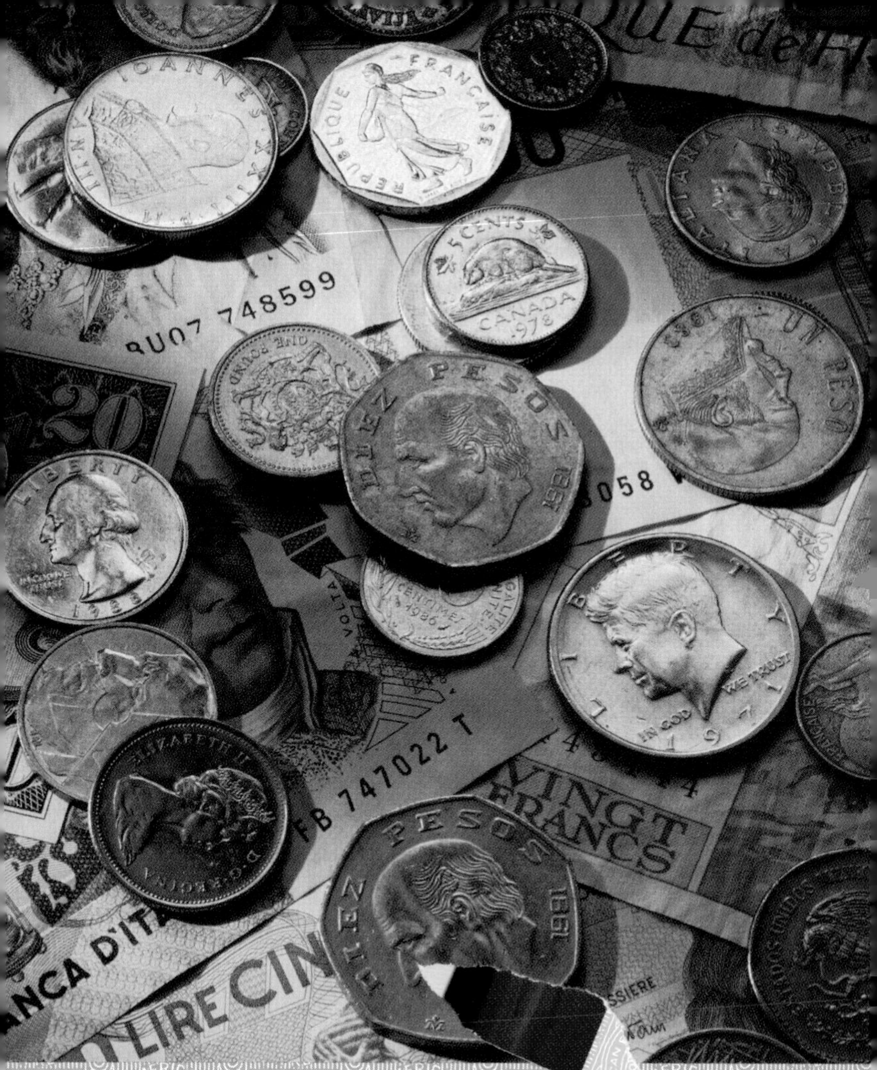
REPUBLIQUE FRANCAISE
5 CENTS
CANADA
1978
DIEZ PESOS
LIBERTY
VINGT FRANCS
FB 747022 T
LIRE

3 Bali

Early seafarers described Bali as a mountainous tropical paradise where maidens walked half nude and entire villages danced for the dead. Bali is still steeped in religious rituals—part Hindu, part animist—that color every belief. Just as colorful are the island's enchanting traditional dancers; its flower-bedecked temples; its elegant hand-woven textiles; and its alluring beaches, volcanos, and jungles.

THE "MAGIC" OF BALI HAS ITS ROOTS in the fact that the island is religiously distinct from the rest of Indonesia: unlike their Muslim neighbors, the Balinese are Hindus. Their faith also contains elements of Buddhism and of ancient animist beliefs indigenous to the archipelago. Hindu culture came to Bali as early as the 9th century; by the 14th century, the island was part of the Hindu Majapahit empire of East Java. When that empire fell to Muslim invaders, Majapahit aristocrats, scholars, artists, and dancers fled to Bali, consolidating Hindu culture and religion here.

To the Balinese, every living thing contains a spirit; when they pick a flower as an offering to the gods, they first say a prayer to the flower. All over the island, from the capital city of Denpasar to the tiniest village, plaited baskets filled with flowers and herbs lie on the sidewalks, on the prows of fishing boats, and in markets. These offerings are made from dawn till dusk, to placate evil spirits and honor helpful ones. *Garudas* (stone figures) guard entries to temples, hotels, and homes. The black-and-white-checked cloths around the statues' waists symbolize the balance between good and evil. Maintaining that harmony is the life work of every Balinese.

The island's geography also contributes to Bali's religion and rituals: the focus of offerings to the spirits is on Gunung Agung, the 9,866-ft "Mother Mountain," which is considered the holiest site on the island. Agung is also known for its deadly eruption in 1963, but other active volcanoes rise 6,560–9,840 ft along Bali's mountainous interior. It's the ash fallout from these high summits, and the dependable rainfall from storms caught between them, that provides fertile valleys for the famed emerald rice terraces. At its edges, Bali is framed by thick mangrove swamps, sweeping white beaches, and lively coral reefs, offering a variety of ecosystems for wildlife such as mousedeer, monkeys, dolphins, giant turtles, and more than 300 bird species, including the rare Bali starling.

Although the island is only 140 km (84 mi) long by 80 km (48 mi) wide, a week wouldn't be enough to fully appreciate Bali's beaches, temples, volcanoes, and towns. With Indonesia's most developed tourist infrastructure, Bali has several beach areas on its southern coast, where 90% of its visitors stay. Each has its own appeal, and all are within easy reach of one another.

Pleasures and Pastimes

Architecture

One of the pleasures of being in Bali is walking through its temples and dwellings built in vastly different styles. Pura Besakih, the island's holiest temple, is a maze of stone steps that graces the slopes of Gunung Agung (if you have time for just one temple, this should be it). The sunsets from such religious spots as Pura Ulu Watu, on the island's southwestern nub, and Pura Tanah Lot, along the curve of the southwestern coast, are breathtaking. Other intriguing architectural sites include the Kertagosa palace in Klungkung, with its detailed murals of history and the afterlife, and the temples at Goa Gajah near Ubud. If you have time, stroll through the grounds of some of the major hotels on the island, many of which have won awards for their unique designs.

Beaches

Many travelers never bother to even leave the beaches; little wonder given each perfect and unique tropical setting. The best are on the island's west side, including the resort area of Jimbaran and the high-energy Kuta strip. Classic eastern beaches are Nusa Dua and Sanur. The black volcanic sands of northern Lovina continue to attract many travelers as well.

Dining

Although seafood is plentiful on Bali, the island specialty is *bebek* (duck)—a dark, succulent meat that is frequently grilled or steamed with spices and always must be ordered a day in advance. Black rice pudding is another island favorite; like the duck, it should be ordered a day ahead. One of the most memorable ways to sample Balinese food is to attend a special feast, whether as part of a village ceremony or a planned restaurant event. Note that since this is a Hindu island—not Muslim—you'll see pork (and alcohol) on the menu.

Lodging

Bali has accommodations for every budget. However, since several resorts are consistently rated the best in the world by top travel and leisure publications, luxury is the way to go if you can. The classic village setting of Ubud's Amandari and Four Seasons, the lovely seascapes of Manggis' Amankila and Jimbaran's Ritz-Carlton, an the Amanusa's hilltop overview of Nusa Dua truly *are* worth the cost of $500 a night. There are also plenty of classy choices for less, though you may have to forego the private plunge pools, sunken tubs, and other deluxe comforts. Ubud's Kokokan Hotel and Kuta's Poppies Cottages all offer a slice of serenity for less than $100 a night.

Outdoor Activities

Despite the hazards of narrow country lanes and rugged mountain highways, bicycling is popular on Bali. A two-week circuit covers the island, and most large hotels have mountain bikes on hand for short jaunts. Both of Bali's world-class golf courses—one is in Nusa Dua, the other in Bedugul—offer special hotel and golf packages. River rafting is a growing sport in the central valleys near Ubud, and several companies offer day and overnight trips from southern tourist areas as well. Nearly every southern beach hotel offers water sports—boating, parasailing, scuba diving, snorkeling, surfing, windsurfing—and many travel agencies offer tours that include lessons. Serious divers (and trekkers) can head for the reefs and trails of Bali Barat National Park on the west coast.

Shopping

Bali has always been a shopper's paradise, and with the fall of the rupiah, quality crafts and merchandise have become affordable even for those on the lowest of budgets. *Everything* is a bargain here; the trick is to get the best quality. Classic items include wood carvings, silver filigree, masks, paintings, batik, and furniture, all of which can be found or made to order in artisans shops along the road from Denpasar—through Batubulan, Celuk, Mas, and Batuan—to Ubud.

Exploring Bali

Bali is a worthwhile stopover for any amount of time—a couple of days as part of an Indonesian or Asian circle tour, a couple of weeks as an individual holiday, or a couple of months as a relaxing sabbatical. Regardless of how much time you have, the secret to enjoying this island is to take things slowly; choose a single venture for each day, and totally immerse yourself in the experience.

Great Itineraries

IF YOU HAVE 3–4 DAYS

Spend two nights at one of the southern beach areas—**Jimbaran Bay** ① if you want lovely sunsets and luxury hotels, **Nusa Dua** ② or **Sanur** ④ if you desire quiet beaches and large resorts, and **Kuta** ③ if you want to party with the crowds. Kuta is also known for its shopping and its fine restaurants, so make time to browse or enjoy a meal. If you're more interested in culture than souvenirs, consider spending sundown at either **Pura Luhur Ulu Watu** at the end of the Bukit Peninsula or **Pura Tanah Lot** near Canggu on the main southwestern coast. Early on the third morning, head north to **Ubud** ⑦ and have lunch in town. Then take an afternoon temple tour or a stroll through the Monkey Forest. The next morning, stop in **Batubulan, Celuk,** and **Mas** to shop for carvings, jewelry, and other souvenirs before taking a late afternoon flight out.

IF YOU HAVE 7 DAYS

Settle into a southern beach resort for three nights, taking a day to enjoy the scenery; also plan two late-afternoon trips, one to either **Pura Ulu Watu** or **Pura Tanah Lot** for the sunset and one to **Kuta** ③ for shopping and nightlife. Head north to **Ubud** ⑦ the fourth day, pausing in **Celuk, Mas,** and **Batubulan** for craft shopping along the way. Spend three nights in Ubud, using the first full day for a scenic tour that includes the **Gunung Batur** ⑨ area and **Pura Besakih.** On the second day, rent a bicycle, pack a picnic, head for **Bedulu** ⑥ and the **Goa Gajah** and discover the village backroads. Or book a cultural tour that includes Goa Gajah and **Klungkung** ⑪ before heading out by air the next morning.

IF YOU HAVE 10 DAYS

Fly in and head immediately to **Ubud** ⑦, where you can spend four days exploring temples and craft villages at your leisure. Make the **Gunung Batur** ⑨ area and the **Pura Besakih** priorities, and be sure to catch at least one dance performance and temple ceremony while you're in Bali's cultural core. Head east for a historical tour of **Klungkung** ⑪ before spending the night on the eastern shores in **Balina Beach and Manggis** ⑭ or **Candidasa** ⑮. The next morning, stop by **Padangbai** ⑬ to view the fishing boats before heading to the southern beaches. Spend the next three or four nights in the south sunning, sightseeing, or shopping. Don't miss **Pura Luhur Ulu Watu, Pura Tanah Lot** (with tea or dinner at the Hotel Tugu), and a day trip to **Denpasar** ⑤.

IF YOU HAVE 14 DAYS

Spend your first two nights in the south for a taste of the beaches before heading north to **Ubud** ⑦ for four nights. Here, you can visit the temples and villages on tours or with your own vehicle, then spend a day traveling north through Kintimani to **Lovina** ⑱. Spend two nights here and then take the northern coastal road to **Balina Beach and Manggis** ⑭ as well as **Candidasa** ⑮, where you can spend two nights enjoying eastern views of Lombok's Gunung Rinjani. Finally, take a morning tour of cultural sights in **Klungkung** ⑪ and make an afternoon of the museums and markets in **Denpasar** ⑤ before heading south to the beaches again for your final days.

THE SOUTH AND DENPASAR

Jimbaran Bay

★ ❶ *1,100 km (682 mi) southeast of Jakarta, 3 km (2 mi) south of Ngurah Rai Airport, 20 km (12 mi) southwest of Denpasar.*

Once a sleepy fishing village, Jimbaran Bay is now a playground for guests of several luxury resorts. On the western side of the Bukit Peninsula to the south of Kuta, the area's white-sand beaches, glowing sunsets, and sapphire waves with colorful fishing boats create a captivating scene. An offshore reef offers makes the waters gentle enough for swimming.

OFF THE BEATEN PATH

PURA LUHUR ULU WATU – About 15 km (9 mi) south of Jimbaran—at the end of the Bukit Peninsula—is this cliff-side temple overlooking the ocean. Originally constructed in the 11th century as one of Bali's six main territorial places of worship, Ulu Watu was rebuilt 500 years later and has been renovated several times since, giving the current structure a mix of old and new styles. The split-gate entrance imitates a curving set of garuda wings and leads to the outer courtyard, where a second gate is framed by statues of Ganesha (the elephant-headed god and son of Shiva) and topped by a fearsome guardian. The inner court houses a smaller, three-tier temple. The sunsets from here are spectacular (visitors arrive in droves to view them), and the nearby beaches offer fine surfing.

Dining and Lodging

$ ✕ **Kakul Cafe.** This upbeat, open-air café brings the cuisine of the southwestern United States to one of Bali's poshest corners. Its bright, mango-color exterior makes it hard to miss; its mango-color tablecloths, moss-green chairs, and funky geometric wall art make it hard to forget. The hearty fare includes a tasty shrimp-and-pepper salad; baked-potato soup; pepper steak; and the familiar pizza, pasta, and quesadillas. ✉ *Jl. Bukit Permai 5c,* ☎ *0361/702815. AE, MC, V.*

$$$$ ★ ✕🏨 **The Ritz-Carlton, Bali.** The breathtaking opulence here is apparent as soon as you step into the entryway: a series of pools descend in falls toward a stunning view of the Indian Ocean. Unpolished marble surrounds the fountains and koi ponds; carved antique wooden benches adorn the hallways; and a replica of Klungkung's Kertagosa Palace mural graces the lobby ceiling. The pool area not only has a two-tiered pool but also a walk-through grotto with an 11,000-gallon saltwater aquarium. Most rooms in the four-story main building have ocean views; all have a Western-style decor with a slightly Balinese flair. The thatched-roof villas have striking Balinese accents, *bale bungong* (cushioned lounging areas), and private plunge pools. At the 130-seat Langit Theatre and open-air restaurant, you can watch Balinese dancing while dining. The intimate Padi's restaurant overlooks the bay and is next to a pond lined with yellow and red heliconias. Try the sweet-and-sour shrimp with turmeric or the yellow chicken curry in a clay pot. There's also a rijsttafel buffet that offers a taste of Indonesia's most famous dishes. ✉ *Jl. Karang Mas Sejahtera, 80364,* ☎ *0361/702222,* FAX *0361/702555. 277 rooms, 16 suites, 36 villas. 6 restaurants, 6 bars, pool, massage, spa, putting green, tennis court, beach, snorkeling, windsurfing, boating, children's programs, meeting rooms. AE, DC, MC, V.*

$$$ ✕🏨 **Bali Cliff Resort and Hotel.** The grounds here are a little run down, but you can't beat the locale along rough-hewn cliffs, 10 km (6 mi) southeast of Jimbaran and at the very tip of the island. Rooms are done up tastefully in pastels; suites and villas offer more space and elegance, with marble floors; hand-carved furnishings; sitting areas; spa baths; and balconies. You can stroll through mazes of gardens and fountains to an on-site temple. Dances are performed on the lower beach as you dine by candlelight in a nearby cave—an unusual and memorable experience. A ride down a sloping, glass-enclosed tram takes you to the multilevel Ocean restaurant, whose tables are in thatched-roof pavilions overlooking the surf. Although portions aren't huge, the food is tasty—spring rolls are crispy and hot, and the grilled fish is very fresh. Just beware of the mean local macaque troop, which will rush the tables for tidbits if not shooed away from afar. ✉ *Jl. Purah Batu Pageh, Ungasan,* ☎ *0361/771992,* FAX *0361/771993. 180 rooms. 3 restaurants, 3 bars, coffee shop, in-room safes, pool, spa, health club, shops, theater, laundry service, meeting rooms. AE, MC, V.*

Bali

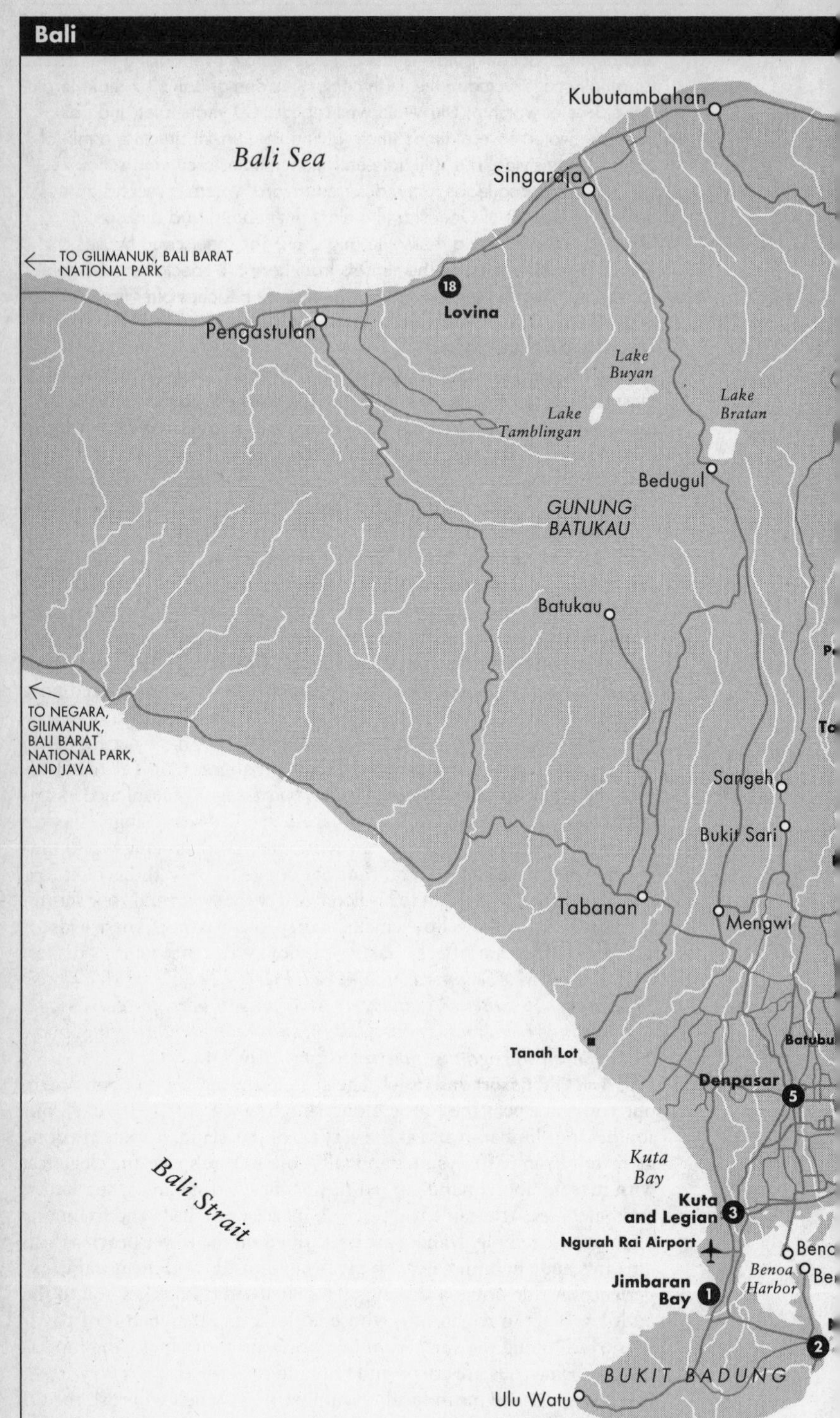
Kubutambahan
Bali Sea
Singaraja
TO GILIMANUK, BALI BARAT NATIONAL PARK
18
Lovina
Pengastulan
Lake Buyan
Lake Bratan
Lake Tamblingan
Bedugul
GUNUNG BATUKAU
Batukau
TO NEGARA, GILIMANUK, BALI BARAT NATIONAL PARK, AND JAVA
Sangeh
Bukit Sari
Tabanan
Mengwi
Tanah Lot
Denpasar
5
Kuta Bay
Kuta and Legian
3
Ngurah Rai Airport
Benoa Harbor
Jimbaran Bay
1
2
BUKIT BADUNG
Ulu Watu
Bali Strait

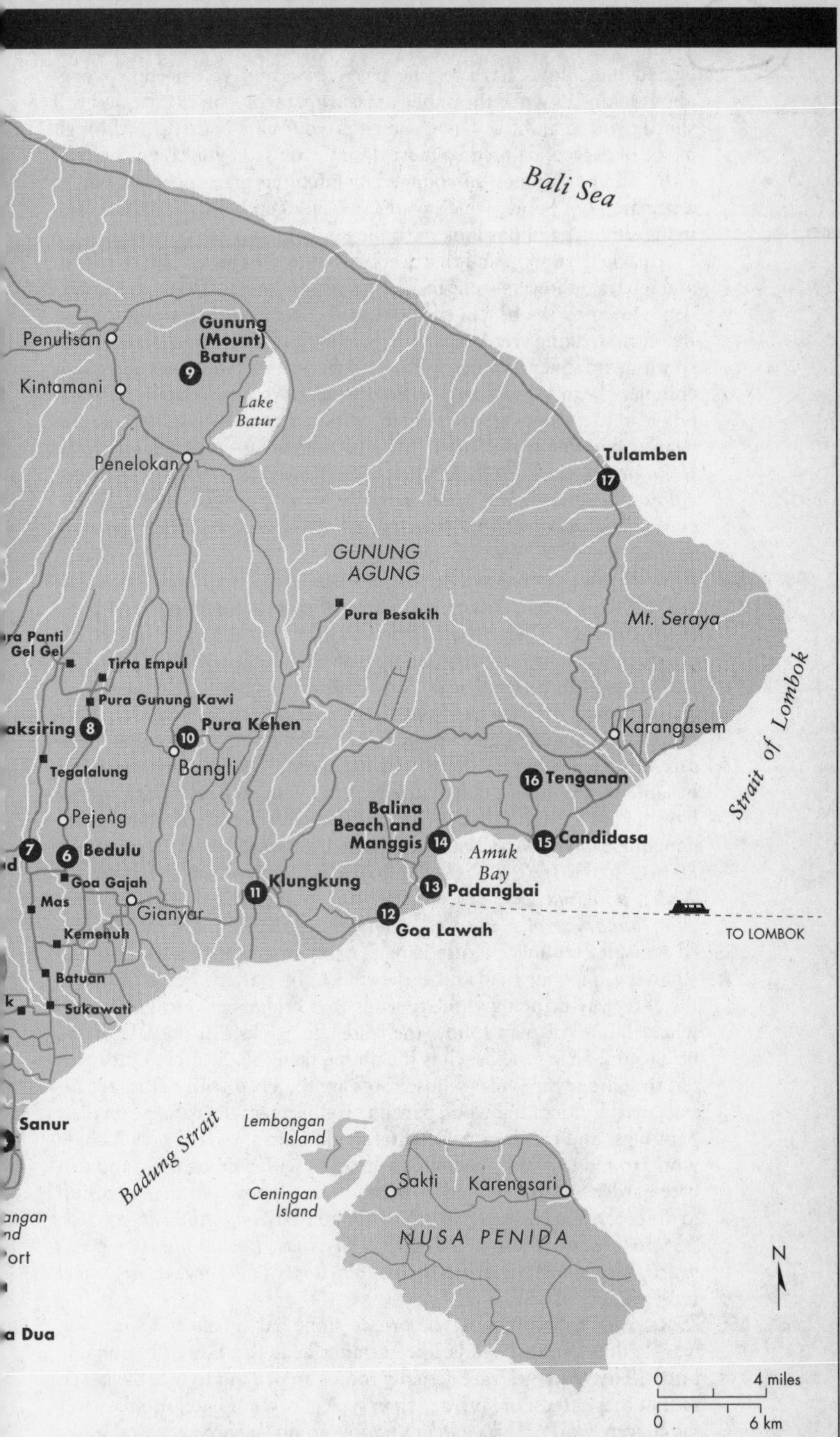

Bali Sea
Gunung (Mount) Batur
9
Penulisan
Kintamani
Lake Batur
Penelokan
Tulamben
17
GUNUNG AGUNG
Pura Besakih
Mt. Seraya
ra Panti
Gel Gel
Tirta Empul
Pura Gunung Kawi
aksiring
8
10
Pura Kehen
Bangli
Karangasem
Strait of Lombok
Tegalalung
16
Tenganan
Pejeng
Balina Beach and Manggis
14
15
Candidasa
7
6
Bedulu
Amuk Bay
Goa Gajah
11
Klungkung
13
Padangbai
Mas
Gianyar
12
Goa Lawah
TO LOMBOK
Kemenuh
Batuan
Sukawati
Sanur
Badung Strait
Lembongan Island
Ceningan Island
Sakti
Karengsari
NUSA PENIDA
N
a Dua
0
4 miles
6 km

$$$$ ★ **Four Seasons Resort.** Set on 35 acres, this veritable village of luxury bungalows rises from the shore some 150 ft up a hill. The most elevated bungalows have terrific bay views, and you needn't worry about hiking down to the public areas from them—an electric taxi will shuttle you to and fro. Once you enter your villa courtyard (through a pair of carved, painted Balinese doors), you're in your own personal oasis. Stepping stones, surrounded by luminous green pebbles, lead to a private pool beside which water splashes gently in a fountain. The living-dining pavilions look onto the pool and bay beyond. Bedrooms have peaked bamboo-and-thatch roofs; bathrooms have huge, deep tubs and separate showers—one inside and one out in a small courtyard garden. Down by the beach, the pool spills over a 20-ft waterfall into a free-form soaking area below. A new 10,000-square-ft spa features nine spacious treatment rooms, a fitness facility, a refreshment center, and complete beauty services. The Four Seasons is very much a self-contained resort; there are no villages within a couple of miles, and the nearest building is the Ritz-Carlton, a mile or so down the beach. ✉ *Jl. Bukit Permai, 80361,* ☎ *0361/701010,* FAX *0361/701020. 147 bungalows. 5 restaurants, pool, massage, spa, 2 tennis courts, beach, snorkeling, windsurfing, boating, shops, laundry service, meeting rooms, travel services. AE, DC, MC, V.*

$$$–$$$$ **Hotel Inter-Continental Bali.** Five stone garudas wrapped in black-and-white checked cloths greet you from their posts in a large lotus pond at the entrance. Their brooding presence conveys a deeper sense of Indonesian formality here than is found at other large resorts nearby. Opulence readily mixes with tradition in the ornate building's design, from the intricately detailed pavilions to the carefully chosen interior decorations that highlight every room. Hardwood floors, light-wood furniture with cream and rose cushions, and carefully hewn stone and metal ornaments adorn the guest quarters. A blue-tile pool rests just over the bay; next to it, a large thatch-roof pavilion with oversize decorative fish dangling from its eaves is an ideal place for sunsets. ✉ *Jl. Uluwatu 45, 80361,* ☎ *0361/701888,* FAX *0361/701777. 214 rooms. 2 restaurants, 2 bars, pool, massage, beach, snorkeling, windsurfing, boating, dance club, laundry service, meeting rooms, travel services. AE, MC, V.*

$$$ ★ **Pansea Puri Bali.** Luxury is reasonably priced at this resort down a narrow, one-lane road and at the edge of Jimbaran's beach. A black-tile entryway dripping with ivy leads to a bridge between two ponds where large koi play follow-the-leader in packs. To the left of the bridge and facing the beach is the dining pavilion. Scattered throughout the gardens are villas whose roofs are thatched with rice straw. Inside, marble floors and wood paneling complement the Balinese textiles, paintings, and carvings. Special treats that are standard here include wraparound terraces, spacious bathrooms with sunken tubs, and private gardens with open-air showers. A free-form pool that edges up to the beach and lagoon makes the best of the bay. ✉ *Jl. Uluwatu, 80361,* ☎ *0361/701605,* FAX *0361/701320. 41 villas. Restaurant, bar, pool, beach, snorkeling, windsurfing, boating, library, laundry service, travel services. AE, MC, V.*

$$–$$$ **Keraton Bali Cottages.** The ornate stone bas-reliefs and sparkling marble floors of its pagoda-like entrance belie this hotel's reasonable prices. The "cottages" are actually rooms angled out to face the beach so that they offer more privacy than typical rows of hotel rooms—and the concept works. Thick gardens tumble around a narrow central walkway lined by the dwellings' small raised porches. All rooms have garden views—but no tubs (only showers); suites also have balconies, sitting rooms, and whirlpool tubs. The decor is simple and neat, and the large grounds, numerous facilities, and reasonable rates attract many European and Indonesian guests. ✉ *Jl. Mrajapati (Box 2023), 80361,* ☎

0361/701961, FAX *0361/701991. 89 rooms, 10 suites. 2 restaurants, 3 bars, coffee shop, pool, snorkeling, windsurfing, boating, billiards, theater, laundry service, travel services. AE, MC, V.*

$ **Puri Bamboo Bungalows.** This small hotel offers comfortable accommodations and a convenient location without the added expenses for opulent facilities. Each neat, two-story cottage has four rooms—two upstairs and two down—all with small, simply furnished bedrooms. Bathrooms have tubs and stone gardens; sinks are in the main room. Superior suites have porches, and deluxe suites include a sitting area. In the middle of the cottages, a pool with a swim-up bar is the center of activity, even though the beach is just steps away. ✉ *Jl. Pangeracikan, 80361,* ☎ *0361/701377,* FAX *0361/701440. 20 rooms, 18 suites. Restaurant, bar, pool, beach, gift shop, laundry service, travel services. AE, MC, V.*

Nightlife

Nightlife here is centered on resort bars. If you tire of the bars at your hotel, barhopping from resort to resort is an option. The **Kakul Kafe** (✉ Jl. Bukit Permai 5c, ☎ 0361/702815) attracts a crowd on weekends. The **Monkey Forest Fun Pub and Disco** (☎ 0361/701888) at the Hotel Inter-Continental Bali is a popular hangout. The **Tarian Open Stage** (☎ 0361/701961) at the Keraton Bali Cottages offers cultural dances on Saturday nights, including an Indonesian buffet dinner.

Nusa Dua

❷ *10 km (6 mi) southeast of Jimbaran Bay, 8 km (5 mi) southeast of Ngurah Rai Airport, 30 km (18 mi) southeast of Denpasar.*

Nusa Dua, a former burial ground, consists of two tiny islands linked to the mainland by a reinforced sand spit. Unlike Kuta and Sanur, this is an entirely planned resort, with no indigenous community. Although you have to travel inland from here to see the real Bali, Nusa Dua's beaches are wide and peaceful, and its self-contained hotels are luxurious.

Dining and Lodging

$ ✕ **Cafe Gong Bali.** At a bend in the road leading into Benoa (3 km/2 mi north of Nusa Dua), you'll come to a wooden temple–style structure with a fish-shape sailboat out front. Although the busy roadside locale and loud reggae music add little to the ambience, this watering hole is still popular with Westerners. The reasonably priced Indonesian fare includes snacks of spring rolls and gado gado, a rijsttafel buffet, and à la carte entrées such as crispy Balinese duck or fresh lobster. ✉ *Jl. Pratama 88, Tanjung Benoa,* ☎ *0361/773738. AE, MC, V.*

$ ✕ **Ulam.** Right on Nusa Dua's prime shopping street, Ulam is favored by travelers for its Indonesian dishes and seafood. Upon being seated in the dark, cozy dining room, women diners receive flowers to put in their hair—and after dinner a free glass of local whiskey is served. Set meals are a specialty: the "seafood parade" consists of juice or soda; avocado-and-shrimp cocktail or crab-and-corn soup; a selection of grilled fish, shrimp, crab, and squid; and fresh fruit or a Balinese pancake. The busy bar caters to the Western crowd, and there's free transportation to and from Nusa Dua hotels. ✉ *Jl. Pantai Mengiat 14,* ☎ *0361/771590. AE, MC, V.*

$$$$ ★ ✕ **Amanusa.** The rough, winding road through the Bali Golf & Country Club and to the Amanusa disguises the resort's opulence. Shining marble floors and thick columns welcome you into the stone main building, which towers above a reflection pond and a wide, sapphire-tile swimming pool. From here, the views of the forested peninsula stretch to the Indian Ocean, and most of the enormous villas—built into the land's gentle folds—share this vista at least partially. Each also has checkered-marble floors; rich teak furniture; a canopy bed; a garden; a

sunken marble tub; and an outdoor shower. Individual bale bungong are outside on the terraces; eight villas also have plunge pools. Chauffeurs will drive you to the resort's beach club—on a pristine strip of sand five minutes' away—where there are sun chairs, cushioned *bales* (raised, open resting pavilions), and a restaurant. You can toast the sunset—seated beneath a canopy of bougainvillea beside the pool—while gamelan music is played. Afterward, the Terrace restaurant's candle-lighted tables provide a romantic dinner setting above the peninsula's twinkling lights. Indonesian and Thai food are the highlights. Try the prawn salad with coconut, chili, lemon, and basil and the rich, red curry with chicken, peanuts, and coconut. Sumptuous desserts include chocolate-caramel-mousse cake and date pudding with butterscotch sauce. ✉ *Jl. Nusa Dua Selatan (Box 33), 80363,* ☎ *0361/772333,* FAX *0361/772335. 35 villas. 2 restaurants, pool, golf privileges, 2 tennis courts, spa, windsurfing, boating, mountain bikes, library, laundry service, meeting rooms. AE, DC, MC, V.*

$$$–$$$$ ★ ✕🏨 **Sheraton Laguna.** The garden setting here attracts an international crowd intent on relaxation and seclusion. (Those here on business stay next door at the Sheraton Nusa Indah convention center complex.) The central courtyard has free-form swimming pools, lagoons, and waterfalls that are connected by stone steps and curving wooden bridges. Ground-level rooms have balconies or patios; upper suites have large balconies that drip with bougainvillea; and suites have large sitting areas and marble baths with oversize tubs. One staff member is assigned to take care of all your needs. If that's not enough pampering, visit the spa, where you'll find indoor and outdoor whirlpool baths; a long bathing pool with several waterfalls; and a massage and treatment villa with marble floors and a cushioned bale. La Trattoria restaurant has a familiar Italian look, and its bright decor and garden views make it a popular gathering place. The breakfast buffet includes meats, fresh baked goods, and local fruits. Indonesian, Italian, and other Western specialities are offered throughout the day, and theme buffets and live entertainment are scheduled nightly. ✉ *Jl. Raya Nusa Dua (Box 2077), 80363,* ☎ *0361/771327; 800/325–3535 in the U.S.;* FAX *0361/771326. 211 rooms, 65 suites. 4 restaurants, in-room safes, pool, wading pool, 2 tennis courts, spa, exercise room, business services, travel services. AE, DC, MC, V.*

$$$ ✕🏨 **Hotel Melia Benoa.** The furnishings at this hotel just north of Nusa Dua are more Pier One than local Bali, but the decor goes well with the casual, international atmosphere. (Owing to the optional all-inclusive rates, this hotel is popular with tour groups.) Open lounges and terraces, tall white buildings, and pools create a sense of space. Rooms are large and have marble floors, wood trim, and balconies with garden or sea views. The gardens are full of cattails and lotus ponds, and there are bread boxes for feeding the koi. The open-air Dwarawati Coffee House offers reasonable prices and a comfortable family atmosphere. The decor is no-frills—basic round tables, dark wood chairs, and a stone floor—but the breakfast buffet is well-rounded, the mix of Indonesian and Western dishes fresh and creative. Entrées include *puscilli al tono* (pasta salad with tuna, olives, tomato, and parsley) and paprika chicken with roasted potatoes and seasoned vegetables. ✉ *Jl. Pratama, Tanjung Benoa (Box 52, Nusa Dua 80363),* ☎ *0361/771714,* FAX *0361/771713. 156 rooms. 2 restaurants, 2 bars, coffee shop, in-room safes, pool, massage, spa, health club, laundry service, meeting rooms, travel services, car rental. AE, MC, V.*

$$$–$$$$ 🏨 **Bali Hilton International.** At this resort, set on 30 acres of landscaped gardens along 984 ft of beach, a spectacular floodlighted waterfall sets the scene. Five-story buildings on either side of the vast, open reception area create a "U" around Balinese-theme courtyards and an enormous lagoon. All rooms in the enormous, pagoda-style, red-tile-roof main buildings have balconies that look onto the lagoon or the sea. Interior corridors connect the structures, which also feature central gardens, pools, and fountains that are open to the sky. Ayodya Club rooms are slightly larger and have a separate check-in area. The Hilton also caters to Japanese visitors with such special amenities as a Japanese-speaking staff, Japanese newspapers, green tea, and slippers. Travelers with disabilities will also be pleased by the hotel's facilities. ✉ *Jl. Raya Nusa Dua (Box 46), 80363,* ☎ *0361/771102; 800/HILTONS in the U.S.;* FAX *0361/771616. 538 rooms. 7 restaurants, in-room safes, 3 pools, spa, 4 tennis courts, exercise room, squash, theater, meeting rooms. AE, DC, MC, V.*

$$$–$$$$ **Grand Hyatt Bali.** Forty acres of gardens and cascading waterfalls are the setting for the Hyatt's four "ethnic village" compounds, each with its own small lagoon or swimming pool. Rooms are large and have a traditional Balinese decor, king-size beds, and small sitting enclaves with banquette seats. Bathrooms have separate shower stalls and wooden shutters that open to the bedrooms. Regency Club rooms feature balconies, marble bathrooms, private pools, butler service, and the Club Lounge, where complimentary breakfast and cocktails are served. The hotel's Balinese character is heightened by the Pasar Senggol open-air night market of 11 food stalls and an amphitheater where traditional dances are performed. ✉ *Jl. Raya Nusa Dua (Box 53),* ☎ *0361/771234; 800/233–1234 in the U.S.;* FAX *0361/772038. 750 rooms. 5 restaurants, 4 bars, in-room safes, 6 pools, putting green, 3 tennis courts, health club, squash, shops, theater, children's programs, playground, meeting rooms. AE, DC, MC, V.*

Nightlife and the Arts

Some of the livelier resort locales include: **Club Taboh** (✉ Nusa Dua Beach Hotel, Jl. Raya Nusa Dua next to the Sheraton Nusa Indah, ☎ 0361/977120), which features karaoke and an all-night disco Tuesday through Sunday; the Grand Hyatt's **Lila Cita** (☎ 0361/771234), which has weekly fashion shows and live bands; and the Sheraton Laguna's **Quinn's** (☎ 0361/771–1237), which offers live entertainment nightly.

Along Jalan Pantai Mengiat, the jazz bar at **Poco Loco** (☎ 0361/773923) rocks on weekends in peak season, **Ulam** (☎ 0361/771590) is always crowded, and **Koki Bali** (☎ 0361/772406) has Balinese dancing at 8 PM every Tuesday and Thursday. There are several bars in the Nusa Dua Galeria shopping plaza (all offer free transport to and from area resorts), including: **Arak Bali** (☎ 0361/774612), **Uno** (☎ 0361/773654), and **Harry's** (☎ 0361/772655).

Balinese cultural performances are scheduled regularly at the **Galeria stage** (✉ Galeria Nusa Dua Shopping Centre, Jl. Raya Nusa Dua, ☎ 0361/771662). In summer live bands also perform here on Saturday night.

Outdoor Activities and Sports

The 18-hole, 6,839-yard course of the **Bali Golf & Country Club** (☎ 0361/771791), on the Bukit Peninsula in Nusa Dua, has $125 greens fees (including caddy) and $27 club rental. Most of the hotels have mountain bikes and maps for the area's numerous cycling paths.

Shopping

Each Nusa Dua resort has at least one shop where you can pick up postcards and souvenirs, but you'll find the best prices and selection outside the hotels. Along Jalan Pantai Mengiat, in the center of town, clothing shops and trinket stalls filled with carvings and textiles are tucked between small, open-air restaurants. If you're shy about bargaining, head for the **Galeria Nusa Dua Shopping Centre** (✉ Jl. Raya Nusa Dua, in the center of town) where you'll find clothing at **Bali Lotus** (☎ 0361/772539), pretty lace creations at **Uluwatu** (☎ 0361/771309), textiles at **Batik Shanti** (☎ 0361/771308) and **Tenun Ikat Bali** (☎ 0361/772081), art at **Batik Keris** (☎ 0361/771303), and jewelry at **Unique Gold & Silver** (☎ 0361/771038) and **Surya Silver** (☎ 0361/773856). Be sure to get a discount book from the Galeria Information desk before you shop or eat.

Shops and bargains abound in the village of **Benoa** (not to be confused with the Tanjung Benoa ship port on the opposite side of Benoa Harbor), a five-minute drive north of Nusa Dua along the eastern peninsula's beach strip. The busy, two-lane road to the northeast end of the beach buzzes with traffic and tour buses from dawn to long past dusk. The village markets, including the **Pasar Seni art market** at the bend in the road into town, offer a refreshing change of scenery if you've been cooped up too long in your resort.

Kuta and Legian

❸ *8 km (5 mi) km northwest of Nusa Dua, 4 km (3 mi) northeast of Ngurah Rai Airport, 12 km (7 mi) southwest of Denpasar.*

In recent years, Bali's first resort area, Kuta, has become extremely commercial and somewhat tawdry. Its once-splendid golden swatch of sand is now smothered by people and scattered with litter, and its main street, just 2 blocks from the beach, is crammed with boutiques, Western fast-food chains, bars, discos, and—after hours—ladies of the night. Still, the sunsets are stunning, the energy of the youthful vacationers (including many backpackers) give the town a festive atmosphere, and there are enclaves of the real Bali down many a narrow, quiet street.

Legian Beach to the north is quieter and less congested than Kuta; it's for those who like to be close to the action but not right in it. Just to the south of Kuta is Tuban, another area of hotels designed to attract families and those looking for quieter vacations.

Dining and Lodging

$$ ✕ **Glory Bar & Restaurant.** The Glory stands out for the freshness of its fish, mud crabs, and lobster. The ambience is convivial, and the prices are fair. The Wednesday Indonesian buffet includes corn soup, fried chicken, sweet-and-sour pork, batter-fried fish, satay, and noodles. ✉ *Jl. Legian 445, Legian,* ☎ *0361/751091. AE, DC, MC, V.*

$$ ✕ **Indah Sari.** This seafood-and-barbecue restaurant on the main drag serves well-prepared dishes—from prawns to grouper—that you can order either spicy or bland. The freshness of the food makes up for the impersonal service and lack of intimacy. ✉ *Jl. Legian, Kuta,* ☎ *0361/751834. AE, MC, V.*

$$ ✕ **Poppies.** Surrounded by high-volume, high-energy shops and dives, Poppies is a garden haven enclosed by tall, thin walls. Vines and blossoms tumble through trellises above the well-spaced tables, and the staff is quick to please. The relaxed alfresco atmosphere makes the creative variety of fresh, tasty Indonesian and Western dishes all the more enjoyable. Items range from Greek salads and *tom yam* (spicy Thai prawn soup) to grilled fish and succulent spareribs. ✉ *Poppies La. (off Jl. Legian), Kuta,* ☎ *0361/751059. MC, V.*

$$ ✕ **Un's.** With its pebbled entryway, small trees strung with white lights, and U-shape pavilion lined with Balinese paintings, the feel here is that of a secret temple tucked away in the center of a bustling town. Margaritas are the happy-hour special, and entrées include both Indonesian and Western specialties—mushroom ravioli, Venetian chicken breast, chicken cordon bleu, and grilled snapper and prawns. At day's end, the bar in the center of the garden is a great place to unwind, and strolling Batak musicians occasionally perform. ✉ *Jl. Pantai, Poppies La. (off Jl. Legian), Kuta,* ☎ *0361/752607. AE, MC, V.*

$$ ✕ **Warung Kopi.** Five marble-top tables facing the street and another 10 in the rear garden provide an oasis from the surrounding honky-tonk scene. The menu is eclectic: Indonesian fish, vegetable, and rice dishes; Indian curries; Western beef and lamb. This is also a fine place to stop for just a beer and an appetizer or coffee and dessert. ✉ *Jl. Legian Tengah 427, Legian,* ☎ *0361/753602. MC, V.*

$ ✕ **Bakung Mas Garden.** This peaceful, romantic restaurant belongs to the Segara Village Hotel. There are only six tables under its thatched roof, though there's a tiny bar in case you have to wait. The food has a Chinese influence: try the stir-fried vegetables with pork or the *semur daging* (thinly sliced beef with a rich sauce of mushrooms and onions). ✉ *Jl. Bakung Sari, Kuta,* ☎ *0361/788407. No credit cards.*

$$$$ ★ ✕🏨 **The Oberoi.** At the far western end of Legian Beach, the Oberoi's 15 acres offer tranquility, privacy, and friendly service. Guest quarters dot the gardens of bougainvillea, hibiscus, and frangipani. The thatched cottages have verandas, and the villas have balconies and garden courtyards; some of the luxury villas have private pools and all have traditional Balinese inner courtyards. Hand-carved teak furnishings and locally made silk-screen prints and draperies are used throughout. Balinese dance is performed in the resort's amphitheater two or three evenings a week. Before the show, consider dining beneath the bamboo ceiling of the Kura Kura restaurant, perhaps near the lotus pond and its fountain. A Swiss chef and a Balinese sous-chef turn out both an Indonesian buffet and à la carte items with a Continental flair. The *bebek betutu*—a Balinese favorite of whole duck stuffed with mild spices, wrapped in banana leaves, and slowly steamed—is a standout dish. ✉ *Jl. Kayu Aya, Basangkasa, Legian Beach (✉ Box 3351, Denpasar 80033),* ☎ *0361/730361; 800/5–OBEROI in the U.S.;* FAX *0361/730391. 60 cottages, 13 villas. Restaurant, bar, café, pool, spa, tennis court, health club, beach, windsurfing, theater, laundry service, meeting rooms, car rental. AE, DC, MC, V.*

$$$–$$$$ ✕🏨 **Kul Kul Beach Resort.** This is one of the most interesting and attractive structures on Kuta Beach. The sundeck is built over rocks on one side of the pool, and you clamber down boulders to have a dip or get a drink. The modern bungalows contain deluxe bathrooms as well as sitting rooms and bedrooms furnished in rattan and bamboo. The attentive service adds to the sense of harmony you feel amid the Balinese architecture. The restaurant serves everything from Italian pastas to New Zealand lamb to Indonesian rice dishes. In the evening, a wayang kulit performance is given in English, an Indonesian singer entertains in the bar, and a video is shown on a wide screen. ✉ *Jl. Raya Pantai Kuta, Legian 80361,* ☎ *0361/752520,* FAX *0361/752519. 55 bungalows. Restaurant, bar, pool, dance club. AE, MC, V.*

$$–$$$ ✕🏨 **Bali Dynasty.** At the Dynasty, two wings branching out from the main building house the guest rooms, which have a standard rectangular layout with a double bed or two twins against one wall, a writing table along the other, and a couple of easy chairs; an extra $10 gets you a garden view. The pool is close to the beach. You can take meals in the Western-style restaurant or in the noteworthy Golden Lotus Chinese restaurant, whose Singaporean chef has a sure hand with spices. ✉ *Jl. Dewi Kartika, Tuban 80361,* ☎ *0361/752403; 800/942–5050 in the U.S.; 0181/747–8485 in the U.K.;* FAX *0361/752402. 225 rooms, 12 suites. 2 restaurants, 2 bars, pool, tennis court, beach, dance club, travel services. AE, DC, MC, V.*

$$$–$$$$ **Bali Imperial.** Here you'll find peace and quiet, yet all the action on the Kuta/Legian strip is just a 10-minute walk away. The relaxed, expansive lobby is glass and marble. Guest rooms have high ceilings, lightwood furniture, shining wood floors, two twin beds or one king-size bed, balconies that face the sea or the garden, and marble baths with separate showers. The resort is under the same management as the Imperial Hotel in Tokyo, and there's an emphasis on service (the staff-to-guest ratio is three to one). If you ring your butler for coffee or tea (complimentary), he'll no doubt bring it to you immediately. ✉ *Jl. Dhyana Pura, Seminyak (Box 3384, Denpasar 80001),* ☎ *0361/754545; 212/692–9001 in the U.S.; 0171/355–1775 in the U.K.;* FAX *0361/751545. 121 rooms, 17 bungalows. 2 restaurants, 2 pools, 2 tennis courts, beach, travel services. AE, DC, MC, V.*

$$ **Kuta Palace Hotel.** Set on 11 acres, this hotel consists of two-story buildings that surround a courtyard with gardens and pools. Rooms are simply but pleasantly decorated with Balinese-patterned fabrics and a cream-and-rust color scheme. All have ocean or garden views. ✉ *Jl. Pura Bagus Taruna, Legian (✉ Box 3244, Denpasar 80001),* ☎ *0361/751433,* FAX *0361/752074. 422 rooms. Restaurant, refrigerators, pool, 4 tennis courts, beach, laundry service. AE, DC, MC, V.*

$$ **Poppies Cottages.** At this, one of Kuta's top small hotels, you can stay in a traditional thatched cottage for a fraction of what it would cost at a larger resort. Set amid fragrant gardens—highlighted by arching bridges, hidden pools, and flowing waterfalls—each cottage has one double bed or two single beds and a large, secluded balcony. Bathrooms have sunken tubs and are in screened, private gardens. A set of pools is nestled among rocks with landscaped sunbathing terraces and waterfalls, and the pavilion houses a small library and game area. Convenience is another advantage here: Kuta's shops and beaches are a five-minute walk down the road. ✉ *Poppies La., Kuta (✉ Box 3378, Denpasar 80033),* ☎ *0361/751059,* FAX *0361/752364. 20 cottages. Restaurant, bar, 2 pools, library, travel services, car rental. AE, DC, MC, V.*

Nightlife and the Arts

Tourist life on Bali focuses on sightseeing and beach activities; by late evening, most areas quiet down, with one exception: Kuta Beach. Here the activity begins with drinks at cafés—one of the most consistently popular is **Poppies** restaurant (☞ Dining and Lodging, *above*)—in the early evening, followed by more drinks in cafés or dancing and drinks in discos, most of which charge a modest cover.

A stroll down Jalan Pantai along the beach leads past many small, open-air bars right on the sand. **Cactus Biru** (no phone) and **Geria Cafe** (no phone), next to the Dunkin' Donuts stand on the northern end of the beach, are usually packed. **Kacang Bali** (☎ 0361/754412), otherwise known as "Peanuts," sponsors a weekly pub crawl that hits many watering holes on the strip.

The new **Hard Rock Cafe Beach Club** (✉ Jl. Legian 204, Kuta, ☎ 0361/755661) is one of the most consistently popular places in town. There's no cover unless a live band is playing; generally, the action starts rolling at 9 PM and grinds down at 2 AM.

Some of the old standbys include: **Gado-Gado** (✉ Jl. Dhyana Pura, ☎ 0361/775225), open Wednesday–Sunday, an open-air disco near the ocean; **Kayu Api** (✉ Jl. Legian and Jl. Melasti, no phone), which has live music, often of international caliber; and **Koala Blu** (✉ Jl. Kuta, no phone), which attracts mostly Australians. For informality, drop in at the **Kuta Jaya Jazz Corner** (✉ Jl. Raya. Pantai Kuta, ☎ 0361/752308).

Shopping

Kuta's shopping scene of small stores crammed onto both sides of the main street has moved decidedly upscale and now includes a range of boutiques and specialty shops. However, if you take your time, you'll still find many bargains. Try to buy crafts directly from village workshops; items to look for include silver objects and jewelry, Indonesian crafts, batik clothing and art, paintings, and wood carvings. Skip the fake watches and bogus tapes sold by roving vendors and go for the Indonesian gamelan music CDs, guaranteed to bring back memories when played at home.

Animale (✉ Jl. Pantai Kuta, ☎ 0361/485450) has unique prints for men and women. The **Cleopatra Boutique** (✉ Jl. Pantai Kuta 21, ☎ 0361/755456)—which caters to the Japanese market as well as Westerners—is a good place for textiles, clothes, and accessories. For men, **Handy's** (✉ Jl. Pantai Kuta 20C, ☎ 0361/751247) has an extensive selection of batik shirts and shorts. **Indigo Kids** (✉ Jl. Pantai Kuta, Jl. Legian Kuta, and Jl. Arjuna 23, ☎ 0361/730447 general factory) is the place to buy batik clothing for babies through teens. **Inspirations** (✉ Jl. Pantai Kuta, ☎ 0361/483616) has a terrific variety of knickknacks, carvings, and woven goods.

For customized jewelry, check out **Mayang Bali** (✉ Kuta Square, Blok A-12, ☎ 0361/752902). **Natural Field** (✉ Jl. Tegal Wangi, Kuta, ☎ 0361/752124) sells lovely textiles, sarongs, dresses, and accessories. For a wonderful selection of high-quality batik, ikat, dresses, accessories, and gifts, step into **Pusaka** (✉ Jl. Pantai Kuta 20D, ☎ 0361/761810; ✉ Jl. Legian 338, ☎ 0361/758110). **Sarayu Silver** (✉ Jl. Pantai Kuta, no phone) sells jewelry.

Sanur

4 *12 km (7 mi) northeast of Kuta, 15 km (9 mi) northeast of Ngurah Rai Airport, 9 km (5 mi) southeast of Denpasar.*

Sanur was Bali's second beach resort, and today it's a good mix of Kuta and Nusa Dua: the energy of the former without the frenzy, and the class of the latter without the high prices. Hotels, restaurants, and shops are spread out, and this helps to keep the pace slow. The wide beach, which is framed by a shallow coral reef, is calm—perfect for snorkeling, boating, and windsurfing.

Dining and Lodging

$$$ ★ ✕ **Telaga Naga.** The name means "dragon's pond," though the lily ponds in the tropical garden set a peaceful—rather than fearsome—tone. The Cantonese and Szechuan cuisine is exquisite. Try the sautéed chicken with dried red chili or the fried prawns with Szechuan sauce, both house specialties. ✉ *Jl. Danau Tamblingan, across from Bali Hyatt,* ☎ *0361/288–1234. Reservations essential. AE, DC, MC, V.*

$$ ✕ **Le Gong.** The gong hangs in a central garden, and although the restaurant is on Sanur's main street, its woven bamboo walls and set-back tables give it a relaxing atmosphere. To make the most of the traditional Balinese menu, order a few dishes and share them. Some suggestions: soto ayam, prawns in butter sauce, fish grilled with spices, and nasi goreng. Fresh papaya or pineapple are refreshing desserts, but the coup de grâce is the Balinese equivalent of a banana split, swathed in a honey treacle. ✉ *Jl. Legong,* ☎ *0361/588066. No credit cards.*

$$ ✕ **Lotus Pond.** This thatched-roof restaurant is large and open, with square dining tables along one side, a cushioned lounge area along the other, and an extensive Indonesian buffet in the middle. Gardens with lotus ponds surround the pavilion. The atmosphere is breezy and casual, the service amicable. Western offerings, such as club sandwiches and salads, are popular as are the spiced-down Indonesian dishes; the rijsttafel buffet is outstanding. ✉ *Jl. Danau Tamblingan,* ☎ *0361/289398. AE, MC, V.*

$$ ✕ **Penjor Restaurant.** Set back from the main street, this bamboo-walled restaurant surrounds an open courtyard where tables are set up in fine weather. Each night a different Balinese dance-drama is presented, and the set menu rotates between Balinese, Indonesian, Chinese, and Indian dinners. Owner Ida Bagus Ketut Oka speaks English fluently and loves to chat with his guests. ✉ *Jl. Batu Jumbar,* ☎ *0361/88226. AE, DC, MC, V.*

$$$$ ✕ **Tandjung Sari.** This renowned hotel, whose unique design has been featured in books on architecture, is a peaceful "village" of Balinese-style bungalows on tropical grounds with small stone temples and statues. The open-pavilion lobby is decorated with carvings, and the gardens overflow with blossoms year-round. Bungalows have split-bamboo walls and such touches as minibars, handwoven fabrics, and an antique or two. Most bathrooms have skylights. Prawns, curries, fritters, and a dozen other items are served in a romantic setting just back from the beach; Wednesday night sees a superb rijsttafel. ✉ *Jl. Danau Tamblingan (✉ Box 25, Denpasar 80001),* ☎ *0361/288441,* FAX *0361/287930. 24 bungalows. Restaurant, bar, minibars, beach, pool, windsurfing, snorkeling. No credit cards.*

$$$–$$$$ ✕ **Bali Hyatt.** For a hotel that's part of a large international chain, this has a surprisingly Balinese feel. The green-tile pool has a waterfall replica of the entrance to the Goa Gajah (Elephant Cave); at the nearby pavilion, an Indonesian buffet is served during a Balinese dance performance on Saturday night. In the open-air spa, specialists perform a range of therapeutic treatments native to the archipelago. Tropical gardens cover the expansive grounds to the 6-km-long (4-mi-long) beach esplanade, where colorful *jukung* fishing boats depart each morning. Rooms are in four-story buildings, and though they're slightly worn, each has an island-style decor and a balcony. The Wantilan Cafe is a great place to try Balinese cuisine. An extensive breakfast buffet is served on the terrace overlooking the lily pond and fountain. For dinner, a rijsttafel buffet of 30-plus dishes—all labeled with their ingredients—is laid out on a lotus altar in the center of the room. The hotel is within walking distance of local markets, shops, and restaurants. ✉ *Jl. Danau Tamblingan (✉ Box 392, Denpasar 80001),* ☎ *0361/281234,* FAX *0361/287693. 390 rooms. 5 restaurants, 4 bars, in-room safes, minibars, 2 pools, spa, 3-hole golf course, 2 tennis courts, jogging, beach, snorkeling, windsurfing, boating, children's programs, meeting rooms, car rental. AE, DC, MC, V.*

$$$ **Hotel Sanur Beach.** Most of the action here takes place around the pools, the beach, and the patio bars. All rooms have balconies, and most have large double beds (a few in the older wing have twins); the best rooms face the pool. Twenty-six self-contained bungalows offer more privacy. Classical Balinese dance performances and buffet dinners are offered most nights. ✉ *Jl. Kalianget (✉ Box 3279, Denpasar 80001),* ☎ *0361/288011,* FAX *0361/287566. 298 rooms, 26 bungalows. 3 restaurants, coffee shop, 2 pools, 4 tennis courts, badminton, beach, windsurfing, recreation room, meeting rooms. AE, DC, MC, V.*

$$ **Segara Village.** At the north end of Sanur Beach, this small, family-owned hotel consists of Balinese-style thatch-roof cottages. The open lobby houses both of the hotel's restaurants, so it can be busy. Rooms have balconies or verandas and private baths. The decor is very simple, but the hospitality is genuine. ✉ *Jl. Segara Ayu (✉ Box 91, Denpasar 80001),* ☎ *0361/288407,* FAX *0361/287242. 40 rooms. 2*

restaurants, 4 bars, 2 pools, 2 tennis courts, bicycles, children's programs, playground. AE, DC, MC, V.

Nightlife and the Arts

Most hotels here have some form of entertainment, often a live band. The **Lotus Pond** (✉ Jl. Danau Tamblingan, ☎ 0361/289398) is a tranquil haven where a casual, upscale crowd gathers for evening cocktails. Across the street, Bali socialites and twentysomething tourists meet for drinks at the **Janger** bar (✉ Jl. Danau Tamblingan 21, ☎ 0361/288888) and late-night dancing at the cavernous, techno-modern **Subek** disco (✉ Jl. Danau Tamblingan 21, ☎ 0361/288888).

Outdoor Activities and Sports

BOATING

For yacht charters, contact **Jet Boat Tours** (✉ Jl. Pantai Karang 5, ☎ 0361/28839). Sanur's **Bali Hyatt** (☞ Dining and Lodging, *above*) has two deep-sea fishing boats available for charter. You can hire the ***Bali Hai*** (☎ 0361/720331) for a luxurious excursion around the island as well as for dive and surf trips. The vessel departs from Tanjung Benoa, about 9 km (6 mi) south.

SCUBA DIVING AND SURFING

You can rent scuba equipment and get a ride out to the reef at Sanur from **Bali Marine Sport** (✉ Jl. Bypass Ngurah Rai, ☎ 0361/87872). **Ocean Dive Center** (✉ Jl. Bypass Ngurah Rai, ☎ 0361/88652) organizes dives out to reefs.

Nusa Lembongan, the island opposite Sanur Beach and next to Nusa Penida, has surfing and diving opportunities. For the best surfing, however, you really should head to Pura Luhur Ulu Watu, on the western side of the Bukit Peninsula. Both dive shops listed above rent boards and arrange transportation; you can also rent boards at the beaches, but they tend to be of lesser quality, and you'll be responsible for any damage done to them.

Shopping

There are interesting shops along Jalan Bypass and Jalan Danau Tamblingan. Look for handwoven fabrics, jewelry, ceramics, baskets, and kites. The **Sanur Beach Market** is worth a browse for handcrafted souvenirs. **Bagus Drugstore,** on Jalan Duyung next to the Bali Hyatt, sells groceries and has a large bookshop (with English-language titles) and souvenir area.

Denpasar

❺ *9 km (5 mi) northwest of Sanur, 16 km (10 mi) northeast of Ngurah Rai Airport.*

Most people don't stay overnight in this busy market town of about 400,000 people, but Denpasar is worth a day trip to visit its museums, markets, and monuments. You can book city tours through your resort, or you can see Denpasar on your own, by taxi or bemo.

Where Jalan Gajahmada intersects with Jalan Veteran is a large **statue of Brahma.** Its four faces look in the cardinal directions. To the left is the **Natour Bali Hotel** (✉ Jl. Veteran 3, ☎ 0361/225681), in a building dating from the Dutch colonial period.

Continue through this intersection past Puputan Square—a park on the right-hand side, with its Sukarno-inspired heroic statue of the common man—to reach **Pura Agung Jagatnatha,** Bali's state temple. (Go right at the end of the park onto Jalan Letkol, and the entrance is on your left.) The temple's center stupa is surrounded by a moat and rises eight levels; at the top is a statue of Shiva with flames coming from his shoulders. The stupa is supported by the cosmic turtle (on whose back the real world symbolically sits, according to Balinese legend) and protected by a huge carved face with a red cloth tongue. Nagas entwine the base; around the bottom are relief carvings.

Farther down Jalan Letkol is the **Bali Museum,** with Balinese art dating from prehistoric to present times. The buildings are excellent examples of Balinese temple and palace architecture. ✉ *Jl. Letkol,* ☎ *0361/222680.* 🎫 *Admission.* ⏲ *Tues.–Thurs. and weekends 8–5, Fri. 8–3:30.*

Another Denpasar attraction is **Taman Wedhi Budaya Arts Center,** where year-round dance performances are held (don't miss the island's annual summer arts festival, held here from mid-June to mid-July). Changing exhibits of modern paintings, batik designs, and wood carvings are also on display. ✉ *Jl. Nusa Indah,* ☎ *0361/222776.* 🎫 *Admission.* ⏲ *Daily 10–4.*

OFF THE BEATEN PATH

TANAH LOT – This famous temple stands on a small rocky islet 15 km (9 mi) west of Denpasar (it's accessible via a small causeway except at high tide, when it turns into an island). Though people flock here for the postcardlike setting, the Balinese revere this pagoda-style temple as deeply as they do the mountain shrines. It has the added mystery of snakes that secret themselves in the rock holes and are said to guard the spirits residing at Tanah Lot. Ideally, you should arrive an hour before sunset; this will give you enough time to see the snakes. Cross the causeway to the temple, then return to the shore to watch it become silhouetted against the burning sky as the sun goes down. Not even the hawkers and the lines of snapping cameras can spoil the vision.

Dining and Lodging

$$$$ ★ ✕🏨 **Hotel Tugu Bali.** The island's most memorable hotel is 11 km (8 mi) west of the city in a bucolic landscape of rolling hills and rice paddies along the edge of the Bali Sea. Nearly every element here is a piece of Balinese and Indonesian history—from the ornately carved teak doors and window frames and the ancient Chinese temple reconstructed on the grounds to the 39—the number needed to show respect to and ask protection from the wrath of the gods—*boma* (faces) looking down from teak columns. You enter the lower level of each two-story guest villa by a boardwalk over a lotus pond; access to the upper floors is via an outdoor spiral staircase. Each villa also has a back terrace with a plunge pool. Inside, you'll find marble floors, huge canopy beds, and exquisite antiques. Bath and toilet areas are small but have such winning touches as stained-glass windows. You can also stay in (or just tour) the Puri Le Meyeur, a bungalow and monument to Belgian artist A. J. Le Meyeur De Merpres, and the Pavilion, which commemorates artist Walter Spies and is modeled after his home at the palace in Yogyakarta, Java. Other on-site amenities include an art gallery, the Puputan Museum brimming with artifacts and old photos, and a traditional medicine and spice stall. Even if you don't stay here, pop in for tea at the small Tugu Restaurant. The selection is varied and delightful: crispy rice cakes, fried tempeh, spring rolls, fresh fruit tarts, and chocolate cake squares. Don't miss the ginger tea—truly refreshing on a hot afternoon. A dinner of such Thai dishes as stir-fried chicken with cashews, grilled red snapper, or crab soup is also an option. Just save room for dessert. ✉ *Jl. Batu Bolong, Canggu,* ☎ *0361/731701,* FAX *0361/731704. 25 villas. 2 restaurants, bar, pool, spa, library, business services, meeting rooms. AE, MC, V.*

Shopping

Along the Badung River (near the bridge off Jalan Gajahmada) is the large, two-story **Pasar Badung,** the liveliest market in town. Packed with spice vendors and farmers selling vegetables, meats, and flowers, it's busiest in the early morning, though commerce continues until early afternoon. The little girls who volunteer to guide you around get commissions from any vendor you patronize; of course, the price of anything you buy is raised accordingly. If you're in Denpasar in the evening, head for the **night market** in the riverside parking lot of the multilevel shopping center at Kumbasari. It's a gathering place for locals, who come to chat, shop, and feast on Balinese food. The **Mega Art Gallery** (✉ Jl. Gajahmada, ☎ 0361/224592) sells new and antique puppets, wood carvings, and paintings.

UBUD AND ENVIRONS

Crafts Villages

From Denpasar north, a strand of crafts villages is laced together by slim, twisting roads that slip between mountain folds and fertile rice fields. In just a day, you can cover the main sights; with a little more time, you can explore off-the-beaten-path shops that often double as the artisans' homes. In any case, these crafts villages are among the highlights of any trip to Bali, and the quality, variety, and affordability of the items sold in them will make a venture to these towns truly memorable.

Batubulan

The first crafts village is 19 km (12 mi) northeast of Denpasar on the main road to Ubud. Batubulan is famous for the stone carvers whose workshops and displays line the road. You'll see small, open factories where boys chip at the soft sandstone and sculptures are for sale out front. Wares range from the classic guardian figures that stand before Balinese temples and houses to smaller statues. Most workshops make small carvings that are easier to transport home. **I. Made Sura** (no phone) is one of the better shops; it also carries some wood carvings, old wooden ornaments, and carved doors.

At 9:30 each morning, **dance-dramas** are performed at each of the village's three theaters, along the main road (the same show is done at all three). Travel agencies in Ubud and many hotels can arrange for you to see the show as part of a cultural tour. Admission is around Rp 20,000.

Tohpati

Balinese batik tends to be more colorful than that of Java, and the designs are often floral rather than geometric. A good source of hand-drawn batiks is **Popiler** (☎ 0361/36498) in the village of Tohpati, on the northern outskirts of Batubulan. If you pay cash instead of using a credit card, you increase your bargaining power by around 20% for the yard goods, paintings, garments, and household items here. Behind the shop, you can watch girls outlining the designs with wax.

En Route German businessman and Balinese resident Ed Swoboda chose Singapadu (just north of Batubulan; take the smaller road that runs straight rather than following the main road around the right curve) as the site of the **Taman Burung** (Bali Bird Park). Designed with Balinese thatched roofs, the aviaries of the 4-acre park house birds from around the world, including such rare species native to Indonesia as the Bali starling and birds of paradise from Irian Jaya. A 160-seat restaurant makes a good stop for breakfast in a lush setting. ✉ *Jl. Serma Lok Ngurah Gambir, Singapadu,* ☎ *0361/299352.* 💳 *Admission.* ⊙ *Daily 9–6.*

Celuk

Celuk, 2 km (1 mi) northeast of Batubulan, is a village of silversmiths, and the main road through town is jammed with small shops announcing their specialties. In workshops behind the stores, you can watch boys working the silver and setting semiprecious stones. As a rule, the jewelry you find here is 90%–92% silver, the tableware 60%–70%. Filigree pieces with detailed, imaginative designs—ships, flowers, butterflies—are among the best items to buy, but don't visit in the morning, when all the tour buses stop here; come in the afternoon when prices return to reasonable levels. If you have time, you can custom-order pieces. Remember that with quiet patience and a smile you might drive the cost of a $125 bracelet down to $80. (Bargaining is the rule, especially where price tags are in dollars.)

At least 30 shops line the main road and surrounding streets, although a severe shortage of sidewalks can make browsing on foot potentially life-threatening. The goods vary little from store to store—rings, earrings, pins, and hair clips are perennial favorites—but some establishments display more merchandise. One shop with a large selection is **Dewi Sitha** (no phone, on the left side of the road going north. Other places include: **Antara** (☎ 0361/298091) and **Celuk Ministore** (☎ 0361/298350). Along the same road, stop in **Bali Ayu Batik** (☎ 0361/298193) and the nearby **Bali Pottery Center** (no phone) for an assortment of crafts.

Sukawati

Four kilometers (2 miles) northeast of Celuk, Sukawati is known for its specialized crafts, including kites, mobiles, wind chimes, temple umbrellas, woven baskets, and shadow puppets. Stalls lining the road also sell baskets, hats, and furniture. **Pasar Seni,** the crafts market on the east side of the main road, sells a range of works by some of the island's most talented artisans, but lines of tour buses stop here midmorning, so arrive early to beat the crowds. If you bargain determinedly, you may find some of the best prices in Bali. A kilometer (½ mi) west, the village of Puaya is one of the best places to shop for wayang kulit puppets and wayang topeng wooden masks.

Batuan

Batuan, 2 km (1 mi) north of Sukawati, is a weaving village and a painting center, where the famous black-and-white style of Balinese painting originated. Small galleries line the main road, and the backstreets have signs pointing to artists' homes. Impromptu visits are welcome in both.

The hand-cut, painted, shadow puppets sold on Bali are usually new, but you can buy antique ones at the **Jati Art Gallery** (✉ along the main road, no phone), which also sells paintings, old masks and temple ornaments, handwoven ikat, batiks, wood carvings, and new puppets. **Mario Antique** (☎ 0361/298541) is a huge, open factory on the left side of the same road, where you can watch dozens of workers honing various pieces of furniture. You can't miss the giant elephants outside the **Antique Furniture Warehouse** (☎ 0361/298269) on the right; this is a fine place to search for both antiques and reproductions.

Find time in this village to visit the 10th-century **Pura Puseh Pura Desa** (Temple of Brahma), where the seldom-seen *gambuh*—the oldest known form of dance drama on Bali—takes place at every full moon. Once performed only for royal celebrations or temple festivals, these dances are the ultimate in classical Balinese style and have influenced numerous other dramas, including the wayang *wong*, in which humans perform the roles of the wayang kulit shadow puppets, and the *legong*, a famous court dance performed by young girls. The gambuh dance dramas are accompanied by a gamelan orchestra that features the long, resonant flutes that are unique to the area.

The brick-and-sandstone temple has three parts. You enter the outer courtyard through a classic Balinese split gate. The bell tower, in the second courtyard, is hung with the ubiquitous black-and-white-checked cloth. In the main courtyard, a stone screen protects the temple from bad spirits (because such spirits can't turn a corner, they can't go around the screen). In one corner of this courtyard is a shrine to Brahma, where a hermaphroditic figure is guarded by two nagas. This is the main shrine and, as in every Balinese temple complex, it faces Gunung Agung, the home of the gods. Nearby, another shrine has three roofs representing Brahma, Shiva, and Vishnu. Over the gate entrances, the face of the god Boma guards against evil from the earth, and the nagas provide protection against evil from the sea. ✉ *Jl. Raya, Batuan.* 🎫 *Rp 15,000.* ⏲ *Daily sunrise to sunset except during ceremonies. Dance performances at 8 PM.*

Kemenuh

On the main road in Kemenuh, 3 km (2 mi) northeast of Batuan, the house of **Ida B. Marka** (no phone), a famous wood-carver, is open to the public, providing a rare look inside a Balinese home. The showroom is in front, but there's no pressure to buy. Behind are a courtyard and a cluster of buildings that serve as the family complex. The centerpiece is the building used for weddings and other rites of passage; this is where the oldest family member sleeps. Other structures include the family temple, a granary, and a cooperative workshop where other villagers help to carve and polish.

Mas

There are some 4,000 wood-carvers on Bali, and most of them live in Mas, 5 km (3 mi) northwest of Kemenuh. Unique crafts found here include framed wooden carvings of Balinese rural scenes, intricately detailed wooden statues of Hindu goddesses, wooden chessboards, and carvings of creatures and characters. The village is also known for its mask making, samples of which can be found in shops down the back lanes. The brightly painted masks, most of which represent characters in Balinese folklore, make great wall hangings.

The famous wood-carver **Ida Bagus Tilem** (✉ Ubud Rd., ☎ 0361/6414) lives in Mas; his work, which has been exhibited internationally, is sold in his small shop. In Mas you'll also find **Taman Harum Cottages** (✉ Mailing address: Box 216, Denpasar, ☎ 0361/35242), which consist of 17 compact adjoining duplexes. Here you can take wood-carving classes or just shop for finished products in the Tantra Gallery, which also has displays of work by master carver Nyana. The **Tinem Gallery** (☎ 0361/35136) contains works by Nyana's brother, Ida Bagus Nyana. A variety of quality carvings are found at **Ary Puja Gallery and Workshop** (✉ Jl. Raya, Mas, ☎ 0361/975195), whose collection includes rooms full of polished wood statues, rural scenes, masks, and ornate framed pictures. **Nyoman Nurga** (☎ 0361/975200) carves made-to-order items.

Bedulu

❻ *5 km (3 mi) northeast of Mas, 26 km (16 mi) northeast of Denpasar.*

This was once the capital of the last Balinese kingdom to stand against the conquering forces of Java in the 14th century. Today Bedulu's main claim to fame is the **Goa Gajah** (Elephant Cave), 2 km (1 mi) to the right of the intersection of Jalan Mas and Jalan Pengosekan (the entrance is on the right through a parking lot lined with souvenir vendors). This cave temple, discovered in 1923 by a farmer cultivating his field, is thought to have been built in the 11th century. In the courtyard, water spouts from the hands of six stone nymphs into two pools. It's believed that worshipers purified themselves here before passing through the mouth of the giant face of Boma carved on the entrance. (The Balinese consider the face protective even though it contains the same symbolic features as the face of Kali, the goddess of destruction, found at other Hindu temples.) To enter the cave, worshipers must pass through the mouth.

The cave is pitch dark—hope that your guide has a flashlight. To the left is a niche with a statue of Ganesha, the elephant-headed god and son of Shiva. In the center, to the right of a crumbled statue, are three *linga* (upright carved stones symbolizing male fertility), each with three smaller *yoni* (female forms).

NEED A BREAK? Atop the hill above the cave, is **Puri Suling** (no phone), a pleasant restaurant with a terrace that looks out over the rice fields and down to the cave area. The Western food is dull, but the Indonesian dishes are excellent.

Also of interest in Bedulu is the **Pura Saman Tiga** temple, on the left side of the road several yards beyond the Bedulu junction. Legend has it that this 11th-century temple was the site where a group of holy men once met to establish laws of religious tolerance and unity on Bali. A little farther on is the **Bedulu Archaeological Museum** (no phone), which houses numerous early Balinese artifacts, including pottery and sarcophagi. The museum is open Monday–Thursday 8–2 and Friday–Saturday 8–1.

Ubud

7 *5 km (3 mi) northwest of Bedulu, 25 km (15 mi) northeast of Denpasar.*

Ubud gained fame as an art colony in the 1930s and has since grown into the island's main cultural center of galleries, crafts shops, and traditional Balinese dance troupes (there are performances nearly every day). It has also grown more commercial. Many artists still have workshops in the region, but hotels, restaurants, ice-cream parlors, and souvenir stalls are taking over more and more ground. Ubud may no longer be a quiet place in which to immerse yourself in Balinese culture, but it still offers many more opportunities to experience authentic Balinese life than do the coastal resort areas. It's also an excellent base from which to explore Bali's interior. Step out of town and walk the many trails that lead through the countryside to small villages, and you'll find the "real Bali."

Ubud was placed on the world map when artists Walter Spies from Germany and Rudolf Bonnet from Holland introduced the Balinese to the three-dimensional form and convinced them that using real people, not courtly officials, in a free-flowing background was legitimate art. From that point on, a naturalism was seen in Balinese art. Exhibits at the ★ **Puri Lukisan Museum,** set in gardens at the west end of the main street, show the evolution of this art style from the 1930s to the present. Works are arranged chronologically, so you can see the transition from formal religious art to more natural, realistic depictions of dances, festi-

Ubud and Vicinity

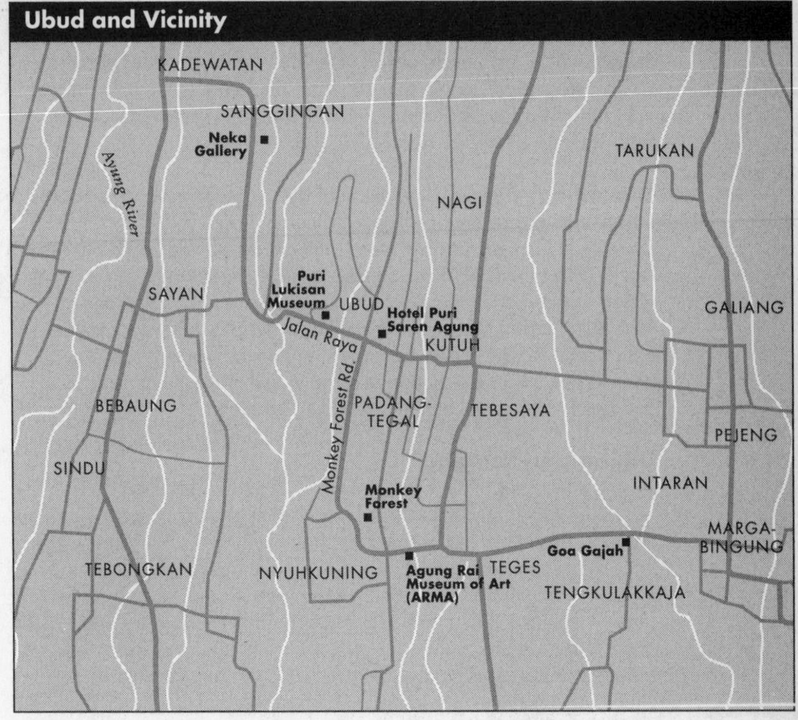

vals, and rice harvesting. ✉ *Jl. Raya (west of intersection with Monkey Forest Rd.),* ☎ *0361/975136.* 🎫 *Admission.* ⏲ *Daily 8–4.*

For an overview of Balinese and Indonesian art styles, visit Ubud's finest collection of paintings at the **Neka Gallery,** at the east end of the main street. The works are organized by style in seven buildings, one of which has paintings by foreign artists, including Spies and Bonnet. Be sure to visit Building 6, devoted to works by Affandi, an Indonesian artist of international renown. Building 4 houses works by I Gusti Nyoman Lempadi, who is recognized as one of the first true Bali artists. ✉ *Jl. Raya,* ☎ *0361/975074.* 🎫 *Admission.* ⏲ *Daily 9–4.*

The **Agung Rai Museum of Art (ARMA)** in Pengosekan, a small community just southeast of Ubud, is a cultural complex whose emphasis is on the Balinese arts. Here you'll find several galleries with permanent displays by Indonesian and European artists; a library; a bookshop; workshops; and the elegant Kokokan Hotel (☞ Dining and Lodging, *below*). The museum offers dance, art, and music classes, and arts performances take place throughout the week; call or stop by the museum for a current schedule. ✉ *Jl. Pengosekan,* ☎ *0361/976659.* 🎫 *Free.* ⏲ *Daily 9–6.*

In the center of town is the beautiful **Hotel Puri Saren Agung,** which was once part of the palace of Ubud's royal family. The structure was rebuilt after it was decimated by a 1917 earthquake; the current prince's living quarters are at the end of the courtyard. There are slightly run-down guest pavilions on the grounds; better to just stop by for a look at the fine antiquities or for a listen to the gamelan music that's played here nightly.

Across from Puri Saren is Monkey Forest Road, which has many souvenir and T-shirt shops and inexpensive restaurants. Farther along are small hotels and losmen, where you can find simple and very affordable accommodations. Keep walking and you'll reach the **Monkey Forest,** where a small donation gets you a close-up view of monkeys so accustomed to people that the little monsters will steal your camera from your hands or tear jewelry from your neck and scamper off with their loot into the trees.

OFF THE BEATEN PATH

TEGALALUNG – The roads north out of Ubud pass through lovely countryside with patchwork rice fields in different stages of cultivation. Men ankle-deep in mud plant and weed while ducks paddle and dip for their lunch. Out in the fields stand shrines to Dewi, the goddess of rice, and raised wooden platforms where farmers rest or eat. In the village of Tegalalung, artisans carve intricate flower designs into wood. It's delicate work, where a slip of the chisel can ruin the whole piece. You don't have to buy anything—though to do so would make the artisans happy. Just watch and marvel at the incredible craftsmanship.

Dining and Lodging

$$ ★ ✕ **Ary's Warung.** This Ubud classic is right on the main street. The open, multilevel layout is welcoming, but in peak season the small tables are placed so closely together that you'll probably bump elbows with the person sitting next to you. Still, the delicious Indonesian and Western fare—including salads, sandwiches, and snacks—is worth putting up with the close quarters. On quieter days, Ary's is a great place to browse through your guidebook or people-watch while sipping tea or coffee. The desserts are fabulous (one taste of the white-chocolate cheesecake, and you'll be hooked). ✉ *Jl. Raya,* ☎ *0361/975053. AE, MC, V.*

$$ ✕ **Café Lotus.** Owned and managed by a Balinese man and his Australian wife, this peaceful, charming restaurant in the center of Ubud has tables in the courtyard gardens of a royal temple. You can't beat the setting: cool stone floors, intimate tables, small waterfalls hither and yon, and a magnificent lotus pond in back. From the creative menu consider ordering the avocado with diced peanuts, the roast chicken, or a homemade pasta dish. ✉ *Jl. Raya,* ☎ *0361/975660. AE, MC, V. Closed Mon.*

$$ ★ ✕ **Kokokan Club.** Bali's best Thai restaurant is hidden in a corner lot next to the ARMA (☞ *above*). Tucked into the folds of a forest beside a river that flows through rice terraces, the two-story, thatched-roof pavilion is just a quick step across a stone bridge. Both the views and the food are memorable. The steamed spring rolls are fresh, soft, and hot; the onion, tomato, and cucumber salad with lettuce, peanuts, and chilies is crisp and zesty; the fish entrées are fresh and sumptuous. Even the standard *phad thai* (fried noodles) are top-notch and beautifully arranged. Round tables, candlelight, and river breezes make this a popular dinner place, but the views are best in the late afternoon. ✉ *Jl. Pengosekan,* ☎ *0361/96495. AE, MC, V.*

$$ ★ ✕ **Murni's Warung.** Beside a small ravine just outside Ubud, this multilevel restaurant is spacious yet intimate. The street-level dining room bustles with activity; one steep flight of stairs below, a second dining room is often empty and has terrific views (particularly of a nearby waterfall), as does the downstairs bar. Throughout, the shadowy wood interior is complemented by simple bamboo furniture and Indonesian art, creating a rustic and very Balinese feel. Both Indonesian and Western dishes are served, and special buffets are available on Western holidays. The Balinese duck—stuffed with spices and baked so thoroughly that the meat falls off the bones—is tried and true. The friendly, cheerful staff is ready to offer advice on local activities or simply rock ba-

bies while parents eat. A shop on the upper floor is a veritable gallery of Balinese items. Murni's also has some on-site accommodations, including two rooms, a bungalow, and a house—all moderately priced. ✉ *Jl. Raya,* ☎ *0361/975233. AE, MC, V.*

$ ✕ **Kafe Batan Waru.** Expats favor this café for its great service, decent food, and laid-back Ubud ambience. Two dozen or so tables edge right up to the sidewalk, and the wait staff is quick to deliver drinks and plates of food even at the busiest times. A combination of Indonesian and Western fare graces the menu, including a tasty assortment of gado gado, mie goreng, nasi campur, and grilled seafood. ✉ *Jl. Dewi Sita,* ☎ *0361/977528. AE, MC, V.*

$ ✕ **Tutmak.** A stone's toss from Kafe Batan Waru is this small, neat coffee shop and espresso counter, where the beans are roasted fresh daily. Duck in for simple meals or pastries and a real cup of "java." ✉ *Jl. Dewi Sita,* ☎ *0361/975754. No credit cards.*

$$$$ ✕🏨 **Kupu Kupu Barong.** This luxurious complex is on the precipice of a deep valley, with glorious views of rice terraces and the Ayung River. Guest quarters vary in size and cost; all require stout legs, since they're built into the hillside (note because of the many levels, steps, and balconies, this hotel isn't recommended for families with young children). The older bungalows blend with the landscape and have woven rattan or stone-face walls and unique crafted furnishings. Duplexes have wood paneling and indulgently large bathrooms. The path to the restaurant is trellised with banana leaves, hibiscus, and clove. Seated on a rattan chair at a marble-top table, you can make your selection from such dishes as chicken casserole with coconut, chili, and lemongrass; prawn curry with yellow jasmine rice and green mango pickles; or smoked chicken and avocados with tropical fruit and black-current dressing. ✉ *Desa Kedewatan, 80571,* ☎ *0361/975478; 800/561–3071 in the U.S.; 0171/742–7780 in the U.K.;* FAX *0361/975079. 19 suites. Restaurant, 2 bars, 2 pools, massage, bicycles, travel services. AE, DC, MC, V.*

$ ✕🏨 **Ananda Cottages.** In the rice paddies of Campuan, just up the hill from Ubud, is this friendly, relaxed hotel. The open-air lounge-lobby surrounds a central garden. The thatched-roof brick bungalows have two units above and two below. Room decor is simple, with rattan furniture and ikat bedcovers; upper rooms have not only better views but also better baths. The open-air restaurant serves such specialities as satay and bebek betutu. ✉ *Jl. Raya (✉ Box 205, Denpasar 80364),* ☎ *0361/975376,* FAX *0361/975375. 30 rooms. Restaurant, bar, pool. No credit cards.*

$$$$ ★ 🏨 **Amandari.** The modern architecture here elegantly reflects local culture and customs. As you walk along stone paths and past lotus ponds, the only thing that might break the serenity is an occasional, distant rooster's crow. The spacious public areas include an open-air lobby, a book and CD library, and a restaurant overlooking a dramatic pool that appears to drop off into infinity. Tall stone walls enclose thatched-roof villas, most of which overlook rice terraces. The light-filled suites have dark wood, marble floors, heavy cream upholstery, spacious showers, dressing areas, and sunken outdoor tubs; six suites have private plunge pools. In duplexes, a spiral staircase leads to an upstairs bedroom. After a workout in the gym—with all its modern equipment—you might head to the spa for a traditional Balinese treatment. If you'd like do some shopping afterward, drivers are available to take you to and from downtown Ubud. ✉ *Desa Kedewatan (Box 33), 80571,* ☎ *0361/975333; 800/447–7462; 212/223–2848 in the U.S.; 0800/282684 in the U.K.;* FAX *0361/975335. 30 suites. Restaurant, bar, pool, spa, tennis court, health club, hiking, bicycles, library, travel services. AE, DC, MC, V.*

$$$$ ★ **Four Seasons Resort at Sayan.** The journey to this 17-acre property begins with a walk along a wooden bridge above rice-terraced mountain slopes and the Ayung River. The path ends at a large elliptical lotus pond on the roof of the central three-story structure. A polished wood staircase descends to the reception area and a lounge and bar with a spectacular 180-degree vista. Two-story suites are in the main building; villas are set into the hillside all the way down to the riverbank. Rooms are accented with rich teak and stone and have custom-made furnishings and tapestries from Bali and Java. The very modern spa offers Balinese massage and natural treatments. There's also a health club and, on a curving terrace, two sunken whirlpools that seem to hang out over the valley. Golf carts transport you along cement paths to the main building, the villas, and the free-form pool beside the river. Garden plots along the way contain ginger, corn, chilies, and other spices and vegetables used in the kitchen; rice grown on site is given away to local villages. ✉ *Desa Sayan, 80571,* ☎ *0361/977577,* FAX *0361/977588. 18 suites, 28 villas. 2 restaurants, bar, pool, hot tubs, spa, health club, shops, library, meeting rooms. AE, DC, MC, V.*

$$$$ **Ibah Luxury Villas.** Tucked into the hills above a bend in Ubud's main road, Ibah is an unexpected pleasure. To reach the thatched-roof villas you stroll through stone archways, follow stepping stones across lily ponds, and hike trails that wind up the slopes. Villas have large windows with heavenly views, wood floors, ornate antique wood doors, and bathrooms with marble tubs and garden vistas. The picturesque pools across the parking lot are surrounded by cushioned seating areas carved into a stone wall built into the hill. The cozy spa above the restaurant is secluded and intimate, with treatment rooms right beneath its eaves. ✉ *Jl. Raya (Box 193), 80571,* ☎ *0361/974466,* FAX *0361/974467. 11 villas. Restaurant, bar, 2 pools, hot tub, spa, health club, laundry service, travel services. AE, MC, V.*

$$$$ **Pita Maha.** A member of Ubud's royal family modeled the Pita Maha after a Balinese village and built it on the edge of the Oos River valley. The architecture of the villas is traditional, the interior touches tastefully luxurious: marble floors, ornate window panels, wicker furniture with cream-color cushions, woven mats. Tall, sliding glass panels open to private terraces; most villas also have plunge pools. Bathrooms have curving sunken tubs, decorative stone walls, and open gardens. The restaurant and large, "infinity-edge" pool look onto the river valley. A stay at this hotel also gives you privileged access to local museums, temples, tours, and activities—compliments of your royal host. ✉ *Jl. Sanggingan (Box 198),* ☎ *0361/974330,* FAX *0361/974329. 29 villas. Restaurant, 2 bars, in-room safes, pool, spa, shop, library, laundry service, travel services. AE, MC, V.*

$$–$$$ **Kokokan Hotel.** Scattered in the hills above the sacred Tirta Tawar River like small, forgotten temples, the stone-and-brick buildings of this charming hotel reflect the aura of their magical setting. Rooms have marble floors; terraces; huge bathrooms (no tubs, though, only showers); and ornate, hand-carved wooden doors and window panels. Balinese textiles and paintings accent the warm wood. Deluxe rooms have carved sandstone walls and sliding door panels that separate the large bedroom area from the bath. Room rates include a full breakfast; you can also dine in the poolside café or at the nearby Kokokan Club (☞ *above*). The on-site museum offers workshops that teach Balinese art forms such as gamelan playing, puppet and mask making, weaving, and dance—an excellent opportunity for parents to learn about Bali with their children. ✉ *Jl. Pengosekan, 80571,* ☎ *0361/975742,* FAX *0361/975332. 15 rooms. Restaurant, pool, laundry service, children's programs. AE, MC, V.*

$$ **Puri Bunga Village Hotel.** This quiet oasis offers the same views as the Amandari and the Kupu Kupu for a fraction of the price. Although the furnishings aren't spectacular, rooms are spacious, and all but two face the Ayung River valley. Two junior suites have whirlpools; the Honeymoon Suite is the most luxurious and private. A small pool in the garden is beside an open-air restaurant. You're better off having your own wheels here; otherwise it's a 10-minute taxi ride into Ubud's center. ✉ *Desa Kedewatan (Box 141), 80000,* ☎ *0361/975448,* FAX *0361/975073. 14 rooms. Restaurant, pool. MC, V.*

$$ **Tjampuhan.** On the main road just out of Ubud—atop a ravine overlooking a holy river—Tjampuhan was once an artists' colony, and the grounds still contain the former house of German painter Walter Spies. The lobby is no more than an open terrace off the road; paths lead to the bungalows, which are set in lovely gardens and have carved and gilded wood doors, woven bamboo walls, bamboo furniture, and handwoven fabrics and batiks. During the rainy season, rooms tend to be a little damp. You can ring for breakfast with bamboo bells. A new spa down the lane from the restaurant offers a variety of traditional treatments in a tropical setting. ✉ *Jl. Campuan (✉ Box 15, Denpasar 80364),* ☎ *0361/975368,* FAX *0361/975137. 63 bungalows. Restaurant, bar, pool, spa, 2 tennis courts, bicycles, car rental. MC, V.*

$–$$ **Puri Gong.** The front is an art gallery, but beyond a slim stone doorway, a path leads back to three large villas overlooking rice terraces. Rooms are bright, spacious, and breezy (there are four in each building, two on the upper level and two on the lower); each has tile floors, large teak canopy beds, and private bathrooms. Lower rooms have verandas, but upper ones have wonderful views through large windows that pull in the afternoon light. Breakfast is included in the price. ✉ *Jl. Hanoman, Raya Pengosekan, Ubud,* ☎ *0361/975343,* FAX *0361/298269. 12 rooms. Restaurant, bar, pool, laundry service, travel services. MC, V.*

$ **Agung Raka.** Four rooms at this lodging in a developing area off Monkey Forest Road are duplexes: downstairs are a covered patio and a small lounge area; up steep wooden steps is the main bedroom with a canopy bed and a small balcony overlooking the rice fields. The bathroom and shower are outside, enclosed but open to the sky. The remaining rooms, which cost about a quarter less, are in small two-story houses; those on the ground-floor have patios, those upstairs have balconies. Rates include breakfast. ✉ *Jl. Pengosekan, 80571,* ☎ *0361/975757,* FAX *0361/975546. 12 rooms. Restaurant, pool. MC, V.*

Nightlife and the Arts

Ubud shuts down early—by the time most dance performances let out, around 9 or 9:30, many cafés and restaurants are closing. One or two spots along Jalan Raya stay open later, including **Ary's Warung** (☎ 0361/975053) and **Café Lotus** (☎ 0361/975660), which often have live jazz or Indonesian music. **Rai Bar** (no phone) on Monkey Forest Road attracts a crowd after everything else has shut down. The **Kokokan Club** (✉ Jl. Pengosekan, ☎ 0361/96495) in Pengosekan has live music on Saturday.

Ubud is the dance center of Bali, and you should see more than one of the varied performances during your visit—not a problem, as at least three troupes perform nightly. Dance shows at hotels are often commercially adapted and shortened; those held elsewhere around Ubud are more genuine. (☞ Pleasures and Pastimes, *above,* for a discussion of the most popular dances.) Try to attend at least one performance in the village of Peliatan (it's just east of Ubud), whose troupes enjoy some renown. The Puri Saren, Ubud's palace, is a pleasant, atmospheric venue. Avoid the Kecak dance in the village of Bona, 3 km (2 mi) east of Blahbatuh, as traffic noise distracts from the chant.

Consult your hotel or the *Bali Tourist Guide* and the *Bali Guide to Events,* available free at most hotels and travel agencies, for current schedules. **Ubud Tourist Information** (☞ Visitor Information *in* Bali Essentials, *below*) has a weekly dance-performance schedule and sells tickets (Rp 5,000–Rp 7,000) that include transportation to shows not held in Ubud proper.

Outdoor Activities and Sports

GOLF

Forty-five minutes north of Ubud, the 18-hole, 6,432-yard **Bali Handera Country Club** (✉ Bedugul, ☎ 0361/788994) is in a volcanic crater and has beautifully landscaped gardens along its fairways. Greens fees are $87 on weekends and $72 during the week. Caddies cost $7 a round.

RAFTING

It takes 2½ hours to drift and bump through gorges and rapids down the Ayung River, ending in the gentle valley near Ubud. Several companies organize rubber-raft trips for around $55, including the reliable Australian outfit **Bali Adventure Rafting** (✉ Jl. Tunjung Mekar, Legian, ☎ 0361/751292). For agencies that specialize in adventure and rafting tours, *see* Travel Agencies *in* Bali Essentials *below.*

Shopping

Ubud's main street is lined with shops that sell art, textiles, clothing, and other handicrafts. On most days you'll also find a street market, but the big "market day" takes place every third day from dawn until noon. The clusters of shops along Jalan Monkey Forest and the surrounding streets are also filled with bargains on jewelry, batik clothing and textiles, and handcrafted bags. **Ary's Book Shop** (☎ 0361/96351) is the best place to find English-language publications on regional culture and nature. For clothing and books, try **Mutiara** (☎ 0361/975145). **Kunang-Kunang I and II** (☎ 0361/975714 or 0361/975716, respectively) have wonderful collections of textiles, carvings, art pieces, and antiques for sale.

The **Puri Gong Art Gallery** (✉ Jl. Raya, Pengosekan, ☎ 0361/974697) purveys antique sculptures, furniture, ceramics, and masks. The gallery next to the **Rudana Museum** (✉ Jl. Cokgederai, ☎ 0361/26564) sells collectors' pieces of hand-painted batik and paintings at reasonable prices. The **Seniwati Gallery of Art by Women** (✉ Jl. Sri Wedari, ☎ 0361/975285) displays and sells the works of many local female artists.

Ubud has its own style of wood carving; it's somewhat more ethereal than the work done in Mas. The slightly dusty shops of **Kamasan** (✉ Jl. Raya, Peliatan, ☎ 0361/974697) have an array of hand-carved items in endless themes, sizes, and styles. Look for handcrafted furniture at **Mario Antiques** (✉ Peninjauan Sukawati, Gianyar, ☎ 0361/98541), just outside Ubud. A good place to see both old and new work is the **Nyana Tilem Gallery** (✉ Jl. Raya, Mas, no phone). **Siadja** (✉ Jl. Raya, Mas, ☎ 0361/975710) is a small shop with numerous colorfully painted items.

En Route Pejeng fell to the Javanese in the mid-1300s, but its temples still stand as testament to a great kingdom. Take time to walk through the **Pura Penataran Sasih,** Pejeng's former state temple, with its centuries-old Moon of Pejeng bronze drum. Also interesting is the **Pura Pusering Jagat,** possibly the crux of an ancient Balinese kingdom in which carvings and a large urn depict tales of the Mahabharata. Don't miss the **Pura Kebo**

Edan, the "crazy buffalo" temple, with its famous 10-ft statue of its namesake.

Tampaksiring

8 *19 km (12 mi) northeast of Ubud.*

This town is an excellent base for visiting three sacred Balinese sites. Since there are few accommodations or restaurants in the area, it's best to make Tampaksiring a day trip from Ubud.

Outside of town follow signs to **Pura Gunung Kawi,** a monument to an 11th-century ruler and one of the oldest temples in Bali. From the access road, a stone stairway leads down to a lush valley. You pass beneath a stone arch to the canyon floor where there are two rows of memorial temples, carved in niches in the face of two cliffs. According to legend, the giant Kebo Iwa carved these in one night with his fingernails.

Beyond the outskirts of Tampaksiring, the road forks. To the right is the famous temple at **Tirta Empul,** where people from all over Bali come to bathe in the holy spring. According to legend, the spring was created when the god Indra pierced a stone to produce magical waters that revived his army, whose soldiers had been poisoned by the demon king Mayadanava.

At the **Pura Panti Pasek Gel Gel** holy spring, a few miles north of Tirtal Empul, the hawkers are less demanding, and fewer visitors interrupt the sanctity of the temple than at Tirtu Empul. The temple is dedicated to Vishnu, whose many responsibilities include water and irrigation. The main shrine stands in the center of a pool filled with holy water and fat goldfish. Bathing pools are segregated by sex and age.

Gunung Batur

9 *11 km (7 mi) north of Tampaksiring, 62 km (37 mi) north of Ubud.*

West toward the villages of Penaka and Sebatu and north of Tampaksiring, the vanilla- and clove-bordered road climbs quickly. Roadside stalls sell fruits and vegetables rather than souvenirs and handicrafts. And then there's the majestic bulk of 5,632-ft Gunung Batur (Mt. Batur). Dark lava flows are visible within the volcano's vast crater—nearly 29 km (18 mi) in diameter and 600 ft deep—where a new volcano has arisen and cool Lake Batur has formed. Penelokan, a village at the edge of the old crater, affords a great view of the lake and caldera.

An alternative route to Gunung Batur that captures Bali's enchanting rural scenes can be done in an afternoon, leaving around 3 PM to catch the best light of the day. The narrow, two-lane Sayan–Kedewatan road along the eastern border of Ubud passes a gathering of resorts through Payangan. Women carrying baskets of vegetables on their heads walk along the forest-lined route. As the lane heads north, you'll glimpse the Ayung River valley to the left; banana and palm trees crowd the right. The terrain then evens out into steeply stacked rice terraces that shine in the late afternoon light. Flocks of cranes cruise through the blue sky above them. About 12 km (8 mi) from the town of Kintamani (☞ *below*), the forest occasionally opens to offer views of the river valley to the left and mountains to the right. The truly breathtaking scenes, however, begin 3 km (2 mi) outside Kintimani, when the triumvirate peaks of Gunung Agung, Gunung Batur, and Gunung Abang appear east to west. A thin pine forest surrounds the road as it climbs into the mountains and comes to the junction with the main northern road. Here, you can't help but stop to gape at the shadowy slopes surrounding Lake Batur far below.

Quiet **Kintamani** is used as a rest stop by hikers who climb Gunung Batur. Guided hikes cost of about Rp 10,000 per person with a minimum of four in the group. To find a guide, inquire at the **Yayasa Bintang Danu tourist office** (☎ 0366/23370) opposite the turnoff to Lake Batur from Penelokan.

In the village of Penulisan, an old stairway leads up a hill to the ancient temple of **Pura Sukawana.** Most of the decaying sculptures are from the 11th century, but look closely and you will find older, pagan phallic symbols. The view, which stretches across Bali to the Java Sea, is breathtaking, especially at sunrise.

Dining and Lodging

$ ✕▦ **Lakeview Restaurant and Homestay.** Of the cluster of small, inexpensive hotels and restaurants beside the volcano's rim in Penelokan, this very simple hotel is one of the most popular. Rooms are very basic but clean, and the proximity to local activities makes up for the lack of amenities. Budget quarters are without bath; superior rooms are the largest and have private baths. The indoor-outdoor restaurant has decent Indonesian fare and memorable views—tour buses often stop here for a buffet lunch en route through the mountains. ✉ *Jl. Raya, Penelokan,* ☎ *0366/51464. 20 rooms. Restaurant, bar, laundry service. No credit cards.*

$ ✕▦ **Segara Bungalows.** Six kilometers (4 miles) down the caldera road past Penelokan, this pleasant hotel is almost at the edge of Lake Batur. The no-frills rooms are clean; all have private baths but not all have hot water, so make sure to specify your preference. An open-air restaurant offers tasty Indonesian and Western dishes in a quiet mountain setting. Tours of the area are available, and the management is very helpful. The hotel is often used as a base for hiring trekking guides. ✉ *Jl. Danau Batur, Penelokan,* ☎ *0361/958001. 38 rooms. Restaurant, travel services. AE, MC, V.*

Pura Kehen

⑩ *35 km (21 mi) south of Gunung Batur. The drive south from Penelokan to Bangli is a quick run downhill. On the outskirts of Bangli is an S-curve; here take a left, and at the foot of the hill is Pura Kehen.*

Pura Kehen, a 12th-century temple dedicated to Shiva, is considered one of Bali's most beautiful: it rises up the mountainside and culminates in an 11-tier shrine. You step through an ornate entrance and into a courtyard with a giant holy banyan tree and a bell tower used to summon the villagers for ceremonies. The entrance to the inner courtyard is up steep steps. At the top center are the "closed gate" and a boma, which blocks evil spirits. Within the inner courtyard, the main shrine sits on a cosmic turtle, symbolizing the spiritual world, entwined by nagas, symbolizing the material. Material binds the spiritual—another example of Balinese harmony.

OFF THE BEATEN PATH

PURA BESAKIH – Known as the Mother Temple of Bali, Pura Besakih is the most sacred of all. Situated on the slopes of Gunung Agung, the complex has 30 temples—one for every Balinese district—on seven terraces. It's thought to have been built before Hinduism reached Bali and subsequently modified. The structure consists of three main parts, the north painted black for Vishnu, the center white for Shiva, and the south red for Brahma. You enter through a split gate.

Much of the temple area was destroyed in 1963 when Gunung Agung erupted, killing 1,800 of the faithful, but diligent restoration has repaired most of the damage. You aren't allowed into the inner courtyard, but there's enough to see to justify the steep 2-km (1-mi) walk from the parking lot past souvenir stands and vendors. Besakih is 40 km (25 mi) northeast of Bangli, 45 km (28 mi) north of Klungkung, and 60 km (35 mi) north of Denpasar. The temple can be reached from Bangli (if you're coming from Gunung Batur), Klungkung (the best route if you're coming from Ubud, Denpasar, or points south), or Candidasa—take the road inland to Amlapura, where the road splits; keep going to Rendang, then turn right to climb the 11 km (7 mi) to the temple.

EAST AND NORTH

Klungkung

11 *28 km (18 mi) southeast of Ubud, 46 km (29 mi) east of Denpasar.*

Klungkung is a former dynastic capital. In the center of town stands the **Kerta Gosa** (Hall of Justice), part of the 18th-century Royal Palace destroyed by the Dutch in the early 20th century and restored again by the remorseful Dutch two decades later. The raised platform in the hall supports three thrones—one with a lion carving for the king, one with a dragon for the minister, and one with a bull for the priest. The accused brought before this tribunal could look up at the painted ceiling and contemplate the horrors in store for convicted criminals: torches between the legs, pots of boiling oil, decapitation by saw, and dozens of other punishments to fit specific crimes. To the right of the Hall of Justice is the **Bale Kambang** (Floating Pavilion), a moat-encircled palace that was also decimated and rebuilt by the Dutch. Part of the motif of its painted ceiling relates stories of the hero Sang Sutasoma, whose supernatural powers could turn arrows and spears into flowers. The **Museum Semarajaya,** across the courtyard, is also worth a look for its collection of island relics as well as black-and-white photos and newspaper clippings that depict palace life and relate historic events.

Goa Lawah

12 *10 km (6 mi) southeast of Klungkung.*

East of Klungkung, the road drops south to run along the coast and through the area of Kusamba, speckled with the thatched roofs of salt-panning huts. Just beyond is Goa Lawah, the bat cave. Unless you really long to see thousands of bats hanging from the ceiling, you may not want to subject yourself to the aggressive hawkers, postcard sellers, and young girls who throw you a flower, then angrily demand payment when you leave. The cave is said to lead all the way to Gunung Agung.

Padangbai

13 *5 km (3 mi) northeast of Goa Lawah.*

Continuing east from Goa Lawah along the coast will bring you to Padangbai, a quiet village next to one of the island's main ports. Because most people simply pass through it en route to other sights, Padangbai has remained a charmingly offbeat center for water sports and romantic getaways. The only time the town seems at all frenzied is right after the four-hour ferry from Lombok arrives or when the occasional cruise ship docks—hawkers set up stands and set to work as passengers disembark. There's a tourist office at the docks, and there are plenty of boats for hire. There are also plenty of small losmen where you can while away the afternoons walking along the thin brown crescent of beach filled with colorfully painted fishing pontoons.

Balina Beach and Manggis

★ 14 *5 km (3 mi) north of Padangbai.*

The curving stretch of Balina Beach, at the other end of Amuk Bay, is just as serene as Padangbai—but with the feel of an upscale resort. Several luxury hotels are set back into the forested slopes along the road between the village of Manggis, 11 km (7 mi) north of Padangbai, and Candidasa.

Dining and Lodging

$$$$ ★ **Amankila.** This hillside resort has views of the Bandung Straits. Luxurious thatched-roof pavilions are connected by long, raised, cement walkways. Each guest villa has a terrace, a bedroom with a king-size canopy bed, and a spacious bath with a sunken tub and separate shower; some villas have private pools. You'll feel like royalty basking in the sun beside the tri-level communal pool, whose waters rush down in wide falls from one level to the next. The beach is a stiff downhill climb, or you can ride to it in a chauffeured Jeep. The large, warm library has an extensive collection of books on Indonesian and regional travel and history; in its cushioned sitting area, experts often present slide shows or give talks on topics related to local culture. At the Terrace restaurant, you choose from three menus—Indonesian, Nonya (Malay), and Western. The chef comes to your table to make recommendations tailored to your tastes, and the rest of the staff maintains this high level of service throughout your meal. Savory appetizers include the Thai-style crab and coconut salad and the *bosonboh,* a light, crispy, stir-fried salad with squid, tofu, bean sprouts, and vegetables. Succulent pork satay, juicy beef rendang, and curry *kapitan* (a wild-chicken curry flavored with lemongrass) are standout entrées. Each night a gamelan trio plays as the sun sets. ✉ *Pantai Buitan (3 km/2 mi northeast of Padangbai turnoff), Manggis 80871,* ☎ *0366/21993; 800/447–7462; 212/223–2848 in the U.S.; 0800/282684 in the U.K.;* FAX *0366/21995. 35 villas. 2 restaurants, bar, pool, massage, hiking, beach, snorkeling, windsurfing, library, travel services. AE, DC, MC, V.*

$$$–$$$$ **The Serai.** When sunlight washes the pale golden walls and marble floors, you get a true sense of this resort's warmth. Rooms are in the two-story buildings with gold walls, wood furnishings, and cream-color upholstery. Superior rooms don't have tubs (only showers), but they do have outer sitting areas that face the pool and beach; in deluxe rooms the baths are fully equipped and the balconies have built-in sofas overlooking the pool and gardens. A range of outdoor activities and tours to local sights are available so you can readily experience the local flora, fauna, and culture. In the restaurant, small square tables and butterscotch wicker chairs are arranged in a raised, sheltered pavilion surrounded by a lotus pond. Must-try Asian dishes include steamed duck breast, spicy prawn mango curry with yellow rice, and Thai green chicken curry. If you crave a Western dish, try the wild-rice mushroom risotto or the grilled peppered tuna. Round woven mats, deep-blue cups and plates with lemon-color starfish, and yellow spice and sugar bowls accentuate the food's artistic presentation. The on-site cooking school gives you a chance to learn more about Indonesian cuisine. ✉ *Pantai Buitan (6 km/4 mi northeast of Padangbai turnoff), Manggis 80871,* ☎ *0363/41011,* FAX *0363/41015. 58 rooms. Restaurant, bar, beach, dive shop, travel services. AE, DC, MC, V.*

$ **Balina Beach Bungalows.** Popular with scuba and snorkel enthusiasts for its diving club, this hotel has one- and two-story thatched cottages near a sandy beach 3 km (1.8 mi) west of Candidasa. All rooms have private baths and ceiling fans. The best rooms, upstairs in the two-story bungalows, have sitting areas and terraces; the one-story garden-view rooms have open-air bathrooms and large corner tubs as well as large cushioned bales overlooking the rice fields. ✉ *Pantai Buitan (8 km/5 mi northeast of Padangbai turnoff), Manggis 80870,* ☎ *0363/41002,* FAX *0363/41001. 42 rooms. Restaurant, bar, pool, beach, dive shop, travel services. AE, DC, MC, V.*

Outdoor Activities and Sports

The **Balina Diving Association** (✉ Balina Beach, ☎ 0361/80871) arranges dives out to Nusa Penida.

Candidasa

15 *3 km (2 mi) east of Balina Beach, 6 km (4 mi) east of Manggis, 14 km (9 mi) northeast of Padangbai.*

Candidasa, once a budget traveler's escape from the 24-hour partying of the southwestern beaches, now encompasses a throng of small hotels, restaurants, tourist shops, and travel agencies. Still, the area is more peaceful than Kuta or Legian, and less expensive than Nusa Dua or Jimbaran. A lively coral reef 300 yards offshore calms the waves and makes the water ideal for snorkeling. If you prefer scuba diving, you can easily hire one of the many fishing boats that park close to the beach.

Dining and Lodging

$ ✕ **TJ's.** Don't let the dressed-down setting of chipped blue chairs, a mishmash of tables, and scuffed brick floors put you off—the food is terrific. There is Asian and Western fare, and a bar along the side wall serves up every drink you can imagine (it's a popular evening hangout). Among the best dishes are the Thai green chicken curry, the spicy Thai red prawn curry, and the nasi campur. ✉ *Jl. Raya, no phone. AE, MC, V.*

$ ✕ **Warung Candi Agung.** Fresh, tasty food and very affordable prices have made this eatery on the main road popular with travelers. With a very basic decor and motorcycles and trucks flying by, there isn't much ambience. But the list of Western, Indonesian, and seafood dishes is long; the service is prompt; and the staff is eager to please. A stage is the site of free weekly Legong performances, and the restaurant operates a free shuttle to and from town. ✉ *Jl. Raya,* ☎ *0363/41157. No credit cards.*

$$ ★ **The Watergarden.** This resort's name couldn't be more appropriate. Cool, thatched-roof cottages with high ceilings, marble floors, warm brick walls, and simple island furnishings are complemented by wide wooden terraces overlooking lily ponds. Each dwelling is nestled into tropical gardens, with rushing waterfalls and koi ponds around every corner. From the white-sand beach across the road, the views of Gunung Agung are superb. Friendly staffers might offer to take you to their villages so that you can see Balinese culture and ceremonies up close. ✉ *Jl. Raya,* ☎ *0363/41540,* FAX *0363/41164. 13 rooms. Restaurant, bar, pool, beach, snorkeling, library, laundry service, travel services. V.*

$ **Fajar Candidasa Beach Bungalows.** Whistling songbirds and chuckling mynahs welcome you to this small hotel; indeed, dozens of birdcages decorate the back of the reception area. Tall, redbrick, templelike bungalows and neat gardens line the walkway. All rooms have small terraces and oversize sunken tubs; only deluxe rooms have air-conditioning, however. The small swimming pool and terrace are right next to the ocean breakwater. The facilities are clean and the grounds are quiet. ✉ *Jl. Raya,* ☎ *0363/41539,* FAX *0366/41538. 33 rooms. Restaurant, bar, pool, beach, boating, laundry service, travel services. AE, MC, V.*

$ **Pandan Bungalows.** Here cozy bungalows with bamboo doors and walls are connected by red-tile terraces beneath a thatched roof. The garden setting stretches to the sea. Bathrooms are open and feature a shower and small stone garden. There's no air-conditioning, but fans are available, as is hot water. You can dine in the restaurant that's next to a small pool and the ocean or in the dining area out front. Continental breakfast is included in the price. ✉ *Jl. Raya (✉ Box 126, Amlapura 80801), ☎ 0363/41541, FAX 0363/41541. 24 rooms. 2 restaurants, bar, pool, laundry service. MC, V.*

Tenganan

⑯ *8 km (5 mi) northwest of Candidasa.*

On the western side of Candidasa, the road turns inland to Tenganan, an ancient walled village of the Bali Aga—the people who lived on the island well before the conquerors of Java's Majapahit kingdom arrived. The village consists of two parallel streets lined on either side with identical walled compounds. Inside the compounds, houses face each other across a grassy central strip, where the public buildings stand (no cars are allowed). Tenganan people seldom marry outside the village, and they adhere to their traditions—it is, for example, one of the few places in Indonesia where double ikat is still woven and traditional Balinese script is transcribed onto palm leaves. Several unique and sacred types of music and dance are still performed here: the gamelan *selendeng,* the orchestra of the ancient Balinese; the gamelan *gambing,* composed of a pair of seven-key bronze xylophones and four wooden-key xylophones; and the *rejang* dance, which features ornate headdresses and costumes made of the fine *geringsing* cloth woven only in Tenganan.

Tulamben

⑰ *40 km (24 mi) northeast of Candidasa.*

The main road from Candidasa cuts west around the foothills of 3,854-ft Gunung Serai and continues up and around the north coast. Although Tulamben isn't a large town, it's visited by many people who have one goal in mind: to dive the wreck of the *Liberty,* a World War II ship that sank just offshore. The reefs here add to the attraction, and the beaches are more serene than others nearby.

Dining and Lodging

$–$$ ✕🏨 **Mimpi Resort.** The accommodations are basic and pleasant at this dive resort set between the sea and the foothills of Gunung Agung. Rooms have a traditional Balinese design with understated island decor; all have air-conditioning and private outdoor showers. The on-site restaurant has Indonesian and Western fare that's hearty enough to please the appetites of underwater adventurers. In addition to dive tours and snorkeling, the hotel also offers sea kayaking. ✉ *Desa Kubu, Karangasem, ☎ 0363/21642, FAX 0363/21939. 40 rooms. Restaurant, bar, pool, spa, beach, snorkeling, dive shop, travel services. AE, MC, V.*

Lovina

★ ⑱ *70 km (42 mi) northwest of Tulamben.*

Calm seas, black-sand beaches, and lovely sunrises and sunsets are what you'll find at these peaceful northern settlements. The cluster of villages here—including Anturan, Bunut Panggang, Kalibukbuk, Temukus, and Tukad Mungga—is known as "Lovina," a pleasant name bestowed on this stretch of coastline in the 1950s by Prince Anak Agung Panji Tisna simply in honor of love. Although a number of hotels and restaurants line the main road, the landscape to the south is all mountains and farmland, and that to the north is all ocean. Travelers have long headed to Lovina for respite, but the large resorts have only laid down roots in the last decade. Diving, dolphin-watching, trekking, and cultural explorations are the prime activities.

Dining and Lodging

$ ✕ **Lian.** Savory scents from this restaurant's satay grill waft into the large dining pavilion, tantalizing you as you wait for your Indonesian, Western, or Chinese fare. If you arrive when it's busy, the wait can be long. Have a beer and relax amid the cheerful chatter and loud Western music. Prices are inexpensive, but portions are small. Note that some of the best dishes—such as the Balinese duck—have to be ordered in advance. ✉ *Jl. Raya,* ☎ *0362/41480. MC, V.*

$ ✕ **Puri Ratus Restaurant.** Guarded by two large chickens in woven cages and a pair of carved wooden lions, this red-tile-roof pavilion has decent, reasonably priced Indonesian and Western fare. Menu items are basic—mie goreng, seafood, curries, and fruits. Breakfast and lunch buffets are offered daily. ✉ *Jl. Raya Lovina,* ☎ *0362/41059. MC, V.*

$$–$$$ **Hotel Aneka Lovina.** It's worth visiting this resort just to see the variety of ornately carved wooden doors. Each room has a traditional Balinese entry, honed with different images and painted in different colors. A winding brick walkway runs through the gardens between the rows of thatched-roof, two-story buildings; fuchsia and orange bougainvillea trickle over their balconies. Rooms are clean and simple with peach curtains, white-tile floors, and Balinese paintings. The seafood restaurant and the large pool are at the end of the resort grounds, next to the ocean. ✉ *Jl. Raya Seririt,* ☎ *0362/41121,* FAX *0362/41827. 59 rooms. Restaurant, 2 bars, pool, beach, dive shop, windsurfing, boating, playground, laundry service, travel services. AE, MC, V.*

$$–$$$ **Sol Lovina.** Set in slightly overgrown grounds, this large resort is all-inclusive, so you never need leave. Rooms are decorated in gold and pale green, with pale peach floors and wood furniture. All have triangular terraces with garden views. Secluded behind high stone walls and ornate green wood doors with gold trim, villas are also decorated in gold and have ample dressing areas, large bathrooms, and outdoor gardens; some have private plunge pools. The communal pool, seafood grill, and garden restaurant are down by the sea. ✉ *Jl. Raya Seririt,* ☎ *0362/41775,* FAX *0362/41659. 118 rooms, 10 villas. 2 restaurants, bar, pool, health club, beach, dive shop, meeting rooms, travel services. AE, MC, V. All-inclusive.*

$–$$ **Hotel Mas Lovina.** Also known as Las Brisas Cottages, these two-story, bullet-shape, traditional Balinese villas are made of dark wood. Bedrooms, which are upstairs, have long windows and views of the pool and the bay. Downstairs, some accommodations have a living area, others have a kitchen—be sure to specify your preference when booking. Each cottage has a redbrick terrace, bamboo furniture, and a large shared backyard with fruit trees. A restaurant serving Indonesian, Western, Chinese, and Japanese food catches the breeze off the water. Breakfast is included in the price, and discounts are available in low season. The Spice Islands Dive Center office is in the reception building. ✉ *Jl. Raya Seririt,* ☎ *0362/41237,* FAX *0362/41236. 20 rooms. Restaurant, bar, pool, beach, dive shop, travel services. AE, MC, V.*

$ **Aditya Bungalows.** The ornate reception building right on the main road in central Lovina has an Indian flair but is actually an old Balinese structure. Guest quarters are down long paths through well-maintained gardens, and many have yards just steps from the sand. Rooms are large and open, with back entrances, raised front porches, tile floors, and very basic furnishings. Note: check the toilet, tub, and refrigerator to make sure they're working, and keep food wrapped up, as ants can be a problem in this area. The staff is very helpful and friendly, and a breakfast buffet is included in the price. ✉ *Jl. Raya Lovina (✉ Box 134, Singaraja 81101), ☎ 0362/41059, FAX 0362/41342. 80 rooms. Restaurant, bar, refrigerators, pool, spa, laundry service, car rental, travel services. AE, MC, V.*

$ **Baruna Beach Cottages.** Off the main road at the edge of the beach, this hotel's dark-stone, two-story, thatched-roof bungalows face the ocean. Agung Rooms have red-tile floors; carved, dark-teak furniture; woven rattan walls and ceilings; terraces overlooking the bay; and bathrooms with a half-tub and a shower hose. The cottage-style rooms are in the back garden and have redbrick terraces with small, temple-style doors; large baths with stone gardens; and batik sarong towels. The pavilion restaurant has a stage for dance performances. ✉ *Desa Pemaron (Box 149), ☎ 0362/41745, FAX 0362/41252. 18 rooms. Restaurant, bar, pool, spa, beach, dive shop, travel services. AE, MC, V.*

Bali Barat National Park

90 km (54 mi) southwest of Lovina, 140 km (87 mi) northwest of Denpasar.

With 188,491 acres of arid forests and mangrove swamps, Bali Barat (West Bali) National Park is a valuable natural treasure. It's one of the few areas left unsculpted by rice terraces, tourist complexes, and other human endeavors. In addition, it's home to several very rare species; foremost is the Bali starling—the island's mascot. Also known as Rothschild's mynah, this soft, white bird has a band of blue around its eyes; the world's last 100 or so of these winged creatures are here, and an on-site breeding program is trying to save the species. Bali Barat also protects approximately three dozen rare Javan *banteng* (buffalo).

There are several unspoiled coral reefs off Menjangan Island, which is just north of the park's mainland. Local dive shops organize scuba and snorkeling trips. If you prefer to stay on land, there's a network of fairly flat trails around the park's edges. You can arrange guided treks at the park office in Cekik, 6 km (4 mi) west of the park entrance at Labuan Lalang (at the crossroads of the main Denpasar and Singaraja roads and on the left side just before Gilimanuk). Permits are required for travel within the park—dive shops usually take care of this formality, but for hiking trips, you'll need to stop at the park office yourself. Another option is a boat trip. You can hire craft at Labuan Lalang, along the Singaraja road, where there are also simple guest houses.

BALI A TO Z

Arriving and Departing

By Airplane

About 13 km (8 mi) southwest of Denpasar, Bali's airport, **Ngurah Rai,** handles international and domestic flights. **Garuda** (☎ 0361/227825) is the main domestic carrier, with flights from Jakarta, Surabaya, Yogyakarta, Medan, Mataram, Ujung Pandang, and Banjarmasin, among other cities. Although most of its flights were suspended at press time, you could also check with **Merpati** (☎ 0361/221188) to see whether its service between Bali and other Indonesian cities has resumed. For details on international carriers, *see* Air Travel *in* Gold Guide.

BETWEEN THE AIRPORT AND HOTELS

Most hotels will have a car or minivan waiting to meet you if you let them know in advance. Otherwise, order a taxi at the counter outside customs; the fixed fare varies depending on the location of your hotel. You can also catch a bemo outside the airport, but make sure that you're going in the right direction and that if you enter an empty van you're not hiring it for yourself—unless that's your intention.

By Boat

Ferries make the 35-minute crossing every hour between Ketapang in eastern Java and Gilimanuk in western Bali for about Rp 1,000 for passengers and Rp 11,000 for vehicles. *See* Nusa Tenggara Essentials *in* Chapter 4, for information on ferry service between Bali and Lombok.

By Bus

Buses from Yogyakarta to Denpasar (16 hours) use the ferry; an air-conditioned bus costs around Rp 17,000. Bus service is available also from Jakarta and Surabaya. You can buy tickets in advance through any travel agent, or you can simply show up at the bus terminal a few hours before you'd like to depart and ask an agent of one of the many bus companies.

Getting Around

By Bemo

Bemos (minibuses) ply the main routes from Denpasar to Sanur and Kuta and from Kuta to Ubud. You can catch them at the main bemo terminals, where fares and schedules are posted, or simply flag one down along the road. Bemos can be crowded with people and goods, but they are quite inexpensive and give you a glimpse of everyday Balinese life.

By Car

Renting cars or Jeeps in Bali is convenient. Daily rates vary from Rp 540,000 at Avis to Rp 454,000 at a small operator, including insurance and unlimited mileage. If you rent from an upscale hotel, the cost of the car will be considerably higher than if you rent off the hotel property. Legally you have to have an international driver's license, though some agencies will not ask for it. Note: if you plan to travel farther than Bali—to Lombok or Java, say—you need a special permit from your rental agent, so be sure to mention your itinerary before you sign the contract. Although prices vary, depending on the places you wish to visit (and the distance covered), a car with a driver will run about Rp 702,000 for 12 hours. Most hotels and agencies can provide drivers.

Try **Andika** (✉ Jl. Batur 12 A, Denpasar, ☎ 0361/240032), **Bagus Rent Car** (✉ Jl. Duyung, Sanur, ☎ 0361/287794), or **Lina Biro Jasa** (✉ Jl. Bakungsari, Kuta, ☎ 0361/51820). **P. T. Multi Sri Bali** (✉ Jl. Raya Uluwatu 8A, Jimbaran, ☎ 0361/701770) represents Avis, which also has branches in several hotels.

Though there is a highway along the island's perimeter, most roads run north to south owing to the mountainous interior. One of the two main north–south thoroughfares heads from Denpasar out toward Sanur and Gianyar, traveling up through Ubud to Gunung Batur; the other cuts off the southwestern highway to head north through Bedugul to Singaraja. On the Bukit Peninsula, the main highway splits just beyond the Ngurah Rai Airport; the east road goes to Nusa Dua, the west to Pura Uluwatu, and a smaller road links points in between.

By Taxi

Taxis are available in the main tourist areas; you can flag one down on the street or book one from any hotel or restaurant. Kuta, Sanur, Nusa Dua, and Denpasar have metered taxis. Make sure that the meter is used. The charge is Rp 450 per km (½ mi). The 15-minute ride from Kuta to Nusa Dua, for example, is Rp 9,000; from Sanur to Nusa

Dua, Rp 15,000. For longer journeys, set rates are negotiable—count on about Rp 15,000 per hour in the southern tourist towns, Denpasar, and Ubud. To order a cab, call the **dispatcher** (☎ 0361/701000 or 0361/289090). You can also try the **airport taxis** (☎ 0361/751011) for rides to and from Ngurah Rai Airport, and **Praja Taxi** (☎ 0361/289090) or **Bali Taxi** (☎ 0361/701111) to travel elsewhere.

Contacts and Resources

Emergencies

Ambulance: ☎ 118. **Fire:** ☎ 113.

Doctors and Dentists: Denpasar: Sangleh Public Hospital (✉ Jl. Sangleh, ☎ 0361/227911) and Kasih Ibu (✉ Jl. Teuku Umar 120, ☎ 0361/223036). Kuta: Kuta Clinic (✉ Jl. Raya Kuta, ☎ 0361/753268), or Dr. N. Sugita (✉ Jl. Tuban, ☎ 0361/751301) for pediatric emergencies. Nusa Dua: Nusa Dua 24-hour Clinic (✉ Jl. Pratama 81A, ☎ 0361/771324) and Nusa Dua Dental Clinic (✉ Jl. Pratama 81A, ☎ 0361/771324). Sanur: Clinic Bali Hyatt Sanur (✉ Bali Hyatt Hotel, Jl. Danau Tamblingan, ☎ 0361/288271). Ubud: Ubud Clinic (✉ Jl. Ubud, Campuhan, ☎ 0361/974911).

Scuba-Diving Emergencies: Baruna (✉ Jl. Raya Seririt, Lovina, ☎ 0362/41084) has a decompression chamber. **Pharmacies:** Bali Farma Apotik (✉ Jl. Melatig, Denpasar, ☎ 0361/22878) provides reliable service and advice. Indonesia Farma Apotik (✉ Jl. Diponegoro, Denpasar, ☎ 0361/27812) is another recommended pharmacy. **Police:** ☎ 110.

English-Language Bookstores

Most large resorts sell some cultural and mass market fiction books, and in major budget tourist areas, such as Kuta, used-book shops thrive on the main strip. Sanur's **Bagus Drugstore** (☎ 0361/287794) has a good selection of culture and nature books. The **Nusa Dua Galeria** supermarket has an entire section of books on regional travel and culture, as well as paperback best-sellers and magazines. **Ary's Bookstore** (☎ 0361/96351) in Ubud is one of the best for regional culture and history.

Tour Operators

The best way to explore Bali is with a private car *and* a knowledgeable guide. Should you visit the crafts villages north of Denpasar, note that most guides get a commission on your purchases. If your guide stops at every shop along the road, speak up—there's too much to see in Bali to spend all your time in such a way. A car, driver, and guide can be hired through local or international car rental agencies, as well as most travel agencies or hotels. For a personal guide, contact **I Made Ramia Santana** (✉ Jl. Planet 9, Denpasar, ☎ 0361/725909).

Many group tours by bus or van are conducted daily. They range from full-day trips into the countryside—stopping at temples, volcanos, and caves—to short in-town Denpasar tours or those that take you to Ubud's arts sights and nearby handicrafts villages. Companies with a great variety of tours include: **Kunang–Kunang** (✉ Jl. Pengosekan, Ubud, ☎ 0361/977388), **Kuta Emas** (✉ Jl. Pantai Kuta 23D, Kuta, ☎ 0361/751925), **Mesti Oriental** (✉ Jl. Nangka Paksimas, Denpasar, ☎ 0361/722283), and **P. T. Putri Mandalika Tours & Travel** (✉ Jl. Hang Tuah Raya II, Sanur, ☎ 0361/297450).

Cruises around the island and to Nusa Lembongan are specialties of: **Bali Hai Cruises** (✉ Benoa Harbor, ☎ 0361/720331), **P. T. Island Explorer** (✉ Jl. Sekar Waru 14D, Sanur, ☎ 0361/289856), **Quicksilver**

(✉ Jl. Segara Kedul 3, Benoa Harbor, ☎ 0361/771997), and **Waka Louka** (✉ Jl. Pratama, Tanjung Benoa, ☎ 0361/723629).

Agencies that specialize in dive trips are: **Bali Club Diver** (✉ Jl. Tamblingan 110, Sanur, ☎ 0361/287263), **Bali Diving Perdana** (✉ Jl. Danau Poso, Gang Tanjung, Sanur, ☎ 0361/286493), **Baruna** (✉ Jl. Raya Seririt, Lovina, ☎ 0362/41084), **Geko Dive** (✉ Jl. Silayukti, Padangbai, ☎ 0363/41516), **Nusa Dua Dive Center** (✉ Jl. Pratama 93A, Tanjung Benoa, Nusa Dua, ☎ 0361/774711), and **Sea Star Dive Center** (✉ Jl. Bypass Ngurah Rai 45, Sanur, ☎ 0361/286492).

For adventure tours—including white-water rafting, kayaking, trekking, and cycling—try: **Ayung River Rafting** (✉ Jl. Diponegoro 150B, Denpasar, ☎ 0361/283789), **Baleraf** (✉ Jl. Tamblingan 82, Sanur, ☎ 0361/287256), **Bali Adventure Tours** (✉ Jl. Bypass Ngurah Rai, Kuta, ☎ 0361/721480), **Bali International Rafting** (✉ Jl. Tirta Ening 7, Bypass Ngurah Rai, Sanur, ☎ 0361/281408), and **Sobek** (✉ Jl. Tirta Ening 9, Bypass Ngurah Rai, Sanur, ☎ 0361/287059).

Travel Agencies

Nitour (✉ Jl. Veteran 5, Denpasar, ☎ 0361/736096) is a reliable travel agency and tour operator. **Pacto Ltd. Tours and Travel** (✉ Bali Beach Hotel, Jl. Tanjung Sari, Sanur, ☎ 0361/788449) provides tour and travel services and also represents American Express. **Satriavi Tours & Travel** (✉ Jl. Cemara 27, Semawang, Sanur, ☎ 0361/287494) offers a comprehensive selection of tours and also arranges custom tours. Since Satriavi is a subsidiary of Garuda Indonesia Airlines, it's well equipped to handle onward flight reservations.

Additional travel agencies with a range of services include: **Bali Griyasari Tours & Travel** (✉ Jl. Gatot Subroto 49, Denpasar, ☎ 0361/461910), **Bintang Balindo Tours & Travel** (✉ Jl. Legian, Gang Meubel, Blk 14, Kuta, ☎ 0361/758402), and **P. T. Lis Bali** (✉ Jl. Tamblingan 32, Sanur, ☎ 0361/286014).

Visitor Information

Denpasar: Dipardi Bali (✉ Jl. Raya Puputan Renon, ☎ 0361/238184). **Kuta:** Bali Tourist Information Center (✉ Central Tourist Plaza, ground floor, Jl. Benasati 7, Legian, ☎ 0361/754090). **Ubud:** Ubud Tourist Information (✉ Jl. Raya, west of Monkey Forest Rd., ☎ 0361/973285).

4 Nusa Tenggara

More than 500 islands trickle eastward from Bali in the Nusa Tenggara archipelago, and the main stepping stones—Lombok, Sumbawa, Komodo, and Flores—are beginning to beckon a steady stream of travelers. Lush Lombok is home to the majestic Gunung Rinjani volcano; Sumbawa offers scenic coastlines and forests; Komodo is known for its dragons; and Flores has fabulous dive sites.

DOZENS OF ISLANDS THAT SPILL OUT EASTWARD from Bali are part of the Nusa Tenggara, the southeastern (*tenggara*) islands (*nusa*). They were formed eons ago when shards of land broke from Sulawesi 300 km (180 mi) to the north and Australia, just 500 km (310 mi) south. Best known are the stepping stones immediately east of Bali: Lombok, a serene tropical haven whose tourism industry is slowly growing; Sumbawa, a golden arc of mountains and plains; Komodo, home of the dragons; Flores, a dive paradise ringed by coral reefs; Timor, site of an ongoing struggle for independence; and Sumba, island of bold ikat patterns and site of ancient battles between warriors on horseback. Between these islands are a smattering of islets: Rinca, Roti, and the Solor and Alor archipelagos, to name a few.

Despite their relatively diminutive size, these arid islands are home to many superlative natural sights. More than 40 volcanoes jut upward from the sea in this province. The explosion of Sumbawa's Gunung Tambora in 1814 was one of the largest in world history, and the 12,221-ft summit of Lombok's Gunung Rinjani still rumbles threateningly from time to time. Tiny Komodo is a mass of parched, dormant slopes smothered in long, green-gold grasses. Flores has 14 active volcanoes of its own. The islands' main wildlife includes birds—cockatoos, parrots, lories, and other Australian types—insects, and reptiles, such as the famous Komodo dragon.

Most Nusa Tenggara inhabitants, like the people throughout much of Indonesia, adhere to Islam. Still, there are subtle differences. The Sasaks of Lombok resisted the influx of Hindu Balinese from the west and have maintained unique brands of Islam: Wektu Telu (Three Prayers) and Wektu Lima (Five Prayers). Farther east, the Sumbawanese have upheld the more traditional Muslim rites brought by the Bugis and Makassarese of Sulawesi—although many people incorporate a healthy dose of animism into their practices. Animism is also evident in the beliefs of the 1,000 or so villagers who live on Komodo. On Flores, 85% of the people are Catholic, thanks to missionaries who have been coming to this island since the 16th century.

The earliest outsiders were the intrepid 12th- and 13th-century traders who discovered the islands' treasures of cinnamon, tortoiseshell, and sandalwood during voyages around the Spice Islands of Maluku to the north. To this day, Nusa Tenggara remains well off the travelers' beaten path. Life has continued here in much the same way for five centuries. Even the modes of travel haven't changed much: aside from a few air routes (whose schedules are undependable), access is by daily ferries or weekly ships. Although there are long-distance buses that journey—on dusty mountain roads—between towns, in-town transport is primarily by horse-drawn cart or by bicycle. Development will no doubt work its way east from Bali. But these sunny islands are likely to remain untainted for a little while longer.

Pleasures and Pastimes

Beaches

Lombok's Senggigi has one of the prettiest white-sand, western-facing beaches in the archipelago, which is why a string of large resorts now adorns most of it; the Gili islands, off Lombok's northwest coast, are a more private setting. Loh Liang Bay, the entryway to Pulau Komodo, has lovely eastern views—and the occasional dragon strolling over the sand or swimming up from the surf. Just outside of Labuanbajo on

Flores, you'll find a classic stretch of tropical beach that attracts both divers and sun worshippers.

Dining

Indonesian food is all you'll find on the menu outside of tourist areas, and don't expect it to be tempered to Western tastes. In addition, as you move east, there will be less meat and more rice and vegetables. Main dishes on Lombok—an island named after a tiny chili pepper—can be hot; here, you'll find lots of grilled and fried seafood, curries, and vegetarian dishes, as well as a surprising number of Chinese restaurants. On Sumbawa, look for *ayam taliwang,* a fried chicken dish, as well as the Indonesian staples of fried rice and noodles. On Flores, the specialties consist of fresh, grilled seafood of any sort as well as the sweet *martabak manis* chocolate-peanut pancake.

Lodging

Outside of Senggigi on Lombok, the Gili islands off Lombok's coast, and Pulau Moyo off Sumbawa's northwest coast, don't expect luxury (or anything close to it). Although there are plenty of decent hotels and *losmen* (small rooming houses with shared facilities) throughout the islands, as a rule, the farther east you go, the fewer the hotel amenities. Main towns with airports usually have at least one small establishment with rooms that have private baths, if not Western toilets; in small towns you'll probably get a clean, simple room with a shared Indonesian-style bath. Since these establishments are meant for sleeping rather than a vacation stay (indeed, most guests are either gone by morning or out all day on business or pleasure activities), all but the most discerning visitors find such quarters acceptable.

National Parks

Lombok's Gunung Rinjani, Indonesia's second-highest (and still active) volcano, attracts thousands of climbers and local religious pilgrims each year. Pulau Moyo, off Sumbawa's northwest coast, sees perhaps only a few hundred travelers annually, but is a peaceful haven with trails through forest and beaches. Pulau Komodo, one of Indonesia's premier national parks, offers the unique experience of viewing wild dragons; the island is easy to reach from both Sumbawa and Flores, and there are plenty of overnight package tours from Java, Bali, and Lombok.

Scuba Diving and Snorkeling

Great dive sites are threaded throughout Nusa Tenggara, and many have only been discovered in the past decade. More popular areas include the Gili Islands, Komodo Island, and several islands off Labuanbajo on Flores. Dive operators (many in hotels) in Senggigi on Lombok and Labuanbajo offer lessons and day trips; operators on Java and Bali often offer package trips.

Exploring Nusa Tenggara

Given the varied activities, religious traditions, and cultural practices in the Nusa Tenggara, each island is almost its own country. Fortunately, travel on and between islands is easy, with decent roads, convenient connection points, and transport options by air, land, and sea. However, this balances out the unpredictable elements that often make travel in this region challenging—your trip may be affected by weather; the cost of fuel; the availability of maintenance workers and parts; and the whims of the air, bus, or ship personnel. Some travelers make the mistake of planning to quickly hop between the islands on a cultural fast track, but this is the sure way to a stressful trip. If you have the time to visit, use it to enjoy each island at a slow pace; if your stay is limited, choose one island and explore it to the fullest.

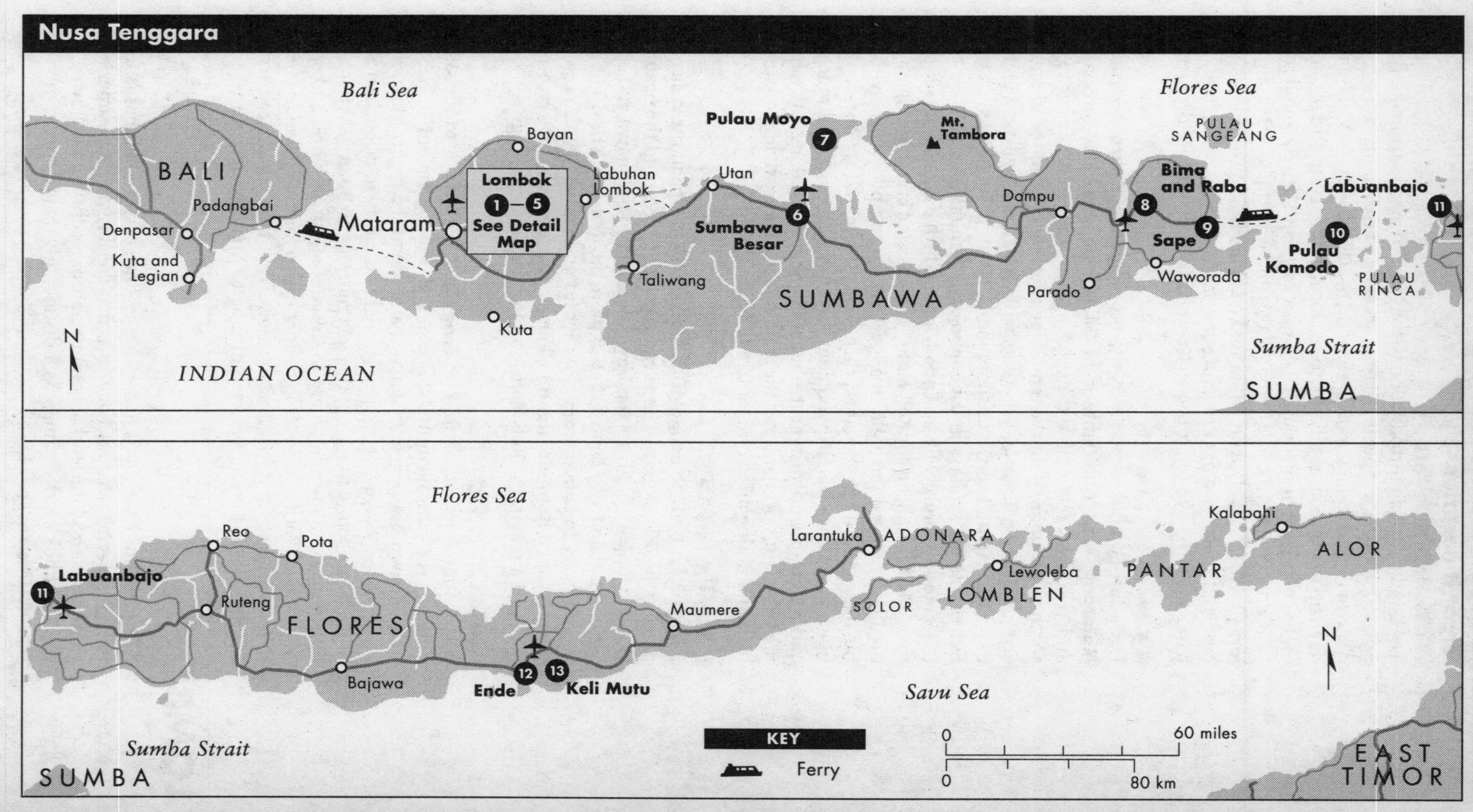

Nusa Tenggara
Bali Sea
Flores Sea
BALI
Padangbai
Denpasar
Kuta and Legian
Mataram
Bayan
Lombok
1–5
See Detail Map
Labuhan Lombok
Kuta
Pulau Moyo
7
Mt. Tambora
Utan
6
Sumbawa Besar
Taliwang
SUMBAWA
Dampu
Parado
PULAU SANGEANG
Bima and Raba
8
9
Sape
Waworada
Labuanbajo
11
10
Pulau Komodo
PULAU RINCA
N
INDIAN OCEAN
Sumba Strait
SUMBA
Flores Sea
Reo
Pota
11
Labuanbajo
Ruteng
FLORES
Bajawa
12
Ende
13
Keli Mutu
Maumere
Larantuka
ADONARA
SOLOR
Lewoleba
LOMBLEN
PANTAR
Kalabahi
ALOR
N
Savu Sea
Sumba Strait
SUMBA
KEY
Ferry
0
60 miles
0
80 km
EAST TIMOR

Great Itineraries

IF YOU HAVE 3–4 DAYS

Try Lombok for an introduction to the Nusa Tenggara by making **Senggigi** ② your base. Spend a day snorkeling and sunning, then take a day trip for snorkeling or diving around the **Gili Islands** ③. Make a third day trip to the central villages to see local architecture and to shop in crafts markets. On the fourth day, start early and drive around the island's northwestern curve to the villages and waterfalls of **Gunung Rinjani** ④. Alternatively, you could make **Labuanbajo** ⑪ on Flores your base and spend two days relaxing and snorkeling or diving here, then make a day or overnight trip to **Komodo Island** ⑩ before departing.

IF YOU HAVE 7 DAYS

For a full Lombok experience, fly into **Ampenan, Cakranegara, and Mataram** ① and head right for the **Gili Islands** ③ to spend three nights and two days relaxing and exploring the beaches and reefs. Head south to **Senggigi** ② for the remaining three nights and spend one day around **Gunung Rinjani** ④, one day in the central craft villages, and one day lounging and souvenir shopping in town. If you'd prefer to visit Flores, spend two days in **Labuanbajo** ⑪, then take an overnight trip to **Komodo Island** ⑩. Fly to **Ende** ⑫ on the fifth day, stay overnight in town, and then head for **Keli Mutu** ⑮, a volcanic crater with gem-colored lakes. Spend the night in a local village and hike up the volcano for the sunrise over the lakes, then return Ende and fly out. If you'd like to visit both islands, you could fly into Ampenan, Cakranegara, and Mataram and spend three nights in Senggigi, taking day trips to the Gili islands, Rinjani, and the craft villages, before flying to Labuanbajo and taking an overnight trip to Komodo.

IF YOU HAVE 10 DAYS

Begin on Lombok in **Senggigi** ②, where you can spend three days exploring the **Gili Islands** ③, the central craft villages, and the beauty of **Gunung Rinjani** ④. Fly to **Sumbawa Besar** ⑥ on Sumbawa and spend the night, then fly to **Bima** ⑧ and explore the town for a day. The next morning, fly to **Labuanbajo** ⑪ on Flores and spend two days, working in a trip to **Komodo Island** ⑩. Finally, fly to **Ende** ⑫ for a two-night stay and a trip to the **Keli Mutu** ⑮ crater, before departing.

IF YOU HAVE 14 DAYS

Spend four days on Lombok in **Senggigi** ②, with trips to the **Gili Islands** ③, the central cultural villages, and **Gunung Rinjani** ④. Next fly to **Sumbawa Besar** ⑥ on Sumbawa and spend the night. Make a trip out to **Pulau Moyo** ⑦ and spend a night either there or back in Sumbawa Besar before flying out the next morning to **Bima** ⑧. After a day in Bima, take a morning flight to **Labuanbajo** ⑪ on Flores and spend three days. Work in an overnight boat trip to **Komodo Island** ⑩ before flying to **Ende** ⑫ and spending the night. Take two days to trek around the **Keli Mutu** ⑮ crater before returning to Ende for departure.

LOMBOK

The island of Lombok is just 45 km (27 mi) east of Bali, but it seems to exist several decades back in time. The beaches are superior to those of Bali and the level of commercialism is substantially lower. Further, Lombok's drier climate is a distinct advantage during the rainy season (December–May).

Lombok, named for the island's well-known *lombok* (chili pepper), is home to two cultures: the Balinese Hindu and the Sasak Muslim. Most of the Balinese, who ruled the island until 1894, live on the western side of the island around Ampenan, Mataram (the provincial capital), and Cakranegara (known for its handwoven textiles). Here you will find Balinese temples of interest, though none are as fully developed as in Bali. The Sasaks, who centuries ago came to Indonesia from northern India, live mainly in Lombok's central and eastern regions and comprise the majority of the island's 2.4 million population. Although they're included in the country's census of Islamic peoples, their religious practices are more animist and Hindu than Muslim. They're divided into two sects: the Wektu Telu (Three Prayers), whose rituals display more of a mix of doctrines, and the Wektu Lima (Five Prayers), who more stringently follow the guidelines of Islam.

Enjoy Lombok while you can, as the unspoiled atmosphere is changing fast: Senggigi Beach is now crowded with hotels, the beaches on the Gili coral atolls are already lined with low-priced bungalows, and at press time there were plans in the works for an international megaresort at beaches to the south.

Ampenan, Cakranegara, and Mataram

1 *24 km (14 mi) north of Lembar (the port for Bali ferries), 1,200 km (744 mi) southeast of Jakarta.*

Most visitors are introduced to Lombok by way of Ampenan, Cakranegara, and Mataram—the string of towns that make up the most populated area on this serene island. Each settlement has a separate function: Western Ampenan is the port where travelers arrive by ship, ferry, and hydrofoil; Cakranegara, the former capital of Lombok, today is a trading center; and Mataram is the island's administrative core and the site of the airport.

On the central town border between Mataram and Cakranegara is **Pura Meru,** the largest Balinese temple on Lombok. Constructed in 1720, Puru Meru is arranged around three courtyards full of small Meru shrines. The three most important—those to Shiva, Vishnu, and Brahma—are in the central courtyard.

Across from Pura Meru is **Taman Mayura,** once a Balinese royal palace, now a large artificial pool filled with lotus. In the center of the pool is Bale Kembang, a floating pavilion that's similar to, but smaller and less ornate, than the one in Klungkung, Bali.

The **Museum Negeri Nusa Tenggara Barat** (Museum of West Nusa Tenggara) has intriguing displays of island weaponry, decorative arts, and artifacts. ✉ *Jl. Panji Tilar Negara, no phone.* 💴 *Rp 200.* ⏲ *Tues.–Sun. 8–4.*

OFF THE BEATEN PATH

NARMADA TAMAN – Lombok's most famous temple-palace complex is Narmada Taman (10 km/6 mi east of Cakranegara), built in 1727. The architecture is an interesting mix of Hindu, Islamic, and Sasak, but the temple is notable for its man-made lagoon, which symbolizes the lake of the holy mountain, Gunung Rinjani, in north Lombok. The faithful explain that the replica's purpose was to permit an aging king to fulfill his religious obligations of throwing offerings into the mountaintop lake when he became too old to make the climb. However, more likely it was built so that the monarch could spy on the maidens washing in the pools.

Five kilometers (3 miles) north of Narmada is **Lingsar Temple,** built in 1714 by the first migrating Balinese and reconstructed in conjunction with Sasak Muslims as a symbol of their unity. Nearby is **Suranadi,** a cool hill town with a Hindu temple, especially venerated for its spring water and eels. Both promise good fortune to the pilgrim.

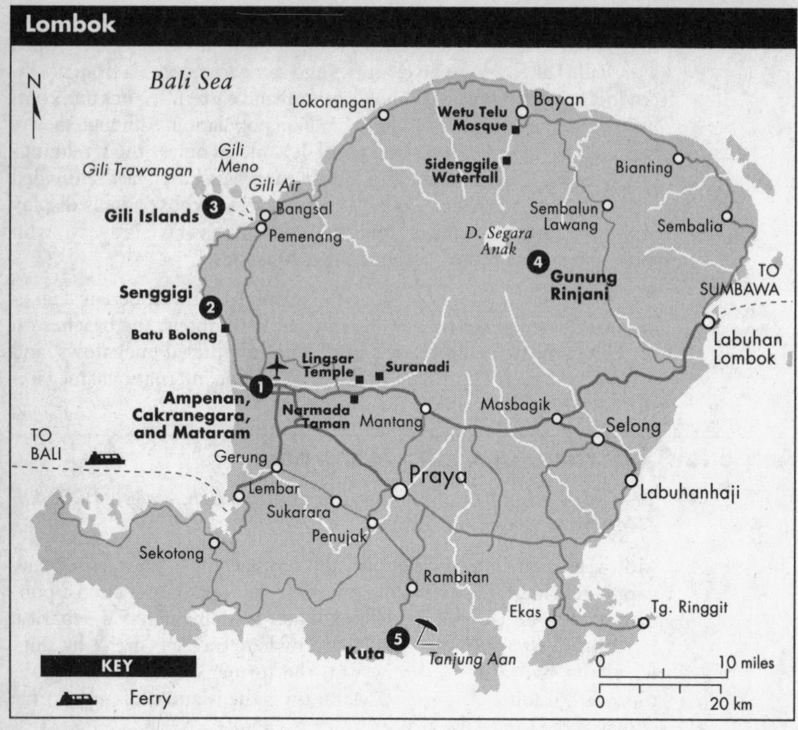

Shopping

The public market in Cakranegara has many silver and gold items and straw baskets. In Sweta, just outside Cakranegara, you can shop for spices and beautifully made cane baskets that entrepreneurs buy and take back to Bali to sell at inflated prices. (Note that Sweta is also a hub for buses to other points east.)

Artha Studio and Gallery (✉ Jl. Arjuna 12, Mataram, ☎ 0370/36715), owned by a local painter, has a collection of wonderful pastels of Lombok life, some of which grace the walls of the island's finest resorts. For a glimpse of the region's handwoven textiles, head to **Pertenunan Rinjani** (✉ Jl. Pejanggik 46, Mataram, ☎ 0364/23169). **Sasak Pottery** (✉ Jl. Koperaso 102, Ampenan, ☎ 0370/31687) has traditional handmade pottery.

En Route As you approach Senggigi from Mataram, you can spot the **Batu Bolong** (Rock with a Hole) temple from alongside the road just a short way south. Perched above the ocean upon a huge outcrop that does, indeed, have a natural hole, the temple faces west toward Gunung Agung and the sunset. Beautiful maidens were supposedly tossed into the sea (as divine sacrifices) here in ancient days, reason enough why residents claim that sharks haunt these waters.

Senggigi

★ ❷ *12 km (7 mi) northwest of Mataram.*

The narrow, curving strip of sand that comprises Senggigi was once a backpackers' escape from the crowded beaches of Bali. Inexpensive accommodations are still available, but expensive resort hotels have begun to dominate the beach. Senggigi is still a pleasant place to relax, but it's no longer a quiet hideaway.

Dining and Lodging

$–$$ ✕ **Graha Restaurant.** The red-tile floors and red-check tablecloths add cheer to this thatched-roof restaurant. An outdoor terrace looks right out over the sea, and soft jazz plays in the background. Specialties include grilled shrimp, *graha lumpia* (deep-fried spring rolls with sweet-and-sour sauce), and ikan *bumbu kuning* (fried and with a yellow sauce). Entrées come with garlic sauce and a choice of four kinds of sambal. ✉ *Jl. Raya Senggigi,* ☎ *0370/93101. MC, V.*

$–$$ ✕ **Restaurant Naga.** The Chinese lanterns and eye-popping, vivid-yellow sign—CHINESE FOOD THAI FOOD SEAFOOD—out front compel you to stop for a bite. Specialties include cashew chicken, Hong Kong duck, and Szechuan crab; specials might include Japanese seafood stew or baked spareribs. Free transport is available to and from area hotels. ✉ *Jl. Raya Senggigi,* ☎ *0370/93207. MC, V.*

$ ✕ **Cafe Alberto.** For a quick meal of pizza, barbecued items, sushi, or sashimi, try this basic, open-air restaurant in a pavilion behind the Dynasty (☞ *below*). Business booms at lunchtime. ✉ *Jl. Raya Senggigi,* ☎ *0370/93758. MC, V.*

$ ✕ **Dynasty.** Two locally carved and painted wooden horses at the entrance beckon you to climb the steps into the casual dining room. Westerners come for the familiar fare of pasta—spaghetti, tagliatelli, ravioli—all of which is homemade. Seafood is also a specialty. Red couches and candlelight make this a popular evening spot. There's karaoke nightly and traditional dancing lessons and performances of Joget Gandrung and Putri Mandalika Thursday at 7. ✉ *Jl. Raya Senggigi,* ☎ *0370/93313. MC, V.*

$ ✕ **Lombok Coconut.** Over a meal of seafood, pizza, or pasta, you can chat about the dozens of stone carvings that decorate this restaurant's facade, about the birds that twitter in their cages, or about the eclectic collection of tables in assorted sizes and shapes. Eavesdropping on the oft-interesting conversations of other travelers is also an option. ✉ *Jl. Raya Senggigi,* ☎ *0370/93195. No credit cards.*

$ ✕🏨 **Hotel Panorama.** Although it's not on the beach, this hotel does have captivating views of the bay from the hills on the eastern side of Senggigi's main road. The brown and white cottages with red-tile roofs are clean and simply furnished. All have tile floors, wood furniture, and garden bathrooms; lower rooms have terraces and upper ones have balconies. Six deluxe bungalows offer more space and privacy. Rich food and reasonable prices make a meal—or afternoon tea—in the restaurant memorable. Consider ordering the steamed fish in a clay pot with hot garlic sauce or the chicken topped with chopped prawns and butter sauce. For dessert you'll find mocha cake, apple pie, lemon pie, and raisin and banana breads. ✉ *Jl. Raya Senggigi, Km 8 (*✉ *Box 1063, Mataram 83015),* ☎ *0370/939000,* FAX *0370/93603. 30 cottages. Restaurant, bar, pool, laundry service, travel services. MC, V.*

$$–$$$ 🏨 **Lombok Intan Laguna.** Beside the ocean it may be, but the Itan's focal point is really its curving pool with an arched stone bridge and round, thatched-roof bar. The two-story cottages have a mix of traditional and modern architecture. Their rooms are spacious, with tile floors, wood furniture, and indoor-outdoor bathrooms. Less-expensive rooms are in a more modern, white, three-story building. At the open-air restaurant, the smell of flowers from the gardens is carried along on cooling sea breezes. A stay here also puts you within walking distance of Senggigi's main shopping area. ✉ *Jl. Raya Senggigi (*✉ *Box 1049, Mataram 831235),* ☎ *0370/93090,* FAX *0370/93185. 146 rooms. 2 restaurants, bar, pool, 2 tennis courts, exercise room, beach, shops. AE, DC, MC, V.*

$$–$$$ 🏨 **Senggigi Beach Hotel.** Sunsets from here are splendid. On a peninsula that juts into the Lombok Straits, this resort has thatched-roof cottages—each with several guest rooms—on 25 acres of grass, coconut trees, and white-sand beach. Modest rooms have twin beds, tables, chairs, and TVs; bathrooms have shower stalls rather than tubs. The open-sided dining room, overlooking the pool, serves mostly buffet-style breakfasts and dinners. ✉ *Jl. Raya Senggigi (✉ Box 1001, Mataram 83125), ☎ 0364/93210, FAX 0364/93200. 182 rooms. Dining room, pool, 2 tennis courts, badminton, beach, snorkeling, windsurfing, boating, travel services. AE, DC, MC, V.*

$$–$$$ ★ **Sheraton Senggigi Beach Resort.** The lobby, with its polished antiques and bay views, immediately conveys the subtle elegance found throughout. Landscaped grounds, thick with blossoms, embrace the three-story terraced buildings. Rooms have sumptuous wood and wicker furniture and Lombok craftwork; all look onto the gardens and free-form pool, and many offer a glimpse of the beach beyond. The main restaurant offers indoor and outdoor dining, and the on-site stage is used for dance performances. ✉ *Jl. Raya Senggigi (✉ Box 1154, Mataram 83015), ☎ 0370/93333; 800/325–3535 in the U.S.; FAX 0370/93140. 156 rooms. 3 restaurants, 2 bars, 2 pools, 2 tennis courts, health club, beach, snorkeling, windsurfing, boating, travel services. AE, DC, MC, V.*

$$ **Holiday Inn Resort Lombok.** This familiar Western establishment does a good job of mixing local traditions with foreign comforts. It has an exotic location on a lovely sweep of sand with rolling blue waves. Stone walkways lead through gardens to connected chalets and the larger, separate bungalows (each with several guest rooms); both types of accommodations have porches and large garden bathrooms. A layered pool surrounds a swim-up bar and a hot tub. Beside the pool is a dining terrace where local musicians stroll nightly. Upstairs in reception, the adept travel staff can help you arrange tours anywhere on the island. ✉ *Senggigi Beach (✉ Box 1090, Mataram 83015), ☎ 0370/93444, FAX 0370/93092. 145 rooms, 14 bungalows. 2 restaurants, 3 bars, pool, massage, spa, health club, beach, snorkeling, windsurfing, boating, shops, laundry service, meeting rooms, travel services, car rental. AE, DC, MC, V.*

$ **Graha Beach.** Set on the beach, the Graha is one of the best of several inexpensive hotels and losmen in Senggigi. Clean, air-conditioned rooms have twin beds, tile floors, TVs, and private showers and toilets. There's a restaurant, small souvenir shop, and money exchange counter. Tours of the island can be arranged—prices are negotiable. ✉ *Senggigi Beach, ☎ 0364/93401, FAX 0364/93400. 29 rooms. Restaurant, beach, travel services, car rental. No credit cards.*

Nightlife and the Arts

Senggigi's main strip, Jalan Raya Senggigi, has a number of small bars and dance places that are busy on weekends. The **Dynasty** (☎ 0370/93313) is a popular hangout with a curving wood bar, cozy red couches, candlelight, and karaoke nightly. On Thursdays at 7, you receive free traditional dance lessons before the Joget Gandrung and Putri Mandalika dance performance. The **Tropical Bar and Restaurant** (☎ 0370/93712) is particularly crowded on Saturday, especially the **C. V. Discotheque** on the first floor. The **Sheraton Senggigi** (☎ 0370/93333) features various cultural performances weekly.

To explore local art, check out the shops at the **Pasar Seni** art market at the center of town, right on Jalan Raya Senggigi. Across from the art market, the **Pamour Art Gallery** (☎ 0370/93104) has exhibitions of Lombok and regional art, craft-making demonstrations, and an extensive collection of crafts and furnishings.

Outdoor Activities and Sports

For scuba and snorkeling trips to the Gilis, many travelers begin from Senggigi. Try **Baruna** (✉ Jl. Raya Senggigi, in the Holiday Inn, ☎ 0370/

93314), an extension of one of Bali's best-known operations. Also on Jl. Raya Senggigi are **Albatross** (☎ 0370/93399), **Blue Coral** (☎ 0370/93251), and **Batu Surya Utama** (☎ 0370/93345).

Gili Islands

❸ *5–8 km (3–5 mi) off the coast from Bangsal-Pameneng, which is 31 km (19 mi) northeast of Senggigi.*

A 30-minute drive north of Senggigi brings you to the Bangsal ferry dock, near Pameneng, where a small boat will zip you across to one of three coral atolls known collectively as the Gili Islands. All three islands have cottage bungalows that are popular with backpackers. Most of these lodgings are simple bamboo huts (Rp 108,000–Rp 216,000) with a cold-water *mandi* (dip-bucket bath) and squat toilets; a few of the more upscale places have electricity. Most losmen rent snorkeling equipment, and dive trips can be arranged. Bring cash as, outside of a few hotels, credit cards are rarely accepted and travelers checks can be difficult to exchange.

Gili Air

Gili Air is closest to shore and requires only a quick 10-minute sea crossing in a motorized prahu. Here dazzling white sand meets crystal-clear water, and the coral reef is home to brightly colored tropical fish. The atmosphere is calm and uncluttered, the scenery simple and rural—a great place to clear your head.

DINING AND LODGING

$ ✕🏨 **Hotel Gili Air and Restaurant.** Gili Air's largest hotel has bungalows encircled by tropical gardens. The modest, clean rooms have basic furnishings accented with touches of island decor. Private bathrooms with flush toilets and running water are standard and most rooms have beach and sea views; only 14 have air-conditioning and hot water, however. Continental breakfast is included in the price, and the on-site restaurant is open all day; pizzas are a specialty and beachfront barbecues take place weekly. There's good snorkeling right off the beach, and the friendly staff can help with tours around the islands. ✉ *Desa Gili Indah, Pameneng,* ☎ *0370/34435. 26 rooms. Restaurant, beach, snorkeling, travel services. MC, V.*

$$$$ ★ 🏨 **The Oberoi, Lombok.** Hidden away on Lombok's northwest coast and within sight of the palm-fringed beach of Gili Air just across the strait, this resort offers the ultimate in upscale seclusion. Spacious terrace pavilions with lovely views are set on well-groomed grounds. High stone walls surround the private villas, each with a garden, fountain, and raised dining pavilion; some have plunge pools. Interiors have high, thatched-roof ceilings; marble floors; dark teak furniture; oversize canopy beds; wicker seating areas; and sliding glass panels that open to garden or ocean views. Bathrooms are of a good size and have separate toilet and shower compartments enclosed by glass doors, double marble sinks, large walk-through closets, and sunken tubs near a lotus pond in the garden. Service is discreet and unobtrusive. The spa and fitness center offer deluxe traditional treatments in open-air bales or air-conditioned rooms. Two large pools face the ocean, and a boat is available to take you snorkeling at nearby reefs or to the Gilis. ✉ *Pantai Medana, Tanjung (*✉ *Box 1096, Mataram 83001),* ☎ *0370/38444,* FAX *0370/32496. 20 villas, 30 terrace pavilions. 5 restaurants, bar, in-room safes, 2 pools, beauty salon, spa, health club, beach, snorkeling, windsurfing, library, laundry service, car rental. AE, DC, MC, V.*

OUTDOOR ACTIVITIES AND SPORTS

Blue Marlin (no phone) has an office in south Gili Air and can coordinate trips out to the reefs. On the east side of the island you'll find **Reefseekers Pro Dive** (☎ 0370/34387).

Gili Meno

For even more pristine waters, the next atoll, Gili Meno, has a greater abundance of sea life—red-lined triggerfish, starfish, five-line damsel, and the occasional shark—and, for scuba divers, there's unique blue coral 50–80 ft below the surface. This is the quietest island, and it has earned its place as a divers' haven. Its accommodations and restaurants are basic, but that's part of its charm.

Gili Trawangan

Although it's the farthest island from Lombok, Gili Trawangan is the party island of the three Gilis, where most visitors come to get away from Bali crowds. The beaches are excellent here, and the diving is memorable. Despite the rapid rise in tourism, there are plenty of inexpensive accommodations and restaurants.

OUTDOOR ACTIVITIES AND SPORTS

Located nearly on top of one another on the east side of Gili Trawangan are **Albatross** (☎ 0370/30134), **Blue Coral** (☎ 0370/34497), and **Blue Marlin Dive Center** (☎ 0370/32424), which make regular dive excursions around the islands. A two-dive day trip is about Rp 540,000 and introductory through full-certification courses are available.

En Route Back on the mainland, on the way to Gunung Rinjani, consider a stop in **Bayan.** Its mosque stands on a stone platform and is said to be more than three centuries old—Lombok's oldest religious structure. This village is also rumored to be where the island's indigenous Wektu Telu (the less stringently Muslim of the island's two Hindu-Muslim-animist Sasak sects) religion was born. Among the highlights of Bayan and its environs are the tall, spade-shape, traditional houses and rice barns that loom above the arid landscape. The settlements here are small, quiet clusters of life where men till the wide fields and women create beautiful original textiles. This is also a burgeoning tourist area where you're welcome to learn about and interact with the Sasak way of life.

Gunung Rinjani

❹ *77 km (50 mi) southeast of Bangsal, 82 km (51 mi) northeast of Mataram.*

The second-highest mountain in Indonesia, after Puncak Jaya (16,564 ft) in Irian Jaya, 12,221-ft Gunung Rinjani is one of the most revered and feared summits in the country. Revered because, like Gunung Agung on Bali, it's considered a sacred summit, a place of the gods; feared because the mountain still shudders and spews fiery lava from time to time. Its beauty is stark and magnificent, a smoldering peak against blue sky and ocean, with the green crescent of Lake Segera Anak shimmering 6 km (4 mi) across outside the crater. The trek up the slope is breathtaking, both for the natural views and village scenes as well as the physical effort. (The hike to the rim and down to the lake can be dangerous and should only be attempted by those who are in good shape and who are blessed with good balance.)

From Bayan, the trail around the rim has several approaches through the village settlements of Batu Koq and Senaru, 5 km (3 mi) and 8 km (5 mi) farther on. A 2-km (1-mi) side trip between them is to the Sendang Gila (Sindanggile) waterfall, where monkeys peer down from the trees alongside the path. Simple losmen abound here, as well as in the eastern villages of Sembulan Lawang and Sembulan Bintang. Most trekkers plan on a three-day journey from Senaru or Batu Koq, taking time to explore nearby hot springs and falls one day and hiking up to the crater the next.

Take comfortable hiking boots, warm layers, a sleeping bag, a tent, a stove, cooking utensils, and a flashlight—most of which you can rent from losmen in Batu Koq and Senaru. Stock up on foodstuffs and water in Mataram, where there's more variety and where prices are lower. Several outfitters arrange organized treks (☞ Tour Operators *in* Nusa Tenggara Essentials, *below*).

Kuta and Environs

★ ❺ *143 km (89 mi) southwest of Bayan, 30 km (18 mi) southeast of Mataram.*

Once a tiny village on the shores of the Indian Ocean, **Kuta** is still quiet, but development plans by large hotels are on the horizon. The curving sandy beach, known as Putri Nyale Beach, is now cluttered with the activity of budget travelers who made this area famous, most of whom stay at one of the many losmen on the other side of the road.

Five kilometers (3 miles) southeast along the coast is the horseshoe-shape **Tanjung Aan,** one of the island's most beautiful beaches. Its fine, soft, white sands are usually deserted, except for a few hopeful vendors selling watermelons and brave hearts windsurfing. All this may change—at press time the beach was slated for development, with wealthy Jakarta businessmen putting up the money for several luxury hotels.

There are several small Sasak settlements just north of Kuta on the road to Mataram, including the village of **Rambitan.** Here, the long, sloping thatched roofs of traditional Sasak houses and *lumbing* (a type of rice barn) are clustered together, and a few of the villagers sell batik sarongs at surprisingly low prices. Try to get a glimpse inside the houses, each of which has two main areas: the outer area where the men sleep and the inner one reserved for the women.

Farther north along the main road is **Penujak,** where lovely terracotta *gerabah* pottery is created; you'll also spot *gentong* (vessels), *jangkih* (traditional stoves), and wooden masks here. Cruise the main street to get a sense of design, selection, and quality. Although **Sukarara**'s fame as a traditional textile center has made it something of a tourist attraction (the costumed weavers at the looms in front of shops are just for show; the real weaving is done in the villages), it's definitely *the* place to see the creative, colorful works of Lombok artisans.

Dining and Lodging

$ ✕🏨 **Matahari Lombok Hotel and Restaurant.** Owned by a Lombok man, his Swiss wife, and their three boys, this friendly establishment caters mainly to budget travelers, although its lovely setting and cleanliness make it seem more upscale. Three houses are available, one with 12 double rooms, one with four, and one with three—all with basic but pleasant local decor, but not all with private baths. A bungalow with two double rooms is also available. Two on-site restaurants offer a mix of Indonesian and basic Western dishes; one has a dance floor that hops in high season. The hotel is in the village but is within walking distance of the beach; a pool is in the hotel's future plans. ✉ *On Kuta's main thoroughfare,* ☎ *0370/54832,* FAX *0370/54909. 19 rooms, 1 bungalow. 2 restaurants. MC, V.*

SUMBAWA, KOMODO, AND FLORES

Sumbawa

Sumbawa is an island of strict Islamic beliefs and stunning scenery, where boys race wild horses through golden plains, men practice bare-fisted *berempah* boxing in the high mountain villages, water buffalo are still used to pull plows through rice fields, and the lavender shadow of Gunung Tambora towers over the bright central shoreline.

Sumbawa Besar

6 *100 km (62 mi) east of Labuhan Lombok, 1,360 km (843 mi) southeast of Jakarta.*

Once the center of the Sumbawa sultanate that dominated the western half of the island, Sumbawa Besar, or Big Sumbawa, is, despite its name, a rather small settlement. Located on the northwest coast, a two-hour drive from the ferry terminal at Poto Tano and less than an hour's flight from Mataram, it's usually just a pass-through point for those heading to the wildlife reserve at Pulau Moyo (☞ *below*). Still this clean, quiet, welcoming town has a few noteworthy sights.

On Jalan Batu Pasak, the **Dalam Loka,** or old sultan's palace, is an assembly of raised, gray, wooden, structures with tiered roofs built in 1885 and restored in the early 1980s. The original structure has 99 pillars to honor the 99 names given to Allah. You can stroll around the outer grounds for a look at Sumbawan architecture, or ask around for the manager, who can give you a tour of the various rooms and explain the significance of the few vestiges of palace days—mostly drawings and decorations—on display inside. Sumbawan dances are performed here most Sunday mornings; at press time plans were afoot to refurbish the buildings and create a museum.

Today, the sultans' descendants reside at the **Bale Kuning** on Jalan Wahidin, where many of the royal families' possessions are still kept; the tourist office (☞ Visitor Information *in* Nusa Tenggara Essentials, *below*) can arrange a visit with advance notification. A black-sand beach at **Kencana** 11 km (7 mi) west of town has decent reefs for snorkeling and views of northern Pulau Moyo.

LODGING

$–$$ 🏨 **Tambora Hotel.** This midsize hotel, just five minutes from the airport, is your best option for a stay right in town. Rooms are simple and clean, and service is attentive. The hotel is a good base for day trips around the area, and it also has a minimart, an art shop, and a copy center on site. Rooms rates include breakfast. ✉ *Jl. Kebayan,* ☎ *0371/21585. 49 rooms. Restaurant, travel services. AE, MC, V.*

$ 🏨 **Kencana Beach Cottages.** Just 15 minutes from the airport, this pleasant hotel is set in gardens surrounded by bamboo and palm trees. A gathering of colorful and very spacious traditional bungalows face a black-sand beach where the clear water offers hints of the coral below. Wooden floors, white walls, high ceilings, and traditional woven art and paintings complete the elegantly simple decor. The location is quiet, but if you need more activity than just sipping drinks from coconut shells by the pool all day, there's plenty to keep you busy. The amicable staff at the on-site travel office can arrange trips to buffalo races, traditional villages, waterfalls, and Pulau Moyo. Before you set out, you can have a good breakfast, which is included in the price of your room. ✉ *Jl. Raya Tano, Km 11, Badas,* ☎ *0371/22555,* FAX *0371/22439. 25 bungalows. Restaurant, bar, pool, massage, beach, dive shop, snorkeling, laundry service, travel services. No credit cards.*

Pulau Moyo

★ 7 *20 km (12 mi) northeast of Sumbawa Besar.*

The focal point of the nature reserve on Moyo Island, just off Sumbawa's northeastern coast, is 402-ft Gunung Moyo. Although wildlife spotting is a draw, the main attraction is diving and snorkeling, and the island's remote location, extensive reefs, and upscale resort have made it the the darling of expensive package tours. Some of the best reefs are around Tanjung Pasir and Aik Manis. For maps and permits, contact the **Dinas Perlindungan dan Pengawetan Alam (PHPA)**—otherwise known as the Forest Authority—office in Sumbawa Besar (☞ Visitor Information *in* Nusa Tenggara Essentials, *below*). For package tours, try the **Tambora Hotel** or the **Kencana Beach Cottages** (☞ *above*), the latter of which can charter a speedboat for two dozen people at a daily rate of about Rp 350,000. If you'd like to visit the island independently, you can take a half-hour ride in a local fishing vessel (around Rp 10,000 each way) from Aik Bari on the coast.

DINING AND LODGING

$$$$ ★ ✕☒ **Amanwana.** Its name, which means "peaceful forest," couldn't be more appropriate. Nestled into a wooded setting facing a secluded beach, the large, luxurious tents mimic a mix of camping and island-bungalow features: simple yet spacious individual bale pavilions are surrounded by smooth terraces and protected by graceful, sloping canvas roofs held up by strong ropes and wooden poles. Despite their simple appearance, rooms are opulent and comfortable, with collectors' pieces of traditional art; polished wood floors; soft, sumptuous couches; king-size beds; writing desks; and large bathrooms. Although the pavilions are enclosed, only one wall is solid; the rest are panels that slide back to reveal huge glass windows, which afford a spectacular 270-degree view of the surrounding forest and bay. A library in the main building has spotless wood floors and glowing golden walls, as well as an intriguing selection of books and works of art. The open-air bar-lounge has a thatched roof and overlooks the bay—an intimate setting amid the wilds. ✉ *Pulau Moyo,* ☎ *0371/22233; 0361/771267 (for reservations);* FAX *0371/22288. 20 luxury tents. Restaurant, bar, dining room, lobby lounge, hiking, beach, snorkeling, windsurfing, boating, library, laundry service, travel services, airport shuttle. AE, DC, MC, V.*

Bima and Raba

8 *230 km (143 mi) east of Sumbawa Besar.*

Seven hours' drive from Sumbawa Besar, the neighboring towns of Bima and Raba are Sumbawa's main eastern settlements. Bima is the island's major port and the former sultanate that shared power over the island with the royal family of western Sumbawa; Raba is the main bus transit point 5 km (3 mi) east.

Things to see in these towns include the old **Sultan's Palace** in Bima on Jalan Sultan Ibrahim, which doubles as a museum of artifacts from the royal family and the region. Included in the collection here are books, furniture, and weaponry. The palace is open 7–5 daily except Islamic holidays. There's a suggested donation of Rp 1,000; guides will be grateful for another Rp 1,000. For a contrast, explore the new **Royal Palace** on Jalan Sumbawa, where the sultans' descendents have a collection of formal attire, decorative jewelry, and royal valuables on display. Book an appointment to visit through the tourist office (☞ Visitor Information *in* Nusa Tenggara Essentials, *below*).

Sape

9 *50 km (31 mi) southeast of Bima and Raba.*

The muted clip-clop of horses' hooves on soft dirt roads echoes through the hills of Sape (*sah*-pay), the easternmost town of Sumbawa. This sublime port—teeming with lively markets selling produce and colorful woven crafts—is the road traveler's stopping point en route to Komodo. Low, one-story homes line narrow streets traversed by horse-drawn carts (known here as Ben Hurs because they resemble the chariots used in the movie); occasionally, soulful Islamic music can be heard. The nearby rough, grassy mountains make for a good day's hike to supreme views over the town and the bay. Ferries to Komodo and Flores leave at 8 AM daily except Friday, and the morning crowd at the docks can be quite festive. For those stuck in town when the ferry breaks down—not an uncommon occurrence—things to do include visiting local weaving workshops, hiking in the hills, and practicing Indonesian with local tour guides who want to polish their English.

DINING AND LODGING

Most losmen will dish up a home-cooked meal for their guests. Fried rice, fried noodles, fried vegetables, or grilled fish with white rice are what you'll find across the board. There are a number of small losmen along the main road, each offering a half dozen clean, quiet rooms with private Indonesian cold-water baths. Try **Losmen Friendship,** near the port, or **Losmen Mutiara,** a two-story, shared-bath hotel next to the docks.

Pulau Komodo

★ 10 *320 km (198 mi) east of Sumbawa Besar, 90 km (56 mi) east of Bima, 40 km (25 mi) east of Sape.*

On the approach to Komodo, a tiny island just 36 km (22 mi) long and 16 km (9 mi) across at its widest point, it's hard to imagine that it's home to the fearsome dragons described by explorers of the late 1800s. Komodo's soft curves and parched golden grasses slide up over the topaz bay of lively coral reefs, glass-clear waters, and white-sand beach. But then you remember that this innocent looking island is, indeed, inhabited by 13-ft, 220-pound adult *ora,* as the dragons are known locally. Don't be frightened, though: although stories of European tourists and village children disappearing run rampant, a trip here is quite safe. The park office is right at the docks, and from it a mild 2-km (1-mi) walk along a sandy path brings you to the dragons' lairs. You'll see them sunning themselves in forest ravines or snuggling up in shallow caves inside cliff walls.

Local legends say that the dragons are descendents of a lost child who once took refuge in one of their burrows. Modern science reports that the dragons evolved from dinosaurs that lived in Asia some 130 million years ago. They're the largest lizards on earth, with a population of around 2,000, and they live only on Komodo, the nearby island of Rinca, and parts of Flores. Their soft, white eggs hatch in April or May, with a three-to-one ratio of males to females. The dragons have sharp hearing and a keen sense of smell (they can pick up the scent of carrion, their favorite treat, 7 mi away). They're fast, too, running at speeds of up to 18 mph and eating at a rate of six pounds of meat a minute. (At one time goats were slaughtered twice a week to attract the dragons, but these slaughters now take place much less frequently so that the dragons can be observed in the wild.) The dragons are also excellent swimmers—to the chagrin of those who are tempted to snorkel in the calm bay at the park's eastern edge. But the dragons aren't the only danger here: this is also an island of giant spiders, vipers, and scorpions. Thus, a guide must accompany everyone outside the main park compound, and you're encouraged to walk carefully and be aware of your surroundings at all times.

Travel to Komodo doesn't have to be the arduous journey of days past, thanks to luxury tour packages via speedboats from Bali, Lombok, and Flores. However, these are only short ventures; to stay longer and explore this fascinating island, you must prepare for a much simpler lifestyle. Komodo does have its amenities, namely an open-air restaurant that serves up simple fare, sells supplies, and rents six wooden cabins. A 2-km (1-mi) low-tide beach walk from the park office, Kampung Komodo is a local settlement of a few dozen raised huts and colorful fishing boats. Here you can meet the islanders and hear their stories. English-speaking guides can be hired at the park office to translate.

Dining and Lodging

$ ✕▣ **Pulau Komodo Bungalows.** A half dozen simple, raised wooden cabins grace the edge of a wide lawn and overlook grazing deer and scampering pigs by dusk and dawn. Each structure has four small bedrooms, a shared cold-water mandi, a common living area, and a wide balcony; the double rooms in front are the largest and coolest. The afternoon breeze eliminates the need for fans, as does the shortage of electricity, which only runs from 6 PM to 10 PM. A restaurant across the yard serves basic Indonesian fare, but you may want to bring your own food supplements if you're staying more than one night. Note: keep all luggage sealed and all food out of the rooms, as animals have been known to raid the cabins in search of cracker crumbs and banana peels, among other things. This is the only place to stay on the island; otherwise, it's necessary to stay aboard a tour boat in the bay. ✉ *Loh Liang, 100 yards northwest of PHPA office, no phone. 12 rooms. Restaurant, beach, snorkeling. No credit cards.*

Outdoor Activities and Sports

Komodo may be small, but there's plenty to do if you're the intrepid sort and you have a few days. You can hire guides (Rp 20,000 for up to five people) to hike to the 1,731-ft **Gunung Ara** and other peaks. Overnight camping trips can also be arranged. You can spot still more wildlife on a side trip to **Pulau Rinca.** The snorkeling around this island's reefs is also spectacular. Divers can organize trips from Labuanbajo, Flores (☞ Outdoor Activities and Sports *in* Labuanbajo, *below*). Since there's no regular boat transport to Rinca, you must sign up for an organized tour or hire your own boat from Labuanbajo.

Flores

Originally named Cabo de Flores, or Cape of Flowers—owing to its blossoming coastlines—by 16th-century Portuguese traders, Flores is a rugged, arid island of smoldering volcanic peaks and teal bays ripe for exploring. Although they were once under the control of Sulawesi's Bugis and Makassarese peoples, the inhabitants of Flores are actually closer in culture to Melanesia the early Melanesian civilizations that migrated west to the Indonesian archipelago; this heritage is reflected in their physical features. In addition, Flores's population is 85% Catholic, a significant statistic in an archipelago that's 90% Muslim. However, the island's draw is not really its culture, but rather its diving. The reefs here are some of Indonesia's best.

Labuanbajo

⓫ *100 km (62 mi) northeast of Sape on Sumbawa.*

A tiny settlement of one-story shops, homes, and losmen now does brisk business as a tourist jumping-off point for travelers heading by boat or plane west to Komodo, east to the gem-color lakes of Keli Mutu, or around the island on lengthy dive trips. Don't miss the Pasar Malam night market at the south end of town, where you can pick up a cheap bite to eat while finding numerous inexpensive souvenirs. There are many simple, comfortable places to stay and numerous beaches and reefs to explore.

If you have an afternoon, check out **Batu Cormin,** a cave 4 km (2 mi) outside of town. Several nearby islands have beaches that are worth a visit, including **Batugosok, Kanawa, Bididari, Sabolo Besar,** and **Sabolo Kecil**; the latter three also have excellent reefs for diving and snorkeling.

DINING AND LODGING

Most losmen have their own small restaurants, and on a scenic stroll along the main road you peruse the diverse menus. There are more than a dozen small losmen along Jalan Yos Sudarso as well. Touts will try to strike bargains with you as you step off the ferry. Always insist on seeing the accommodations first before making a deal, though; most places are simple and clean, but you never know if it's what you want until you see it. Walking along the main road is also a good way to check out the many travel booths and find out about the trips that they offer, as well as learn about additional accommodations and activities on the islands within an hour's boat ride of town.

$ ✕ **Gardena Bungalows.** Just a few yards from the ferry dock, this hotel offers traditional wooden bungalows with verandas above the bay in a setting of tropical gardens. There's no air-conditioning, but fans are provided; all rooms also have beds with mosquito nets and private bathrooms with showers. This is a popular place, and the friendly staff can assist you with tours to Komodo and Rinca, snorkeling trips to Bididari and Sabolon islands, and bus and ferry tickets. A small restaurant serves Indonesian, Chinese, and Western fare; breakfast is included in the price. ✉ *Jl. Yos Sudarso, 86554,* ☎ *0385/41258,* FAX *0385/41200. 19 bungalows. Restaurant, laundry service, travel services. No credit cards.*

$ **New Bajo Beach Hotel & Cottages.** This hotel is on the secluded, white-sand Phe'de Beach, with its thriving coral reefs, about about 2 km (1 mi) from Labuanbajo. Rooms are simple, clean, and decorated with Nusa Tenggara carvings and textiles; cottages have air-conditioning, private baths with hot water, and TVs. You can make tour arrangements—by car, speedboat, and fishing boat—at the travel desk. The restaurant offers a mix of Asian and Western dishes. ✉ *Pantai Pede 86554,* ☎ *0385/41047,* FAX *0385/41069. 16 rooms, 10 bungalows. Restaurant, beach, snorkeling, travel services, airport shuttle, car rental. No credit cards.*

$ ★ **Puri Komodo Resort.** On a peninsula at the northwest tip of Flores, this back-to-nature retreat is a relaxing hideaway. The 50-acre resort sits on a long stretch of sugar-white sand at the edge of a huge coral reef, making it a prime spot for dive trips. The 12 basic, clean bungalows (at press time, 12 more were being built) are surrounded on three sides by breezy balconies and are equipped with American-style spring mattresses. Bathrooms are outside of the rooms and include traditional bamboo showers; the toilet facilities are Western, however. The spacious two-story chalet has six rooms, two on each level and each with a private indoor bathroom. The serene gardens are a lovely place to walk in the cool evenings before dining in the seaside restaurant. The resort is 20 minutes by boat from Labuanbajo, but transfers and trips into town are free. Tours to Komodo, Rinca, and other area attractions can be arranged on site. ✉ *Batu Gosok, 86554,* ☎ *0385/41319,* FAX *0385/41030. 12 bungalows, 1 chalet. Restaurant, beach, snorkeling, travel services. No credit cards.*

OUTDOOR ACTIVITIES AND SPORTS

Puri Komodo Resort (☞ Dining and Lodging, *above*) offers trips to Komodo and Rinca, as well as dive tours around Flores. The **Sea Transportation Cooperative** (no phone) organizes boat trips to Komodo, Rinca, and other points around Flores, as do **Kencana, Perama,** and **Suamarnik.** All of these are on Jalan Yos Sudarso, the town's 2-km (1-mi) main strip. Not all tours offer the same amenities, so it pays to check out what you'll get for your money; accommodations, food, equipment, supplies, entrance fees, and souvenirs may or may not be included.

Ende

12 *250 km (155 mi) southeast of Labuanbajo.*

At the base of a mountain slope and the edge of the sea, Ende is a waiting point for many travelers catching ships to other parts of Nusa Tenggara and those heading east to Keli Mutu (☞ *below*). You can wander the lively **daily market** on Jalan Pasar at the waterfront for a taste of local culture and walk through the town to see its amazing variety of tailor shops with ancient Singer sewing machines. The **Ende Museum** on Jalan Perwira is actually a house where former President Sukarno was exiled by the Dutch in 1933. Knock on the door, and the manager will let you in to view the old photographs that are on display. For those interested in architecture, the neighboring village of **Wolotopo** is a good place to have a look at traditional woven textiles and the local style of raised wooden houses.

SHOPPING

To find quality ikat textiles from both Flores and Sumba, try the **market** on the corner of Jalan Pasar and Jalan Pabean. Eight kilometers (5 miles) east of Ende, the village of **Ndona** is the home of many traditional weavers. The blankets sold here are good buys.

Keli Mutu

★ 13 *66 km (41 mi) northeast of Ende.*

A volcanic crater filled with a triad of gem-color lakes, Keli Mutu has attracted visitors worldwide for more than a century. The magic of the site is that these three lakes change color—and no one knows why. (Scientists have theorized that the variations are caused by minerals in the soil or water.) In the 1960s, they were rust, navy, and cream; now they are teal, olive, and ebony. The view of the sunrise over the crater is one of the archipelago's most memorable.

The mountain is reached from Ende via the town of Moni, which is 14 km (9 mi) from the mountaintop. Trucks and minibuses make the journey up the 14-km (9-mi) road before dawn and return between 7 and 8 AM, but many visitors prefer to ride up and then make the 2½-hour walk back down to Moni. There are also a number of hot springs and waterfalls just outside of Moni. You can stay in a losmen in Moni or make this a day trip from Ende.

NUSA TENGGARA A TO Z

Arriving and Departing

By Airplane

Garuda (☎ 0364/22226) and its subsidiary, **Merpati** (☎ 0364/22226), run shuttle service, with flights every hour beginning at 7 AM, from Denpasar to Lombok's **Selaparang Airport** in Mataram. The last flight is at 3 PM. You can buy tickets at the airport an hour before departure. For trips from Lombok to Denpasar, Bali, you can only reserve a seat if you have a connecting flight. Note that flights tend to be late and are frequently canceled.

Elsewhere in the Nusa Tenggara, the main airports are at Sumbawa Besar, Bima, Labuanbajo, and Ende. Flights to Mataram on Lombok, Denpasar on Bali, Ujung Pandang on Sulawesi, and Jakarta on Java depart several times weekly, but schedules are unpredictable and flights are often canceled. For details on air transport, contact **Merpati** (☎ 0371/21416 in Sumbawa Besar; 0374/42697 in Bima). The airport in Sumbawa Besar is just yards from the Tambora Hotel, but bemos make the journey from other points in town for around Rp 250. Bima's airport is 16 km (10 mi) from town, Rp 10,000 by taxi. The Labuanbajo airport is 3 km (2 mi) from town, a Rp 5,000 taxi ride. Ende's airport is just outside town at the junction of Jalan Ahmad Yani, Jalan Keli Mutu, Jalan El Tari, and Jalan Gatot Subroto; backpackers walk it, but you can also take a bemo for about Rp 400.

By Boat

Ferries make the four-hour crossing from Padangbai, east of Denpasar on Bali, to Lembar, south of Ampenan on Lombok, every two hours around the clock; the fare is Rp 5,000. Since the ferry docks some distance from the tourist centers on both Bali and Lombok (it takes three bemos to travel from Lembar Harbor to Senggigi), a bus/ferry package—between Ubud, Kuta, or Sanur on Bali and Mataram or Senggigi on Lombok—is a good idea. Fares are reasonable (e.g., Rp 13,000 from Kuta to Senggigi), and most travel agents can make the bookings. Try **Dewi Sri Murni Tours** (☎ 0361/730272) in Kuta on Bali. On Lombok, contact **Perama Travel** (☞ Tour Operators *in* Contacts and Resources, *below*).

The ***Mabua Express*** (☎ 0370/81195 in Lembar) luxury hydrofoil takes just 2½ hours to cross from Tanjung Benoa in southern Bali to Lembar. It leaves at 8 AM and 2:30 PM from Tanjung Benoa and at 10:30 AM and 5 PM from Lembar. The fare is Rp 119,000 in economy, Rp 216,000 in Emerald Class, and Rp 302,000 in Diamond Class; the latter includes transport from to Kuta, Nusa Dua, or Sanur on Bali and to Bangsal, Mataram, or Senggigi on Lombok.

Ferries depart hourly between dawn and dusk for the 1½-hour journey to Poto Tano on the west coast of Sumbawa; fares are around Rp 3,600 for air-conditioned (and smoke-filled) quarters and Rp 2,300 for deck class; vehicles transport costs Rp 6,000–20,00. On the west end of Sumbawa, it costs Rp 10,000 to make the seven-hour ferry crossing to Komodo and Rp 11,500 for the 10-hour continuing journey to Labuanbajo, Flores. In theory, the ferry departs at 8 AM every day but Friday, but check on the schedule and the condition of the ferry with locals before you show up at the docks (crossings have been canceled for weeks at a time for boat repairs).

The national fleet of Pelni ships (large, cruise ship–type vessels) stop at Sumbawa Besar's satellite port of Badas, 7 km (4 mi) to the west, every two weeks. Pelni also pauses at Sumbawa Besar weekly, alternating journeys between Lembar on Lombok and a route that encompasses Waingapu, Sumba, Ende, Flores, Kupang, and Timor. Costs range from about Rp 15,000 per segment for economy class (bunk beds in shared rooms of 100 or more, shared baths, and three simple meals a day) to about Rp 70,000 or more per segment for first-class (a two-bed cabin and more elaborate meals).

From Labuanbajo, regular ferries depart daily at 8 AM (except Friday) for the three-hour journey (Rp 4,000) west to Komodo; they then continue on seven more hours to Sape on Sumbawa (Rp 11,500). In Ende, the Pelabuhan Ipi dock is 3 km (2 mi) from town; the Pelni office at Jalan Kemakmuran and Jalan Pabean has schedule details. A regular ferry also cruises south to the island of Sumba on Tuesday and east to Kupang on Timor on Saturday.

By Bus

Buses/ferries are an important form of transportation between islands in Nusa Tenggara. Sumbawa Besar has a new terminal 6 km (4 mi) northwest of town; vehicles leave for Lombok at 6, 8, and 9 AM and again at 9 PM and depart for Bima between 7 and 9 AM and at 8 PM. Bima's terminal for points west is just outside of the town center; buses to Lombok leave in the evening and smaller buses to towns on Sumbawa run between 6 AM and 5 PM. Express buses to Lombok and Bali meet the ferries from Labuanbajo in Sape, Sumbawa's eastern port. Buses from Sape transfer in Bima for towns west. Those from Labuanbajo head east for Ende around 7 AM and then again around 4 PM when the ferry from Sape arrives.

Getting Around

By Bemo and Horse-Drawn Cart

Public transport on Lombok consists primarily of crowded bemos and the *cidomo,* a horse-drawn cart that seats four or five and costs approximately Rp 500 per km (½ mi). Elsewhere in the Nusa Tenggara, bemos are the way to get around towns and to nearby sites; most cost around Rp 250 for short distances; you can bargain with drivers for longer jaunts. Many areas still have horse-drawn carriages called *dokars,* also known as Ben Hurs in Sape.

By Bus and Taxi

The central terminal on Lombok is in Sweta, just outside Cakranegara. Government-set fares are posted, although they may be out of date, so don't balk if you're charged slightly more. Do bargain, however, if the price seems outrageous. Metered taxis are available from the airport and at hotels (though you can also hire them for a flat fee to take tours); a taxi from the airport to Senggigi should cost less than Rp 7,000 (though you'll be asked for at least Rp 10,000 initially). There's a taxi stand in Senggigi, right on the main road next to the art market.

Unless you've hired your own vehicle to drive east through the other islands, buses are the only way to reach the small towns. Taxis are available in the larger settlements, but usually only for short-distance trips.

By Car

On Lombok, rental cars cost about Rp 45,000 a day or Rp 75,000 with driver. Try **Rinjani Rent Car** (☎ 0370/32259), on Jalan Bung Karno in Mataram across from the Hotel Granada, or **Metro Rent Car** (☎ 0370/32146) on Jalan Yos Sudarso in Ampenan, which rents Suzuki Jimmys for Rp 45,000–Rp 60,000 including insurance. You can also rent a car or hire a car and driver through major hotels.

Contacts and Resources

Emergencies

Scuba-Diving Emergencies: The closest decompression chamber is operated by Baruna (✉ Jl. Raya Seririt, Lovina, ☎ 0362/41084) in northwest Bali.

LOMBOK

Ambulance: ☎ 118. **Medical:** Klinik Senggigi Medical Services (☎ 0370/93210). **Fire:** ☎ 113. **Police:** ☎ 110.

OTHER ISLANDS

Medical and Police. Bima: Bima Police Station ☏ 0374/21110. **Labuanbajo:** Public Hospital of Labuanbajo (✉ heading away from docks on the main road, take first left after BRI Bank). **Sumbawa Besar:** Public Hospital of Sumbawa (☏ 0371/21087); Sumbawa Besar Police Station (☏ 0371/21142).

English-Language Bookstores

Most major Lombok resorts have at least a few books, news magazines, and international papers available. Used bookstores come and go in the tourist areas of Senggigi and Kuta; ask at your hotel. The **Senggigi Supermarket and Department Store** (☏ 0370/93738) on Jalan Raya Senggigi sells books and maps. Aside from this, however, you will find few bookshops selling English-language material on the island.

If you're desperate for reading material on the other islands, local hotels usually have a few books to trade, or you can trade with fellow travelers. Unfortunately, outside of the more touristed areas, the bookstore concept hasn't caught in Indonesia.

Tour Operators

LOMBOK

Baruna (✉ Holiday Inn Lombok, Jl. Raya Senggigi, Senggigi, ☏ 0370/93093) arranges dive trips. **Bidy Tour and Travel** (✉ Jl. Ragigenep 17, Ampenan, ☏ 0370/32127) offers treks, island cruises, dive packages, visits to cultural villages, and fishing trips. **Dream Divers** (✉ Jl. Raya Senggigi, Senggigi, ☏ 0370/93738; ✉ Gili Air, ☏ 0370/3454) has dive trips around the island. **Satriavi Tours & Travel** (✉ Senggigi Beach Hotel, ☏ 0364/23430 ext. 8602) organizes different tours of the island, including treks to Gunung Rinjani. **Perama** (✉ Jl. Pejanggik Mataram, ☏ 0370/35936; ✉ Jl. Raya Senggigi, Senggigi, ☏ 0370/93007) coordinates treks to Gunung Rinjani, day tours of Lombok, and land/sea adventure tours to Komodo. Golf tours are available through **Rinjani Country Club** (✉ Jl. Sriwijaya 396, Mataram, ☏ 0370/37316).

FLORES

Grand Komodo Adventures and Diving (✉ Jl. Sukarno-Hatta 45, Bima, ☏ 0374/42018; ✉ Jl. P. W. Papu, Labuanbajo, ☏ 0385/41277) organizes dive trips throughout Nusa Tenggara on live-aboard boats. **Puri Komodo Resort** (✉ Batu Bosok, Labuanbajo, ☏ 0385/41319) coordinates a variety of tours and treks.

Travel Agencies

The following Lombok companies can make travel arrangements and organize guided tours: **Bidy Tour and Travel** (☞ Tour Operators, *above*), **Discover Lombok** (✉ Pasar Seni market, Jl. Raya Sengiggi, Senggigi, ☏ 0370/36781), **Lombok Indah Tour and Travel** (✉ Jl. Raya Senggigi, Senggigi, ☏ 0370/93838), **Lombok Wisata Indah** (✉ Pasar Seni market, Jl. Raya Sengiggi, Sengiggi, ☏ 0370/32815), **Nazareth Tours and Travel** (✉ Jl. Raya Senggigi, Sengiggi, ☏ 0370/93033). **Perama** (☞ Tour Operators, *above*) also has an office on Jalan Yos Sudarso in Labuanbajo on Flores.

Visitor Information

LOMBOK

The **Regional Office of Tourism** (✉ Jl. Singosari 2, Mataram, ☏ 0364/21730) is open Monday–Thursday 8–3 and Friday–Saturday 8–noon.

FLORES

The **Labuanbajo Tourist Office** (✉ Off Jl. Yos Sudarso, ☏ 0385/41170) keeps odd hours, though they're supposed to be open daily 10–6; if you want information, it's best to stop by as soon as you get off the ferry from Sape.

SUMBAWA

The **Bima Tourist Office** (✉ Jl. Soekarno Hatta, ☎ 0374/44331) is open 7–3 Monday through Friday. The **PHPA Office Information Booth** (✉ Jl. Yos Sudarso, Bima, no phone) provides general information on Komodo and Rinca. It's open Monday–Thursday 8–4 and Friday–Saturday 8–11. The **Sumbawa Besar Tourist Office** (✉ Jl. Garuda, near Hotel Tambora, ☎ 0371/21632) has hours Monday–Thursday 8–4 and Friday–Saturday 8–11. For information on the national parks, try the **PHPA Office** (✉ Jl. Garuda 12, Sumbawa Besar, ☎ 0371/21358), which is open 8–2 weekdays.

5 Sulawesi

Sulawesi consists of bits of Borneo, New Guinea, Antarctica, and Australia that were joined eons ago. The oddly shaped island is filled with volcanoes and a mix of tropical Asian and arid Australian plant and animal species. Its Bugis and Bajau peoples come from a long line of seafarers, and the Tanatoraja inhabitants honor the dead with elaborate, ancient rituals that are the stuff of legends.

TO THE NORTH AND EAST OF BALI AND JAVA is the island of Sulawesi, formerly called the Celebes. Four long peninsulas radiate from a central mountainous area, giving the island an orchid shape. Its topography is dramatic—from rice fields, rain forests, and mountains to bays where crescents of sugar-white sand gently slip into sapphire water and dazzling coral reefs. Sulawesi is actually a puzzle of land masses that were pieced together over millions of years, its arms once connected to Borneo, New Guinea, and even Antarctica. The island also inherited plenty of natural power from the "ring of fire" into which it was born, for Sulawesi has 11 active volcanoes. The crushing tectonic forces that pushed the island's arms into place resulted in a chain of mountains that stretch 1,300 km (806 mi) from north to south. Still, no point on the island is more than 100 km (62 mi) from the sea.

With its pieces sliding together from all over the earth, Sulawesi is the home of many unique species; in fact, two-thirds of its mammals and one-third of its birds are found nowhere else in the world. Included in its rare cast of wildlife are the *babirusa* (deer pig), and two types of *anoa* (pygmy buffalo). Several national parks, including Morowali, Lore Lindu, Tangkoko Batuangus Dua Saudara, and Pulau Manado Bunaken Tua, are prime spots for trekking and wildlife watching—if you're the adventurous sort. At present, Sulawesi is virtually unspoiled, its tourist infrastructure confined mostly to the southwestern port of Ujung Pandang, central Tanatoraja, and northeastern Manado.

The earliest human inhabitants were seafaring tribes who sailed through the straits from other parts of Asia and from Australia. The first major settlement was southern Soppeng, which was soon overshadowed by Mankasara—now Ujung Pandang—and northern Manado, both busy trading hubs on the way to and from the Spice Islands of Maluku. Mankasara in particular rose to prominence in the 16th century as the aggressive Bajau "sea gypsies" and Bugis tribes took over the waters. In fact, the Bugis were so feared by Asian and Western traders venturing into the region that they became the basis for the modern-day term "Boogey (Bugi) Man." However, it took just a century or so for the Dutch to dominate trade in the region and later take over much of the island, changing the capital's name to Makassar in the process. As Islam spread through the lower peninsula in the early 1600s, the Dutch began working their way north and inland to a region the Bugis called Tanatoraja, the fabled "Land of the Kings"—a secluded, mountainous area where head-hunting, witchcraft, human sacrifice, and elaborate funeral rites were practiced. It was well into the 1900s before missionaries arrived bringing Christianity with them, and well into the 1940s before the Dutch relinquished power, allowing the island to become part of the Republic of Indonesia.

Today, more than 12 million people live on Sulawesi; around four-fifths follow Islam, and the rest—mostly in Tanatoraja and northern Manado—are Christian. The people's physical attributes and their traditions have Arabic, Austronesian, Chinese, and Indian roots; indeed, the island's culture is its primary attraction. There are the southern Bugis, who once sent bands of pirates to prowl the waters and raid ships and whose glorious 200-ton, dual-masted *pinisis* can still be seen in the water at Ujung Pandang and at the shipyards of Maru Masa, 7 km (4 mi) from Bira at the peninsula's opposite end. The Bajau, too, are expert sailors who still spend nearly all their time on the water; their village homes are clustered together over the bays of the south coast. Perhaps the most famous culture here, though, is that of Tanatoraja, where traditional clan houses—the carved and painted *tongkonan*—are built on stilts and topped by massive, curving roofs like a graceful pair of buffalo horns soaring skyward. To the north, the Minihasans around Manado follow Christian beliefs (20% of them are Catholic, 80% are Protestant) introduced by 15th-century Spanish and Portuguese missionaries.

Travel on Sulawesi is challenging at best. Most of the numerous flights between the southwest peninsula and Tanatoraja and northeastern Manado were, at press time, suspended owing to the economic crisis. With the Ujung Pandang–Manado highway recently completed, buses are a viable alternative until the airlines reestablish service; however, the central terrain is mountainous, vehicles are rarely in good condition, and trips are often arduous. Sea travel is the third, and perhaps most pleasant option if you have the time—ships only call weekly or biweekly at various island ports. Renting a car and driving yourself isn't advised and, unfortunately, if you're planning to venture far from Ujung Pandang, long-distance drivers aren't always available. On this island, perhaps more than any other, you must keep your traveler's sense of humor, making every effort to consider the journey as much a part of the fun as the destination.

Pleasures and Pastimes

Architecture

The long, raised *tongkonan* Tanatoraja homes—with their graceful, upswept roofs in the shape of curving bull horns—are Sulawesi's signature structures. On a drive through the region you'll find fine examples of such homes in many villages, including Lemo and Marante.

Dining

Anything and everything is on the menu on Sulawesi. Dishes differ greatly from south to north, though: pork is a rarity around Muslim Ujung Pandang, where seafood reigns; Toraja specialties include buffalo, *pa'piong* food cooked in bamboo tubes, and combinations cooked in blood; Manado market finds might be birds, bats, or rats, depending on what the merchant hunted the previous night. Take heart, though: Most restaurants offer tame—albeit spicy—fare and there are many Chinese and even a few Japanese establishments to fall back on should you find the food too exotic or hot. Don't miss the strong, dark Torajan coffee.

Lodging

Large international hotels with all the trimmings are springing up in the island's three main tourist regions—Ujung Pandang, Tanatoraja, and Manado—with many more in the works. Travelers of all budgets will find comfort in these areas. Outside of here, though, accommodations range between small, well-kept guest houses to spartan losmen—you may trade some creature comforts for a lot of local charm. In the Tanatoraja, several hotels offer individual tongkonan as guest quarters.

Scuba and Snorkeling

Pulau Bunaken Manado Tua Marine Park is the prime place for underwater explorations here. Just a half-hour by boat from Manado, this park draws divers worldwide and is rife with shipwrecks, sandy beaches, and sea life. Many Indonesian and international dive operations offer packages here; for those who arrive impromptu, most scuba enthusiasts stay and rent equipment from dive hotels at Molas Beach 30 km (19 mi) northwest of the city.

Shopping

You can find artwork and crafts from all over the archipelago in Ujung Pandang, including ceramics, hand-woven cloth, brassware, antiques,

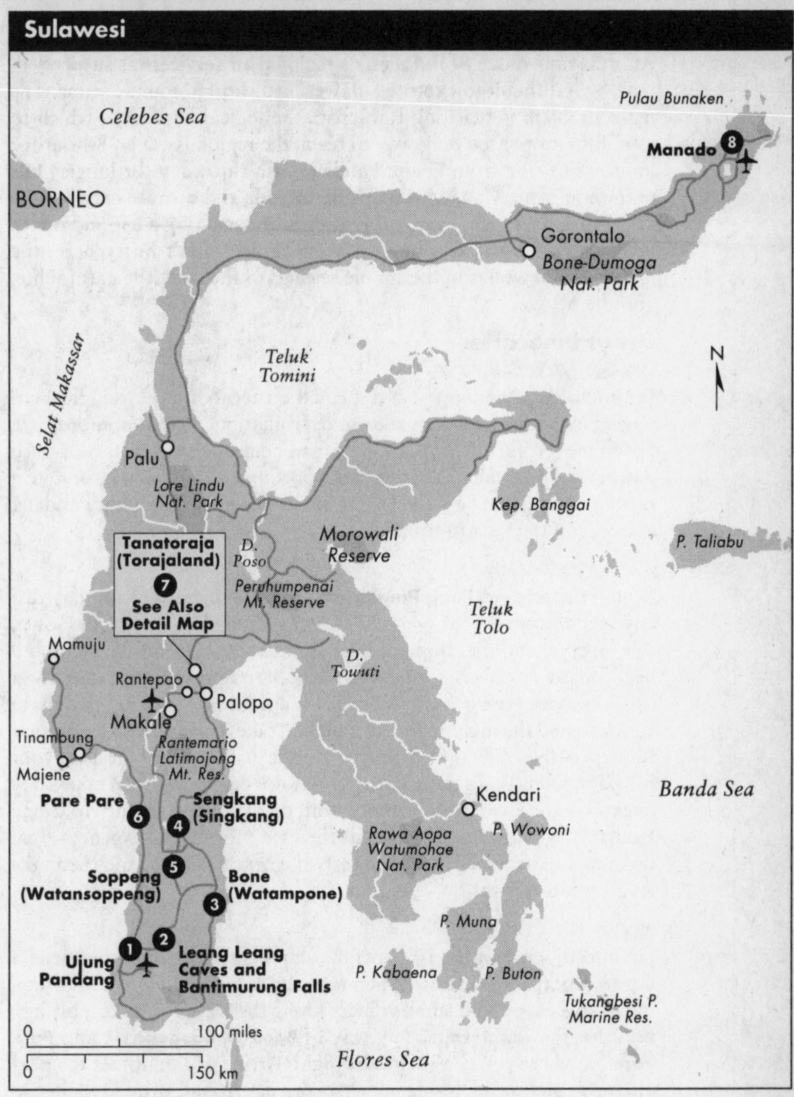

and gold and silver filigree jewelry. In the Tanatoraja, the most valuable and significant souvenirs include the beautiful Torajan textiles with their strong motifs and dark colors, decorative items of woven leaves or carved bamboo, and the ubiquitous bamboo flutes. Rantepao has flourishing shops, but the best market rotates every six days between Rantepao, Makale, and other nearby towns; check with your hotel for a schedule.

Wildlife Watching

Several island creatures are found on only Sulawesi such as the anoa "dwarf buffalo," the *babirusa* (pig deer), and the black Celebes macaque. Not only are these some of the world's rarest animals, but they're also among the most unusual. Sulawesi has a number of world-class national parks for trekking and wildlife watching. They often have basic accommodations, an extensive network of trails, and local guides available for hire. Check with the national parks office in Ujung Pandang for details on transportation, accommodation, and adventure options.

Exploring Sulawesi

At press time much of Indonesia's regional air service was suspended, making it difficult to explore Sulawesi in a short amount of time. The main problem is reaching Rantepao, the logical base from which to visit Tanatoraja; the only way to reach the region is via an 8-hour (or longer) bus ride from Ujung Pandang or a three day (or longer) bus marathon from Manado. Flights on Garuda still operate between the two main cities, however, and renting a car or hiring a car and driver are also possibilities. Whatever your choice, don't hurry here; the magic of Sulawesi is in the simple settings of the land, the natural life, and the people.

Great Itineraries

IF YOU HAVE 3–4 DAYS

Fly into **Ujung Pandang** ① and spend the afternoon exploring the Benteng Ujung Pandang, then take an overnight bus to the **Tanatoraja** ⑦. Spend the second day exploring the major cultural stops. On your third day, try to find a local ceremony or sporting event to watch, or take a rafting trip on the Sa'dan. Take a night bus back to Ujung Pandang and fly out the next morning.

IF YOU HAVE 7 DAYS

Begin your trip in **Ujung Pandang** ① and spend the first full day discovering the city's history at the Benteng Ujung Pandang, Old Gowa, the harbors, and the shops of Jalan Somba Opu. Spend the night and head by car or bus to the **Tanatoraja** ⑦ stopping along the way for a break in **Pare Pare** ⑥; bring plenty of film for the amazing mountain views. Spend the night in Tanatoraja and take a day to wander around Rantepao, then take the next day to see the main cultural sites. On your fifth day, attend a Torajan sporting event or ceremony, then take a day to explore the local trails by foot or raft on the Sa'dan. Return to Ujung Pandang by night bus and fly out the next morning; or, spend a final night in Tanatoraja, drive back early the next morning, and then take an afternoon flight.

IF YOU HAVE 10 DAYS

Fly into **Ujung Pandang** ①; spend a day sightseeing; and then take a day to tour the southwestern peninsula by car, including Bantimurung, the Maros caves, and small villages along the way. The next morning, head for the **Tanatoraja** ⑦ by way of **Bone** ③, **Soppeng** ⑤, and **Pare Pare** ⑥, where you can spend the night. Arrive in Tanatoraja the next afternoon and spend the night, then take a day to walk around Rantepao and the nearby sites. Spend two days touring the Toraja highlands, then head back to Ujung Pandang and catch a flight to **Manado** ⑧. Spend the night and embark on an overnight trip to Bunaken Manado Tua National Marine Reserve the next morning, then head back to Manado to catch a flight out.

IF YOU HAVE 14 DAYS

Fly into **Ujung Pandang** ① and take two days to explore the city and the lower southwestern peninsula, then two days to drive north to **Tanatoraja** ⑦. Spend five days here, perhaps a day for the Rantepao area, two days of sightseeing, a day for attending a local ceremony, and a day for trekking or river rafting. Return to Ujung Pandang on the 10th day and fly north to **Manado** ⑧, spend the night and join a two-night, three-day boat trip to Bunaken Manado Tua National Marine Reserve, where you can snorkel or dive around the islands before heading back to Manado for a return flight. (Note: do not scuba dive within 24 hours of flying).

UJUNG PANDANG AND ENVIRONS

Ujung Pandang

❶ *1,630 km (1,011 mi) northeast of Jakarta, 770 km (477 mi) northeast of Denpasar, 322 km (200 mi) north of Labuanbajo.*

Most visitors fly into Ujung Pandang and use it as their base for travel throughout Sulawesi. The city has several old forts and palaces that can easily be seen on short trips along the coast just outside of town. Ujung Pandang's port is busy and colorful, with everything from small, slim prahu outriggers to sleek pinisi to huge modern Pelni (a state-owned company) ships. Natural wonders are also plentiful, including vast, empty beaches, waterfalls, and tropical gardens less than a two-hour drive away.

Benteng Ujung Pandang, better known as Ft. Rotterdam, is by the harbor in the center of the Old City. Once a fortified trading post for the Sulawesi Gowan dynasty, the fort was captured and rebuilt by the Portuguese in 1545, then captured by the Dutch in 1608 and reinforced again. Several municipal offices are housed in the complex, including the Conservatory of Dance and Music. You can occasionally see unofficial dance performances (the children practice on the stage in the fort's center) as well as the official ones frequently held on Saturday night at 8; the staff at your hotel should have a schedule. The fort also includes the **Galigo Museum,** the state's museum, which is divided into ethnology and history sections. The ethnographic museum is the more interesting, with a large collection of artifacts from different areas of Sulawesi. 🎫 *Free to fort; admission fee for museums.* ⏲ *Fort: Daily 8–5. Museums: Tues.–Thurs. 8 AM–1 PM, Fri. 8 AM–10 AM, weekends 8–4.*

The lovely blossoms at the **Clara Bundt Orchid Garden,** just south of the fort off Jalan Hasanuddin, include varieties from all over the world. Some of the plants here grow to more than 13 ft high. There's also an extensive seashell collection that includes several giant clams. ✉ *Jl. Mochtar Lufti 15,* ☎ *0411/22572.* 🎫 *Free.* ⏲ *Daily 10–4.*

Across the harbor from Ujung Pandang is **Samalona Island,** which has been developed into a recreational center, mostly appealing to locals. It can be reached in 45 minutes. The sports you can participate in here include snorkeling and waterskiing.

For a look at southern Sulawesi's culture and crafts, head for **Taman Mini Sulsel,** southeast of the ports and Benteng Ujung Pandang and about 5 km (3 mi) east of the Orchid Garden (☞ *above*). This combination amusement park and cultural complex includes examples of architecture, textiles, and costumes from all over the archipelago, but it makes a decent introduction to the area's history and sights, including the curved-roof tongkonan of Toraja. ✉ *Jl. Dangko.* 🎫 *Admission.* ⏲ *Daily 10–10.*

For an overview of exquisite silk textiles, visit the **Tenunan Sutera Alam** silk factory in the city's southern Chinese quarter. Here, women still practice their craft each step of the way, from gathering and dyeing the strands to spinning and weaving the garments. ✉ *Jl. Ontah 408, no phone.* 🎫 *Free.* ⏲ *Daily 10–3.*

For those interested in religion and architecture, there are also a number of Chinese temples in the southern part of the city, particularly around Jalan Sulawesi. You can wander through them at anytime during daylight hours, as long as there are no religious ceremonies taking place; the friendly caretakers will most likely be pleased to provide a quick tour. **Ibu Agung Bahari** (✉ Jl. Sulawesi 41), is a 350-year-old structure filled with carvings and colorful paintings. The brilliant colors and ornate detailing of the 18th-century **Tian Hou Gong Temple** (✉ Corner of Jl. Sulawesi and Jl. Serui) make it hard to miss. The large, wooden building is dedicated to Tian Hou, the "Heavenly Queen," who is both a goddess of fertility and a patron of the sailors who still worship here. Her figure, which graces the central altar, is surrounded by three lower levels, where the faithful also worship venerated deities of medicine and motherhood as well as of fertility. Just down the street is **Long Xian Gong Temple** (✉ Corner of Jl. Sulawesi and Jl. Bali), or "Dragon Ghost" temple, built in 1868. This temple has classic Chinese architectural lines and houses three altars: the left one is dedicated to Tu Di Gong, the god of the earth and wealth; the right one to Mi Lo Fo, the protector of jewelers; and the central one to Xian Mu, a mother of the gods.

About 4 km (2 mi) southeast of town is the **Diponegoro Tomb,** the grave of and monument to a great Javanese hero. Prince Diponegoro of Yogyakarta led the fight against the Dutch successfully for five years during the Java War (1825–30). The Dutch finally put a stop to his leadership by summoning him to their headquarters on the pretense of negotiating peace and then taking him prisoner. His sentence was exile to Sulawesi and imprisonment at Ft. Rotterdam, which was where he spent his final 26 years. ✉ *Jl. Diponegoro.* *Free.* *Daily sunrise–sunset.*

Four centuries ago, the kingdom of Gowa—which merged with the kingdom of Tallo to form the island's first true center of power—was the site of the palace of the Makassar rulers and a key port. The ruins of "Old Gowa" begin 7 km (4 mi) south of Ujung Pandang at **Sombaopu,** the fort that protected the sultanate with massive brick walls (10 ft thick and 23 ft high) and a clever locale overlooking the sea. The Dutch—in cohorts with Makassar rival Bugis troops—decimated the fort in 1669 and the elements pounded the ruins for the next three centuries. Indonesian archaeologists restored them in the late 1980s. Besides strolling around the fort area, you can also visit the historical museum, which displays artifacts and ammunition uncovered in the excavation, as well as four "living cultural villages" that represent four of the region's ethnic groups' crafts and rituals. ✉ *Off Jl. Tallo along the Ujung Pandang–Sunguminasa Hwy., no phone.* *Admission.* *Daily 8–5.*

The **Tomb of Sultan Hasanuddin** and other kings of Gowa are in a cemetery between the fort and the Sungguminasa Palace (☞ *below*). Besides the grave of Hasanuddin, the most famous of the Gowan kings and a national hero for his ferocious battle against the Dutch, you'll also find the **Pelantikan stone,** or *tomanurunga,* the coronation stone of the Kingdom of Gowa. Legends of the kingdom tell of the goddess Tomanurunga, who started the line of Gowan kings when she married a mortal named Karaeng Bayo at this site. Afterward the stone became the place where the sultans were crowned. Fifteen minutes' walk from the tomb is the 1603 **Mesjid Katangka,** Ujung Pandang's oldest mosque (now rebuilt) and the site of more graves.

The traditional, raised, wooden palace of **Sungguminasa** (4 km/3 mi south of Sombaopu) was built in 1936. The **Ballalompoa Museum** here is a must-see, full of ornate royal jewelry and ceremonial costumes. ✉ *Jl. Cenderawasih, off Jl. Tallo and the Ujung Pandang–Sungguminasa Hwy., no phone.* *Admission.* *Mon.–Thurs. 8–1, Fri. 8–10:30, Sat. 8–12.*

North of the city are several noteworthy sights. The remains of **Tallo,** Gowa's 16th-century satellite kingdom and ally are 3 km (2 mi) north of Ujung Pandang in the rice paddies off Jalan Tallo Umar. Just 4 km

(2 mi) north of town is **Paotare,** the harbor where the Bugis bring their pinisi to unload cargo, mend sails, and prepare for the next voyage. Watching these elegant wooden schooners set off along the warm, bright water is a timeless sight. Sunsets from here are singular, but the pier has missing planks and gaping holes, so watch your step. **The ports of Sukarno and Hatta** along Jalan Martadina southwest of Paotare are a good place to watch large modern ships and two-masted prahu glide in from all parts of Indonesia.

Dining and Lodging

$$ ✕ **Shogun.** On the waterfront road, Sulawesi's original Japanese restaurant is clean and busy. Menu items include such traditional fare as sushi and sashimi. Try anything served with the fresh local seafood—especially the fish. Sake is a nice complement to an evening meal. ✉ *Jl. Penghibur 2,* ☎ *0411/324102. AE, MC, V.*

$$ ✕ **Surya Supercrab.**This restaurant serves some of the best seafood in Ujung Pandang—count on crowds and a wait for a table. The large, bright room has no notable decor or atmosphere, but the crab-and-asparagus soup is delicious, as are the gigantic prawns. ✉ *Jl. Nusakambangan 16,* ☎ *0411/317066. No credit cards.*

$$–$$$ ✕🏨 **Radisson Ujung Pandang.** What this hotel lacks in charm it makes up in efficiency and a grand location on the waterfront. Rooms are boxlike but comfortable and well equipped, with such amenities as hair dryers and in-room safes. The coffee shop looks out onto the water and offers a combined taste of the West and of Asia—tiger prawns with a hint of lemongrass and barbecued duck in a light curry sauce. There's also a Chinese restaurant that serves both Szechuan and Cantonese fare. ✉ *Jl. Somba Opu 235, 90111,* ☎ *0411/333–3111,* FAX *0411/333222. 90 rooms. Restaurant, coffee shop, health club, meeting rooms. AE, DC, MC, V.*

$$–$$$ 🏨 **Hotel Sedona.** This comfortable, deluxe, 10-story hotel has a scenic location on the southern Losari Beach. The spacious lobby has beige polished-marble floors and floor-to-ceiling windows that offer sweeping sea views. Rooms and suites are awash in pastels and decorated with contemporary furnishings tailored for modern travelers, including queen-size beds, desks, minibars, and sizable baths; six rooms have terraces. A large ballroom and meeting rooms with many facilities make this hotel popular with business travelers. ✉ *Jl. Somba Opu 297, 90111,* ☎ *0411/870555,* FAX *0411/870222. 218 rooms, 12 suites. 3 restaurants, 2 bars, pool, health club, beach, shops, laundry service, business services, meeting rooms. AE, MC, V.*

$$–$$$ 🏨 **Makassar Golden Hotel.** Right on Losari Beach, this hotel has Toraja-style roofs on its main building. Most of the comfortable rooms and cottages face the sea and have wall-to-wall carpeting, with beige decor and woven bedcovers in a Toraja design. All rooms have private baths, minibars, and TVs. ✉ *Jl. Pasar Ikan 50, 90111,* ☎ *0411/314408,* FAX *0411/320951. 50 rooms, 10 cottages. Restaurant, coffee shop, minibars, pool, beach, dance club, laundry service, meeting rooms. AE, DC, MC, V.*

$$ 🏨 **Makassar City Hotel.** Toraja-style carved-wood panels are the focus here. The hotel is affordable and centrally located, but its facilities and furnishings have seen better days: rooms are spacious, with sitting areas, king-size beds, TVs, and minibars, but stains on the carpets and scuff marks on the walls attest to their age. The lounge has tired crushed-velvet sofas and lumpy leather chairs. ✉ *Jl. Khairil Anwar 28, 90111,* ☎ *0411/317055,* FAX *0411/311818. 89 rooms. Restaurant, bar, pool, meeting rooms. AE, DC, MC, V.*

$ 🏨 **Hotel Ramayana.** Between the airport and Ujung Pandang, this place is clean but purely utilitarian. It's conveniently located across from the Liman Express office, which runs buses to Tanatoraja. ✉ *Jl. G. Bawakaraeng 121, 90111, ☎ 0411/442479, FAX 0411/322165. 35 rooms. Restaurant, travel services. No credit cards.*

Nightlife and the Arts

Sunset viewing and snack munching are the prime activities on the patios of the expat hangouts **Kios Semarang** and **Eva Ria** along Jalan Penghibur. Local bands often play at the **Makassar Golden Hotel** (✉ Jl. Pasar Ikan 50–52, ☎ 0411/314408). Dancers can try the disco at the **Marannu City Hotel** (✉ Jl. Sultan Hasanuddin 3-5, ☎ 0411/315087).

Shopping

Ujung Pandang's position at the crossroads of trade routes between east and west Indonesia, as well as those north and south between Asia and the South Pacific, makes it one of the most diverse shopping spots in the country. Start east of the waterfront and south of Benteng Ujung Pandang at **Jalan Somba Opu,** which is lined with crafts shops filled with shells, spices, carvings, silks, gold, fine Gowan brasswork, and musical instruments. **Asia Art and Curio** (✉ Jl. Somba Opu, no phone) has a variety of antiques. **Asia Baru** (✉ Jl. Somba Opu, no phone) is a good place for porcelain. **Kanegbo Art Shop** (✉ Corner of Jl. Somba Opu and Jl. Pattimura, no phone) sells silk textiles, baskets, and pieces of fine jewelry made in the region. The **Maryam Art Shop** (✉ Jl. Pattimura 6, 2nd floor, no phone) also has old pieces.

Leang Leang Caves and Bantimurung Falls

❷ *38 km (24 mi) northeast of Ujung Pandang.*

The extensive underground chambers of the **Leang Leang Caves** (also known as the Maros Caves) make up an archaeological park that protects some of the archipelago's most valuable prehistoric artwork. In the midst of breezy, forested hills, the park's rugged limestone cliffs hide Mesolithic paintings of wildlife and human images from 5,000–10,000 years ago. Visit Leang Pettae and Leang Peta Kere to see eerie sets of human handprints in all different sizes, or Ulu Leang and Leang Burung I and II to see fossils. More than 60 caves have been found in the region, including Salukan Kalang, which at 11 km (7 mi) is the island's longest.

Three kilometers (2 miles) northeast of Leang Leang is a serene forest haven with tropical scenery, cool streams, quiet caves, and the thundering **Bantimurung Falls,** made famous by 1800s naturalist Alfred Russel Wallace, who came here to collect butterflies. Although the park is overrun with locals on weekends and holidays and it now takes patience to find the spectacular giant birdwings so common in Wallace's day, the area is nevertheless a good place to observe Sulawesi's natural beauty.

Bone

❸ *79 km (49 mi) northeast of Bantimurung, 110 km (68 mi) northeast of Ujung Pandang.*

In the 17th century, this town (formally known as Watampone) was a regional core of power and a semiautonomous state ruled by the rebel king, Aru Palakka. The Dutch eventually conquered the city—three times—and remnants of their presence include colonial houses along some of the streets.The Dutch weren't the only outsiders to live in Bone, though; the seafaring Bugis also maintained a presence, and an 1881 Bugis house, the **Bola Soba,** can be seen behind the Hotel Watampone on Jalan

Sudirman. The former palace is now the **Museum Lapawawoi,** with an extensive collection of photos, charts of royal successions, and an array of court artifacts. The museum is open daily 8–5; there is an admission fee. Bone is also a base for visiting one of the peninsula's largest cave systems, the **Mampu Caves,** 40 km (25 mi) south of town.

Dining and Lodging

$ ✕ **Pondok Selera.** This small, friendly place is consistently recommended by both visitors and expats as the best restaurant in town. The back garden is a pleasant spot in which to enjoy savory Indonesian and Chinese dishes. Any of the seafood entrées with hot rice and mixed vegetables are guaranteed to satisfy. ✉ *Jl. Biru 28, no phone. No credit cards.*

$ **Wisma Bola Ridie.** Its name means "The Yellow House," and its yellow exterior is a symbol of South Sulawesi nobility. It was owned by a descendent of the last prince of Bone, and is in a charming 1930s Dutch building. Large, comfortable rooms, tile floors, and congenial hospitality all add to the delightful setting five minutes' walk from the main town. Breakfast and tea are included in the price. ✉ *Jl. Merdeka 6,* ☎ *0419/21412. 6 rooms. No credit cards.*

$ **Wisma Watampone.** This modern-style building with touches of Sulawesi decor offers more Western comforts than expected outside of Ujung Pandang, including air-conditioning and private baths in all rooms. Quarters are simple, spacious, and clean, and the English-speaking staff members are happy to assist with travel plans. ✉ *Jl. Biru 14,* ☎ *0419/21362. 20 rooms. Restaurant, coffee shop, pool, laundry service. AE, MC, V.*

En Route Forty kilometers (25 miles) northwest of Bone (via Uloe) are the **Mampu Caves,** a network of underground limestone passages that comprises Sulawesi's largest cave system. You can hire guides in the village next to the site, and they will point out an imaginative variety of characters found in the unusual stalactite and stalagmite shapes. Local lore has it that these images are the former court of a lazy local princess, turned to stone when she dropped her spool and promised to marry whoever picked it up for her but then broke her vow when it was returned by a dog.

Sengkang

❹ *65 km (40 mi) northwest of Bone, 175 km (109 mi) northeast of Ujung Pandang.*

Sengkang (Singkang) is an unexpectedly pleasant lakeside resort town in the center of the southwestern peninsula. A large, shallow lake—Danau Tempe—gives the town a relaxed, mountain-hideaway feel, and the, scenic gardens, lush hills, and "floating" houses (Bugis houses that are raised on stilts) have made it quite a draw. There are also numerous weaving cooperatives in the area where you can observe the creation of silk textiles from the worm to the loom to the market shelves. Check out **Toko Sumber Sutera** (✉ Jl. Magga Amirulla 140, no phone) for an idea of selection and price.

Soppeng

❺ *25 km (15 mi) southwest of Sengkang, 75 km (46 mi) northwest of Bone.*

Soppeng, or Watansoppeng, is another silk-production hub. Along the northern road from here to Pangkajene are groves of mulberry trees where silkworms are cultivated; many of the worms that hatch here are sent to Sengkang. Among the town's other attractions are its gardens, some of the most prized in the region, and the hundreds of fruit bats that live in the trees near the central mosque. Soppeng's true richness, however, lies in its cultural treasures, such as the **Taman Purbakala Kompleks Makam Kuno** (Sultans' Graves), a gathering of unique stone structures just outside town on the road to Ompo.

Pare Pare

6 *70 km (43 mi) northwest of Soppeng, 180 km (108 mi) north of Ujung Pandang.*

From Ujung Pandang the four-hour drive north to Pare Pare—halfway between Ujung Pandang and Rantepao in the Tanatoraja region—takes you through rice fields and past the Makassar Strait. Bugis houses, which are built on stilts and have crossed roof beams, line the road. At some you'll see fish hanging from the rafters, curing in the sun. With 90,000 people, Pare Pare is Sulawesi's second-largest town. The Bugis *bago* ships—smaller and more agile than the 100-ton pinisi cargo ships—and other craft sail from its port, perhaps on their way to Kalimantan on Borneo. At the **Museum Bangenge,** 2 km (1 mi) south of town at Cappa Galung, you'll find a collection of traditional weapons, costumes, and ornaments overseen by curator Haji Hamzah, a descendent of the last ruler of the region's Bacu Kiki kingdom. ✉ *Desa Cappa Galung, no phone.* 🎟 *Admission.* ⏲ *Daily 10–4.*

Dining and Lodging

$ ✕ **Sempurna.** On Pare Pare's main street is a clean, Formica-furnished, air-conditioned restaurant that serves tasty Indonesian and Chinese fare. Seafood dishes dominate the menu; try the sweet-and-sour shrimp. ✉ *202 Jl. Bau Massepe,* ☎ *0421/21573. No credit cards.*

$ ✕🏨 **Bukit Indah.** Perched on a hill, this smart, pristinely clean restaurant has a view of the bay and catches a nice breeze. The crab-and-corn soup is delicious; if you're feeling daring, try the fried frogs' legs. To reach Bukit Indah, take a right turn up the hill from the main street just before entering downtown Pare Pare. (Note that six clean, simple rooms are available if you wish to stay the night.) ✉ *Jl. Sudirman 65,* ☎ *0421/21886. No credit cards.*

En Route The route from Pare Pare north to Tanatoraja wasn't paved until 1980; before then, the rutted, stony track took hours to cover. Even today, travel on this thin, two-lane road can be arduous, if not terrifying, as it winds along steep, jagged cliffs before it twists and turns inland, climbing into limestone hills forested with tropical pines and palms. Shimmering in the distance are the steely blue mountains that locked out intruders for centuries. Farther north are the smooth tucks and folds of soft, green, mountain slopes. The sky is enormously wide and, in the dry season, the air is clear and warm, allowing a glimpse of what regional legends maintain is the realm of gods.

NEED A BREAK? About 54 km (32 mi) before Makale is a roadside restaurant, **Puntak Lakawan,** with a terrace that affords spectacular views of Tanatoraja. Stop for the vistas, the strong coffee, and the "tourist only" Western toilet facilities—not for the food.

Tanatoraja (Torajaland)

★ 7 *Makale is 328 km (205 mi) northeast of Ujung Pandang, 110 km (68 mi) northeast of Pare Pare; Rantepao is 17 km (11 mi) northeast of Makale.*

The so-called Land of the Kings, which dominates south-central Sulawesi, was put in the international limelight in the early 1900s, when word of its animist cultures and their traditions first reached the West. Then, as now, people were captivated by tales of Tanatoraja's graceful tongkonans, whose curving roofs point east and west to the heavens out of respect for ancestors; of its life-size *tau tau* (wooden effigies) that mark graves in limestone cliffs; of its wedding ceremonies and their elaborate costumes of gold and silk brocade; of its exciting *sisemba* kick-boxing contests and buffalo fights; and of its funerals involving hundreds of people and dozens of animal sacrifices.

The more popular sights are between Makale, the administrative center, and Rantepao, the commercial and tourist hub to the north. From Rantepao a network of roads peels off into the countryside to Toraja villages. To see the highlights, you'll need at least three full days; plan on a week to visit the more remote villages. If you drive to the area, add a day each way for the trip to and from Ujung Pandang. Although the dry season runs from April to October, many of the celebrations take place in July and August when the crops are harvested. This is when most people visit the area—particularly the towns around Rantepao. To avoid crowds, schedule a trip around these months or venture into the northwestern or eastern regions, which are the least infiltrated by Western visitors.

A good way to experience Tanatoraja is by hiking from one village to the next through hills and rice paddies along small, rugged paths. (Be sure to wear strong, ankle-supporting shoes and a hat—for sun protection—and bring binoculars so that you can clearly see the tau tau.) A trip that combines bus travel and short hikes is another option, though the going will be slow. You can also hire a minivan or a Jeep. Regardless of how you travel, a good, professionally trained guide is essential. Such a guide will not only serve as your translator, but also your ambassador and teacher—explaining the culture's beliefs and ceremonies, relating local legends, and introducing you to the lesser-known settlements.

Of all the rituals, the funeral ceremony is probably the most important to the peoples of the Tanatoraja, and you should attend one if you get the chance. Funerals here are celebrations of life after death rather than a lament for the departed soul. They can take months to arrange, with relatives arriving from all over the archipelago, and can last for days. Palm wine is drunk, feasts are shared, and animals are slaughtered. Wealth is measured in buffalo (it's believed that the dead arrive in the hereafter riding a large white buffalo): the more buffalo sacrificed at the funeral, the more honor to the dead, the family, and the clan. Even those who have converted to Christianity continue the funeral ritual to demonstrate their prestige, keep tradition, and make sure the dead have plenty of influence with the gods.

Another large ritual takes place when a clan erects a new tongkonan. At these housewarming ceremonies the whole clan—often hundreds of people—is present. Buffalo, chickens, and pigs are sacrificed, both as dishes for the huge feast and as a show of prestige. All tongkonan face north—toward the land of the gods, according to one legend. Another legend contends that they face the direction from which the first settlers sailed (they are then purported to have used their upturned boats as shelters, hence the buffalo-horn shape of the roofs today). Houses are raised and have high gables with geometric designs and, perhaps, a few buffalo skulls; they also usually face a row of large rice barns.

Makale

Set amid the mountains and around a man-made lake, Makale is the entrance to Tanatoraja. Although it gleams with whitewashed Dutch churches and has an interesting market, this cool highland town attracts few visitors. Indeed, if you're in the area during peak season, you might consider making this your hub rather than crowded Rantepao. Although Makale isn't within walking distance of the main sights, you can easily hire a vehicle and a guide here. The **town market,** held every six days off Jalan Pasar Baru, is a riot of color and activity. Several trails on the outskirts of town lead to small villages—perfect for day hikes and picnics. A path from Jalan Ihwan Rambe runs west toward **Tondon,** where there are several secluded tau tau.

Rantepao and Environs

Rantepao is a small, easygoing town of dirt roads, cool mountain breezes, and a quietly booming tourist business year-round. Its big event occurs every sixth day, when the "weekly" market at the town crossroads attracts shoppers from miles around. Even on off days, the market shops sell wood carvings, cloth, and other Toraja-crafted goods. Rantepao's inexpensive restaurants and hotels are clean, comfortable, and friendly, and its semi-backwoods location and Christian-animist character give it an honest, genteel aura.

Some of the best-known Tanatoraja villages and sights are a short walk or drive from Rantepao. (Note: When you visit a village, plan to give a small donation of at least Rp 1,500, as tourism helps with these communities' upkeep. Also bring gifts of cigarettes or food to show your respect.) In **Karasik,** a traditional village on the southern outskirts of town, a group of elegant tongkonan surround several megaliths. Four kilometers (2 miles) south of Rantepao is **Kete Kesu,** a wood-carving village with hanging graves beneath the cliffsides; you'll also spot coffins and piles of bones along the thin forest paths. Ten minutes' walk from Kete Kesu is **Sulukeng,** where megaliths mark several graves.

In **Londa,** 8 km (5 mi) south of Rantepao, long, twisted passageways run deep into the cliffs and are lined with piles of skulls and bones. Coffins are tucked into some of the cave shelves as well, many with more than one body inside (it's customary to bury family members together). You don't need a guide for the caves, but you will need a bright flashlight; if you don't have one, there are plenty of guides—many of whom speak English and are excellent storytellers—with gas lamps for hire near the snack stands outside. Within walking distance of the Londa caves is **Pabalsenam,** a tree of hanging graves for babies who died before teething. Five kilometers (3 miles) south of Londa is **Lemo,** one of the best places for viewing tau tau in the cliff faces; try to arrive here early in the morning, because the figures face east and are bathed in shadows by midday.

At **Marante,** 5 km (3 mi) northeast of Rantepao, you'll find burial caves in a limestone cliff as well as the remnants of poles used to support hanging coffins, some old carved coffins, and a funeral bier shaped like a traditional house—a ship to carry the deceased to the next life. At one end of the village is a modern home with a prow projecting from the roof and a wooden buffalo head attached to its front post—a fabulous anachronism.

Ten kilometers (6 miles) east of Rantepao is quiet **Nanggala.** Here the tongkonan are built on poles with soaring prow-shape roofs and are lined up facing north; *lumbung* (granaries, smaller than the houses but similar in shape) stand opposite. The tongkonan is cared for by the clan leader. A noble clan may decorate all the walls with carved and

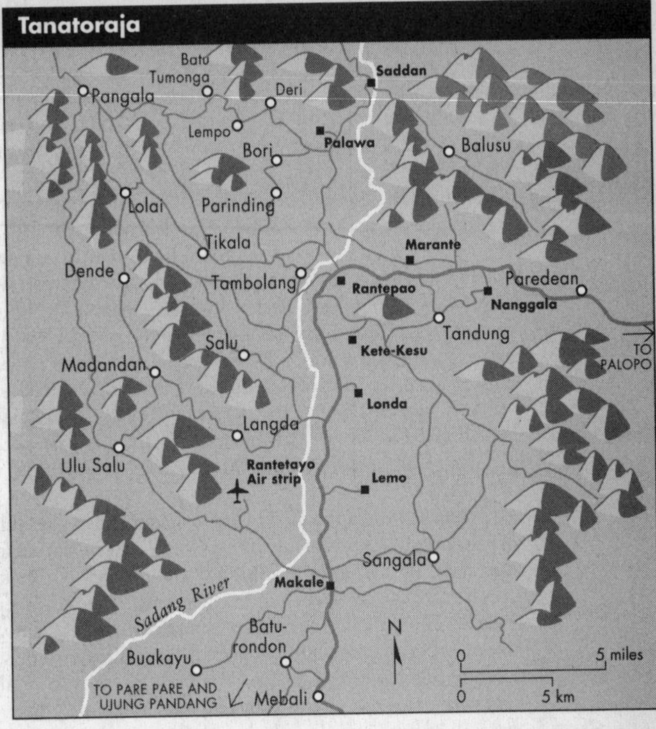

painted designs symbolizing the buffalo, the sun, and important crops. A middle-ranking clan is permitted to decorate only the front gable. When you see a wooden buffalo head or the horns of sacrificed buffalo affixed to the front pole of the house, you're looking at the house of a noble clan.

In the very old village of **Palawa,** 7 km (4 mi) north of Rantepao, hundreds of horns of sacrificed buffalo hang on the houses. Eight of the traditional homes contain shops that sell Toraja carvings, textiles, old coins, and, well, junk. In **Saddan** (3 km/2 mi northeast of Pulawa), Toraja women weave and sell their colorful textiles, which have mainly primary colors in geometric patterns.

DINING AND LODGING

$ ★ ✕ **Pondok Torsina.** A few miles south of Rantepao, this small hotel and restaurant serves good Indonesian food on a veranda overlooking the rice paddies. Try the asparagus soup, shrimp in spicy butter sauce, or grilled fish. If possible, make arrangements a day in advance to have the *piong,* a traditional Toraja meal cooked in bamboo. The Toraja owner is very helpful in filling in any information gaps left by your guide. ✉ *Tikunna Malenong,* ☎ *0423/21293. No credit cards.*

$ ✕ **Restaurant Rachmat.** Right across from the traffic circle in the center of town, this Chinese-operated restaurant has design elements based on a traditional Toraja house. The menu includes standard Indonesian, Toraja, and Chinese dishes and caters to tour groups, so it can be busy and noisy. Local specialties include fried buffalo steak and black rice. ✉ *Jl. Abdul Sari 8. No credit cards.*

$$$ ✕🏨 **Marante Highland Resort.** At this hotel just outside Marante, request a room in one of the traditional structures with roofs that look like upside-down boats. These have Indonesian fabrics and terraces that overlook the landscaped grounds, and all rooms have good, long bath-

tubs. The pool has an adjoining terrace café, the coffee shop serves Western food and a few Indonesian dishes, and the barbecue restaurant offers an array of Southeast Asian dishes. The hotel staff can arrange excursions to the surrounding villages and cliffside graves. ✉ *Jl. Jurusan Palapo (✉ Box 52, Rantepao 91831),* ☎ *0423/216169,* FAX *0423/21122. 111 rooms. 3 restaurants, pool, shops, travel services, meeting room. AE, DC, MC, V.*

$$ **Hotel Misiliana.** The lovely setting for this massive collection of traditional bungalows is a hilly, landscaped area 4 km (2 mi) northeast of town. The courtyard garden has a row of tongkonan with rice barns opposite; guest rooms surround the courtyard and are in two- or four-unit bungalows designed to complement the houses. The rooms themselves are spotless and have twin beds with colorful native spreads as well as modern tile baths. Set-menu breakfasts and dinners are included in the room price. A cultural show takes place some evenings. ✉ *Jl. Pongtiku 27 (Box 01), 91831,* ☎ *0423/21212,* FAX *0423/21512. 96 rooms. 2 restaurants, bar, coffee shop, pool, tennis court, laundry service, business services, meeting rooms, travel services, car rental. AE, DC, MC, V.*

$$ **Toraja Prince Hotel.** This large complex in the hills 4 km (2 mi) northeast of town is as upscale as you'll get in the region. The buildings have flourishes of traditional architecture. Rooms are spacious, comfortable, and clean; bright Torajan textiles complement the dark woods. The Japanese restaurant is a refreshing alternative to the abundance of Indonesian fare in town; a second restaurant serves Torajan, Chinese, and Western dishes. The friendly, professional management team operates a very thorough travel service; they take great pride in being helpful. ✉ *Jl. Pakubalasalu, 91831,* ☎ *0423/21430,* FAX *0423/21304. 95 rooms. 2 restaurants, bar, pool, shop, laundry service, travel services. AE, MC, V.*

$ ★ **Pia and Poppies Hotel and Restaurant.** Mr. Paul worked for years as a chef at different Bali resorts before returning to Rantepao and opening this inn. His wonderful property is sleepy and serene, with panoramic valley views from the terrace, and skylighted, rock-inlaid showers. Mr. Paul and his family also preside over one of the most sophisticated Torajan dining rooms around; save room for the pumpkin soup. ✉ *Jl. Pongtiku 27A (a few blocks south of Rantepao on the road to Makale), 91831,* ☎ *0423/21121,* FAX *0423/25059. 10 rooms. Restaurant, bar. No credit cards.*

$$ **Toraja Cottages.** Just 3 km (2 mi) east of Rantepao, and set among tropical gardens, this hotel consists of rows of attached cottages around the main building. The small, clean rooms have twin beds. Westernized Indonesian food is served in a veranda restaurant with rattan furniture, and, amusingly, a model of the Statue of Liberty on a corner table. People like to gather in the small bar off the lobby. ✉ *Kampung Bolu (reservations:* ✉ *Jl. Somba Opu 281, Ujung Pandang 91831),* ☎ *0423/21089; 0411/84146 in Ujung Pandang;* FAX *0423/21304; 0411/873083 in Ujung Pandang. 58 rooms. 2 restaurants, bar, pool, shops, travel services. AE, DC, V.*

MANADO AND ENVIRONS

Manado

8 *2,500 km (1,550 mi) northeast of Jakarta, 1,900 km (1,178 mi) northeast of Ujung Pandang, 1,600 km (992 mi) northeast of Rantepao.*

As the hub for ships sailing between the Philippines, Borneo, and the Spice Islands and as the capital of a collection of northern states united in the province of Minihasa, Manado is a cosmopolitan city. Yet despite its international flavor and port town status, it's a surprisingly clean, open, congenial place.

For most people, *the* reason to come here is scuba diving.The waters and reefs of the nearby Bunaken Manado Tua National Marine Reserve offer some of the world's most spectacular dive sites. Live coral gardens and diverse marine life make for some fascinating and colorful exploration. Most trips begin from Manado or Malayang village, ★ where powerboats zip you out to **Pulau Bunaken,** the main island of this archipelago (10 km/6 mi off shore), in just over an hour. Dive operations know this territory well and offer a variety of trips to the reefs around Pulau Bunaken. Area dive sites include the **Manado Wreck,** the 196-ft skeleton of a Dutch ship that sunk during World War II; the reefs off **Pulau Manado Tua,** a dormant volcano now covered with forest; and the coral gardens around **Pulau Siladen, Pulau Montehage,** and **Pulau Nain.**

When you come up for air, Manado has an abundance of markets, little shops, museums, and memorials. The **Sam Ratulangi Monument,** on Jalan Sam Ratulangi, honors the "father" of the Minihasan people, who was the first governor of east Indonesia. The **Ibu Walanda Maramis Monument** memorializes a pioneer of the Indonesian women's movement. The **Toar Lumimuut Monument** on Jalan Sudarso commemorates the legendary goddess Lumimuut and her son—who, as the stories go, mistakenly married each other. **The Provincial Museum of Northern Sulawesi** on Jalan Supratman provides a good overview of the region's culture. *Museum* ⏲ *Mon.–Thurs. 8–5, Fri. 8–11, Sat. 8–2.* 🎫 *Admission fee.*

Lodging

$$–$$$ 🏨 **Novotel Manado.** Right on the waterfront esplanade near the Matahari Department store, this large hotel is one of the town's newest and most luxurious. Standard rooms are comfortable and have touches of local decor amid the mainly Western furnishings. Suites have spacious sitting areas; for a fine bay view, request one of the two suites that have balconies. A sixth-floor pool also commands a stunning view of the water; the bar here is an early-evening hot spot. Blue Banter Marina, Tour, and Diving Center, in front of the hotel, offers dive tours to area reefs as well as dive classes and provincial tours. ✉ *Jl. Piere Tendean, 95111,* ☎ *0431/855555,* FAX *0431/868888. 190 rooms, 14 suites. Restaurant, 2 bars, coffee shop, pool, health club, dive shop, children's programs, laundry service, business services, meeting rooms, travel services. AE, DC, MC, V.*

$$ 🏨 **Hotel New Queen.** Just 10 minutes from the airport, this newly renovated establishment offers clean, convenient accommodations at reasonable prices. Rooms are basic in decor but have such amenities as refrigerators. The price includes airport transfers, breakfast, dinner, or laundry service. ✉ *Jl. Wakeke 12-14, 95111,* ☎ *0431/855551,* FAX *0431/864440. 35 rooms. Restaurant, bar, coffee shop, refrigerators, laundry service, meeting room. AE, DC, MC, V.*

$$ ★ 🏨 **Nusantara Diving Center (NDC).** Manado's best-known dive organization also runs a hotel and restaurant right on Molas Beach, 5 km (3 mi) north of town. You can check in, make your scuba plans, and be out on the Bunaken reefs the next day. Rooms are basic and small and not all of them have air-conditioning. But the place is friendly, and most guests don't mind the limited indoor space as they're here solely for the underwater action. The on-site dive shop has all the equipment necessary for dive and snorkel tours and classes, and the travel desk can organize trips to the countryside, including visits to area volcanoes.

All-inclusive dive, boat, and hotel packages are available. ⊠ *Molas Beach, 95001,* ☎ *0431/863988,* FAX *0431/860638. 43 rooms. Restaurant, 2 bars, beach, dive shop, dance club, travel services. AE, MC, V.*

Outdoor Activities and Sports

Package rates for the three top dive operators in the area run Rp 648,000–Rp 972,000, including equipment, boat, and meals. **Barracuda** (⊠ Jl. Sam Ratulangi 61, Manado, ☎ 0431/62033) has a fleet of dive boats as well as several chalets on Molas Beach so that you can put together hotel and boat dive packages. **Murex** (⊠ Jl. Sudirman 28, Manado, ☎ 0431/66280) also has a dive resort and a number of boats that run to the Sangihe and Talaud islands north of Manado, among other places. The **NDC** (☞ Lodging, *above*), considered one of the friendliest and most professional outfits in the region, offers all-inclusive hotel, dive tour or class, and boat packages.

SULAWESI A TO Z

Arriving and Departing

By Airplane

Garuda (☎ 0411/322543) flies to Ujung Pandang's **Hasanuddin Airport** (☎ 0423/62411) from Jakarta and Surabaya on Java and from Denpasar on Bali, among other places.

Merpati (☎ 0411/24114 in Ujung Pandang; 0423/21485 in Rantepao) once flew each morning between Ujung Pandang and the **Rantetayo Airport** (☎ 0423/62423) near Rantepao; this is the only air route to Tanatoraja, and at press time flights were suspended. However, due to the popularity of this region, service was expected to resume; contact your travel agent or Merpati for updates. In any case, even when flights are scheduled, the runway can become unserviceable in the rainy season, causing frequent cancellations.

All flights to Manado's **Sam Ratulangi Airport** (☎ 0431/51060) from the south are via Ujung Pandang on **Garuda** (☎ 0431/51544). **Merpati** (☎ 0431/64027) may also have flights to different points on the island. **Bouraq** (☎ 0431/62757) serves the city from Gorontalo on the northeast peninsula, Palu in the central area, and the northeast island of Ternate. Internationally, you can enter Manado nonstop from Davao in the Philippines or from Singapore (☞ Air Travel *in* Gold Guide).

BETWEEN THE AIRPORT AND DOWNTOWN

The Hasanuddin Airport is 22 km (14 mi) east of Ujung Pandang; a taxi to town costs about Rp 15,000. You can buy a coupon inside the terminal, next to the baggage claim. You can also hire a minivan—perfect for groups or those with lots of dive gear—outside the arrivals area for around Rp 10,000. Rantetayo Airport is 24 km (15 mi) southwest of Rantepao. You can catch a bus into town or book one for a ride to the airport from your hotel for about Rp 5,000. From Sam Ratulangi Airport, 13 km (8 mi) east of Manado, metered taxis run roughly Rp 7,000.

By Boat

Pelni (⊠ Jl. Angkasa 18, Jakarta, ☎ 021/421–1921) ships from Surabaya (☎ 031/21041) pass through Ujung Pandang (☎ 0411/331393) every seven days and moor at Pelabuhan Hatta Harbor, a short becak ride from the center of town. Because Ujung Pandang is the gateway to eastern Indonesia, many other shipping companies take passengers from here aboard freighters to Maluku and other eastern islands and to Kalimantan, on Borneo. Manado's port is Bitung, 30 km (19 mi) from town, where **Pelni** (⊠ Jl. Sam Ratulangi 7, Manado,

(☎ 0423/62844) ships pass through en route to Ambon, Jayapura, Ujung Pandang, and other points along the Sulawesi coast.

Getting Around

Because the country between Ujung Pandang and Rantepao is breathtaking both from alongside and above, the ideal way to visit Tanatoraja is to make the outbound journey by road and return by air (that is, of course, if there's air service).

By Becak

For short journeys bicycle rickshaws are popular. Bargain hard—a trip in a town should cost about Rp 1,000, even if the driver begins by asking Rp 5,000.

By Bemo

In Ujung Pandang, bemo minivans run along Jalan Jendral Sudirman/Ratulangi; Jalan Hasanuddin/Cenderawasih; and Jalan Bulusaraung/Mesjid Raya to Leang Leang (sometimes detouring to the airport). Public minibuses to towns outside Ujung Pandang leave from Jalan Sarappo whenever they're full.

By Bus

The best bus service north from Ujung Pandang to Tanatoraja and points in between is **Liman Express** (☎ 0411/315851). Buses run from Manado to Gorontalo and all the way south to the Ujung Pandang; however, as the "highways" are often unpaved, in a state of disrepair, or washed out altogether, for road trips in the Minihasa province it's far more convenient to hire a car and driver from one of the many travel agencies; for longer distances it's far more convenient to fly.

The bus to Tanatoraja from Ujung Pandang takes nine to 12 hours, depending on weather and road conditions, plus an hour lunch break. There are morning and evening departures in both directions. At Rp 15,000, it's an economical way to go. Since the countryside is not to be missed, make sure to make at least one trip during daylight.

By Car

You can hire a car and a driver through most hotels and travel agencies in Ujung Pandang, Rantepao, Makale, and Manado. For in-town and short regional excursions from Ujung Pandang, taxis are the most widely used form of transport; ask at your hotel for recommendations and count on Rp 324,000–Rp 540,000 per day. In Tanatoraja, travelers often hire minibuses to shuttle them between sights, with prices around Rp 54,000 and hour or Rp 432,000 a day. Taxis may be hired for around Rp 32,500 an hour in Manado.

By Taxi

You can hail cabs on the street in Ujung Pandang or pick one up outside a hotel. Taxis are metered; the fare is roughly Rp 1,000 per km (½ mi). Two large companies are: **Amal Taxi** (☎ 0411/313131) and **Omega** (☎ 0411/22679). Taxis are available in Tanatoraja and Manado, but the more popular public transport modes are bemos and *mikrolets* (a Manado-style bemo), respectively. In Manado, you can also try **Dian Taksi** (☎ 0421/862421).

Contacts and Resources

Emergencies

Ambulance: ☎ 118. **Hospitals:** Elm Hospital (✉ Jl. A Yani, Rantepao); Pancaran Kasih (✉ Jl. Sam Ratulangi, Manado); **Rumah Sakit Umum** (✉ Jl. Yos. Sudarso, Manado); **Rumah Sakit Umum** (✉ Jl. Gunung

Bawakaraeng, next to Hasanuddin University, Ujung Pandang); **Stella Maris Hospital** (✉ Jl. Panghibur, Ujung Pandang).

Pharmacy: Kimia Firma (✉ Jl. A Yani, Ujung Pandang). **Police:** ☎ 110 or 7777. **Scuba Diving Emergencies:** The only public decompression chamber is operated by **Baruna Watersports** (✉ Jl. Bypass Ngurah Rai 300B, Kuta, ☎ 0361/753820) on Bali.

English-Language Bookstores

All the major hotels in Ujung Pandang and Manado have shops or kiosks with English-language newspapers, magazines, and the occasional guidebook or novel.

Tour Operators

In Ujung Pandang, **Toraja Highland Tours and Travel** (✉ Jl. Rambutan 3, ☎ 0411/852495) offers a full range of tours throughout the southern province and specializes in trips to Toraja. **Intravi** (✉ Jl. Urip Sumoharjo 225, ☎ 0411/319747) is also a reputable agency. Besides arranging tours, **Pacto Ltd. Tours and Travel** (✉ Jl. Jendral Sudirman 56, ☎ 0411/873208) represents American Express. **Ramayana Tours** (✉ Jl. Bulukunyi 9A, ☎ 0411/871791) is particularly good for tours into Tanatoraja because many of its guides come from there. It also offers excursions to the southeast peninsula, famous for boatbuilding and a reclusive Muslim village, and arranges customized trips such as Jeep treks across the island or canoe visits to the weavers of Galumpang in central Sulawesi. In Manado, try **Helista Tour and Travel** (✉ Jl. Bethesda 75, ☎ 0423/628880), which also offers dive tours, or **Manado Land and Sea** (✉ Jl. Diponegoro 5, ☎ 0431/64476).

Travel Agencies

Ceria Nugraha (✉ Jl. Usmar Jafar 9, 90111, ☎ 0411/311846) and **Limbunan** (✉ Jl. Gunung Bawakaraeng 40–42 [Box 97], 90111, ☎ 0411/323333) are reliable agencies in Ujung Pandang. In Tanatoraja, try **Ramayana Satrya** (✉ Jl. Pong Tiku, Rantepeo, ☎ 0423/21615). In Manado, **Natrabu** (☎ 0431/853716), **Pandu Express** (✉ Jl. Sam Ratulangi 91, ☎ 0431/851188), and **Pola Pelita Express** (✉ Jl. Sam Ratulangi 113, ☎ 0431/852231) offer a range of travel services.

Visitor Information

In Ujung Pandang, the **South Sulawesi Tourist Office** (✉ Jl. Sultan Alauddin 105 B, ☎ 0411/83897) is open Monday–Thursday and Saturday 7–2, Friday 7–11. The **North Sulawesi Provincial Tourism Office** (✉ Jl. 17 Augustus, ☎ 0431/64911) can help with maps and dive details; it's open Monday–Thursday 7–2, Friday 7–11, and Saturday 7–12:30. The **Manado Tourist Office** (✉ Jl. 17 Augustus, ☎ 0431/64299) has general information on the area and is open Monday–Thursday 7–2, Friday 7–11, and Saturday 7–12:30. If you're headed to one of the region's national parks, contact the **National Parks Office** (PHPA; ✉ Jl. Babe Palar 67, ☎ 0431/62688). It's open Monday–Thursday 9–4, Friday 9–11, and Saturday 9–12:30. The **Tourist Information and Booking Center** (✉ Bunaken Souvenir Shop, Jl. Sam Ratulangi 178, Manado) also has maps and regional information available. It's hours are Monday–Thursday 9–4, Friday 9–11, and Saturday 9–4.

6 Sumatra

Indonesia's largest island is also its most rugged. Sumatra's spine is constructed of more than 90 volcanoes and nearly three-quarters of its land is smothered in rain forest. Settled at the edges but mostly untouched at its heart, Sumatra is the modern explorer's dreamland with many rare plants and animals, including species of tiger, rhino, and elephant unique to the island.

ALTHOUGH SUMATRA'S AMENITIES HAVE IMPROVED in recent years, this is still an island for the adventurous and the tolerant—not for those who need exact schedules, fixed prices, and luxury. The world's fifth-largest island (about the size of Japan or Spain), and Indonesia's most northern one, lies off the west coast of the Malaysian peninsula. Its rubber and palm-oil plantations and oil and gas fields make it a gold mine for the country. Medan, the capital of North Sumatra province, is an important commercial center. The capital of West Sumatra province, Padang, is a large port. But not all of Sumatra's resources have been exploited, not all of its lands developed: it has rain forests that teem with wildlife as well as beautiful lakes, mountains, and beaches.

Before Jakarta exploded into the violence that led to the end of President Suharto's 32-year-rule, riots in Medan (in early May 1998) caused large business areas of the city to close. Medan is a commercial center and has one of Indonesia's largest ethnic-Chinese populations (the Chinese, who many believe receive unfair government protection and assistance, are often the target of disenfranchised Indonesian workers). The city is also home to several universities whose student bodies often agitate for more political freedom. And then there is Aceh—the province on the northern tip of Sumatra—whose zealous Muslim inhabitants have always wanted more independance from Jakarta. (The Dutch never fully controlled this region, and the Indonesian government only did so with strong-arm tactics.) All the turmoil aside, the Sumatrans are an intriguing and diverse people—from the former headhunter Bataks in the north to the matrilineal Miningkabau tribes in the west. Many islanders are also freewheeling entrepreneurs who understand the value of tourism; some speak a little English, and most are friendly and quick to offer help and information.

To do Sumatra right, you'll need at least a week. It's best to enter at Medan in the north and travel overland to Padang on the west coast (or vice versa). Taxis and a comprehensive bus system link small towns, and domestic airlines connect provincial capitals. (Note that, at press time, the airports in Medan and Padang had not been greatly affected by the economic crisis, though air service elsewhere was less comprehensive than in better financial times.)

Pleasures and Pastimes

Architecture

The traditional wooden *rumah gadang* (big houses) of the Minangkabau peoples—carved and painted with intricate decorative motifs and topped by high tapered, curving roofs—are among Sumatra's main attractions. Bukittinggi and the surrounding hills are the place to find these beautiful structures.

Dining

Sumatra is the birthplace of the Padang-style restaurant, where dozens of small dishes—each containing a different entrée—are placed before you to sample at your leisure, always with loads of steamed rice and side dishes of fiery *sambal* sauces. The fare may include beef, chicken, and seafood curries; grilled fish; boiled eggs; and a variety of vegetables. Prices are based on the number of dishes you taste. Be careful before you sample, though: Sumatran food is on the very hot side, but this can be tempered slightly by leaving the red and green peppers and their seeds in the sauce before you scoop a taste onto your plate. Satay (also spelled "saté") is a common snack found everywhere, and there are numerous Chinese restaurants in the main cities.

Lodging

All the major cities have large hotels with reasonable amenities. What small-town hotels lack in amenities that make for in local flavor; homestays are also an option in small communities as are cheap *losmen* (small guest houses with shared facilities). Popular tourist areas, such as Gunung Leuser, Lake Toba, and Bukittinggi, have a wide range of accommodations for every budget.

National Parks

Sumatra's premier natural playground is Gunung Leuser National Park, a half-day's drive from Medan. Trekking, wildlife watching, river trips, and observing orangutan at the Bukit Lawang rehabilitation center are popular activities. This is one of Indonesia's best-organized parks, with a full-scale visitors center, plenty of guides, a good trail network, and activities for all ages.

Shopping

There are many unique crafts created on this island, such as silver filigree and songket textiles from Bukittinggi and ikat weaving from the Lake Toba region and southeastern Sumatra. A wide selection of merchandise is available in the local markets, but many repeat travelers often go directly to the villages to order textiles woven to their preferences in pattern and color. Other interesting souvenirs include wood carvings and woven baskets.

Exploring Sumatra

Although its terrain is rough and its main cities are far apart, Sumatra's numerous entry and exit points make travel planning here a puzzle whose pieces fit together in numerous and surprisingly convenient ways. Make your itinerary flexible, though, for there are frequent delays and cancellations even on the most well-traveled routes. Most people enter through Medan, the largest city; Padang is another good gateway city. From your entry point, it's best to choose one or two destinations and spend your time fully enjoying them rather than trying to cover several places. Keep in mind that much of the island is still unexplored and uninhabited, so take the opportunity to enjoy the uncomplicated, unhurried lifestyle found in few other regions of the world.

Great Itineraries

IF YOU HAVE 3–4 DAYS

Fly into **Medan** ①, spend the night, and head for **Gunung Leuser National Park**—bring comfortable clothes, hiking shoes, binoculars, and lots of film. Take the first day to relax by the river and visit the Bukit Lawang orangutan rehabilitation center. Spend the second day exploring the shorter trails with a guide. On the third day, take a rafting trip and attend one of the visitor programs before heading out the next morning.

IF YOU HAVE 7 DAYS

Fly into **Medan** ①, spend the night, and get to **Gunung Leuser National Park** the next afternoon. Take two days to visit the orangutan rehabilitation center, raft the river, and view the wildlife along the shorter trails, then head for **Danau Toba and Pulau Samosir** ④ the next morning. Spend two days exploring the lakeside villages and enjoying Batak culture before returning to Medan for a flight out.

IF YOU HAVE 10 DAYS

Fly into **Medan** ① and take three days for walks and wildlife at **Gunung Leuser National Park,** then head for **Danau Toba and Pulau Samosir** ④ and spend three more days. From Lake Toba, take a day to go south by road through the beautiful, mountainous terrain to **Bukittinggi** ⑥, where you can spend your final three days exploring the Minangkabau highlands before going two hours by road to **Padang** ⑨ for flights back to Medan and off the island.

IF YOU HAVE 14 DAYS

Fly into **Medan** ① and spend the night, then take a day to look around town before heading for **Gunung Leuser National Park** the next morning. Spend three days here, then move south for three days at **Danau Toba and Palau Samosir** ④ to enjoy the area's serene ambience and Batak culture. Take a day to go by road to **Bukittinggi** ⑥, and spend three days in the Minangkabau highlands visiting villages and discovering the area's natural wonders. Make the two-hour drive to **Padang** ⑨ the next day and spend the afternoon wandering around town before catching a flight back to Medan and off the island the next morning.

NORTH SUMATRA

Outside of Medan, the provincial capital and a bustling commercial center, much of North Sumatra remains wilderness. Among its highlights are the 100-km-long (62-mi-long) Danau Toba and its island, Samosir, which are in the caldera of a massive volcano; the rain forests of Gunung Leuser National Park; and the Bukit Lawang Orangutan Rehabilitation Center. Although many sights are along the Trans-Sumatran Highway (also called the Asian Highway), which runs the length of Sumatra from north to south, others take a lot more effort to reach. Luckily North Sumatra's people are friendly and helpful, making much of the island a joy to see—regardless of problems with the infrastructure.

Medan

❶ *1,350 km (840 mi) northwest of Jakarta, 625 km (390 mi) northwest of Singapore, 575 km (360 mi) northeast of Padang.*

Medan, the capital of North Sumatra and the fourth-largest city in Indonesia, developed into a bustling plantation town early this century and is now only second (after Jakarta) in terms of business importance. The general population of more than 2 million people jostles about in a city designed for 500,000. Cars, taxis, bemos, motor scooters, bicycles, and pedestrians compete for positions on streets that are in various states of repair.

The two major in-town sights are the large, multidome **Mesjid Raya Mosque** (⊠ near the intersection of Jl. Mesjid Raya and Jl. Sisinga Mangaraja in the southeast of town) built in 1906 and one of Indonesia's largest, and the Sultan's Palace, the **Istana Sultan Deli** (⊠ Jl. Katamso just west of the mosque) built in 1880. Special permission from the tourist office (☞ Visitor Information *in* North Sumatra Essentials, *below*) is required to visit the inside of the palace.

The **Orangutan Rehabilitation Station** in Gunung Leuser National Park is just a 2½-hour drive outside of town. You can hire a taxi and a guide for about Rp 810,000. It's best to leave Medan by about 11 AM to reach the park by 2 PM. You will then have a 30-minute walk in tropical heat up to the ranger's hut. A further 15-minute hike up the mountain takes you to the feeding platform where rangers, at 3:30 PM, spend 35 min-

North and West Sumatra

utes feeding and inspecting the orangutans, preparing them for life in the wild. You need to be relatively fit to make the 45-minute hike, which involves rugged terrain and crossing a creek by raft, but the experience is well worth the effort.

Dining and Lodging

Western fast food has arrived in Medan. There's a McDonald's near the Mesjid Raya Mosque, a Pizza Hut in Deli Plaza, and, it seems, Kentucky Fried Chicken is everywhere else. For more upscale Western fare, try the restaurants in the larger hotels. On the Asian side, many eateries—including the food stalls in the park across from the mosque—serve good Padang cuisine. Padang food originated, of course, in Padang on Sumatra's west coast, but it is known throughout the archipelago. Dishes are similar to curries, and most are quite spicy.

$$–$$$ ✕ **Miramar.** Near several antiques shops in central Medan, this restaurant serves Chinese and Padang dishes (seafood is a specialty) in an air-conditioned dining room with big padded chairs around large tables. The menu has pictures so you get a good idea of what you're ordering, and the service is good. ✉ *Jl. Pemua 11,* ☎ *061/325491. AE, MC, V.*

$$ ✕ **RM Famili.** A short walk down Jalan Sisingamangaraja from the Mesjid Raya Mosque, this is a great place to sample Padang food. There are many selections in a glass display case as you walk into the large, open-air dining room. Smiling waiters will bring small plates and bowls of food to your table and serve you rice. You eat what you want and pay accordingly. It's best to get a seat close to the waterfall fountain to drown out the traffic noise outside. ✉ *Jl. Sisingamangaraja 33,* ☎ *061/718787. No credit cards.*

$–$$ ✕ **Tip Top.** Opened in 1935, Tip Top is a Medan institution. It offers a selection of Indonesian, Chinese and Padang food (all of it good) and some Western food (not as good). The front dining room opens onto a very busy street, but there are quieter, air-conditioned dining rooms in the back. The cake and coffee are tops. ✉ *Jl. Jendral A. Jani 92,* ☎ *061/24442. No credit cards.*

$$$ **Hotel Danau Toba.** The city's first major hotel (circa 1972) is more like an urban resort with its lagoonlike pool (complete with landscaped islands), its many restaurants, and its karaoke bar and disco. Despite their age, public areas and guest rooms are well maintained. ✉ *Jl. Imam Bonjol 17, 20235,* ☎ *061/557000,* FAX *061/530053. 268 rooms, 4 suites. 4 restaurants, 4 bars, pool, massage, health club, dance club, meeting rooms. AE, DC, MC, V.*

$$$ **Novotel Soechi.** This central Medan establishment has the city's only cybercafé (with eight computer terminals), making it a good choice for those who can't bear to be disconnected from the rest of the world. Rooms are of a good size and some have doors that connect them to other rooms—perfect for families or other groups traveling together. There's a 24-hour restaurant on site, and you have a good selection of both dining and shopping options in the adjoining Hong Kong Plaza. ✉ *Jl. Cirebon 76-A, 20235,* ☎ *061/561234,* FAX *061/57222. 232 rooms, 15 suites. Restaurant, 4 bars, café, pool, tennis court, health club, business services, meeting rooms. AE, DC, MC, V.*

$$$ **Tiara Medan Hotel.** Although Medan's many new hotels have given it a run for the money, the clean, smart Tiara has remained Medan's best. Guest rooms are spacious and well maintained, and the staff is friendly and quick to help. The lobby restaurant offers standard Chinese, European, and Indonesian fare for lunch, and the more formal Amberita Restaurant serves dinner. ✉ *Jl. Cut Mutia, 20152,* ☎ *061/516000,* FAX *061/51076. 316 rooms, 16 suites. 2 restaurants, bar, pool, 2 tennis courts, health club, squash, business services, meeting rooms, travel services. AE, DC, V.*

$$ 🏨 **Natour Dharma Deli Medan.** Although this hotel, part of Indonesia's Natour chain, is right in central Medan, it has a lovely pool with bar service and shaded areas—the perfect escape from urban buzz and equatorial sun. Though rooms are on the boxy side, each is comfortably furnished with two queen-size beds, two chairs, a coffee table, a desk, and satellite TV. The coffee shop serves Indonesian, Chinese, and Western food. ✉ *Jl. Balai Kota 67, 20111,* ☎ *061/327011,* FAX *061/327153. 180 rooms. Coffee shop, pool, massage, exercise room. AE, DC, MC, V.*

$ 🏨 **Hotel Sri Deli.** This wooden, brightly painted, four-story hotel is near the mosque. Rooms are clean and each has its own bath (with hot water)—a real plus in a budget hotel; some rooms have air-conditioning as well. A few members of the friendly staff speak a little English, and many tour guides hang out downstairs. ✉ *Jl. S. M. Raja 30, 20214,* ☎ *061/713571. 53 rooms. Café. No credit cards.*

Shopping

For a variety of contemporary goods, try **Deli Plaza** (✉ Jl. Guru Patimus) in the north of town. In central Medan, the many shops in the **Hong Kong Plaza** (✉ Jl. Cirebon) are your best bets.

Jalan Jendral A. Yani has several good curio and antiques shops. Among them they offer goods from all corners of Indonesia. Note that only good, old-fashioned, hard currency is accepted, and haggling is de rigueur: **Toko Bali** (✉ Jl. Jendral A. Yani 68, ☎ 061/512556), **Dagang Sepalat** (✉ Jl. Jendral A. Yani 61, no phone), **Rufino** (✉ Jl. Jendral A. Yani 56, ☎ 061/567165), and **Selatan** (✉ Jl. Jendral A. Yani 44, ☎ 061/518149). If the heat and the bargaining tire you, take a break at the nearby Tip Top or Miramar restaurants (☞ Dining and Lodging, *above*).

Brastagi

❷ *68 km (41 mi) southwest of Medan.*

Brastagi, two hours from sweltering Medan on one of two routes to Danau Toba, is a refreshing hill station 4,600 ft above sea level and set between two volcanoes. It retains an Old World air from the days when Dutch planters came here to escape the heat.

Several groups of the Karo Bataks have their villages in the highlands, and one worth a visit is **Lingga,** 15 km (9 mi) southwest of Brastagi and just a little off the road to Danau Toba. Here you can see 250- to 300-year-old multifamily tribal houses that are still used today. Karo Bataks, as well as the Toba Bataks, are descendants from proto-Malay tribes who originally inhabited the border areas of what is now Myanmar (Burma) and Thailand. They chose this mountainous region for its isolation, and their patrilineal society remains virtually intact—despite the increasing numbers of sightseers.

Dining and Lodging

$$–$$$ ★ ✕🏨 **Bukit Kubu Hotel.** This wonderful, old, colonial-style hotel is the area's best. Ask for a double suite with a view of the mountains (the price is only Rp 54,000 more than that for a standard room). Lunch is served on a breezy terrace; dinner, inside, is in the formal dining room. Starched linen and billowing lace curtains are reminiscent of the 1930s, when Dutch planters came here to relax. Today, the hotel is popular with wealthy folk from Medan who come for weekends in the cool mountain air. ✉ *Jl. Sempurna 2, 22151 (booking office:* ✉ *Jl. Jendral Sudirman 36, Medan 20100),* ☎ *0628/20832; 061/519636 in Medan. 40 rooms. Restaurant, laundry service. AE, V.*

Prapat

❸ *120 km southeast of Brastagi, 176 km (110 mi) south of Medan.*

From Brastagi it's an easy two-hour bus or taxi ride south to Prapat, the resort town near Danau Toba where ferries leave for Pulau Samosir. The last 30 minutes of the journey are the most dramatic. The road winds through tropical vegetation to a pass, where the lake suddenly appears below. (Note that if you're coming directly from Medan—a four-hour drive—you can take the Trans-Sumatran Highway. The views aren't quite as fantastic and you'll miss charming Brastagi, but the route is fast.) If you arrive in Prapat late and miss the last boat (about 4:30 PM) there are a few good places to eat and to rest your travel-weary bones.

Dining and Lodging

$$–$$$ ✕ **Singgalang.** The first version of this family restaurant opened 40 years ago. This new edition, an air-conditioned dining room just off the highway, carries on the tradition of offering good Chinese and international fare. (There are also a couple of fan-cooled guest rooms if you're stuck for a place to stay.) ✉ *Trans-Sumatran Hwy. 52,* ☏ *0664/41260. AE, DC, MC, V.*

$ ✕ **Trogadero.** For good Indonesian cuisine—satays, nasi goreng, and the like—try this one-room restaurant near the water. You'll find it easy to relax in the easygoing atmosphere. ✉ *Jl. Haranggaol 110,* ☏ *0664/41148. No credit cards.*

$$$–$$$$ 🏨 **Niagara.** One of Prapat's best hotels—as many a tour group has discovered—is on a hill behind town with spectacular views of the lake and a big pool. Guest rooms are spacious and comfortable, and the huge dining room has an international menu. There's a free shuttle bus into town. ✉ *Jl. Pembangunan 1, 21174,* ☏ *0664/41028,* FAX *0664/41233. 178 rooms, 4 suites. Dining room, bar, pool, 4 tennis courts, bicycles, dance club. DC, MC, V.*

$$ 🏨 **Natour Hotel Prapat.** The best quarters here are in the bungalows on landscaped slopes that face the lake. Rooms, though worn, are comfortably large and well furnished and have patios. Like all Natour hotels, this one is not spectacular but it is a bargain. ✉ *Jl. Marihat 1, 21174,* ☏ *0664/41012,* FAX *0664/41019. 85 rooms. Dining room, bar, beach. AE, V.*

$ 🏨 **Risis Hotel.** This clean, whitewashed hotel on the street that leads to the market square is a good bet if you're on a tight budget. Some rooms have private baths; all have bare walls and floors and minimal furniture. Although there's no on-site restaurant, Trogadero (☞ *above*) and all its Indonesian fare is nearby. ✉ *Jl. Haranggaol 39, 21174,* ☏ *0664/41392. 20 rooms. No credit cards.*

Danau Toba and Pulau Samosir

★ ❹ *Samosir Island is 45 minutes by boat from Prapat.*

Danau Toba, the largest lake in Southeast Asia and one of the highest in the world, sits 2,950 ft above sea level, surrounded by steep slopes that plunge headlong into the water to depths of 1,475 ft. Prapat may be the major resort town *on* the lake, but most visitors prefer to stay *in* the lake—on Samosir, a hilly 777-square-km (300-square-mi) island that's home to the Toba Bataks. The island remains agriculturally based. Even the people who run guest houses in touristed Tuk Tuk (☞ *below*) continue to plant their rice fields.

In **Tomok,** you'll find the tombs of King Sidabutar, who ruled in the 1800s; his son; his grandson; and several warriors of rank. Nearby are several Batak houses with curving roofs and intricately carved beams and panels. To reach these attractions, walk ½ km (¼ mi) up from the ferry dock past stalls selling souvenirs, artifacts, and batik cloth. Keep in mind that the actual purchase price is 30%–40% of the initial asking price.

Tuk Tuk, on a peninsula that juts into the lake, has been greatly developed as a tourist hub during the last 10 years (indeed, some areas are virtual guest-house ghettos, with one lodging after another). Still, quiet retreats remain and a stay in one can be pleasant. There are few vehicles; many visitors get around by bicycle, just as the easygoing locals do. (Note that the locals are fond of chess and are usually eager to play. If you're good you might give them a game; if you're *very* good you might even win.) To reach Tuk Tuk, it's best to take the passenger ferry (a 45-minute ride), which stops at several hotels on the peninsula. **Ambarita** is a village where, in the past, miscreants had their heads lopped off. You can still see the courtyard where the king held council. Ancient, weathered stone chairs and tables form a ring in front of the chief's traditional house. The village is a nice two-hour bicycle outing from Tuk Tuk.

At the northern tip of Samosir is **Simanindo,** site of a fine old traditional house, once the home of a Batak king. The village has been declared an open-air museum, and the one house not to miss is the Long House (Rumak Bolon), with its fine carvings and the sculpted depiction of the god Gajah Dompak. His job was to frighten off evil spirits, and by the look of him, he must have been good at it.

In nice weather, consider making the pleasant ride (by motorcycle) to the small **Danau Sidihoni** toward the center of Pulau Samosir island. On the way, you can contemplate the fact that you'll soon be visiting what has to be the world's only lake on an island in a lake on an island.

Passenger boats cost Rp 1,500 one-way to Tuk Tuk, slightly more for Ambarita and Simanindo. They leave from Prapat's lakeshore market. A little ways down the coast there's a car ferry to Tomok. The passenger boats are more frequent and enjoyable. For a more extensive look at the island you can charter a powerboat for a three-hour trip to Tomok, Tuk Tuk, Ambarita, and Simanindo, which will cost about Rp 40,000. It could be your only opportunity to get seasick at 3,000 ft. For travel around Samosir, minibus taxis make irregular trips, and there are motorbikes for rent (about Rp 20,000 a day).

Dining and Lodging

Accommodations here are pleasant, albeit a bit rustic. All the hotels have restaurants, but you should trying eating at a few places because the best lodging doesn't necessarily have the best food.

$–$$ ✕ **Bagus Bay.** For a good selection of Indonesian food, very edible pizza and sandwiches, and terrific fruit shakes, check out this big open-air eatery. You'll also find an extensive used bookshop with some English-language titles. Once a week (the days vary) there's an evening performance of traditional dance and music put on by local Bataks. ✉ *Jl. Slamet Riyadi, Tuk Tuk, 0625/41481. No credit cards.*

$–$$ ✕🏨 **Toba Vegetarian Restaurant.** Toba has seven guest rooms, four of them in a Batak house that was moved here and refurbished. It has hot water and a balcony facing the lake. Room 7, on the second floor, is the best room. The food here is good, especially the freshly baked cakes and the dark German bread. ✉ *Jl. Slamet Riyadi 111, Tuk Tuk 22395,* ☎ *0271/37603. 7 rooms. Restaurant. No credit cards.*

$$$ 🏨 **Toledo.** This is one of the bigger resorts, but the owners have done a reasonable job fitting it into the environment. Though the hotel caters to tour groups, you can stay here without feeling overwhelmed.

Ask for a room with a patio facing the lake; make your second choice a room next to the pool. Activities here include boat rides on the lake and outings to island sights. ✉ *On both sides of the road along the northeast side of the Tuk Tuk peninsula, Tuk Tuk 22395,* ☎ *0271/46356,* FAX *0271/44788. 140 rooms. Restaurant, bar, pool, massage, beach, boating, shops, meeting rooms, travel services. AE, DC, MC, V.*

$$ ★ **Carolina Cottage.** Tuk Tuk's first accommodation remains its best. Rooms—in Batak houses at the edge of the lake—all have spectacular views and baths; most also have hot running water. The service is friendly and helpful. For convenience and a great view, request a room down by the beach and the swimming area. Continental breakfasts, snacks, and dinners are served. ✉ *On a small lane off Jl. Slamet Riyadi, Tuk Tuk 22395,* ☎ *0625/41520,* FAX *0625/41521. 50 rooms. Restaurant, bar, beach. No credit cards.*

En Route On the Trans-Sumatran Highway from Prapat to Bukittinggi is Binanga (sometimes known as Lumban Binanga) and 15 km (9 mi) southwest of Prapat are five traditional houses. Park at the side of the highway (you'll see a sign), and walk down the hill past some new houses and terraced paddy fields to these 100- to 200-year-old Batak houses. Few tourists come here, so Binanga has much less bustle than the villages on Samosir.

North Sumatra Essentials

Arriving and Departing

BY AIRPLANE

Air service in Indonesia went into a tailspin with the financial crisis in 1997. Several airlines folded, others cut routes, and all adjusted their schedules. Flights are sure to continue to Medan, but you should double-check schedules. **Garuda Indonesian Airways** (☎ 061/516066) and **Silk Air** (☎ 061/537744) have daily hour-long flights from Singapore to Medan's **Polonia Airport** (☎ 061/538444) right on the south edge of town. **Malaysia Airlines** (☎ 061/519333) flies from Penang, Malaysia. There are also flights to Jakarta on Java and Padang in West Sumatra. **Merpati** (☎ 061/514102) also serves Medan. The only way into Medan from the airport is by taxi. A fixed rate of Rp 4,800 applies.

BY BOAT

The least expensive and more adventurous way to reach Medan is on one of the daily five-hour "fast boats" from Penang, Malaysia. At 96 Malaysian ringgit it's a bargain, but the Melaka Straights often get rough. Contact **Kuala Perlis-Langkawi Ferry Service** (☎ 04/262–5630) in Penang or **Perdana Express** (☎ 061/545803) in Medan.

Getting Around

BY AIR

If you only have enough time for a few of Sumatra's highlights, the best strategy is to use Medan as a sightseeing hub and then fly to Padang to see its area sights—or vice versa.

BY BUS

Buses range from the air-conditioned express variety to crowded local vehicles. Long-distance bus travel—such as the 14- to 16-hour journey from Medan's Amplas bus station to Padang—can be an adventure. (Motion sickness is a concern, as is all the smoke from the clove Kretek cigarettes that are popular with so many passengers.) Short day trips by bus are quite tolerable, however. Bus stations are never far from town centers, and you'll generally find a bus leaving for nearby destinations within 30 minutes of your arrival at the station. A travel agent can arrange the bus trip, too. In Medan, contact **Trophy Tours** (☞ Tour Operator and Travel Agent, *below*).

BY CAR

Although many sights are along the Trans-Sumatran Highway—a well-sealed two-lane (for the most part) highway—renting a car and driving yourself is a risky business on Sumatra. It's best to hire a car and a driver—leaving the work to someone who knows the terrain and the language. A travel agent (☞ Tour Operator and Travel Agent, *below*) and the staff at major hotels can make arrangements for you.

BY TAXI

In Medan, you'll find car and motorcycle taxis at hotels, the bus station, the airport, and the dock. Some taxis have meters; with others, you must negotiate the fare before you get in. The original asking price will usually be about 20% to 40% higher—if you look gullible, it will be higher still—than what you should pay. For a shared taxi, try **Indah Taxi** (✉ Brig-jen Katamso 60, ☎ 061/510036).

Contacts and Resources

EMERGENCIES

Ambulance: ☎ 118. **Fire:** ☎ 113. **Hospital:** Dr. M. Jamil (✉ Jl. Perintis Kemerdekaan, ☎ 061/22355 for English speakers). **Police:** ☎ 110.

ENGLISH-LANGUAGE BOOKSTORES

Try the bookshop in the **Tiara Medan Hotel** (✉ Jl. Cut Mutia, Medan, ☎ 061/574000). The **Toko Buku Bookshop** (✉ Jl. Ahmad Yani 48, Medan, no phone) is another good bet.

TOUR OPERATOR AND TRAVEL AGENT

Trophy Tours (✉ Jl. Brig-jen Katamso 33, Medan, ☎ 061/555666) can help you with tours and trips on Sumatra as well as with other travel arrangement.

VISITOR INFORMATION

The **tourist office** at Polonia Airport—between the domestic and international terminals—has lists of accommodations in the region. The staff will happily make reservations and arrange ground transportation.

Some information can be obtained from **North Sumatra Regional Office of Tourism** (✉ Jl. Alfalah 22, Kampung Baru, Medan, ☎ 061/762220). More helpful is the **Provincial Tourist Service** (✉ Jl. Jendral A. Yani 107, Medan 20151, ☎ 061/511101).

WEST SUMATRA

Much of mountainous West Sumatra remains covered in virgin jungle with volcanoes, rivers, elephants, endangered tigers, and rhinos—a nature-lover's delight. It has three regions: the volcanic highlands, a coastal plain, and islands covered in jungle. The long plain is heavily inhabited, the highlands and islands less so. Nearly 90% of the population are members of the matrilineal Minangkabau tribe (here women inherit the family property). Extended families live in *rumah gadang* (big houses) with roofs that have a series of curving spikes—similar to buffalo horns—that point skyward.

Bonjol

5 *600 km (372 mi) south of Medan, 220 km (136 mi) north of Padang.*

There's really not much here—just a funky concrete globe of the world, a park, some coffee stalls, and a souvenir shop—but it *is* the site of the equator and hence merits at least a little respect. You can get a certificate that you visited at the souvenir shop, which might make Bonjol worth a stop if you're driving south from Medan to Padang on the

Trans-Sumatran Highway. If you're a geography junkie, you can also make Bonjol a day trip from Bukittinggi (☞ *below*).

Bukittinggi

6 *120 km (75 mi) southeast of Bonjol, 550 km (341 mi) southwest of Prapat, 94 km (58 mi) north of Padang.*

Nestled in the highlands north of Padang, picturesque Bukittinggi is the area's cultural and tourist hub. At 3,051 ft above sea level on the Agam Plateau it offers cool relief from the heat. The Dutch called it Ft. de Kock; although some foundations and a few rusty cannon are all that remain of the actual fort, their hilly site offers good views.

The **Jam Gadang** clock tower is the landmark of Bukittinggi's center. The nearby town market is a lively place to shop for local items or sample local food at one of the numerous stalls. The **Rumah Gadang Museum,** a refurbished, 19th-century Minangkabau home that's also near the clock tower, offers free dance performances on Sunday and public holidays.

On the south end of town are the extensive **Japanese Tunnels,** dug with forced labor during World War II as a defense against an attack by the Allies. They're worth the small admission charge, and it's easy enough to tour them by yourself because there are lights along the main tunnel. If you want a more extensive look you can hire a guide who knows the history, and perhaps more importantly carries a flashlight so you can see all the nooks and crannies. Nearby the Japanese Tunnels is **Sianok Canyon,** which winds south of the city. A one-hour walk through the canyon from Bukittinggi brings you to the village of Kota Gadang, whose inhabitants are known for their silver work—particularly silver filigree. Even if you're not in the market the walk here makes a nice half-day outing.

Pandai Sikat (12 km/8 mi south of Bukittinggi) is known for its furniture and woodworking factories, but it's also a weaving center, with several hundred looms turning out cloth. The furniture is beautiful to some, a bit overdone for others, and too big for most travelers to transport home. However, there are some smaller wood carvings for sale here, too.

Dining and Lodging

$ ✕ **Lapan Nasi Sederhana.** It doesn't look like much—just a room that's open to the street and food displayed in a glass case—but the Padang dishes are spicy and good. Point to what you want, and it will be brought to your table with a bowl of rice. This place is popular with locals and can be packed. ✉ *Jl. Minangkabau 61, no phone. No credit cards.*

$ ✕ **Simpang Raya.** Like its Padang cousin, this branch serves a good selection of such Indonesian staples as nasi goreng and satays in a simple dining room. Expect crowds at lunchtime. ✉ *Jl. Sudiman 8,* ☎ *0751/22163. No credit cards.*

$$$ 🏨 **Melia Comfort Pusako.** The Melia's location 4 km (2 mi) from the center of town gives it the feel of a resort. Rooms here are spacious and have views of the surrounding mountains. You can bike into town or ask the hotel staff to arrange for transportation—making the location seem less remote. They can also coordinate golf outings at a local course. ✉ *Jl. Soekarno-Hatta 7, 26129,* ☎ *0752/32111,* FAX *0752/32667. 184 rooms, 7 suites. 2 restaurants, bar, pool, massage, 2 tennis courts, health club, bicycles, business services. AE, DC, MC, V.*

$$$ 🏨 **Novotel.** In a building that looks like a cross between a medieval fort and a Middle Eastern palace, this hotel is a commanding presence above the center of town. It also has many of the amenities you would expect of an international chain establishment, including a pleasant pool and gardens. You can walk or bike around town from here, and the on-site Shaan Holidays office will arrange guided tours of the area or trips to the local golf course. ✉ *Jl. Laras Datuk Bandaro, 26113,* ☎ *0752/35000,* FAX *0752/23800. 93 rooms, 6 junior suites, 1 suite. Restaurant, bar, pool, bicycles, travel services. AE, DC, MC, V.*

$–$$ 🏨 **Benteng Hotel.** This budget hotel—a simple concrete structure—offers rich views from its location right next to what remains of Ft. de Kock on the highest hill in town. The basic rooms have TVs, well-kept old furniture, hot water in private baths, and air-conditioning—though you hardly need it with the cool highland breezes. The staff is friendly. ✉ *Jl. Benteng 1, 26113,* ☎ *0752/21115,* FAX *0752/22596. 15 rooms. Restaurant, bar. MC, V.*

Danau Maninjau

❼ *40 km (25 mi) west of Bukittinggi.*

Smaller than Danau Toba and, perhaps, not as spectacular, this lake is still quite beautiful. The steep crater walls are mostly forested, though there are terraced rice fields in places. The drive here from Bukittinggi is something of a thrill; the final descent from the rim of the crater to the lake involves 44 hairpin turns. You can calm your nerves and soothe your soul with a swim in the lake's deep blue waters.

Batusangkar

❽ *50 km (31 mi) southwest of Bukittinggi.*

According to legend, Batusangkar is the cradle of Minangkabau culture, and it has many unique traditional houses as well as a countryside full of terraced rice fields. It's best to visit with a driver and guide from Bukittinggi or Padang. Be sure to stop in Balimbang village, which has many traditional Minangkabau houses, including one reputed to be 350 years old.

Padang

❾ *575 km (360 mi) southwest of Medan, 900 km (560 mi) northwest of Jakarta, and 490 km (304 mi) southwest of Singapore.*

The capital of West Sumatra is also the largest port in the west of the island. Sitting on a coastal plain, it's hot and has the laid-back atmosphere and attitude that often accompanies such a climate. Many of the city's structures have Minangkabu roofs with their hornlike spikes. The clip-clop of horse-drawn carts is a more common sound than the ear-splitting whine of motorcycle taxis so often heard in Medan. The city's old quarter, next to the river, is worth a stroll. The century-old shops look a bit worn (somehow, this adds to their appeal), and the boats in the river are colorfully painted. But the highlight here is the food. Don't miss the chance to sample spicy Padang food *in* Padang.

In a traditional Minangkabu house on the corner of Jalan Diponegoro and Jalan H. O. S. Cokroaminoto, the **Adiyawarman Museum** has a collection of regional antiques. ⏲ *Daily 9–5.*

Although Padang is on the coast, most of its beaches aren't that great. The exception is **Bungus Bay,** 20 km (12 mi) south of town. The sand is soft and white, and the surf is calm. Farther, this crescent-shape bay is surrounded by rice fields and hills. Several islands just off the coast from Padang also have beautiful beaches.

Dining and Lodging

$$–$$$ ✕ **Sari.** One of Padang's fancier restaurants is near a quaint little mosque with loudspeakers that blast the call to prayer early in the evening. Seated in the air-conditioned dining room or on the patio (which is nicer if it's not too hot) you can order local and imported steaks or Indonesian and Padang dishes. ✉ *Jl. Thamrin 71B,* ☎ *0751/31838. MC, V.*

$$ ★ ✕ **Simpang Enam.** This restaurant tops the competition that surrounds it. Although the menu has a selection of Chinese dishes, anything made with the fish, fresh from the waters nearby, will be delicious (the pepper crab is a good choice). You order in the simple air-conditioned dining room, and then watch the chefs cook your meal through a window. ✉ *Jl. H. O. S. Cokroaminoto 44,* ☎ *0751/25044. AE, V.*

$–$$ ✕ **Simpang Raya.** In an old house off a busy road Simpang Raya offers a good selection of Indonesian staples, including a noteworthy chicken satay. There are tables in an air-conditioned room, in a fan-cooled room, and on a patio. ✉ *Jl. Aziz Chan 24,* ☎ *0751/24894. No credit cards.*

$$$ 🏨 **Bumi Minang.** Opened in 1995 as a Sedona chain hotel, this impressive seven-story property was bought by local owners in 1997—although people still often refer to it as the Sedona. It's centrally located and offers all the amenities you'd expect from a hotel with international roots. A band plays local music in the lobby, the rooms are comfortable, and the staff is professional. ✉ *Jl. Bundo Kandung (Box 135), 25118,* ☎ *0751/37555,* FAX *0751/37567. 138 rooms, 26 suites. 5 restaurants, pool, 2 tennis courts, business services. AE, DC, MC, V.*

$$$ 🏨 **Sol Inn Pusako, Sikuai Island Resort.** A 20-minute boat ride from Padang, this resort has 99-acre Sikuai Island all to itself. Each of its 54 timber cottages has a balcony view of white sandy beach and gentle surf. Though the decor is nothing fancy, rooms are spacious and comfortable with air-conditioning, hot water, and TVs. The restaurant serves Indonesian, Japanese, Chinese, and Western cuisine. You can work off all that food by participating in one of the resort's many water sports activities. ✉ *Jl. Muara 38, Padang 25118,* ☎ *0751/35311; 800/336–3542 in the U.S.;* FAX *0751/22895. 54 cottages. Restaurant, 3 bars, 2 pools, jogging, beach, dive shop, snorkeling, boating, jet skiing, fishing. AE, DC, MC, V.*

$$–$$$ ★ 🏨 **Batang Arau Hotel.** In Padang's old quarter and next to the river, this former bank—yes, bank (circa 1808)—was converted into a hotel in 1995. It's run by a German, Norma Dulfer, and a stay here is a memorable experience. Though each room is unique, all are outfitted with solid wooden furniture and iron beds (with mattresses, of course) and decorated in local Minangkabau style. Two rooms have balconies. Breakfast is included in the rate. ✉ *Jl. Batang Arau 33, 25118,* ☎ *0751/27400,* FAX *0751/31404. 6 rooms. Bar, billiards. AE, V.*

$$ 🏨 **Paradiso Village, Cudadak Island.** For a very basic island escape—one where your days are filled only with sunbathing and reading—try Paradiso Village, a 90-minute boat ride or a 90-minute drive and a 10-minute boat ride from Padang. Built by an Italian scuba diver who fell in love with the area in the early 1990s, the resort offers two-story bungalows with mosquito nets and fans, although sea breezes usually keep things cool enough. The reasonable room rates include all your meals—very reasonable, indeed. ✉ *Rimbun Sumatra Tours, Jl. Batang Arau 33, Padang 25118,* ☎ *0751/31403,* FAX *0751/31404. 10 bungalows. Restaurant, beach. AE, MC, V.*

$–$$ ☎ **Wisma Mayang Sari.** On a busy Padang street, this small establishment in an old Dutch-era house still feels like someone's home—right down to its front yard and its living room. Rooms are basic, though each has air-conditioning or a fan, a private bath with hot water, and a refrigerator. Breakfast is included in the price of a room. ✉ *Jl. Jendral Sudiman 19, 25118,* ☎ *0751/22647. 15 rooms. V.*

West Sumatra Essentials

Arriving and Departing

BY AIRPLANE

Though service to Padang will no doubt continue despite the economic crisis, service to other destinations may be cut back or even discontinued; always double-check schedules. Padang's **Tabing Airport,** north of town, is served by **Garuda** (☎ 0751/58487), **Merpati** (☎ 0751/32010), and **Silk Air** (☎ 0751/38122), a Singapore airline.

BY BOAT

If you're a patient traveler and have a lot of time, arriving and departing by boat travel is another option. Check with **Pelni** (☎ 0751/33624) about its service. The line travels weekly to many of the nearby islands and also has service to Jakarta and coastal cities on mainland Sumatra.

BY BUS

If you're a glutton for punishment there are overnight buses on the Trans-Sumatran Highway from Jakarta to Padang. The Padang bus station is on Jalan Pemuda near the intersection with Jalan M. Yamin.

Getting Around

BY AIRPLANE

There are regular flights between Padang and Medan. For more information, *see* Arriving and Departing *in* North Sumatra Essentials, *above.*

BY BUS

There are 14- to 16-hour bus trips between Padang and Medan—not the most comfortable way to go. For hops between nearby towns, however, bus travel is fine, though some local buses don't have air-conditioning and can be crowded. You can buy your ticket at the bus station—usually near the town center—right before you depart or you can have a travel agent make arrangements for you in advance. In Padang contact **Lintas Andalas Terminal** (✉ Jl. Pemuda, ☎ 0751/23216).

BY CAR

Despite the relatively good condition of the Trans-Sumatran Highway, driving a rental car yourself can be dangerous unless you already know the country and you speak the language. It's best to make arrangements to hire a car and a driver through a travel agent (☞ Tour Operators and Travel Agencies, *below*) or the staff of a major hotel.

You can pick up cabs or becaks at hotels, bus stations, airports, and docks. If your cab isn't metered, be sure to negotiate the price before you get into the car; don't hesitate to bargain hard. In both Padang and Bukittinggi, horse-drawn carts are another public transport option. You can also share a cab with four or five strangers and split the cost. For a shared taxi in Padang, contact **Safa Marwa** (✉ Jl. Pemua 33, ☎ 0751/25244). **Patax** (✉ Jl. Pintu Kebun, ☎ 0752/21163) is a good company in Bukittinggi.

Contacts and Resources

EMERGENCIES

Ambulance: ☎ 118. **Fire:** ☎ 113. **Hospitals:** RSUP Dr. M. Djamil (✉ Jl. Perintis Kemerdekaan, Padang, ☎ 0751/26585), or General Hospital (✉ Jl. A. Rivai, Bukittinggi, ☎ 0752/21013). **Pharmacy:** Yani (✉ Jl. A Yani 42, Padang, ☎ 751/27948). **Police:** ☎ 110.

ENGLISH-LANGUAGE BOOKSTORES

In Padang try **Gramedia** (✉ Jl. Damar 63, ☎ 0751/37003) a few blocks north of the museum and bus station. It has a few English-language pulp-fiction titles. In Bukittinggi there are several used bookshops with some English-language novels on Jalan Ahmad Yani.

TOUR OPERATORS AND TRAVEL AGENCIES

In Padang, **Pacto** (✉ Jl. Tan Malaka, ☎ 0751/33335) can help you with a variety of travel arrangements. **Rimbun Sumatra Tours** (✉ Jl. Batang Arau 33, ☎ 0751/31403) is, as its name suggests, good for tours.

In Bukittinggi try: **Pt. Maju Indosari** (✉ Jl. Muka Jam Gadang 17, ☎ 0752/21671), or **Shaan Holidays** (✉ Jl. Pemuda 9, ☎ 0752/32530).

VISITOR INFORMATION

In Padang, contact the **Indonesian Tourist Promotion Office** (✉ Jl. Khatib Sulaeman, ☎ 0751/55711). In Bukittinggi, contact the **Bukittinggi Tourism Information Office** (✉ Jl. Syech Bantam 1, ☎ 0752/22403).

INDEX

L

M

N

O

P

NOTES

NOTES

NOTES

NOTES

NOTES

NOTES

NOTES

Fodor's
EXPLORING
VIETNAM
upCLOSE
europe
getting the most from your grand tour
Coastal Califor
PHOTOGRAPHY BY GALEN ROWE
Fodor's
New
Aruba
ALL THE BEST OF THE ISLAND WITH A SIDE TRIP TO CURAÇAO
CITYPACK
Chicago
A COMPLETE POCKET GUIDE PLUS A FULL-SIZE COLOR MAP
Fodor's
"The King of Guidebooks"
Fodor's
Italy
The Complete Guide with the Cities, Lakes, Tuscan Hills and Baroque and Renaissance Treasures
RAND McNALLY
New England's Best Bed & Breakfasts
DELIGHTFUL PLACES TO STAY
WONDERFUL THINGS TO DO
WHEN YOU GET THERE

Fodor's Travel Publications

Available at bookstores everywhere. For descriptions of all our titles and a key to Fodor's guidebook series, visit www.fodors.com/books

Gold Guides

U.S.

Alaska
Arizona
Boston
California
Cape Cod, Martha's Vineyard, Nantucket
The Carolinas & Georgia
Chicago
Colorado
Florida
Hawai'i
Las Vegas, Reno, Tahoe
Los Angeles
Maine, Vermont, New Hampshire
Maui & Lāna'i
Miami & the Keys
New England
New Orleans
New York City
Oregon
Pacific North Coast
Philadelphia & the Pennsylvania Dutch Country
The Rockies
San Diego
San Francisco
Santa Fe, Taos, Albuquerque
Seattle & Vancouver
The South
U.S. & British Virgin Islands
USA
Virginia & Maryland
Washington, D.C.

Foreign

Australia
Austria
The Bahamas
Belize & Guatemala
Bermuda
Canada
Cancún, Cozumel, Yucatán Peninsula
Caribbean
China
Costa Rica
Cuba
The Czech Republic & Slovakia
Denmark
Eastern & Central Europe
Europe
Florence, Tuscany & Umbria
France
Germany
Great Britain
Greece
Hong Kong
India
Ireland
Israel
Italy
Japan
London
Madrid & Barcelona
Mexico
Montréal & Québec City
Moscow, St. Petersburg, Kiev
The Netherlands, Belgium & Luxembourg
New Zealand
Norway
Nova Scotia, New Brunswick, Prince Edward Island
Paris
Portugal
Provence & the Riviera
Scandinavia
Scotland
Singapore
South Africa
South America
Southeast Asia
Spain
Sweden
Switzerland
Thailand
Toronto
Turkey
Vienna & the Danube Valley
Vietnam

Special-Interest Guides

Adventures to Imagine
Alaska Ports of Call
Ballpark Vacations
The Best Cruises
Caribbean Ports of Call
The Complete Guide to America's National Parks
Europe Ports of Call
Family Adventures
Fodor's Gay Guide to the USA
Fodor's How to Pack
Great American Learning Vacations
Great American Sports & Adventure Vacations
Great American Vacations
Great American Vacations for Travelers with Disabilities
Halliday's New Orleans Food Explorer
Healthy Escapes
Kodak Guide to Shooting Great Travel Pictures
National Parks and Seashores of the East
National Parks of the West
Nights to Imagine
Orlando Like a Pro
Rock & Roll Traveler Great Britain and Ireland
Rock & Roll Traveler USA
Sunday in San Francisco
Walt Disney World for Adults
Weekends in New York
Wendy Perrin's Secrets Every Smart Traveler Should Know
Worlds to Imagine

Fodor's Special Series

Fodor's Best Bed & Breakfasts

America
California
The Mid-Atlantic
New England
The Pacific Northwest
The South
The Southwest
The Upper Great Lakes

Compass American Guides

Alaska
Arizona
Boston
Chicago
Coastal California
Colorado
Florida
Hawai'i
Hollywood
Idaho
Las Vegas
Maine
Manhattan
Minnesota
Montana
New Mexico
New Orleans
Oregon
Pacific Northwest
San Francisco
Santa Fe
South Carolina
South Dakota
Southwest
Texas
Underwater Wonders of the National Parks
Utah
Virginia
Washington
Wine Country
Wisconsin
Wyoming

Citypacks

Amsterdam
Atlanta
Berlin
Boston
Chicago
Florence
Hong Kong
London
Los Angeles
Miami
Montréal
New York City
Paris
Prague
Rome
San Francisco
Sydney
Tokyo
Toronto
Venice
Washington, D.C.

Exploring Guides

Australia
Boston & New England
Britain
California
Canada
Caribbean
China
Costa Rica
Cuba
Egypt
Florence & Tuscany
Florida
France
Germany
Greek Islands
Hawai'i
India
Ireland
Israel
Italy
Japan
London
Mexico
Moscow & St. Petersburg
New York City
Paris
Portugal
Prague
Provence
Rome
San Francisco
Scotland
Singapore & Malaysia
South Africa
Spain
Thailand
Turkey
Venice
Vietnam

Flashmaps

Boston
New York
San Francisco
Washington, D.C.

Fodor's Cityguides

Boston
New York
San Francisco

Fodor's Gay Guides

Amsterdam
Los Angeles & Southern California
New York City
Pacific Northwest
San Francisco and the Bay Area
South Florida
USA

Karen Brown Guides

Austria
California
England B&Bs
England, Wales & Scotland
France B&Bs
France Inns
Germany
Ireland
Italy B&Bs
Italy Inns
Portugal
Spain
Switzerland

Languages for Travelers (Cassette & Phrasebook)

French
German
Italian
Spanish

Mobil Travel Guides

America's Best Hotels & Restaurants
Arizona
California and the West
Florida
Great Lakes
Major Cities
Mid-Atlantic
Northeast
Northwest and Great Plains
Southeast
Southern California
Southwest and South Central

Pocket Guides

Acapulco
Aruba
Atlanta
Barbados
Beijing
Berlin
Budapest
Dublin
Honolulu
Jamaica
London
Mexico City
New York City
Paris
Prague
Puerto Rico
Rome
San Francisco
Savannah & Charleston
Shanghai
Sydney
Washington, D.C.

Rivages Guides

Bed and Breakfasts of Character and Charm in France
Hotels and Country Inns of Character and Charm in France
Hotels and Country Inns of Character and Charm in Italy
Hotels of Character and Charm in Paris
Hotels of Character and Charm in Portugal
Hotels of Character and Charm in Spain
Wines & Vineyards of Character and Charm in France

Short Escapes

Britain
France
Near New York City
New England

Fodor's Sports

Golf Digest's Places to Play (USA)
Golf Digest's Places to Play in the Southeast
Golf Digest's Places to Play in the Southwest
Skiing USA
USA Today The Complete Four Sport Stadium Guide

Fodor's upCLOSE Guides

California
Europe
France
Great Britain
Ireland
Italy
London
Los Angeles
Mexico
New York City
Paris
San Francisco